Heaven Can Indeed Fall

Political Theory for Today

Series Editor: Richard Avramenko, University of Wisconsin, Madison

Political Theory for Today seeks to bring the history of political thought out of the jargon-filled world of the academy into the everyday world of social and political life. The series brings the wisdom of texts and the tradition of political philosophy to bear on salient issues of our time, especially issues pertaining to human freedom and responsibility, the relationship between individuals and the state, the moral implications of public policy, health and human flourishing, public and private virtues, and more. Great thinkers of the past have thought deeply about the human condition and their situations—books in Political Theory for Today build on that insight.

Titles Published

Heaven Can Indeed Fall: The Life of Willmoore Kendall, by Christopher H. Owen
The Politics of Private Property: Contested Claims to Ownership in U.S. Cultural Discourse, by Simone Knewitz
The Political Philosophy of the European City: From Polis, through City-State, to Megalopolis, by Ferenc Hörcher
John Locke and the Uncivilized Society: Resistance and Individualism in America Today, by Scott Robinson
Welcoming the Other: Student, Stranger, and Divine, edited by N. Susan Laehn and Thomas R. Laehn
Cosmopolitanism and Its Discontents: Rethinking Politics in the Age of Brexit and Trump, edited by Lee Ward
Eric Voegelin's Asian Political Thought, edited by Lee Trepanier
The Spartan Drama of Plato's Laws, by Eli Friedland
Idolizing the Idea: A Critical History of Modern Philosophy, by Wayne Cristaudo
Eric Voegelin Today: Voegelin's Political Thought in the 21st Century, edited by Scott Robinson, Lee Trepanier, David Whitney
Walk Away: When the Political Left Turns Right, edited by Lee Trepanier and Grant Havers
Plato's Mythoi: The Political Soul's Drama Beyond, by Donald H. Roy
Democracy and Its Enemies: The American Struggle for the Enlightenment, by Paul N. Goldstene
Tradition v. Rationalism: Voegelin, Oakeshott, Hayek, and Others, edited by Gene Callahan and Lee Trepanier
Aristocratic Souls in Democratic Times, edited by Richard Avramenko and Ethan Alexander-Davey

Heaven Can Indeed Fall

The Life of Willmoore Kendall

Christopher H. Owen

LEXINGTON BOOKS
Lanham • Boulder • New York • London

Published by Lexington Books
An imprint of The Rowman & Littlefield Publishing Group, Inc.
4501 Forbes Boulevard, Suite 200, Lanham, Maryland 20706
www.rowman.com

86-90 Paul Street, London EC2A 4NE

Copyright © 2021 by The Rowman & Littlefield Publishing Group, Inc.

All rights reserved. No part of this book may be reproduced in any form or by any electronic or mechanical means, including information storage and retrieval systems, without written permission from the publisher, except by a reviewer who may quote passages in a review.

British Library Cataloguing in Publication Information Available

Library of Congress Cataloging-in-Publication Data

Names: Owen, Christopher H., author.
Title: Heaven can indeed fall : the life of Willmoore Kendall/ Christopher H. Owen.
Description: Lanham : Lexington Books, [2021] | Series: Political Theory for Today / series editor, Richard Avramenko, University of Wisconsin, Madison | Includes bibliographical references and index. | Summary: "Willmoore Kendall was a man against the world, a "maverick," an "iconoclast," a man "who never lost an argument or kept a friend." He co-founded National Review, helped turn the word liberal into an insult, and became the chief theorist of conservative populism. Understanding Kendall helps us understand America"— Provided by publisher.
Identifiers: LCCN 2021034319 (print) | LCCN 2021034320 (ebook) |
 ISBN 9781793624444 (Cloth : acid-free paper) | ISBN 9781793624451 (ePub) |
 ISBN 9781793624468 (Pbk : acid-free paper)
Subjects: LCSH: Kendall, Willmoore, 1909-1967. | Conservatives—United States—Biography. | Journalists—United States—Biography. | College teachers—Political activity—United States. | Military intelligence—United States—History. | Kendall, Willmoore, 1909-1967—Mental health. | Conservatives—Family relationships—United States. | Conservatism—United States.
Classification: LCC JC573.2.U6 O94 2021 (print) | LCC JC573.2.U6 (ebook) | DDC 320.52092 [B]—dc23
LC record available at https://lccn.loc.gov/2021034319
LC ebook record available at https://lccn.loc.gov/2021034320

TO HOPIE

Contents

List of Illustrations ... ix

Preface: 1959: Willmoore Il Magnifico ... xi

Acknowledgments ... xix

List of Abbreviations ... xxi

Introduction: Tribune and Teacher of the American People ... 1

1 1909–1929: Sightless Senior and the "Boy Wonder" ... 13

2 1929–1935: "I Beg to Disagree" ... 35

3 1935–1942: "A Great Creature of the Earth" ... 57

4 1942–1947: "Spreading Like the Green Bay Tree" ... 79

5 1947–1954: "It Sure Is a Hard World" ... 99

6 1954–1959: "Why Are You So Damn Logical?" ... 123

7 1959–1963: "In Open Air Again" ... 147

8 1963–1967: "Kendall for King" ... 171

Conclusion: 1977: "The Best Man of Bugtussle" ... 201

Bibliography ... 209

Index ... 225

About the Author ... 233

List of Illustrations

Figure 0.1	Making a Point, University of Dallas	4
Figure 1.1	Child Prodigy in Knee Pants. Lawton High School, 1921	19
Figure 3.1	Close Reading, Kendall Marginalia in the *Second Treatise*	68
Figure 6.1	Nellie Cooper Kendall	141
Figure 8.1	Teaching, University of Dallas	174
Figure 8.2	Domestic Harmony, At Last	175
Figure 8.3	Home Again	195
Figure 9.1	Charles Banks Wilson, "Carl Albert"	202

Preface
1959: Willmoore Il Magnifico

On the Saturday evening of May 2, 1959, the weather in Palo Alto was clear, but the wind was blowing with a bit of a chill. As the sun started to set over the Pacific, an expectant crowd gathered at Stanford University's Memorial Hall. This building provided the largest indoor venue on campus and could seat more than seventeen hundred persons. Tonight the Hall was too small. All seats were filled by 7:00 p.m. though the performance was scheduled to start at 7:30. Organizers set up loudspeakers on the lawn and within adjoining buildings to broadcast the event to the overflow crowd. According to one observer, attendees were "hanging from the rafters." And, no, Wilbert Harrison had not shown up to play his current hit "Kansas City." Rather two popular professors, a pacifist and a "warmonger," were debating the morality of war. Student interest in questions of war and peace remained high as the Cold War still cast an ominous shadow.[1]

In one corner stood Mulford Sibley, a University of Minnesota political scientist. He had served the previous year as a visiting professor at Stanford and had won a devoted following among students. Sibley, a Quaker and socialist, was the foremost advocate of pacifism in American academia. He had braved the wrath of the US government during World War II as a conscientious objector. At the height of the Cold War, Sibley continued to argue against war and military preparedness. In the other corner stood Willmoore Kendall, the "well-known Fascist beast" from Yale. Kendall was a veteran of World War II and Korea. He had held a high position in the Central Intelligence Agency (CIA), helped professionalize American principles of psychological warfare, and was a senior editor at *National Review*. Kendall, a Catholic, was finishing up his own visiting professorship at Stanford. He had replaced Sibley and had also won the hearts and minds of many students.[2]

Though the two men's political principles could hardly have been further apart, they were old friends, having grown up together in 1920s Oklahoma. As a boy Sibley had attended the Methodist Church in the small Oklahoma town of Miami, pastored by Reverend Willmoore Kendall, Sr., father of his opponent in tonight's debate. Both men had also received degrees from the University of Oklahoma. Later they crossed professional paths at the University of Illinois where Mulford Sibley got a job teaching political science as Willmoore Kendall was finishing up his doctorate. As evidenced this spring evening, both men were learned, both skilled at disputation, and both possessed strong convictions. Each spoke for 40 minutes, then got 5 minutes to respond to the other. Afterward both speakers took questions from the audience.[3]

Kendall—fifty years old, with a "brindled" military-style crew cut—went first. He noted his social connections to Sibley, suggesting that his dad's example may have inspired his opponent's political views. Kendall pronounced that—together with Sibley and the audience—his object was to seek truth and not to make an oratorical display. Yet, as Kendall proceeded with his speech, he pulled no rhetorical punches. Sibley, he said, could never *win* a debate on this subject because Western civilization, the civilization to which he, Sibley, and the audience belonged, had rejected pacifism for millennia. From Moses onward, said Kendall, the West had often considered but always rejected pacifist arguments. However this event might turn out, no totting up of debater's points would alter this aversion to pacifism. The West *obviously* would not adopt the pacifist proposal, "the mere thought of which strikes terror into the heart."[4]

Kendall then declared that pacifists were barbarians, heretics, and parasites. They were barbarians because they refused to defend their civilization from "enemies from beyond the gates of our Civilization." By refusing to fight, the pacifists were prepared to allow their own civilization to fall and barbarism to triumph. Pacifists were also heretics, that is, "enemies within the gates." Most accepted the Christian roots of Western civilization but put a radical twist on Christian principles which undermined their society's well-being. Pacifism, Kendall argued, "insinuates itself into the body politic as a higher expression of Christian selflessness, [but] is marked throughout by irresponsibility and callous indifference towards the wants and needs and rights of the pacifists' fellow-men." The pacifist was a parasite. He lives "*off* our Civilization" and benefits from "the [martial] commitments it imposes upon others." The pacifist thus "consumes the produce of fields that he does not help to till."[5]

This aversion to pacifism—while instinctual and traditional—was also rational. Here Kendall delved deep. Drawing upon Aquinas, he argued that pacifism meant ontological rejection of society itself, for it denied the "recourse to arms, even by legally constituted states attempting to defend their just interests." Citing Lincoln he maintained that "no state voluntarily wills its own dissolution." Thus, as society was formed to promote human flourishing through establishing a legal order, those who refused to defend society were enemies to human welfare, for they advocated national suicide. Claiming to promote human dignity, then, pacifists were in fact antisocial anarchists who willed "the nothingness of civil society."[6]

Kendall then detailed Augustine's just war theory, which, he claimed, demonstrated how Christians might wage war to defend the social goods of civilization while restraining the violent passions of war to uphold ideals of peacefulness and justice. Indeed, this tradition often required the use of force—including military action—as a positive Christian duty, "the *law of Christian love itself*," to protect the weak from their oppressors. To help the oppressed and to preserve the goods of one's own civilization, nations sometimes had to go to war. Historically, for example, that meant that war had been required to defend the West against Islamic invasion. In the twentieth century, upholders of this tradition possessed a moral duty to battle "the disciplined hordes of World Communism" and to defeat "the abomination known as Nazism."[7] In fact, by refusing to submit to evil, by confronting and vanquishing the evildoer, heroic resistance might help bring that evildoer to embrace the goods of civility and peace.

The advent of nuclear weapons, said Kendall, did not change this moral calculus. God, said Kendall, had "made it *our* business . . . to protect justice, and law, and liberty, and this out of love for our neighbor." Indeed, Kendall argued, the United States, to promote justice, ought to have used its atomic monopoly in 1946 to demand that the communist regime of the USSR stop oppressing its people. It is always "our" job, that is, we the people of the West, to fulfill this moral obligation and "to use the means at our disposal in order to preserve justice in the situations in which 'we' are involved." If God has willed "the destruction of the planet in an atomic *Götterdämmerung*," this moral obligation still remains. Even in a thermonuclear world, therefore, the people of the West must perform "our duty to strike down the Soviet aggressor . . . to prevent him from doing the wrong he is doing"—as previously the West had done against the Nazis.[8]

Sibley, aged forty-seven and with thinning curly brown hair, then stood up. A lifelong socialist, he wore his trademark red tie as a symbol of solidarity with the working class. Saluting the audience as "orthodox, heretics, and friends," he proceeded to deliver his speech. He was unyielding in his defense of pacifism; that is, he claimed to oppose *all* wars. Still, Sibley focused on the contemporary "age of violence." Indeed, said he, the "central faith of American foreign policy today seems to be in the threat of mass violence." Yet Sibley also acknowledged the warlike activities of the Soviet Union, China, and India. None passed pacifist muster. He argued that human values were not absolute but dependent on historical context and that a hierarchy among such values was inevitable. Sibley drew a distinction between force—which was sometimes legitimate and necessary—and war which was never permissible.[9]

Human agreement on "social and political ideals" was, he claimed, more widespread than commonly acknowledged. All sides in the Cold War, for example, claimed to support freedom, equality, brotherhood, progress, and peace. Sibley suggested the existence of a force "continuum" from "nonviolent" civil disobedience to "increasingly violent" forms of force culminating in "the institutional practices which we sum up under the word war." The evils that war lets loose, said Sibley, including deaths of noncombatants, "contradict the kinds of ends (freedom and destruction of tyranny) for which war is usually proclaimed." The "character of a future war," with likely use of atomic weapons, would bring death and destruction to a catastrophic new level. Meanwhile preparations for war undermined peaceful economic development which might make war less likely.[10]

War was "immoral," Sibley argued, "because it involves organized and deliberate . . . killing of human beings." And "the prohibition of killing, would seem to be as close as we can come to a moral absolute in this sub-angelic world." In this light, distinctions between "aggressive" and "defensive" wars had little meaning, for both sides waged war in the same murderous fashion. Also, there were no actual criteria to distinguish an aggressive war from a defensive war. Even when war achieved positive results, as with eliminating Nazi power, these come "at such a cost and with such enormously evil by-products that its positive attainments are far more than counter balanced by its evil."[11]

For nations who accepted that there was no such thing as a good war, Sibley counseled unilateral disarmament (if multilateral disarmament proved impossible). Funds saved from war preparations could be used for education, for "nonviolent resistance," and for helping the "underdeveloped" world. And if "worst came to worst," said Sibley, the people of such a nation "would agree with Socrates that . . . it is better to suffer injustice than to commit it." Thus, nonviolent people might find themselves enslaved, but such results could also occur when a country fought and lost a war. In any case, occupation of a nonviolent nation by a hostile force "would still be preferable . . . to a war." Tyranny might triumph but "with *relatively* little loss of human life." Individuals ought therefore to engage in an "open conspiracy" against "war making governments everywhere."[12]

As regards Christianity and pacifism, Sibley noted that he did not "regard [himself] as a Christian." He maintained that the connection between pacifism and Christianity was not clear but then argued that the earliest Christians had opposed war, as such, on religious grounds. He admitted that after the early Christian period, pacifists were few because "historical so-called Christianity . . . held war to be legitimate under certain circumstances." The "nonkilling" ethos of the New Testament was nevertheless incompatible with war "despite the efforts of men like Athanasius, St. Augustine, and Luther to prove the contrary." Whatever Christianity might say about it, concluded Sibley, "pacifism is the only practical politics in our day."[13]

Sibley next proceeded with a rejoinder to Kendall's talk. He claimed Kendall contradicted himself by claiming that Western civilization would never accept pacifism while fretting about pacifist popularity. Sibley then argued that the present ought not be bound by "the short-sightedness and obtuseness of our ancestors." He argued that pacifists were not irresponsible because they were championing the values they held most dear and were not parasites because war itself contradicted Western values. Contra Kendall, he argued that the just war theory was false because modern "war . . . will always give rise to greater disorder than order." Any ends achieved would be "at a price more than counterbalancing the gains." Western civilization would "have likely reached a higher level more rapidly" if Charles Martel had not resisted the more advanced civilization of Muslim invaders. Sibley closed by suggesting repudiation "of war as a method of resisting tyranny" and urging development of "efficacious and moral means of defense."[14]

Kendall then rose to offer his own rebuttal. Sibley, he said, had told "us that enslavement—*our* enslavement—was preferable . . . to a war fought for the purpose of repelling and crushing the invader." Slavery would not be so bad, Sibley claimed, because most people would survive. Tyrannies do not last forever and could be resisted nonviolently. Kendall then argued, contradicting Sibley, that future wars would not necessarily go nuclear. Meanwhile, our "quasi-pacifist *inhibitions*" had left "millions of Russians . . . in Communist prison camps." Similar inhibitions had prevented the United States from helping "German and Eastern European Jews whom the Nazis slaughtered by the millions." Sibley, he added, would "cheerfully bid us to 'achieve' political freedom by delivering ourselves into slavery." Finally, Kendall asked how "that old complex of errors that learned men call 'historic Christianity'" had misrepresented its teachings for so long until corrected by Mulford Sibley.[15]

As the two men exchanged one highbrow haymaker after another, the crowd got caught up in the excitement. "The hall," said one observer, "sounded like the last quarter of a football game between Stanford and California." Fifty years later graduate student Tom Schrock still recalled the "spectacular" Kendall-Sibley debate. In the question and answer period which followed their speeches, neither professor retreated. Asked how he would save democracy should the Soviets nuke Palo Alto, Kendall responded that he would retaliate in kind. Queried about what he would do if the Soviets demanded capitulation or war, Sibley replied that he would surrender then begin a nonviolent resistance campaign when Russian troops arrived. As spirited defenders of their respective positions, then, Sibley (as proto-hippy peacenik) was sublime and Kendall (as homegrown Dr. Strangelove) magnificent. "Mulford," said Willmoore as they left the stage, "this was a great show. We'll have to take it on the road."[16]

Who won the debate? On one level that depended on whether one thought it better to be red or better to be dead. On another level, the real winners of the debate were the audience members who witnessed its powerful back and forth. Student organizers of the event were surprised by its popularity and praised both participants. It was all too rare, they said, for students to see "the drama" of well-prepared scholars expressing their ideas—powerfully, boldly, and without apology—on a subject of such great consequence. Even after paying Sibley's airfare and offering a similar fee for Kendall to donate to anticommunist Tibetans, the Breakers Club, which had sponsored the event, generated a tidy profit from the overflow crowd. Requests almost immediately arose for transcripts of the respective speeches. Using Kendall's contacts, organizers contracted with the Swallow Press in Denver. When published later that year, the debate proceedings sold rather briskly, especially on the Stanford campus, and talk arose of a second edition. Sibley and Kendall got a bit peeved with one another that evening, but both soon got over it, and in the coming years they would meet on other stages to debate different controversies.[17]

Both scholars were, in distinctive and diametrically opposed ways, too hot for Stanford to handle. In 1958, when the university political science department had declined to offer Sibley a permanent position, students had protested. When the department made a similar decision with Kendall for this following year, a different set of student demonstrators carried signs to object.[18] Sibley soon returned to Minnesota where, though something of a gadfly, he served out a long and distinguished career, never wavering in his pacifism and retiring in 1981. Meanwhile, Kendall, who had hoped to get a full-time job at Stanford, headed off for a two-year research sabbatical at the University of Madrid.

Though disappointed at Stanford's decision, Kendall had had a fruitful year in Palo Alto. Faced with large classes, he had shelved his own uniquely effective Socratic teaching style. Thereby, he had honed his effectiveness and increased his self-confidence as a speaker. His carefully prepared lectures were so popular that his classes became standing room only, as nonenrolled students crowded in to hear. Kendall had also participated in a series of public debates prior to the confrontation with Sibley. Taking the conservative side on a variety of controversial issues, many of these appearances had been well attended and successful. In December 1958, at one of these events, he met local librarian and ex-Marine Nellie Cooper, who first agreed to serve as his research assistant—following him to Spain—and who later became his wife. As the Spring Semester wound down, Kendall received a telegram of congratulations from former student William F. Buckley, Jr., for a "a year of splendid achievements."[19]

During the debate itself, Kendall uttered a telling aside, a throwaway line, referencing his own family background. "My father," said the conservative political theorist, "like Professor Sibley, was a persuasive man, and strongly held Professor Sibley's present ideas." In the context of the debate, this statement affirmed that it was "always good to greet a fellow-townsman whom one has not laid eyes on for a long time."[20] After these opening niceties, of course, Kendall had launched a blistering, root and branch attack on pacifists of Sibley's ilk. Indeed, if one connects the dots of his speech, the Yale professor had called his own father a barbarian, heretic, and parasite. Therein lies a tale.

NOTES

1. Thomas Schrock, Email to Author, October 17, 2017; Kent M. Lloyd, Introduction to *War & the Use of Force—Moral or Immoral, Christian or Unchristian—A Debate at Stanford University* by Willmoore Kendall (hereafter WK) and Mulford Q. Sibley (Denver: Swallow Press, 1959), 2; Oscar Pemantle, *Contrasting Arguments: The Culture War and the Clash in Education* (New York: Peter Lang, 2019), 201.

2. "Plan for Peace," *Hammond Times*, May 15, 1944, p. 6; Paul K. Damai, "Radio Short Circuits," *Hammond Times*, August 13, 1944, p. 8; "Goble to Speak," *Evening Courier*, February 18, 1945, p. 7; Duane L. Cady, "What's On My Mind: Remembering Mulford Q. Sibley," May 20, 2019, duanelcady.com; Letter to the Editor, *YDN*, October 17, 1957, p. 2

3. Lloyd, "Introduction," 2–3; WK and Sibley, *War & the Use of Force*, 5.

4. Letter, *YDN*, October 17, 1957, p. 2; "Kendall-Sibley Debate," *Stanford Daily*, March 1, 1959, p. 1; WK/Sibley, *War*, 5–6.

5. WK/Sibley, *War*, 6–9.

6. Ibid., 7–10.

7. Ibid., 12–13.

8. Ibid., 14.

9. Cady, "Sibley"; "Kendall-Sibley Debate," 1; "Capacity Crowd Attends," *Stanford Daily*, May 4, 1959, p. 1; WK/Sibley, *War*, 15–16.

10. Ibid., 18–21.

11. Ibid., 21–22.

12. Ibid., 22–23.

13. Ibid., 24–25.

14. Ibid., 26–29.

15. Ibid., 30–32.

16. Leo Paul de Alvarez, "Willmoore Kendall: Teacher," Obituary, Clipping from *Phalanx*, 1967, B16F7, Willmoore Kendall Papers (hereafter KP), Hoover Institution Library and Archives; Thomas Schrock, Email to the Author, October 7, 2017; "Capacity Crowd," 2; Oscar Pemantle, "Trial by Drury," Unpublished Manuscript in Possession of the Author, 2019, 1.

17. Lloyd, "Introduction," 3–4; "Professors Will Debate," *San Mateo Times*, May 2, 1959, p. 15; WK to William F. Buckley, Jr., [June] 1959, Box 8, William F. Buckley, Jr. Papers (hereafter BP), Manuscripts and Archives, Sterling Memorial Library, Yale University; Sibley to WK, April 5, 1966, Box 19, Folder 5, KP; Richard L. Noble to Don Lipsett, January 20, 1962 and Noble to Thomas E. Reilly, February 21, 1962, B20, BP; Kristin Serum, "Freedom of Speech," *Minneapolis Star*, April 7, 1967, p. 6.

18. "Professors Will Debate," 15; "Conservative to Debate Liberal," *Stanford Daily*, May 10, 1966, p. 1.

19. American Political Science Association, Oral History Project, Transcripts of Tapes Recording Conversations with Charles S. Hyneman, 1978–79, pp. 37–38, B4F18, Katherine A. Kendall Papers (hereafter KKP), Social Welfare Archive, University of Minnesota Archives and Special Collections; Diana Smith, "Kendall, Ogg Opposed," *Stanford Daily*, January 14, 1959, p. 1; "McCord-Kendall," *The Stanford Daily*, April 9, 1959, p. 1; Bob Frank, "Profs Differ," *Stanford Daily*, April 10, 1959, p. 1; "Kendall-Miller Meet," *Stanford Daily*, April 16, 1959, p. 1; Clipping from *Dallas Morning News*, November 9, 1969, p. 10E, B22F4, KP; Curriculum Vitae of Mrs. Nellie D. Kendall, B30F1, KP; WK to William F. Buckley, Jr. (hereafter WB), [Fall] 1958 and December 23, 1958, B6, BP; WB to WK, June 3, 1959, B8, BP; WB to Richard L. Noble, June 3, 1959, B21F6, KP.

20. WK/Sibley, *War*, 5.

Acknowledgments

Support for this project was received from the Faculty Research Committee, Northeastern State University, Tahlequah, OK 74464. Thanks also to the Carl Albert Congressional Research and Studies Center at the University of Oklahoma which provided support for the project through its Visiting Scholars Grant. Parts of the following narrative have appeared previously in *The Chronicles of Oklahoma*, in *Walk Away: When the Political Left Turns Right* (Lexington Books, 2019) and in *Chronicles: A Magazine of American Culture*.

List of Abbreviations

BDJ	Bertrand de Jouvenel
BP	William F. Buckley, Jr. Papers, Manuscripts and Archives, Sterling Memorial Library, Yale University
CB	Cleanth Brooks
CBP	Cleanth Brooks Papers, Yale Collection of American Literature, Beinecke Rare Book and Manuscript Library, Yale University
CCR	Office of the Coordinator for Inter-American Affairs, Coordination Committee for Colombia Records, 1941–1945
COR	Numbered Correspondence, Coordination Committee for Colombia Records
CH	Charles S. Hyneman
CHP	Charles S. Hyneman papers, Collection C2, Indiana University Archives
EV	Eric Voegelin
FGW	Francis Graham Wilson
FW	Frederick Wilhelmsen
GWC	George W. Carey
HR	Henry Regnery
HRP	Henry Regnery Papers, Hoover Institution, Library and Archives
JH	Jeffrey Hart
KK	Katherine Tuach Kendall
KKP	Katherine A. Kendall Papers, Social Welfare Archive, University of Minnesota Archives and Special Collections
KP	Willmoore Kendall Papers, Hoover Institution, Library and Archives
LB	L. Brent Bozell, Jr.

LS	Leo Strauss
NK	Nellie Cooper Kendall
NR	*National Review*
OxY	Yvona Kendall Mason, ed. *The Oxford Years: The Letters of Willmoore Kendall to His Father*. Bryn Mawr, PA: Intercollegiate Studies Institute, 1993
PGK	Pearl Garlick Kendall
RPO	Revilo Pendleton Oliver
VK	Steven D. Ealy and Gordon Lloyd, eds., "The Eric Voegelin-Willmoore Kendall Correspondence," *Political Science Reviewer* 33 (2004):357–412
WB	William F. Buckley, Jr.
WK	Willmoore Kendall, Jr.
WKC	Willmoore Kendall Collection, Archives and Special Collections, University of Dallas
WKM	John A. Murley and John E. Alvis, eds., *Willmoore Kendall: Maverick of Conservatives*. Lanham, MD: Lexington Books, 2002
WKS	Willmoore Kendall, Sr.
WP	Francis Graham Wilson Papers, University of Illinois Archives
YM	Yvona Kendall Mason

Introduction

Tribune and Teacher of the American People

For democracy to exist as more than a word, Willmoore Kendall insisted that "we the people" must be able to make the most important political decisions. To admirers Kendall was a maverick or an iconoclast, to foes mad, indecent, even a "murderer." One contemporary writer has called Kendall the Fanon of conservatives, the "Ur-Democrat." Anyone who challenged the sovereignty of the people risked his learned and ferocious wrath. Beset by addictions, attractive to women, and notoriously combative, he cheerfully attacked Franklin Roosevelt, Barry Goldwater, John Stuart Mill, John Locke, Albert Schweitzer, Billy Graham, Abraham Lincoln, and Socrates. His anticommunism was fierce, "his enemies," according to his most famous student, "as numerous as the stars above." When the world blackened the name of Joseph McCarthy, Kendall stood almost alone among American academics to defend him.[1] Yet Willmoore Kendall was also one of the most effective and sensitive teachers of his age. As an American official, his ideas shaped Cold War practices of intelligence analysis and psychological warfare. As a political activist and writer, he helped start the conservative movement which toppled the post-World War II liberal consensus. Most important was his political theory—worked out over decades of deep reading and obsessive cogitation—in which he refined the nuances of American democracy.

Throughout the various phases of his career, Kendall viewed his chief work as championing the people. His political theory looked to promote and protect democratic governance in the United States. He sought neither to resurrect ancient institutions, nor to invent new institutions ex nihilo, nor to propose new political solutions of universal application. Rather he believed, together with Rousseau, that "liberty is not one of those fruits that thrive in any just any climate. It is not, therefore, to be plucked by just any people." More than other conservatives, Kendall believed the American people possessed enough virtue to be able to preserve both liberty and democracy.²

A champion of the American people, Kendall served in effect as their tribune, an intellectual defender of their prerogatives. Several scholars have also used the word populist to describe this tendency in Kendall's work, though seldom elaborating on it. Using a populist schematic, however, helps resolve conundrums associated with simply labeling him as a conservative. Many have noted how Kendall's ideas are often at odds with the best-known strains of conservatism. Kendall was not a neocon, not a theocon, not a paleocon, not a country-club Republican, not a state's rights advocate, not a libertarian. Some commentators have regarded Kendall as a follower of Leo Strauss or Eric Voegelin, but he disagreed with both men on many things. Other labels for Kendall's thought have included Catholic, Trotskyist, Burkean, "absolute majoritarian," and "philosopher of the lynch mob." Even among two of his most accomplished students, one saw Kendall as an Aristotelian focused on reasoned discourse, the other as a myth-burdened Rousseauian.³ Some of these labels are more accurate than others, but none do justice to Kendall's intellectual complexity.

Even for those who do not agree with him, reading Kendall is instructive precisely *because* his ideas do not lend themselves to simplistic summary or easy left-right dichotomy. His writing was often apophatic, revealing his own ideas through pointing out the flaws and inconsistencies in the views of others. Yet Kendall's readers and listeners, even those like libertarian economist Murray Rothbard and conservative sociologist Robert Nisbet who were horrified by his theories, often thought: "Hey, I never looked at it that way before." As a young man of the left, Kendall embraced communism but viewed Stalinism as a treacherous death cult. As an established personality of the right, he called himself a conservative but rejected many attacks on big government and supported the economic ideas of John Maynard Keynes. Thus, Kendall's chroniclers (often his friends and students) have sometimes proclaimed that, like St. Athanasius, Willmoore stood alone, *contra mundum*.⁴ It is tempting, therefore, to view Kendall as a quirky and quarrelsome conservative whose ideas fit into no particular school of thought and which are of little lasting interest.

Such judgment would be a serious mistake. In the first place, Kendall's ideas have always maintained a following among conservative intellectuals, several of whom have regarded his political theory as of the highest caliber. Jeffrey Hart, distinguished Dartmouth essayist, called Kendall the "most important political theorist . . . since the end of World War II." U.S. Senator and political scientist John P. East regarded Kendall as "the most original, innovative, and challenging [political] interpreter of any period." According to contemporary conservative journalist Daniel McCarthy, Kendall "is one of the most overlooked founding fathers of the conservative movement and also one of the most interesting." He was "the top Americanist of the postwar conservative movement."[5] When looking at the long span of his life—as one may do in a biography—it becomes clear that Kendall absorbed ideas from many sources, blended them together, and recast them in a way particularly his own. Had he lived longer, he may have been able to create a more sizable school of political theorists. As it happened, his ideas have remained intriguing while standing outside any major school of thought.

Seeing Kendall both as a populist and a conservative makes much of his quirkiness disappear. Viewed through this lens, Kendall's theory demonstrates more coherence and greater consistency over time than most scholars have realized. He was a conservative with "a radical *habitus*," but his steadfast focus on rule by the people calls into question claims, by William F. Buckley, Russell Kirk, and others, that he was simply a contrarian, a conservative because most contemporaries were liberals. Kendall always continued to read and to think, so his political theory continued to change. When one looks at Kendall's evolution as a thinker, movement to the right is obvious. As one observes Kendall journeying from Trotskyist to absolute majoritarian to Madisonian, continuities in his thought emerge. Kendall's *goal*—empowering the people to rule democratically and to uphold a functional, just, tranquil, and cohesive polity—remained the same throughout his career. But his ideas about the best *means* to achieve this goal changed greatly. In trying to clarify those means, he drew on many sources—Burke, Rousseau, Strauss, Voegelin, Aristotle, Madison—then incorporated their insights into his own political theory. Scholars who have proposed labeling Kendall's ideas as populist have seldom pursued the implications of such characterization. Historian George H. Nash, for example, dropped the theme of populism because of "tricky" ambiguities in the term. Indeed, to many scholars, populism has appeared a "thin" ideology. This claim arises chiefly because populism fails to coincide with traditional liberal-conservative divisions, that is, there are both right-wing and left-wing populists. All sorts of groups, with conflicting political programs, have donned the populist mantle. One anthology on American Populism from the 1970s, for example, included excerpts from George Wallace, George McGovern, Joseph McCarthy, and Saul Alinsky.[6]

As a young man, Kendall himself recognized a similar tendency—that political theorists often praised majority rule in the abstract but felt little "obligation to formulate the ideas it represents or to seek out the arguments that might be urged in its favor." Kendall made it his life mission to correct this deficiency. For decades he used his formidable intellect to formulate ways to strengthen the people's ability to rule democratically. If defining populism as "a political philosophy supporting the rights and power of the people in their struggle against the privileged elite," then Willmoore Kendall was a left-wing populist in the Depression years and, as he moved right, he remained a populist until death. Throwing down a populist gauntlet in 1939, for example, Kendall proclaimed "that between those who accept the majority principle as the differentia of democratic government, and those who repudiate it, a wider gulf is fixed than that which separates the latter from the defenders of Fascism." In 1966, shortly before his death, Kendall strongly reaffirmed that he valued democracy over capitalism. In any conflict between political liberty and capitalist efficiency, he proclaimed: "let productivity suffer, and let freedom ring!"[7] Any enemy of the people's right to rule was Kendall's enemy.

Recent scholarship suggesting an "ideational" model for populism linked to Rousseau's notions of the general will applies to Kendall. Indeed, one may understand his career as seeking a long-term solution to Rousseau's conundrum that "man is born free, and everywhere he is in chains." Kendall felt the allure of primitive democracy: Swiss peasants gathering under the oak, or Pilgrims covenanting on the *Mayflower*, in which the people might find consensus reflecting the will of the community. Unwilling to accept that democracy might only exist in such settings, he sought to understand how to preserve it in the modern nation-state. That Kendall did not call himself a

Figure 0.1 Making a Point, University of Dallas. *Source:* University of Dallas Archives & Special Collections.

populist also fits here, for, as scholars Cas Mudde and Cristóbal Kaltwasser have suggested, the term is seldom self-proclaimed. As a mature thinker, Kendall defined populism as a type of progressivism seeking quick enactment of majority will, a position he once held but then abandoned. According to contemporary scholars, populism is a "thin" ideology which "almost always appears attached to other ideological elements." If true, this characteristic again fits the bill for Kendall, a self-proclaimed conservative.[8]

In contemporary political discourse, both inside and outside the academy, the word populism frequently appears as an emotive label used to attack one's enemies. Yet, what many twenty-first-century news commentators and academics now say about populism—that it is incoherent, backward, and anti-intellectual—is what their liberal forbears said about 1950's conservatism. As the incipient American conservative movement began—a movement Kendall helped launch—its detractors disparaged it, not merely as erroneous, but as half-baked, poorly informed foolishness. From the academy, for example, Lionel Trilling of Columbia and Louis Hartz of Harvard argued that all real American thought was progressive in character. In attacking *National Review* in 1956, Dwight MacDonald of *Commentary* and John Fischer at *Harper's* resorted to ad hominem attacks rather than engaging the new magazine's ideas. One may pair most every "scrambled egg-heads of the right" from the 1950s with similar denunciations of populists in the present day.[9]

So by declaring himself a conservative in the 1950s, Kendall opened himself up to attack from the intellectual elite of his day. By proclaiming him a populist thinker—when the study of conservatism, if not conservatism itself, has become semirespectable in American academic circles—this biography will likely prolong his status in some circles as an intellectual untouchable, doubly so by labeling him a conservative populist. If one defines populists as a mindless and irresponsible rabble, then Kendall was not a populist. But Kendall worked for his entire career to develop "a political philosophy supporting the rights and power of the people in their struggle against the privileged elite." It is in using this definition—rather than Kendall's own sense of the word—that I see him as a populist. Anyone who reads Kendall's mature political theory cannot deny that it was meticulously constructed, intricately layered, and sophisticated. Over his career, then, Kendall developed many innovative and provocative ideas, a number of which remain politically relevant. To borrow language from literary critic Cleanth Brooks, Kendall's longtime friend, the man's academic work, whether or not one agreed with its conclusions, constituted a "well-wrought urn."[10] To establish the populist character of Kendall's thought therefore "thickens" the concept of populism itself.

Distrustful of elites, he advocated reliance on the "deliberate sense of the community" for decision-making. His ideal, in the end, was rule by the people through elected representatives who possessed the time and the temperament to consider both national and local interests. He came to fear that ephemeral majorities would enact change rashly. He expressed skepticism about individual rights as a touchstone for public policy, arguing that all societies must and do limit individual activities which that society thinks threaten its survival. Kendall did not merely grumble about elite domination or craft appeals to suit the prejudices of the masses. Rather he sought to show that liberalism was undemocratic and socially destructive. By insisting on rapid realization of unpopular and utopian demands, liberalism (and some types of conservatism) took decision-making out of the hands of the people and undermined existing social goods. Speaking to students at the University of Dallas, Kendall said: "These are the people who are going to do justice, let heaven fall where it may. And I say to them, heaven can indeed fall and that it can hurt some of the heads it hits mighty bad." He then tried to show how the American people might keep control of their government by exercising a "constitutional morality" of "restraint" to prevent the political sky from falling. Such restraint required careful deliberation among elected representatives about the future. It also involved maintaining balance among the six goods enumerated in the preamble to the Constitution—union, justice, domestic tranquility, common defense, general welfare, and liberty. By valuing and talking through each of these goals, but prioritizing no one above the others, the American people might maintain their democracy for the long haul.[11]

Recent political developments have increased the need to appreciate Kendall's work for understanding American conservatism. In 1994, for example, historian Alan Brinkley maintained that American conservatism was Lockean, was focused on individual freedom, and rested on "antistatist assumptions of John Stuart Mill." Yet, Kendall, a key founder of the modern conservative movement, loathed Locke, was skeptical of the Bill of Rights, and despised Mill. In 2010 historian Patrick Allitt wrote a history of American conservatism without mentioning populism or nationalism. He argued that a synthesis of traditionalism, libertarianism, and anticommunism still dominated late twentieth-century conservatism. In 2011 Kim Phillips-Fein downplayed conservative divisiveness by arguing that a seamless fusion existed between free market and traditionalist conservatives. If populism existed among conservatives, she argued, it was a smoke screen disguising the hegemony of big business. By 2016 political scientist George Hawley was telling a new tale. Reagan-era fusionism lay in shreds. Right-wing insurgents—often populist, nationalist, sometimes racist or tribalist in nature—had arisen to challenge the conservative establishment. Insofar as these challenges have been populist, *one must* look to Kendall for instruction. For his ideas, more than those of any other American thinker, provide an intellectual framework for conservative populism. As the conservative synthesis has unraveled, some observers have begun to look anew to Kendall. For example, Matthew Continetti, editor of the *Washington Free Beacon*, recently resurrected Kendall's "battle-line" metaphor of liberal-conservative conflict for describing the hyperpartisanship of present-day American politics.[12]

Historian George Nash noted that Kendall's teaching lay outside the typical conservative paradigm and that he opposed the conservative establishment as soon as one appeared. Kendall's ideas combined Rousseau's concept of the general will, Leo Strauss's views on natural right, Aristotle's ideas on the good, and James Madison's vision of legislative supremacy. Behind it all lay Kendall's notion that the American people ought always to govern itself well, lest a dictator or a judge or a bureaucracy arise to govern instead. If one accepts Kendall's political theory as populist, one must ignore it to claim that populism lacks serious intellectual foundations. His ideas contradict assertions that populists "are not an authentic part of modern democratic politics . . . [because populists] insist that only they themselves are legitimate representatives" of the people. Kendall did no such thing. His ideas had exclusionary elements but so too did those of his liberal opponents. Some leftists also now damn Kendall as a monstrous racist.[13] Yet race was not central to his thought, and, despite occasionally expressing insensitive racial views, he strongly praised Congress for enacting civil rights laws to keep African Americans within the American political system.

However one categorizes it, to focus on Kendall's political theory alone would provide an incomplete picture of his achievements, for he also exercised public influence in other ways. Least known was Kendall's work in intelligence, but he achieved much success in this field. For example, he briefly headed up CIA efforts in Latin America. His ideas about the role of analysts remain central to contemporary debates in the intelligence community. Kendall crafted propaganda and pioneered psywar techniques during the Korean War. The public knew Kendall best as a conservative teacher, writer, and speaker. Teaching at Yale, Kendall inspired William F. Buckley, Jr., and L. Brent Bozell, Jr., into careers of political activism. He cofounded *National Review* in 1955, helping mold it into *the* American platform for sophisticated conservative opinion. As a regular contributor, he excoriated establishment figures in his column, "The Liberal Line." His sharp-edged debates with left-wing academics on issues of the day often left audiences enthralled.

If one were to ask why Kendall should be remembered, the initial response would be (1) because of his insightful political theory and (2) because he helped kick-start the conservative movement which toppled New Deal-style liberalism. Taking this tack, these two contributions are what make Kendall an *important* person. But biography involves more than discussing a man's significance. Rather, a biographer—if true to his craft—must tell the story of a human being, not just chronicle or analyze his subject's accomplishments. Kendall possessed a difficult temperament. He was a man, said one student, "who never lost an argument or kept a friend." According to first wife Katherine Kendall, Willmoore was a "stormy petrel, brilliant and charming." His personal life was chaotic—broken marriages, alcoholism, rage. "The road you must travel if you want to do any serious study of Kendall, the man," said third wife Nellie Kendall, is "a turning, twisting road that has many dead ends, double backs, forks, etc. Studying his political philosophy would be, I think, a simpler matter." Yet two men who knew Kendall quite well—one the Speaker of the House of Representatives and the other a Spanish Trotskyist refugee—both suggested that to understand Kendall's philosophy one needed to dive into his psychology.[14]

In my own view, one cannot understand Willmoore Kendall without engagement with his political philosophy. In the following biography (the first book-length treatment of his life and work), I have therefore described and analyzed his most important works. One finds Kendall's political philosophy scattered about in many essays and articles. He had no single magnum opus which one may consult as definitive or which his other works set out to defend. His scholarship was dense, based on a style of close reading and textual analysis picked up from R. G. Collingwood at Oxford and from the New Critics at LSU. Several scholars have written astute pieces on Kendall's ideas.[15] To do full justice to Kendall's thought, however, requires a separate book in which a single author can gather up and critique Kendall's scholarly work in toto, subjecting it to the techniques of careful reading and analysis which he himself used.

The following biography—a life of Willmoore Kendall—is not that book. However, by helping to know Kendall as a person, it elucidates and deepens understanding of his teaching. His activities as conservative publicist and intelligence officer, for example, became intertwined with his scholarship. That his exotic personality often obscured his work as a thinker makes grasping the complex details of his life all the more important. Neither his brilliance nor his contrariness came out of a vacuum. Kendall's teacher Collingwood maintained that history differs from the physical sciences because historians can understand the past from the inside. Historians study human beings and so can reconstruct the thoughts of their subjects in ways scientists cannot, a process Collingwood called "reenactment." Kendall sometimes applied this technique in his own scholarship, interrogating past thinkers as if witnesses in a trial so he might understand their thought. When reading *The Federalist*, for example, Kendall tried to understand its anonymous author Publius afresh, reenacting his experience to cut through decades of interpretative accretions.[16] By thinking with Willmoore Kendall, then, by reenacting his thought processes and putting ourselves in his shoes, we can imagine the world as he experienced it, through the mind's eye of this one gifted but often troubled man.

To tell Kendall's story well thus requires weaving together distinct strands of his life as he worked to be a teacher and tribune for the American people. One must ponder his psychology, think through his family relationships, delve into his intelligence activities, investigate his journalistic endeavors, and analyze his political theory. The very intricacy of this tale makes it exciting and illuminating. Kendall was a child prodigy, preacher's kid, and bucolic boy scout who became an ambitious military analyst, mesmerizing teacher, razor-tongued polemicist, and profound student of American politics. He loved to talk, think, drink, smoke, and cook. He more than held his own in debates against Ivy League intellectual heavyweights, sat on a stage with Archduke Otto von Habsburg, but also could enjoy conversing "with a garage mechanic named Eddie."[17] By knowing his story, in its untidy particularity, one may, inter alia, better grasp America's Cold War past and better understand certain complexities of the human condition.

NOTES

1. Chris Morgan, "Willmoore Kendall Catches Fire," *Jacobite*, August 22, 2019, https://jacobitemag.com/2019/08/22/willmoore-kendall-catches-fire/.

2. Jean-Jacques Rousseau, *The Social Contract*, trans. Willmoore Kendall (Chicago: Regnery, 1954), 119; John E. Alvis, "The Evolution of Willmoore Kendall's Thought," in *WKM*, 86–94.

3. George H. Nash, "Willmoore Kendall: Conservative Iconoclast (II)," *Modern Age* 19 (Summer 1975): 245; Grant Havers, "Leo Strauss, Willmoore Kendall, and the Meaning of Conservatism," *Humanitas* XVIII, nos. 1 and 2 (2005): 16–21; Garry Wills, *Confessions of a Conservative* (New York: Doubleday, 1979), 22–23; Havers, "Meaning," 17; Alvis, "Evolution," 47–48; Murray N. Rothbard, *Strictly Confidential: The Private Volker Fund Memos of Murray N. Rothbard*, ed. David Gordon (Auburn, AL: Ludwig von Mises Institute, 2010), 44; Alvis, "Evolution," 47; Leo Paul de Alvarez, "The Missing Passage of 'The Vanderbilt Lectures,'" in *WKM*, 153.

4. Rothbard, *Confidential*, 35–36; Nash, "Iconoclast II," 245, 248; WK to WKS, October 16, 1933 in *Oxford Years: The Letters of Willmoore Kendall to His Father* ed. YM (Bryn Mawr, PA, 1993), (hereafter *OxY*), 282; Murley/Alvis, *WKM, passim*; George H. Nash, "Willmoore Kendall: Conservative Iconoclast (I)," *Modern Age* 19 (Spring 1975): 127–35; Nellie Kendall, ed., *Willmoore Kendall Contra Mundum* (New Rochelle, NY: Arlington House, 1972).

5. JH, "Willmoore Kendall: Philosopher of Consensus," *National Review* (hereafter *NR*), September 1, 1978, pp. 1084–85; John P. East, "The Political Thought of Willmoore Kendall," *The Political Science Reviewer* 3 (Fall 1973): 201; Daniel McCarthy, "The Constitution Versus Calhoun: Why Harry Jaffa is Still Wrong

About Willmoore Kendall," *American Conservative*, September 23, 2013, https://www.theamericanconservative.com/mccarthy/the-constitution-vs-calhoun-why-harry-jaffa-is-still-wrong-about-willmoore-kendall/; Matthew Continetti, "'Genuine Civil War Potential:' Willmoore Kendall, Donald Trump, and American Conservatism," *Washington Free Beacon*, July 27 2018, https://freebeacon.com/columns/genuine-civil-war-potential/.; Grant Havers, "Who is to Say Nay to the People? Publius, Majority Rule and Willmoore Kendall," May 28, 2012, https://www.lawliberty.org/2012/05/28/who-is-to-say-nay-to-the-people-publius-majority-rule-and-willmoore-kendall/.

6. Bertrand de Jouvenal (hereafter BDJ) to WK, March 9, 1961, B16F2, KP; John B. Judis, *William F. Buckley: Patron Saint of Conservatives* (New York: Simon & Schuster, 1988), 61; WB, Introduction to *God and Man at Yale*, 50th Anniversary Edition (Washington, DC, Nash, "Iconoclast II," 245; Cas Mudde and Cristóbal Rovira Kaltwasser, *Populism: A Very Short Introduction* (Oxford: Oxford University Press, 2017), 6; George McKenna, *American Populism* (New York: G.P. Putnam's Sons, 1974).

7. WK, "The Majority Principle and the Scientific Elite, *Southern Review* (Winter 1939): 463–73; "Populism," *The American Heritage Dictionary*, https://www.ahdictionary.com/word/search.html?q=populism.; George H. Nash, "The Place of Willmoore Kendall in American Conservatism," in *WKM*, 7; WK, "The Future of Individual Initiative in America," November 29, 1966, 11–21, *WKC*.

8. George W. Carey, (hereafter GWC), "Willmoore Kendall and the Doctrine of Majority Rule," in *WKM*, 25, 37–42; Mudde/Kaltwasser, 2–6.

9. Lionel Trilling, *The Liberal Imagination: Essays on Literature and Society* (New York: Viking Press, 1950); Louis Hartz, *The Liberal Tradition in America* (New York: Harcourt, Brace, Jovanovich, 1955); Dwight MacDonald, "On the Horizon: Scrambled Eggheads of the Right." *Commentary*, April 1956, https://www.commentarymagazine.com/articles/on-the-horizon-scrambled-eggheads-on-the-right/; John Fischer, "Why is the Conservative Voice So Harsh," *Harper's Magazine*, March 1956, 16–22; Anthony R. Brunello, "The Madisonian Republic and Modern Nationalist Populism," *World Affairs* 181, no. 2 (Summer 2018): 128; D.J. Mulloy, *Enemies of the State: The Radical Right in America From FDR to Trump* (Lanham, MD: Rowman & Littlefield, 2018), 183–85.

10. Cleanth Brooks, *The Well-Wrought Urn: Studies in the Structure of Poetry* (New York: Harvest Books, 1947).

11. WK, Classroom Lecture, University of Dallas, Government 201, [1964], B26F3, KP; Grant Havers, "Willmoore Kendall for Our Times," *Modern Age* (Winter/Spring 2011): 123–24; JH, "The 'Deliberate Sense' of Willmoore Kendall," *The New Criterion* (March 2002): 78–79; Francis G. Wilson (hereafter FGW), "The Political Science of Willmoore Kendall," *Modern Age* 16, no. 1 (Winter 1972): 47.

12. Alan Brinkley, "The Problem of American Conservatism." *American Historical Review* 9, no. 2 (April 1994): 415–16; Patrick Allitt, *The Conservatives: Ideas and Personalities Throughout American History* (New Haven: Yale University Press, 2010), *passim*; Kim Phillips-Fein, "Conservatism: A State of the Field." *Journal of American History* 98, no. 3 (December 2011): 734–35; Kim Phillips-Fein, "'As

Great an Issue as Slavery or Abolition': Economic Populism, the Conservative Movement, and the Right-to-Work Campaigns of 1958." *Journal of Policy History* 23, no. 4 (2011): 506; George Hawley, *Right-Wing Critics of American Conservatism* (Lawrence: University Press of Kansas, 2016), *passim*; Matthew Continetti, "War Potential."

13. Nash, "Place," 12; Alvis, "Evolution," *passim*; Jan-Werner Mueller, *What is Populism?* (Philadelphia: University of Pennsylvania Press, 2016), 101; Luke March, "Left and Right Populism Compared: The British Case," *British Journal of Politics and International Relations* 19, no. 2 (March 2017): 300; Jeet Heer, "Racism and the Paradox of Anti-Democratic Populism," May 26, 2021, https://jeetheer.substack.com/p/racism-and-the-paradox-of-anti-democratic.

14. Oscar Pemantle to the Author, Email, June 21, 2019; Katherine Tuach Kendall (hereafter KK) to John W. Fiser, January 21, 1982, B4F18, KKP; Nellie Cooper Kendall (hereafter NK) to George H. Nash, February 27, 1972, B21F13, KP; Carl Albert to Paul P. Berman, October 12, 1972, B92F26, General Correspondence, (hereafter CAC); Juan Andrade to George H. Nash, "About Willmoore Kendall," January 8, 1974, B4F18, KKP.

15. Mark Nugent, "Willmoore Kendall and the Deliberate Sense of Community," *Political Science Reviewer* 36 (2007): 228–65; Nash, "Iconoclast I" and "Iconoclast II:" GWC, "How to Read Willmoore Kendall." *Intercollegiate Review* 8, no. 2 (Winter/Spring 1972): 63–65.

16. GWC, "How to Read," 63; R.G. Collingwood, *The Idea of History* (London: Oxford University Press, 1956), 215–16; GWC, "Doctrine," 31.

17. *Frederick Daniel Wilhelmsen*, UD Profile Series, I (Dallas: University of Dallas, 1998), 10; Leo Paul de Alvarez, "Willmoore Kendall and the Constitution," [1994], 1–2, Willmoore Kendall Collection, Archives and Special Collections, (hereafter WKC), University of Dallas.

Chapter 1

1909–1929

Sightless Senior and the "Boy Wonder"

In March 1929, with winter giving way to Spring, the twenties still roared like thunder in Tulsa. While the nation's economy continued to expand, the "Oil Capital of the World" was booming. With about 140,000 residents its population had doubled in the decade. Tulsa's oil barons—Robert McFarlin, James Chapman, William G. Skelly, and Waite Phillips—were growing immensely rich. J. Paul Getty and Harry Sinclair had made their millions and left town, but the remaining "princes of petroleum" dominated the city's commerce and municipal government, making the key decisions which shaped the city.[1] The Black Tuesday stock market crash lay months in the future while the strikes in the East Texas Oil Field which collapsed global oil prices would not occur for a year after that.

Stylish structures were popping up all over town. After completing a seventy-two room mansion in 1927, for example, Waite Phillips built the Philtower, a neo-Gothic skyscraper which opened for business downtown in 1928. Ten blocks south, and completed a year later, stood Boston Avenue Methodist Church. This stunning exemplar of ecclesiastical art deco, with soaring 225-foot tower and Wesleyan iconography, provided an upscale setting for the services of its prosperous congregation. The same year Frank Lloyd Wright completed Westhope, a 10,000 square foot home of "strange and startling beauty," for his cousin Richard Lloyd Jones, owner and editor of the *Tulsa Tribune*. This flat-roofed, two-story house included a four-car garage, swimming pool, fish pond, fountain, and four patios.[2]

Amid such glitter, however, were indications that dangerous social rifts plagued the city. Brothels, speakeasies, gambling hells, and narcotics dens lined the streets north of downtown. In the nearby Greenwood district, much of the physical infrastructure had been rebuilt from the 1921 Race Massacre, in which angry white mobs had killed dozens of black people and burned hundreds of homes. Gruesome postcards celebrating destruction of "the Black Wall Street" still circulated. Membership in the Ku Klux Klan had surged in Tulsa in the early 1920s. The organization appealed to store owners and professionals squeezed between an ostentatious upper crust and a rowdy working class. Although waning in popularity and power, the Invisible Empire retained a presence in Tulsa in 1929. On the edge of Greenwood stood its newly built Beno Hall. Possessing a few neo-Gothic flourishes and with a seating capacity of three thousand, it was among the largest auditoriums in the region.[3]

A block away stood a speakeasy called the Louvre. Locals knew this venue (later famous as Cain's Ballroom) as much for its alcohol-fueled fights as for its well-attended dances. On the Saturday evening of March 9, 1929, a young man named Willmoore Kendall hit the streets of north Tulsa to celebrate his birthday. He had turned twenty the previous Tuesday, but teaching duties at the Oklahoma Military Academy in Claremore had kept him busy until the weekend. Blue-eyed, razor-thin, 6 feet tall, dressed in academy uniform and riding boots, Kendall cut a snappy figure walking into the Louvre. The locals were not impressed. Entering the honkytonk with a date, Kendall got drunk and, according to one account, "threatened to shoot up the place." The young teacher, still in uniform, then punched someone who insulted his date. Three bouncers hauled him outside and beat him unconscious. When he revived and tried to escape, they dragged him to a police station where—booked for public drunkenness—he spent the night in jail. The next day the story appeared on the first page of the *Tulsa Tribune*. Only a paragraph long, the story made the paper as a "funny feature" because of the novelty of the young man's uniform. The newspaper had mistaken the youthful Kendall for a cadet.[4]

The tyro teacher suffered no lasting legal consequences. The city court dropped the intoxication charge and fined him nine dollars for disturbing the peace. But that initial small paragraph wreaked "ruination" in his life. As a former employee of the *Tribune*, he felt angry about the paper publicizing the incident. Kendall made some calls and got the paper to agree to a retraction. But it was too late. The Oklahoma Military Academy fired him. Even trickier was figuring out how to deal with the reaction of his father. Reverend Willmoore Kendall, Sr., served as the Methodist pastor in Vinita, a small town northeast of Tulsa. As the *Tribune* circulated throughout the area, there was no hiding what had happened at the Louvre. To avoid his father—and without telling anyone where he was going—the young man therefore fled to Chicago. A series of anguished letters between the Kendalls, *père et fils*, followed. The mortified minister demanded his prodigal offspring "appear before" Vinita First Methodist Church to apologize. Kendall, Jr., rejected this demand. Defending his behavior at the nightclub, he declared he was not sorry and that he was angered by his father's "caustic attitude." He then asserted that it would be "quite impossible" for him ever to live again amid the "provincial smugness" of Oklahoma.⁵

Willmoore, Jr.'s arrest and flight appeared, for a time, to crush high hopes that the Kendalls had placed upon their oldest son. This escapade, said Reverend Kendall, constituted the "deepest bitterness I have ever known." Indeed, the entire family had already invested lots of emotional energy into its oldest son's success. Seven years before, for example, news about thirteen-year-old Willmoore had flashed out of small-town Oklahoma to create a national sensation. The American wire services in the summer of 1922 had publicized the story of a prodigy who had blossomed in Mangum, Oklahoma, a cotton town located in the southwestern corner of the state. The boy's name—Willmoore Kendall—was somewhat unusual. In May of that year the lad graduated from Mangum High School at age thirteen, and his story received some local coverage.⁶

When word got out that young Kendall would enroll as a freshman at Northwestern University in Evanston, Illinois, the story went national. Dozens of American newspapers—including major metropolitan dailies—picked up the story. They mentioned that Reverend Kendall was blind, read Braille, and was a superb typist. When he enrolled in Garrett Theological Seminary at Northwestern, his wife, Pearl Kendall, had to read the required books aloud to her sight-deprived husband. Already taking care of Willmoore, then aged two, Mrs. Kendall's life got even busier when daughter Yvona was born in 1911. Given an Oliver typewriter and Montessori blocks to play with—while his mother tended the baby and helped her husband with his studies—Willmoore, Jr. (with some guidance from mom) learned his letters. He started pecking out words on his forty-nine key babysitter, astonishing his parents who decided they had a child prodigy on their hands. For the family, this system worked well. Reverend Kendall got good grades, earned his Bachelor of Divinity degree in 1912, and received a "gold medal in oratory."⁷

Various events before Kendall, Jr.'s birth shaped this path to precocious boyhood. In November 1907, for example, the Oklahoma Conference of the Methodist Episcopal Church, South received Willmoore Kendall, Sr., aged twenty, into its ministerial ranks. Blind from early infancy, Kendall was a young man in a hurry. A native of Kentucky, his family had moved to Indian Territory to the city of Ardmore (near the Texas border). His father Walter Chiles Kendall owned a grocery store there for several years and served on the city council. Born in 1887, Willmoore, Sr., first moved away from home when he was five years old, attending the Kentucky School for the Blind in Louisville. When his family moved to Oklahoma, he enrolled as a boarding student at the better-equipped Texas Asylum for the Blind in Austin. He thrived there, coming to cherish literature, gaining fluency in Braille, and learning to prioritize the life of the mind.⁸

In Austin this ambitious and talented young man overdosed on the American Dream. Dr. Howell Piner, superintendent of the school, convinced him he could achieve anything he set his mind to. Kendall, Sr., became a wholehearted believer—Horatio Alger style—that hard work, talent, and "pluck" overcame all obstacles, even blindness. He relished the attention of admirers who claimed that, through "force of character and ability," he had "overcome every obstacle and handicap." For much of his ministry, he tried "to inspire and encourage the men and women who have lost their ambition and desire to achieve something worthwhile in this life." In 1905 he graduated from the brief-lived Hargrove College in Ardmore as valedictorian. He then moved to Chicago to attend the Moody Bible Institute. But he soon discovered that the Garrett Institute offered a more cerebral approach than the "narrow fundamentalism" of Moody. Because Garrett provided "the kind of education he wanted," he switched schools.[9]

At Evanston, Kendall met Northwestern student Pearl Anna Garlick of Chicago. She belonged to an extended middle-class German American family of devout Methodists. Her friendship, and readiness to read to him, cured the ministerial student of his homesickness. In December 1907, following his ordination, the young minister returned to Chicago to marry Miss Garlick. He then came home to Oklahoma to take up his first ministerial post at Eufaula. The following year he became the pastor of First Methodist Church in Konawa, Oklahoma. On March 5, 1909, the couple, then living in a modest three-room parsonage, had their first child, a son, whom they named Willmoore Bohnert Kendall. Reverend Kendall, however, still hungered to complete his education and so in the summer of 1910, wife and infant in tow, he returned to Garrett to complete his degree. These years in the Chicago area were formative for the new family. Reverend Kendall worked his way through school. He earned money by typing research papers for other students, and he also raised funds by preaching and holding church revivals. In 1912 the family returned and settled back into life in the Sooner State. But ties to the Midwest and connections to Chicago remained important to the family. Mrs. Kendall's relatives lived there, and Reverend Kendall idealized his years at Garrett.[10]

Reverend Kendall possessed a powerful intellect and soaring ambition. With his prestigious theology degree, Kendall received assignments to Oklahoma college towns, including Stillwater, Lawton, and Weatherford. A "pulpiteer of unusual ability," he had, according to one newspaper, "no peer in Oklahoma as an orator." He would, *ad seriatim*, pastor many Oklahoma churches for more than three decades, earning fame as an evangelist and orator. Able to read Hebrew, Greek, French, and German, he was intelligent, passionate, but frustrated. He often expressed plans to better his professional condition by entering politics, working as a journalist, obtaining a prestigious pulpit, or changing denominations. Reverend Kendall was a progressive, a club man, town booster, and prohibitionist who loved urban life and the "smell of gasoline." His favorite place was the "Magic City" of Tulsa. Mostly, however, he served small, unsophisticated towns, which he often hated. Hot and dusty Hobart, in western Oklahoma, was a "wretched hole" with a "stolid, ignorant, self-complacent" citizenry. Poteau (isolated in the Winding Stair Mountains) repelled him. So did Idabel, in the extreme southeast corner of the state, for it possessed "no paved street."[11]

Reverend Kendall, said one reporter, was "not a fundamentalist." Rather he was "an intense modernist" in theology who disavowed belief "in a hell of fire and brimstone." Professing belief in "the immortality of the soul," he remained vague about what happened to souls who "did not establish contact with immortal things." He was not so certain about heaven either, "of which mystics have been so sure." As a postmillennialist and advocate of the social gospel, Kendall, Sr., held that God's "wise Providence" would "transform ... this American continent into an earthly Paradise." The minister identified with the Protestant mainline, "the great Evangelical Churches—Methodists, Presbyterians, Congregationalists, Baptists, Disciples," and looked askance at groups, such as Jehovah's Witnesses, Mormons, Unitarians, and Catholics, who had "special doctrines to propagate." He promoted "the universal fatherhood of God and the universal brotherhood of man," condemned "race-hatred," and proclaimed himself "bitterly opposed to war."[12]

He disparaged the traditional theology of less-educated Methodist ministers and taught his family to do likewise. He spent much of his ministry giving educational talks about history and literature. He sought to modernize Methodism by building ornate and modern church edifices. A man of action, Kendall, Sr., encouraged church festivals and outreach activities to attract those "not moved by old-fashioned gospel sermons." His talks drew lessons from Shakespeare, Ibsen, Broadway plays, popular biographies, and novels. Often speaking at high school and college graduations, he tailored his message to appeal to youth and avoided polemics which might offend non-Methodists. Reverend Kendall could deliver "old time Gospel preaching" but preferred God's own "patient example" of promoting a slower and gentler growth in grace. Willmoore, Jr., later said that his father did not believe in the Bible even as he was explicating it.[13]

As "Tulsa's Blind Prophet of Sunshine and Optimism," Reverend Kendall loved to banter with the worldly minded. He was a regular guest speaker at Kiwanis, Rotary, and the YMCA. Especially active in the Lions Club—which had a long-term commitment to aid the visually impaired—he spoke at its 1926 International Meeting in San Francisco. Even more prominent was his work in promoting prohibition. During World War I, speaking to the Women's Christian Temperance Union, Kendall pushed for this long-cherished progressive reform as "a war measure." In the 1928 presidential election, like many southern Protestants, he took the extraordinary step of voting Republican when Democrat Al Smith focused on legalizing liquor. Later he played a prominent role in opposing the Twenty-First Amendment to repeal prohibition. In this fight he faced down Robert Lee Williams, former governor of the state and prominent Methodist layman. At a 1933 church conference, after Williams gave a speech opposing national prohibition, Reverend Kendall pushed through a resolution to support the Eighteenth Amendment. Kendall continued to work for prohibition even as the amendment was repealed.[14] Partly due to such efforts, Oklahoma never ratified the Twenty-First Amendment and continued to restrict liquor sales tightly for decades to come.

Looking back at his career in 1939, Kendall, Sr., mused that: "Handicaps . . . do one of two things to a person. Either they give him a driving, tireless ambition to achieve something worthwhile or they 'lick' him." Reverend Kendall chose the former option. However, he suffered emotional frustration when lionized as a great speaker, an accomplished scholar, or a talented pastor because the lionizer would usually append a suffix to his comments on the minister with some version of "for a blind man." And, when he felt frustrated in not achieving his own professional goals, the sightless minister exercised his ambition vicariously on Willmoore, Jr.[15] Being upheld as a boy genius by his father would in turn incise the younger man's psyche.

Impressed by the boy's intelligence, Reverend Kendall pushed Willmoore relentlessly. At age four, already reading Hawthorne's short stories, he entered first grade at Hartshorne elementary. In Lawton at age nine, young Willmoore began high school. Since the Methodist polity was connectional instead of congregational, Methodist ministers transferred regularly from one church assignment to another. November was stressful for ministerial families, for in that month the conference met and gave assignments for the coming year. Relocation usually occurred after a preacher had stayed three years or so at one place. In this situation, insofar as the younger Kendall had a particular place in Oklahoma which he considered home, it was the city of Lawton in the southwestern part of the state.[16] Here he completed most of his high school work. He attended school in Mangum for only a few months before graduation, having transferred there when Reverend Kendall received a new pastoral assignment.

At home father and son spent lots of time together, attending baseball games where sighted Junior described the action to sightless Senior. At age ten young Willmoore began to chauffeur his father around town in the family Ford. He sometimes terrified local residents who heard Willmoore Kendall was behind the wheel and thought that the blind preacher was driving. The son also drove his father around the state to preach at revivals. Reverend

Kendall said his oldest child was not "abnormally studious," but "a normal, healthy husky boy who loves to play like other boys." Tellingly, the young man's shelves were full of Horatio Alger books.[17]

Some pictures of the younger Willmoore from these early years have survived. One is a 1921 photo of the Lanier English Club posing on the steps of Lawton High School's splendid new edifice. In front is a severe-looking teacher, surrounded by a passel of smiling high school girls dressed modestly but fashionably. A few high school boys in coats and ties stand to the right. Prepubescent Willmoore stands alone at the base of a Doric Column. He is wearing a sweater and knickerbockers (not old enough yet to wear the long trousers of older boys). In 1922 a cherubic portrait of the young lad appeared in the Lawton High School Yearbook. A caption to the side read: "Willmoore Kendall—Our class baby left us the first semester, and we miss him very much. He was one of the brightest students in school—also the noisiest." At Mangum he soon developed the reputation of a chatty jokester.[18]

In the summer of 1922 this newly minted high school graduate moved in with Chicago relatives. He had an adventurous summer, attending the Pageant of Progress and writing home to his parents almost every day. But he soon

Figure 1.1 Child Prodigy in Knee Pants. Lawton High School, 1921. *Source:* "U.S., School Yearbooks, 1880-2012"; School Name: Lawton High School; Year: 1921 and 1922, Ancestry.com. U.S., School Yearbooks, 1900-1999 [database on-line]. Provo, UT, USA: Ancestry.com Operations, Inc., 2010.

grew homesick and begged to come home. Instead his father insisted that he matriculate at Northwestern University. Some publicity continued as Kendall began classes. One story detailed his humorous attempts to rush a fraternity. Another showed him as a member of Northwestern's ROTC Program. The school newspaper printed his picture—the youngest cadet in America—shaking hands with famed Great War General Van Horne Moseley. Quickly this experience became a disaster. As a thirteen-year-old boy Kendall was not prepared for college. Years later, in a letter to his sister, he noted how mortifying it had been to attend college classes still dressed in knickerbockers. College authorities allowed the country's youngest freshman to be treated as a freak, "to perform in a variety of ways in knee trousers." Meeting the football coach, Kendall "wriggling and screaming was tossed about among the football huskies." Humorous articles appeared about his admiration for Northwestern "Co-Eds." As to academics, he later revealed that his father had written all his high school papers. Failing some classes, the young man did not make it through the semester and returned to Oklahoma right after Thanksgiving.[19] No newswires trumpeted his failure.

Much had happened at home since he left. Reverend Kendall's pastoral charge in Mangum ended disastrously when he angered the Ku Klux Klan by denouncing it from his pulpit. In January 1922 he took out an advertisement in the local paper to announce an anti-Klan talk. In July, after the Mangum branch of the Invisible Empire had grown in size and power, Kendall—once more announcing his lecture in the local paper—criticized the organization again. This time the local Klavern ignited a "fiery cross" to warn him off. In a July letter, writing from Illinois, Willmoore, Jr., advised his father to reconsider his attacks. He feared the Klan "was too strongly organized to be driven out" and hoped his father would not be "tarred and feathered." On Sunday, August 13, at a revival in the nearby town of Granite, twenty-five robed Klansmen paid a call on Reverend Kendall. Ostensibly there to praise his work in promoting Christian "brotherhood," the hooded guests meant to warn the preacher to lay off. They gave him a letter vowing "to maintain forever the God-given supremacy of the white race in all things." Faced with this hostility, Kendall asked for a transfer. Church authorities granted his request, transferring him to eastern Oklahoma. In November Reverend Kendall left town in a hurry, not waiting for his replacement to arrive.[20]

Yet the minister never gave up his views about the desirability of interracial and interreligious harmony. For the rest of his career Reverend Kendall would, by his own account, strive "for cooperation between men of all faiths and all races." He worked for interfaith and Jewish rights groups and berated anti-Catholic forces as "liars and cowards." He also continued to denounce the Klan after leaving Mangum. Even before leaving the Greer County town, Kendall provided a public service which worked against Klan interests. On

October 4, 1922, he introduced a local crowd to John C. Walton, then mayor of Oklahoma City, who was running as the Democratic candidate for governor. The minister said he had examined Walton's record and regarded him as "worthy of trust and honor." A month later Walton, a liberal Democrat, won the election and easily carried Greer County.[21] As governor he proved a fierce enemy of the Klan.

After Mangum, Reverend Kendall began to receive less choice assignments. Previously, members of his churches had expressed their approval of his path onward and upward to bigger and better pulpits. In 1923 and 1924, however, he was assigned to a Tulsa pulpit at a downscale church in a working-class neighborhood, Hagler Memorial Methodist Church at the corner of West Admiral and Phoenix. It was only a few miles from Boston Avenue Methodist Church as the crow flew but worlds away in social class. Receiving this charge did allow the minister to save face. He had proclaimed, as an excuse for leaving Mangum, that he wanted assignment to a town with a college so he could live nearby while his son attended school.[22]

As a boy Willmoore Kendall lived through the worst period of racial strife in the state's history. In July 1922 he wrote home from Illinois upset when relatives attacked his father for pastoring a segregated church. He suggested to his father that his northern relatives could not grasp the intense public pressure to uphold the color line in Oklahoma. In February 1923, shortly after the failed effort at Northwestern, he started work for the *Tulsa Tribune*. There, as the paper's prized "Boy Reporter," he learned "to slap out a thousand words of tolerably clean prose in an hour." With future novelist George Milburn and Cal Tinney (later a humorist and Hollywood actor), he comprised the "three musketeers of words." All were teenage reporters of ability, all trained in the *Tribune*'s sensationalist reporting style, and all remembered fondly by editor Victor Barnett.[23] Embers from the 1921 Tulsa Race Massacre, which his new employer had help spark through inflammatory reporting, were hardly cool.

In March 1923, on his fourteenth birthday, Kendall wrote to a friend about plans to revive a state chapter of the Junior KKK (which a group of boys had started earlier in Lawton), with himself as Grand Wizard. Thereby he endorsed the group which had terrorized his own family nine months before. Discussion of this effort was interspersed with adolescent dating advice and mentioned nothing about race relations. It occurred in a period when Willmoore was rebelling against his father's ideas and at the height of Klan influence in the state, when adolescents were attracted to the group as much by its pageantry as by its message. As a reporter, the young man had critically covered Klan-related events such as the organization whipping citizens who did not abide by its moral code. Yvona Kendall Mason claimed that her brother was "incensed" by Klan violence and established the teen group to protect "abused people" from the adult organization.[24]

Meanwhile, the *Tribune* became involved in a major confrontation with Governor Walton. In 1923, mired in a political battle with the state legislature over corruption and cronyism, the governor decided to attack the Klan. In so doing he ran roughshod over civil liberties. Walton declared martial law for the entire state, suspended habeas corpus in Tulsa County, refused to let the state legislature meet, and appointed a censor for the *Tulsa Tribune*. Walton enforced these provisions with the National Guard. In response the Oklahoma legislature impeached and removed the governor from office. The next year, when Walton ran for the Senate, the Kendall family supported his campaign because they feared "a revivalism of Klanism in Oklahoma." And in 1925 Willmoore, Jr., condemned a masked Klan offshoot at the University of Oklahoma—the Deep Dark Mystery Club—for bullying other OU students. Indeed, this club almost lynched his friend George Milburn.[25] Given his age, one ought not overinterpret these boyhood experiences, one way or another, as a window into the mature Kendall's ideas about civil rights and politics. Yet Kendall's Sooner state boyhood certainly gave him an up close and personal view of the divisive power of race-based politics as well as a glimpse into the power that the legislature possessed to check a wayward executive.

Even in less troubled times, politics stood front and center in the lives of the Kendalls. Members of the family were avid and active Democrats. In 1914, for instance, Reverend Kendall, touting his educational achievements, ran an unsuccessful campaign for county school superintendent in Pittsburg County. He often later mulled running for office. Oklahoma politicians prized his endorsement because of his ability as a speaker to wow crowds. Reverend Kendall's progressive sensibilities pushed him to take an anticorporation stance in politics, but he also opposed socialism. Kendall, Sr., frequently gave partisan speeches for Democratic candidates, introduced politicians at rallies, made political endorsements, and delivered political sermons. According to one Republican commentator he could "make the best speech, for a Democrat, that we ever heard."[26]

After the United States entered World War I, for example, the Methodist minister spoke out against the war. He advised his listeners not to buy Liberty Bonds. He then delivered a speech at a Methodist meeting in Weatherford, Oklahoma, to justify his position. Comparing himself to Lincoln, Savonarola, and antebellum abolitionists, and echoing Martin Luther, Reverend Kendall claimed "he could do no other." It was his job "to lead man toward a time when wars shall cease and when the people of the earth shall be united in one great family by the bond of love." Kendall proclaimed himself willing to die or go to prison rather than support an unjust war based on "greed and avarice." He denounced the notion that Americans should support their country right or wrong, promised to pray for peace, and asked hearers to consider themselves "citizens of the world."[27]

In taking this stance, Kendall was supporting the antiwar position staked out by Thomas P. Gore, Democratic senator from Oklahoma. The Methodist minister's stand for peace did not last long when pacifism proved unpopular. In November 1917—after the *Tulsa World* called for lynching opponents of the war—local vigilantes kidnapped, flogged, then tarred and feathered seventeen members of the Industrial Workers of the World. By December—perhaps not coincidentally—Reverend Kendall had switched over to a safer Wilsonian line of waging "war to make the world safe for democracy." Perhaps annoyed by his original speech, denominational authorities transferred him, in the middle of the year and against his wishes, to the military town of Lawton, where he ministered to soldiers at nearby Fort Sill. Sightless solidarity (Gore was also blind) went completely out the window in 1920 when Kendall supported a challenger in the Democratic primary, "attacking the loyalty of Senator Gore." Gore supporters called out the "preacher-patrioteer" for flag-waving hypocrisy. They noted that his wartime speech had "breath[ed] the very essence of sedition and disloyalty."[28]

In his teens, Willmoore, Jr., followed politics avidly and participated in this partisan activity. Together with other family members, he worked for the operation of his "Uncle Charlie," that is, Democrat Charles C. Childers. Childers, after many years in the state legislature, won election as state auditor in 1922 and as member of the Corporation Commission in 1926. Childers provided numerous jobs for his relatives. Willmoore's grandfather, Walter Kendall, worked twenty years for the state, following Childers from the auditor's office to the corporation commission. In return, these relatives were expected to campaign to get Childers reelected. All involved were faithful Democrats. Indeed, Childers had endangered his career by supporting Walton too long on grounds of party loyalty. On at least one occasion, family members had to lay low when a political rival charged Childers with nepotism. Willmoore, Jr., for example, delayed receiving his pay in the summer of 1926 so that his office-holding relative could deny accusations of impropriety.[29]

Willmoore's grandmother, Gennessee Adams Kendall, was also on the state payroll. She served over twelve years as matron of women at the state penitentiary in McAlester. In January 1923, with Walton's election, she resigned her post. In April the Oklahoma Federation of Labor charged that prisoners at McAlester, including women prisoners, had previously been hung from their wrists for hours if failing to meet quotas for a state-operated textile venture. Reverend Kendall defended his mother and the previous prison administration from charges he claimed were lies. Governor Walton shut down the mill but refused to countenance tales of torture. In a variety of ways, then, the Kendalls were connected to the circle of Democratic politicians who ruled Oklahoma. In 1933, for example, Reverend Kendall presided at the wedding of Johnston Murray, son of Governor William H. "Alfalfa Bill" Murray and himself a future governor of the state. In 1936 he officiated at the wedding of Congressman Lyle Boren, Democratic New Dealer and scion of a prominent Oklahoma political dynasty. That same year the minister also turned down a paid post with the reelection campaign of Governor E. W. Marland.[30]

The two Willmoores identified as white southerners. The Kendalls regarded themselves as descendants of the old southern plantation aristocracy. In fact, they came from a town-dwelling, middle-class background, more real estate developers than planters. Kendall, Jr.'s maternal relatives were German Americans of the Old Northwest. Much of this identity was cultural not genealogical and intertwined with devotion to the Democratic Party. In November 1924, for example, the younger Kendall listened to radio reports and speeches from that year's election. While detailing his amazement about the new technology, he recorded his thoughts on prominent participants in the campaign. He regarded the speech of John W. Davis, Democratic candidate from West Virginia, as competent. Meanwhile, he hated the "nasty voice" and grating New England accent of President Calvin Coolidge but loved the "mellifluous eloquence" of Mississippi Democratic Senato Pat Harrison, a southern orator of the old school.[31] Though everyone was a Democrat, the Kendall home was a stormy one with frequent arguments. Pearl Kendall was an intelligent and "loving" woman who used what tools were available to her to cope with a challenging marriage. Family and friends sometimes saw her as an "appendage" of her longwinded husband. According to her daughter Yvona, Mrs. Kendall "used dependency as a tool," playing the children off against each other and taking sides with them against her husband. Short in stature, she possessed a passive-aggressive personality. According to her husband, she withheld "love and affection" from those she regarded as imperfect. Reverend Kendall's bombastic persona made her life difficult. When boasting about reading over three hundred books a year, her husband appeared to take her efforts—such as reading to him—for granted. Mrs. Kendall engaged in the typical activities of a pastor's wife, sponsoring women's missionary groups, entertaining, giving occasional talks at church functions, while also cooking and taking care of the children. As a youngster, Willmoore showed great affection for his "little mother" as "the embodiment of all that is sweet and lovely and generous," but he mostly talked to her about domestic matters while saving intellectual talk for his dad. Years later, he claimed that any connection the Kendall children had "with what is good and healthy and wholesome in life" came from their mother, and that Reverend Kendall, though courageous, was an intellectual fraud who "had much in him which was abominable."[32]

The family's reasonably pleasant pre-1922 days did not return when its number one son came back from Northwestern. Verbal clashes created tension in the household, as the two Willmoores engaged in regular tabletop political debates. The family's two other children, Yvona and Walter (born in 1915), suffered emotional neglect because of attention paid to their older brother. Both were intelligent and capable. Yvona attended classes at several colleges and received an Associates Degree. Then she worked for some years as a librarian and in state government before her marriage. Her parents, stressed by supporting Willmoore, were unable to finance her academic ambitions. Nor was her older brother much help. Walter was not as good a student as either of his siblings, but he did graduate from Oklahoma A&M in Stillwater. Both younger children, however, received condescending treatment at home because neither possessed the intellectual gifts of their older brother.[33]

Reverend Kendall claimed that he and his wife "maintained an old-fashioned home for our children." By providing "parental guidance," they served their children with the "fruits of our experience." Continuing to speak for himself and Mrs. Kendall, he suggested it unwise "to turn children loose and let them grow up in their own way" and claimed, even with one child arrested for brawling in a honkytonk, that the Kendall kids "have never given us any moral problems." The Kendall parents offered plenty of unsolicited "guidance," but they often failed to provide age-appropriate oversight for their children. Well before turning sixteen, Willmoore walked Tulsa streets without adult supervision, interviewing crime victims and perpetrators and writing mildly risqué stories for the *Tribune*. He "dated" girls when he was only twelve or thirteen, sometimes promising to break off contact with those who were too "tough." Even his father admitted that Willmoore had begun to "look upon life with a man's point of view" by age nine when he accompanied his father for talks with Fort Sill soldiers.[34]

After Willmoore dropped out of Northwestern, Reverend Kendall continued to harbor huge expectations for his oldest son. Enrolling at the University of Tulsa, the youngster completed his freshman and sophomore years. Kendall then transferred to the University of Oklahoma in 1924 when he was fifteen. He knew many people attending school on the Norman campus whom he had met in the towns where his father had preached. During the Spring Semester of 1925, he ran away to New Orleans because his father would not let him join a fraternity. His father called the authorities to have his son arrested. They offered to put the runaway on the next train home to Idabel. Instead, Reverend Kendall had the sheriff confine his son in the municipal "waif's home" until he could travel to New Orleans to collect him. Starting home Reverend Kendall had his son handcuffed. Willmoore, Jr., never forgot this incident and never forgave his father for it.[35]

That summer and fall he stayed in Idabel with his family under close parental supervision. In the Spring of 1926 Willmoore, Jr., again headed off to Northwestern, this time with less fanfare. In 1925 one Northwestern publication had put out the story that the "boy wonder" of Oklahoma had dropped out of college to raise chickens. Yet this second effort at Evanston was more successful than the first. Kendall earned some credits, but he decided to return to Norman to earn his degree quicker. As an undergraduate, Kendall was not a particularly attentive student, often cutting classes, but he had a gift for languages. In February 1927, still only seventeen, he completed his course work and graduated from the University of Oklahoma with a BA in Romance Languages.[36]

Right after graduation, Kendall, Jr., returned to Northwestern to pursue graduate work. Determined to prove his love for his parents by "making good at . . . Dad's alma mater," the third time proved the charm, for in 1928 he earned an MA in Romance languages. Kendall's thesis, "Pio Baroja: A Study," analyzed the work of the most prominent Spanish novelist of the early twentieth century. In it he took issue with existing interpretations of Pio Baroja y Nessi's work. Baroja, a modernist from Spain's famous Generation of '98, was more original, he argued, than most critics realized. Kendall's thesis was workmanlike rather than profound. He cited key authorities on Baroja, analyzed some of his novels, and reached conclusions which differed slightly from those of previous scholars. "Pio Baroja" demonstrated none of the interpretative brilliance of the later Kendall, but it was a creditable piece of scholarship for a nineteen-year-old graduate student. Its ordinariness came about because Kendall's teachers forbade his preferred "journalistic style." The first draft, they said, was "demonstrative of the influence of H.L. Mencken," a mere journalist and not "an authority on anything." Kendall thought the finished thesis "lousy" but had it "been any better," he claimed, "it would not have been accepted."[37]

In pursuing his education, Willmoore received financial help from home, including funds from his grandparents and other relatives, but he struggled to pay his tuition and had to work odd jobs to pay his way through school. He found employment as an elevator operator and busboy at the luxurious Orrington Hotel in Evanston, as a clerk at the Post Office and at a printing company, as a typist and translator for fellow students, even as a "valet" for a business executive. In fall 1928, Northwestern MA in hand, Kendall returned to Oklahoma. With strong recommendations from his father and various family friends, including President Henry G. Bennett of Oklahoma A&M, he accepted an offer to teach at the Oklahoma Military Academy in Claremore. Here he worked for several months before the blowup at the Louvre.[38]

Over his lifetime, Willmoore Kendall, Jr., struck up a series of remarkable friendships with an odd variety of intellectuals. The repartee of clever people attracted him, and his mocking wit in turn often fascinated them. Kendall's first close friend of this sort was fellow Oklahoman George Milburn of Coweta. Milburn and Kendall shared much in common. Both worked as teenage reporters at the *Tulsa Tribune*, attended the University of Tulsa, and graduated from the University of Oklahoma. Each would leave the state in disgust, but each would remain emotionally connected to—even haunted by—the Sooner State. George was three years older but graduated a couple of years later from the university. Kendall and Milburn remained close friends for years. Milburn was a talented writer whose fiction won considerable acclaim in the 1930s. H. L. Mencken became a particular fan, publishing many Milburn stories in the *American Mercury*. Other Milburn tales appeared in the *New Yorker*, *Vanity Fair*, and *Harper's*. His best work came in 1936 with publication of the novel *Catalogue*.[39]

Milburn's writing portrayed deep understanding of Oklahoma's people, the nuances of their language, their oddities, prejudices, rages, and sorrows. Few of his tales were flattering. As a young man he spent lots of time with the Kendalls, and several Milburn pieces drew on the family for inspiration. "The Apostate," for example, appears to be a fictionalized account of Willmoore Kendall's troubled relationship with his father. In "A Position on the Staff," Milburn recalled Kendall, Sr., with his portrayal of "Rev. Herman Roscoe Cartwright." A "militant modern minister," Cartwright delivers a speech to Tulsa boosters on "The Kiwanism of Christ" as they sit munching fried chicken. The same story details the work of an idealistic boy reporter (based on Milburn, Kendall, Jr., or Tinney) who went to work for the *Tulsa Tribune*. On the boy's first day at work, veteran reporters squabble about whose irresponsible article had kicked off the race massacre. Meanwhile they teach the youngster to write speedy, graphic prose devoid of romance. "Gerald Lee Cobb" depicts the pride of a southern-born couple. "Old Man Cobb" was a rough-hewn sort who sent his son, the titular character, for an education at Garrett Seminary. Mrs. Cobb was a southern Methodist lady with aristocratic pretensions. Based on Willmoore, Sr., and his parents, the story ends with a typical Milburn twist. Gerald Lee, jailed for taking a pacifist stance in World War I, becomes a "holy roller" to the disgust of his propriety-focused mother. Playfully but pointedly, Milburn seemed to ask what would have happened if Reverend Kendall had stayed true to his pacifism, been sexually abused in prison, and become a god-obsessed Pentecostal.[40]

In the mid-1920s Milburn went to work writing joke and novelty books for Haldeman-Julius publishers in Girard, Kansas. In the summer of 1927 he commissioned his friend Willmoore Kendall, Jr., to write Little Blue Book No. 440, aka *Baseball: How to Play It and How to Watch It*. Writing as A. Monk, Willmoore thus authored his first book. Yvona, also anonymous as Hans Kueffer, provided the illustrations. The book was a tongue-in-cheek primer on the American pastime, providing tips on how to bunt, steal bases, and so forth. Humorously presaging Kendall's career as a political theorist, the little book discussed how to enjoy the game through watching it intelligently, grasping its principles, rather than mindlessly rooting for one's favorite team. Through enlightened understanding of "the theory of the game," said Monk, one might derive more enjoyment as a fan.[41]

In time, George Milburn became unwelcome in the Sooner State. Fellow Oklahomans recognized truth in his portraits. But they did not appreciate his stereotypes of them as violent, racist simpletons. Willmoore regarded "Georgie" as a close friend, took pride in his success, but did not regard him as a profound writer. He recognized and disliked many of the same flaws in the Sooner State as Milburn did. His break with home was less definitive than that of his friend because he also acknowledged positive aspects to life in his home state. He knew that, for better and for worse, Oklahoma had shaped his views on the larger world. Kendall's intention to escape the Sooner's State's "provincial smugness" in 1929 after getting beaten up and arrested in Tulsa was genuine. Bloodied and embarrassed, he called Oklahoma "hopeless" and expressed determination to forge his own path into manhood. He expressed resentment at Reverend Kendall's "sarcasm" and told his father that he regretted staying in college for "six years . . . when every fibre of my existence cried to get out and find out what I was going to do with myself." From then on, the younger man asserted, "I'm going to be doing my own planning and carry out my own plans."[42] Except for brief interludes, he never again lived with his parents or resided in his home state.

Kendall's Oklahoma boyhood gave him many useful gifts. Aside from his two academic degrees, Kendall was fluent in Spanish and had inherited a lifelong habit of serious reading. On the receiving end of parental censure for much of his youth, he learned how to respond forcefully to criticism. He possessed considerable ambition and wanted to make his own mark on society. Kendall also had developed a hands-on appreciation and understanding of practical politics. From his various jobs, schools, clubs, and churches—and from visits to his grandparents at McAlester State Prison—he knew a wide variety of people from distinct social strata. Kendall had an active social life, attending summer camps with the Boy Scouts and YMCA. In 1921 he rescued a boy from drowning at the Craterville Amusement Park. He knew Tulsa from his reporting work there, sold books for three months in McCurtain County, and worked on political campaigns in Oklahoma City. In Norman he socialized with fraternity lads, attended sporting events, and made lasting friends. He taught school at Claremore.[43]

Having lived in most of Oklahoma's major cities and regions, he developed familiarity with the state and its cultural ethos. Kendall also knew Chicago quite well. From relatives and friends there, he came to understand that larger forces and a greater diversity of peoples and opinion existed in the world than he could have grasped if isolated at home. By twenty, then, the young man had acquired a certain worldliness, possessed a sprightly personality, and loved intelligent conversation. Severing relations with someone as controlling as Reverend Kendall, however, was never going to be simple. And in coming years—with Willmoore, Jr., outside the state—Willmoore, Sr., became a relentless hoverer. Moreover, when Kendall the younger abandoned dad's domicile for the larger world, he bore lots of scars. Some were physical. For example, he suffered from an annoying skin rash, or "chafing," which sometimes flared up enough to make walking difficult. Oklahoma doctors had treated this affliction with X-rays, once giving the teenager enough radiation to make his hair fall out.[44] Perhaps he carried bodily marks from childhood escapades and from his confrontation with the bouncers at the Louvre. Of more lasting significance were emotional wounds inflicted by his overbearing father.

NOTES

1. Angie Debo, *Tulsa: From Creek Town to Oil Capital* (Norman: University of Oklahoma Press, 1943), 97–99; Danney Goble, *Tulsa!: Biography of the American City* (Tulsa: Council Oaks Books, 1997), 85–102.

2. Debo, *Tulsa*, 104–106; Galen S. Frysinger, "Philbrook Museum," "Philtower," "Boston Avenue Church," and "Westhope," http://www.galenfrysinger.com/oklahoma.

3. Goble, *Tulsa!: Biography*, 125; Steve Gerkin, "Beno Hall: Tulsa's Den of Terror," *This Land*, September 3, 2011, http://thislandpress.com/2011/09/03/beno-hall-tulsas-den-of-terror/.

4. Doug Darroch, "Cain's Spirit," *Tulsa Tribune*, December 10, 1975, p. 10B; WK to Willmoore Kendall, Sr. (hereafter WKS), March 16, 1929, B2F1, KP; "Fiery Cadet," *Tulsa Tribune*, March 10, 1929, p. 1; WK to WKS, March 16, 1929, KP; Yvona Kendall Mason (hereafter YM), Unpublished Biography of WKS and WK, 45, B9F6, KP.

5. WK to WKS, March 22, 1929, WK to WKS, April 7, 1929, WK to WKS, March 1929, and WK to WKS, May 29 1929, B2F1, KP; WKS to WK, April 1929, B4F1, KP.

6. WKS to WK, April 3, 1929 and May 17, 1929, B4F1, KP; "Mangum Boy," *Mangum Star*, May 25, 1922, p. 1; "Mangum Prodigy," *Daily Ardmoreite*, August 9, 1922, p. 3.

7. YM, Biography, 30–32, Box 9F6, KP; "Youngest H.S. Graduate," *Mangum Star*, May 25, 1922, p. 1; "Typewriter Makes," *New York Herald*, August 6, 1922, p. 18; "Scholar and Athlete," *New York Times*, October 8, 1922, sec. x, p. 9; "Chiefly About People," *Western Christian Advocate*, February 15, 1911, pp. 6, 28; "The Average Child Can Be A Prodigy," *Tulsa Tribune*, November 16, 1923, p. 13; "Death Claims State Worker," *Daily Oklahoman*, October 28, 1932, p. 12; "Garrett Biblical Institute Graduates 45 Ministers," *Chicago Tribune*, April 25, 1912, p. 8; "Blind from Infancy," *Daily Ardmoreite*, October 24, 1920, p. 2.

8. YM, Biography, 1, B9 F6, KP; "Death Claims State," 12; Betty McMinn, "New Vice President of Scarabia," *Campus*, January 31, 1940, p. 2.

9. YM, Biography, 20–27, Box 9F6, KP; George Meyer, "The Establishment and Superintendency of the Texas Blind Asylum," https://history.tsbvi.edu/ images/ Superintendency.docx; Memorial of Rev. John Walker Piner, https://www.findagrave.com/ memorial/155480680/john-walker-piner; "Commencement Exercises," *Advance Democrat*, May 16, 1918, p. 1; "Blind Evangelist," *Chickasha Daily Express*, October 9, 1916, p. 4; "Blind from Infancy," p. 2; "Hargrove College, Ardmore College, 1895–1913," https://www.lostcolleges.com/hargrove-college.

10. WK to WKS, Summer 1922, B1F1, KP; "Blind from Infancy," p. 2; "Garlick-Kendall," *Daily Ardmoreite*, December 22, 1907, p. 9; YM, Biography, 29–31, 48, Box 9F6, KP; "Bishop Atkins' Appointments," *Daily Ardmoreite*, November 10, 1909, p. 4; "'Dr. Jekel [sic] and Mr. Hyde,'" *Konawa Chief-Leader*, March 12, 1909, p. 1; YM, Biography, 26–29, 44–45, Box 9F6, KP; "Oklahoman Coming," *Waxahachie Daily Light*, October 23, 1941, p. 1; "Blind from Infancy," p. 2.

11. "Blind from Infancy," p.2.; McMinn, "Scarabia," p. 2; "Notices," *Mangum Star*, November 17, 1921, p. 4; "M.E. Revival," *Foss Enterprise*, July 14, 1916, p. 1; WK to WKS, June 17, 1922 and November 11, 1924, B1F1, KP; WK to WKS, April 19, 1929, B2F1, KP; "Kendall Lauds," November 16, 1933, *Kiowa County Review*, p. 8; WKS, "Let Me Live," *Weatherford Democrat*, August 24, 1916, p. 5; "Death Claims Rev. W. Kendall," *Miami Daily News-Record*, June 7, 1942, p. 1; WKS to WK, 1924 and WKS to WK, Spring 1926, B3F8, KP; YM, Biography, 88, Box 9F7, KP; WKS to WK, February 18, 1933, May 6, 1933, and November 24, 1933 in *OxY*, 147, 192, 299.

12. Meredith Williams, "Miami Minister," *Daily Oklahoman*, March 4, 1932, p. 14; WKS to WK, October 26 1932, in *OxY*, 75; "Rev. W. Kendall's July 4th Address," *Hartshorne Sun*, July 17, 1913, p. 1; WKS, "Man Who Brought Light," *Miami Daily News-Record*, August 22, 1930, p. 3; "Warning," *Miami Daily News Record*, February 24, 1930, p. 1; "Money Spent On Wars," *Tulsa Tribune*, July 23, 1923, p. 11; "Tulsa," *Tulsa Tribune*, July 26, 1923, p. 16; WKS to WK, October 15, 1934, in *OxY*, 426; WKS to WK, September 30, 1941, B5F1, KP.

13. "Through the Spiritual Vision," *Lawton News*, May 18, 1919, p. 1; WK to PGK, June 13, 1922, WK to PGK, Summer 1922, and WK to WKS, October 1925, B1F1, KP; YM, Biography, 105–6, B9F7, KP; "Shakespearian Studies," *Miami Daily News-Record*, September 11, 1931, p. 6; WKS, "Church's Share," *Hartshorne Sun*, October 31, 1912, p. 9; "Commencement Exercises, Stillwater Public Schools," The *Advance Democrat*, May 16, 1918, p. 5; "Baccalaureate Sermon," *Miami Daily News-Record*, August 22, 1930, p. 3; WKS to WK, November 22, 1932 and January 19, 1935, in *OxY*, 99, 463; "Blind Pastor Paints Picture," *Tulsa Tribune*, November 19, 1923, p. 5; "Hear Willmoore Kendall," *Tulsa Tribune*, April 26, 1924, p. 2; WK to CH, Summer 1960, B7, CHP.

14. "Tulsa's Blind Prophet," *Tulsa Tribune*, April 26, 1924, p. 2; "Lions Prepare," *Miami Daily News-Record*, March 14, 1930, p. 6; YM, Biography, 160, B10F7, KP; "KVOO To Broadcast," *Miami Daily News-Record*, June 5, 1930, p. 6; YM, Biography, 241, B10F2, KP; "Rev. Kendall Speaks," *Miami Daily News-Record*, March 1, 1931,

p. 3; "Oklahoman Coming," p. 2; "Recovery Road," *Miami Daily News-Record*, January 4, 1934, p. 6; WK to WKS, July 20, 1926, B1 F8, KP; McMinn, "Scarabia," p. 2; Williams, "Miami Minister," 14; "Blind from Infancy," p. 2; "National Prohibition," *Advance Democrat*, July 4, 1918, p. 1; "Wet, Dry Chiefs," *Kiowa County Review*, November 2, 1933, p. 1; "Judge Williams," *Miami Daily News-Record*, November 12, 1933, p. 6; "Wets Invited," *Kiowa County Record*, July 6, 1933, p. 1.

15. Nash, "Iconoclast I," 227, 402; "Blind Evangelist," p. 4; WKS Obituary, Official Record, 4th Annual Session, East Oklahoma Conference, The Methodist Church, Tulsa, Oklahoma, October 21–25, 1942 (Tulsa, E.J. Jorns, 1942), 470; "Blind Pastors," *Daily Oklahoman*, October 27, 1939, p. 1; YM, Biography, 35, B9F6, KP; WKS to WK, October 30, 1932 and WK to WKS, November 5, 1932, in *OxY*, 81, 91.

16. WK to WKS, March 4, 1932, B2F5, KP; WK to WKS, November 27, 1935, B3F3, KP.

17. YM, Biography, 36, 40, B9 F6, KP; Williams, "Miami Minister," 14; "Blind from Infancy," p. 2; WK to WKS, June 6, 1922, B1F1, KP.

18. *"School Yearbooks, 1880–2012" Lawton 1921*, Ancestry.com; "Mangum Boy," p. 1.

19. WK to WKS, July 1922, B1F1, KP; "Mangum Boy," p. 1; YM, Biography, 79–80, 520–23, B9F6 and B10F6, KP; "Typewriter Makes," p. 18; GWC, Prologue, xiv; "Boy Scouts," *New York Times*, October 8, 1922, p. 90; Wills, 18; WK to WKS, August 19, 1922 and WK to WKS, November 1922, B1 and WK to YM [1960], B6F3, KP; "Miami Minister," *Daily Oklahoman*, March 4, 1932, p. 14; "Oklahoma Child Prodigy," *Ardmore Daily Press*, September 15, 1922, p. 1; WK to WKS, Spring 1924, B1F1, KP; Willmoore Kendall, "Pio Baroja: A Study" (Master's Thesis, Northwestern University, 1928), 97; "Prodigy Here!," *Tulsa Tribune*, November 26, 1922, p. 3.

20. WK to WKS, July 18, 1922, July 22, 1922, and August 1922, B1F1, KP; "Does Mangum Need," *Mangum Star*, January 5, 1922, p. 4; "Methodist Church Notes," *Mangum Star*, July 13, 1922, pp. 6–7; "Klansmen Visit Church," *Mangum Star*, August 17, 1922, p. 1; "Ku Klux Klan Commends," *Mangum Star*, August 24, 1922, p. 1; "Methodist Pastor," *Mangum Star*, October 12, 1922, p. 4; Minister History, WKS, Oklahoma United Methodist Archives, Archives and Special Collections, Dulaney-Browne Library, Oklahoma City University; "New Methodist," *Mangum Star*, November 9, 1922, p. 1.

21. "Not Guilty," *Hartshorne Sun*, June 18, 1914, p. 1; "Methodist Church Notes, *Mangum Star*, September 28, 1922, p. 5; "Nov. 11 Speaker," *Waxahachie Daily Light*, October 30, 1941, p. 1; WKS to Editor of *Tulsa World*, February 23, 1930, B3, F8, KP; "Walton Addresses," *Mangum Star*, October 5, 1922, p. 1; "County Vote," *Mangum Star*, November 9, 1922, p. 1.

22. "Local Items," *Hartshorne Sun*, November 8, 1917, p. 5; "Kendall Goes," *Luther Register*, November 12, 1915, p. 1; "Hagler Memorial," *Tulsa Tribune*, February 23, 1924, p. 3; YM, Biography, 88, B9F7, KP.

23. YM, Biography, 89–90, B10F7, KP; WK to WKS, March 5, 1932, B2F5, KP; WK, "Wife of a Confessed Whipper," *Tulsa Tribune*, August 25, 1923, p. 1; "Tribune Cub Reporters," *Sooner State Press*, September 26, 1936, p. 2.

24. "Official Constitution of the Junior Knights of the Ku Klux Klan," March 1923, and WK to "Dick," March 5, 1923, B1F1, KP: YM, Biography, 39, 88–90, B9F6, KP; WK, "Whipper," p. 1.

25. Larry O'Dell, "Walton, John Calloway," *The Encyclopedia of Oklahoma History and Culture*, https://www.okhistory.org/publications/enc/entry.php?entry=WA014; YM, Biography, 110, B9F7, KP; WK to WKS, November 1925, B1F4, KP; "Society Mask," *Daily Oklahoman*, November 28, 1925, p. 1; George Milburn, "Oklahoma," *Yale Review* XXXIV (March 1946): 515–26; WK to WKS, April 18, 1927 and August 1927, B1F6, KP.

26. "Blind But Qualified," *Hartshorne Sun*, July 16, 1914, p. 1; "Victory Dinner," *Miami Daily News-Record*, February 28, 1937, p. 2; WK to WKS, April 4, 1932, B2F5, KP; WK to WKS, January 18, 1932, [March] 1932, and December 23, 1934, in *OxY*, 8–9, 16–17, 447; "Little Daily," *Stillwater Gazette*, November 16, 1937, p. 1.

27. YM, Biography, 37, B9F6, KP; "Kendall Urged," *Lawton News*, July 28, 1920, p. 1.

28. "Kendall Urged," p. 1; Nigel Sellars, "Wobblies in the Oil Fields: The Suppression of the Industrial Workers of the World in Oklahoma," in *An Oklahoma I Had Never Seen Before: Alternative Views of Oklahoma History*, ed. Davis D. Joyce (Norman: University of Oklahoma Press, 1994), 137–38; "Church Services," *Advance Democrat*, December 13, 1917, p. 1; "Local Mention," *Advance Democrat*, July 11, 1918, p. 5; "Among Soldiers," *Stillwater Gazette,* August 23, 1918, p. 5.

29. WK to WKS, November 4, 1914 and November 1924, B1 F1, KP; "Kendall Rally," *Hartshorne Sun*, May 14, 1914, p. 1; Joseph B. Thoburn, *A Standard History of Oklahoma* (Chicago: American Historical Society, 1916), 3: 987–88; "Death Claims State," p. 12; WK to WKS, [July] 1926, B1F4, KP; WK to WKS, [Summer] 1926 and WK to WKS, July 28, 1926, B1F5, KP; WK to WKS, July 20, 1926, B1F8, KP; Arrell Morgan Gibson, *Oklahoma: A History of Five Centuries*, 2nd ed. (Norman: University of Oklahoma Press, 1981), 215–20; WK to WKS, 1926, B1F5, KP; WK to WKS, August 1932, B2F5, KP; WK to WKS, July 20, 1926, B1F8, KP.

30. "Blind Pastor" and "Walton Advised," *Tulsa Tribune*, May 1, 1923, p. 5; "New Warden," *McCurtain Gazette*, January 31, 1923, p. 2; YM, Biography, 13–14, B9F6; "Kendall Reads Vows," *Kiowa County Record*, May 4, 1933, p. 1; "Kendall to Speak," *Okemah Semi-Weekly Herald*, July 3, 1936, p. 5; "Baby Member," *Ogden Standard-Examiner*, December 27, 1936, p. 6; WKS to WK, March 15, 1936, December 27, 1936, and December 1938, B4F3, KP.

31. WK to WKS, April 18, 1927, B1F6, KP, WK to WKS, Summer 1931, B2F3; Joe Kendall, "Historical Sketches," https://www.ancestry.com/mediaui-viewer/tree/13795759/person/-9111512/media/971af842-bf40-42ef-8f22-5de25320707a?destTreeId =105088105&destPersonId= 310043792412&_phsrc=kYA110&_phstart=default; YM to KK, December 27, 1979, B4F18, KKP; YM, Biography, 16, B9F6, KP; WK to WKS, November 3, 1924, B1F1, KP; Allan A. Michie and Frank Ryhlick, *Dixie's Demagogues* (New York: Vanguard Press, 1939), 73–82; WK to WKS, August 1930, B2F2, KP.

32. KK to Walter Earl Kendall, June 2, 1995, KK to YM, May 31, 1977, and PGK to KK, August 8, 1965, B4F18, KKP; WKS to WK, April 3, 1929, B4F1, KP;

McMinn, "Scarabia," p. 2; "Informal Tea," *Miami Daily News-Record*, November 16, 1931, p. 6; PGK to KK, October 1, 1966, B4 F18, KKP; YM to Savoie Lottinville, October 8, 1972, B92F26, General Correspondence, CAC; WK to PGK, 1928, B1F8, KP; WK to PGK, May 12, 1929, B2F1, KP; WK to WKS, B2F3; WK to YM, [1960], B6F2; KP; WK to WKS, May 10, 1934 and WKS to WK, September 30, 1934, in *OxY*, 361, 418.

33. KK to Walter and Barbara Kendall, June 2, 1995, KKP; "Kendall Transferred," *Miami Daily News-Record*, November 7, 1932, p. 1; "Former Miamians," *Miami Daily News-Record*, November 26, 1939, p. 25; "Yvona Kendall," *Daily Oklahoman*, November 26, 1939, p. 57.

34. Williams, "Miami Minister," 14; YM, Biography, 89–90, 105, B9F7, KP; WK to WKS, July 26, 1922, B1F1, KP; WK, "Viela Has a Plan," *Tulsa Tribune*, March 28, 1923, p. 4.

35. WK to WKS, September 1924, B1F1, KP; YM, Biography, 130–37, B9F7, KP; Wills, *Confessions*, 19–20.

36. "Campus Column," *Northwestern Alumni News*, December 1925, pp. 11–12; Nash, "Iconoclast I," 133; YM, Biography, 120, 137–38, 176, B9F7 and B10F1, KP; WK to WKS, December 1924, B1 F1, KP; WK to WKS, July 20, 1926, B1F8, KP; Kendall, "Baroja," 97; YM, Biography, 160–61, B10F1, KP.

37. WK to WKS, Spring 1927, B1F6, KP; Kendall, "Baroja," 89–90, 97; YM, Biography, 229–31, 242, B10F2, KP.

38. YM, Biography, 95, B9F7, KP; WK to WKS, December 1922, B1F1, KP; WK to WKS, May 1, 1927, B1F6, KP; WK to WKS, August 1926, B1F5, KP; WK to WKS, Fall 1922, B1F1, KP; WK to WKS, December 22, 1929, B2F1, KP; WKS to WK, January 23, 1928, B3F8, KP; Kendall, "Baroja," 97; WKS to WK, April 3, 1929, B4F1, KP; YM, Biography, 209, B10F1, KP; YM, Biography, 158–59, 206–11, 244–45, B10F1-3, KP.

39. Steven Turner, *George Milburn, Southwest Writers Series* (Austin: Steck-Vaughan, 1970), 4–5; YM, Biography, 89, B9F7, KP; WK to WKS, March 5, 1932, B2F5, KP.

40. WK to WKS, October 18, 1924, B1F1, KP; YM, Biography, 89, 117, B9F7, KP; YM, Biography, 189, B10F2, KP; George Milburn, *No More Trumpets and Other Stories* (New York: Harcourt, Brace, 1933), 38–46, 262–90; George Milburn, *Oklahoma Town* (Freeport, NY: Books for Libraries, 1931), 94–97.

41. Carl Albert and Danney Goble, *Little Giant: The Life and Times of Speaker Carl Albert* (Norman: University of Oklahoma Press, 1990), 81–82; WK [Alan Monk], *Baseball: How to Play it and How to Watch It* (Girard, KS: Little Blue Books, 1929).

42. Turner, *George Milburn*, 5–8; WK to WKS, March 5, 1932, B5F5, KP; WK to WKS, March 21, 1934, November 27, 1934, and WKS to WK, February 28, 1934, in *OxY*, 332–33, 341–43, 439; WK to WKS, April 7, 1929, B2F1, KP.

43. YM, Biography, 32–33, 41–42, 90–94, B9 F6/F7, KP; GWC, Prologue, xiv–xv; Wills, *Confessions*, 19; WKS to WK, Spring 1926, B3F8, KP; WK to WKS, August 24, 1924, B1F1, KP; "Mangum Boy," p. 1; WK to WKS, March 5, 1925, B1 F4, KP; WK to YM, November 17, 1944, B5F2, KP; Toby La Forge, "Boy Scout

Tribune," *Tulsa Tribune*, July 29, 1923, p. 51; Christopher H. Owen, "Sooner State 'Boy Wonder:' The Oklahoma Roots of Willmoore Kendall's Thought," *Chronicles of Oklahoma* 97, no. 1 (Spring 2019): 86–87.

44. WK to WKS, 1926, B1 F5 B1F5 and WK to WKS, June 30, 1928, B1F8, KP; WKS, "Average Child," *Tulsa Tribune*, November 16, 1923, p. 13.

Chapter 2

1929–1935
"I Beg to Disagree"

On the Friday afternoon of October 15, 1931, Dr. Matthew Thompson McClure, professor of Philosophy at the University of Illinois, was out of the office. Thus, when Willmoore Kendall, then a student in McClure's class, dropped by Lincoln Hall to chat about his term paper, he had to go away disappointed. Wandering off, Kendall passed a bulletin board in an out-of-the-way corner of the building. There he spied a dog-eared prospectus for applying to the Rhodes Scholarship. Kendall decided on the spot to enter the competition for the Rhodes but, as he kept reading, discovered that the application was due the next day. Undeterred, he obtained the application from a university office, completed it, and put it in the mail. He received a short extension from the Rhodes committee to forward required documents.[1]

Still, it took some scurrying around to get the materials in on time. The Rhodes required a reference from a college president from an institution the applicant had attended for at least two years. The University of Oklahoma had maxed out on its share of applicants so Kendall got the letter from Walter Dill Scott, president of Northwestern. Even after he submitted the documents, Kendall faced two more hurdles. Applicants had to appear in Oklahoma City on December 5, 1931, for interviews. Successful candidates then faced another meeting a week later in New Orleans. Informed of Willmoore's initiative, Reverend Kendall discouraged his offspring from this unlikely quest. The minister's mood lifted when his son succeeded at the Oklahoma City prelims. When learning that Willmoore had received the scholarship after a successful interview in New Orleans, Reverend Kendall was ecstatic, seeing the award as a massive "honor to the family." Mrs. Kendall and he had to slip off from friends to have "a big cry."[2]

Offered a special interview in Chicago to avoid taking two long trips in a week, Kendall, Jr., had declined. The New Orleans interview entailed a "frightful grilling." Kendall believed that first-rate letters of recommendation—particularly one from Professor John Van Horne at Illinois—put him over the top. In this assessment Kendall underestimated his own verbal flair. As he described it, the committee must have appreciated his "Socratic reasoning." Kendall, set on a career in journalism, had defended the notion that a good journalist required quality academic training. In the face of committee skepticism, he claimed it not possible for an editorial writer to be "overtrained." Impressed by the other candidates, Kendall was shocked when the committee announced he won to a crowd of applicants and reporters.³

In the two and a half years between his Tulsa disaster and his New Orleans triumph, Kendall had worked hard to make his way in the world. After leaving Oklahoma, he settled in the Chicago area and toiled at a variety of jobs. None were intellectually stimulating or paid well. Some required grueling manual labor. In April 1929, for example, Kendall obtained a job as a clerk with the Western Electric Company in Cicero, Illinois, where he worked for about a year. The company assigned him to a position which required him to be constantly on his feet and irritated his skin condition. When a supervisor proved unsympathetic to his complaints, he quit. In the summer of 1930 he moved to Oklahoma City, helping his uncle Sloan Childers campaign for Sheriff of Oklahoma County. By August Willmoore was back working construction. The new job required carrying "mammoth boards" for building scaffolds, demolishing a "cement wall" with sledge hammer and chisel, and moving bricks with a wheel barrow. After two days, he reported home, the only muscles in his body not sore were those "intended to wiggle the ears."⁴

Given the state of the American economy, Kendall was fortunate to have found any employment. But the physical demands of blue-collar work made other sorts of work more alluring. The United States Census, taken in April 1930, listed Kendall, Jr., as living in Miami, Oklahoma, with his family and recorded his occupation as journalist. Yet, neither his residence nor his vocation was strictly accurate. Although Kendall sometimes stayed for weeks at a time in Miami with his family, he mostly lived and worked elsewhere. Young Kendall's letters—full of charming travel stories and colorful anecdotes—showed a journalistic gift. Reverend Kendall recognized his son's writing talent, suggesting that he should submit his letters to magazines. Nevertheless, labeling Willmoore a journalist was mostly aspirational, for his efforts in that field continued to be sporadic and unrewarding.⁵

Discouraged by his job prospects, Kendall applied for the doctoral program in Romance Languages at the University of Illinois. With good references and possessing an excellent command of Spanish and a reading knowledge of French, he was accepted for the Fall Semester of 1930. He received an instructorship which covered his tuition and paid a $150 stipend per month. The new position let him live "fairly comfortably" and even save money.

While taking graduate classes, Kendall would serve as a "full-time instructor," teaching several sections of first-year Spanish. Rejoicing in a place with more intellectual stimulation than in the workaday world, he thrived as a student and teacher. It was in Champaign where Kendall first came to love the academic life. He had comfortable lodgings and reported that

> the meals at the [University] Club are surprisingly instructive. The man on one's left is a specialist in English history; the man across the table perhaps a fair authority on Shakespeare; the man two seats away on the right is an Economics wizard. All those fellows, I find, know something I'm very glad to know—and they're all glad of a chance to talk.[6]

That fall Willmoore threw himself into his work as a teacher and discovered that he was good at it. He hoped and expected that his students would shine on departmental examinations. Kendall had a low opinion of the other instructors in his department. They were "a feeble lot," he said, and he was confident that his own "children" would outshine them. And, indeed, at the end of the semester—he bragged to his parents—one of his students achieved the highest score on the departmental exam. This student, Katherine Tuach, a red-haired Scottish-born immigrant girl, hailed from Chicago. She became an ardent admirer of Kendall as "the only teacher she had down here who seemed to have anything to give her except cut and dried information out of textbooks." Learning that Katherine was interested in international journalism, Kendall gave her individual reading assignments and meet with her weekly to discuss them.[7]

After a year of teaching, Kendall decided to spend the summer of 1931 in Mexico City. He planned to practice his Spanish and to find a job as a correspondent for the Associated Press. In June he passed through Oklahoma for a short visit with his parents. Having reconciled with them several months after the Louvre blowup, he was again welcome in the family home. Troubled by the eruption of a boil, he visited a local doctor to have it lanced before proceeding on his trip. Once on his journey he suffered quite a bit of discomfort with the "thing keeping [him] in constant misery all the way to San Antonio." A physician there reassured him that "the pain was a natural part of the healing process" and charged him "two and a half bucks for a handsome new bandage."[8]

From there things got more exciting. By the time he arrived in Monterrey, "the inflammation had spread until the soreness extended four or five inches on either side of the original eruption." Kendall checked into a hotel and consulted a physician. Fearful of blood poisoning, this doctor moved into action. After receiving a shot of novocaine, Kendall watched as the Mexican practitioner "lighted a gas jet and began to heat an iron." For such an infection, said the doctor, a scalpel "would not do at all" and instead he would "burn the infection out with an iron." As Kendall "watched him burn it out," he noted the strangeness of smelling the "odor of human flesh wedded to the realization that it's your own. In went the iron—tssssss!—and up in smoke went another quart of pus and another ounce of flesh." The operation took more than an hour. After the doctor bandaged the cauterized wound, Kendall was delighted to receive a bill for "only five pesos—two dollars!"[9] He then continued his journey.

Kendall knew colleagues from Champaign-Urbana would be in Mexico City, but he wanted to live and work on his own. In July, once he had arrived, the young doctoral student paid a visit to the National Museum of Mexico to catch up with an old friend. Asking for Daniel Rubìn, with whom he had washed dishes at the Orrington Hotel back in Evanston, Kendall got a strange look. The perplexed attendant asked Kendall if he meant "Prof. Daniel Rubìn de la Borbolla, of the Dept. of Physical Anthropology." Kendall at first thought not, but then ascertained that his friend worked as professor of anthropology at the Museum. In fact, Rubìn had become an acclaimed scholar, Mexico's leading anthropologist. As it happened, this position at the museum was only the beginning of a long and distinguished career.[10]

The reunion was a happy one, for Daniel and Willmoore had been close friends. Indeed, Kendall had known all three Rubìn brothers—Daniel, Justino, and Gilberto—quite well in his Chicago days. He had roomed with Gilberto at the YMCA as all four young men were working their way through school. The intelligence, work ethic, and family togetherness of the Rubìns had impressed Kendall. He admired them all, but he felt nearest to Daniel whom he had regarded, in those lonely teenage years, as "the dearest friend I have ever had." Getting reacquainted, Kendall used his friend's connections to find better lodgings. He also obtained paid employment working with Rubìn, helping his new patron "work into shape" many "Maya legends he has been collecting" and to put his speeches into "good English." Kendall enjoyed this work but also missed the previous two weeks of "delicious Mexican lethargy" in which he had slept late and done nothing productive.[11]

Kendall loved living in Mexico and regretted having to come home to the United States. Although he never got on with the Associated Press, he did discover opportunities for future employment. Daniel arranged a job for him working with the Guggenheim Foundation in Mexico City which would have allowed time to work on his doctorate at the National University. The salary was adequate but would not have allowed Kendall to repay debts he owed for his previous educational endeavors. Other jobs were also available in the United States. An Oklahoma "teacher's college" wanted to hire Kendall to lead its department of foreign languages, but he declined in order to continue his doctoral study at Illinois.[12]

Kendall's political convictions were beginning to move leftward but remained vague. In 1931 he commented on the bad economic situation in Mexico but also expressed concern about the economic outlook for the United States. He suggested that the Depression might "prove an excellent thing for the country." Something was needed to transform "the execrable financial system under which the country has writhed for so many years." He saw American government as "in the hands of folk who are not concerned about the interests of the great majority of our population." He even began to waffle on prohibition, an issue near his father's heart. Given the need for more government revenue, the younger man found proposals for legalizing and taxing "four per-cent beer" to be "convincing." He then reassured his father that he "was not talking wet," that he was "daily more convinced that some sort of prohibition . . . was absolutely necessary to civilization."[13]

Kendall knew that he was fortunate to return to the United States with the "unutterable security" of a position at Illinois. In the autumn of 1931 Kendall pushed forward with his interactive style of teaching. He fought departmental battles about which grammar text to use, but textbooks in general bored him. Thus, Kendall adopted a version of direct method language instruction—then experiencing a boom of popularity in the United States—with virtually all classroom communication in the target language. This method prioritized verbal communication and intensive interaction between students and instructor, deemphasizing instruction in grammar. With a well-prepared teacher (i.e., fluent in the target language), it was ideal for small classes of intelligent and focused students. "Having stumbled upon [this] classroom manner" Kendall cut free from textbooks. Teaching then became "splendidly satisfactory" for him, "a real delight day in and day out." He began to contemplate "thirty–forty years" of university teaching as a "satisfying thing" in which he could take a "craftsman's pride."[14]

Kendall gained increasing confidence as an instructor. He believed university authorities appreciated his ability enough that his position was "waterproof." Kendall compiled a good record in his academic work, demonstrating greater conscientiousness than in previous efforts at Oklahoma and Northwestern. So impressed were his teachers with his language skills that the department chair waived the French proficiency exam, viewing it as "absurd" in Kendall's case. During these years Kendall continued to work at various literary translations then discovered that publishers viewed such works as unsaleable. He also wrote and translated articles and short stories for publication only to have most of them rejected. Unlike his previous work in journalism, academic writing was hard for Kendall. He refused to dash out narratives as he had done as a boy journalist, but labored over his prose, envisioning academics as his audience.[15]

Rejections of these translations and short stories helped disenchant the young teacher with studying language, literature, and grammar. The coming of the Depression also deepened his interest in politics. Before leaving for Oxford, Kendall had thus decided to shift his academic focus to politics and economics. In part he made this change because he believed it would further his dream to become a world-renowned journalist. He was not straightforward with his academic advisor about these goals. Kendall's intellect had given Professor Van Horne inflated notions about his student's knowledge of Spanish literature. Even in his first year at Illinois, Kendall had begun to take graduate classes in philosophy as his interest in Spanish literature lagged. He therefore applied for the Rhodes as an aspiring journalist not as a would-be expert in Spanish prose. Although he did not lie to Van Horne about his plans, Kendall chose not to disabuse his advisor's assumptions about his career trajectory.[16]

Kendall made important long-term friendships at Illinois. He became close friends with Revilo Oliver, a brilliant but eccentric polyglot from Corpus Christi, who specialized in the study of Sanskrit. The two men would keep up a humorous and occasionally highbrow correspondence after Kendall went to Oxford. Kendall, already a man of the left, regarded the Oliver of the early 1930s as an arch-reactionary monarchist. Despite their many disagreements, their friendship survived for many years. Oliver's attacks on the New Deal (labeling the NRA as No Results Anticipatable or calling the president "Frenzied Frankie") amused Willmoore.[17]

Receiving the Rhodes was a life-changing event for Kendall. After getting notice of the award in 1931, Kendall showed himself ready to turn the page on many aspects of his former life. In an interview with the *Daily Oklahoman* he asked the paper not "to revive that child prodigy stuff," because he had "about lived it down."[18] Kendall regarded his upcoming time in England as a chance to forge his own path away from the smothering attentions of Reverend Kendall. The Rhodes Scholarship also provided the Illinois instructor with a chance to pursue subjects which interested him, rather than continuing in an academic direction which he had fallen into because of fluency in Spanish. The young man also knew going overseas would broaden his outlook. In spite of extensive travel and possession of an MA from a prestigious university, Kendall still retained a certain provinciality. In 1932 he was still only twenty-three and lacked maturity and direction as he headed to Oxford.

The scholarship came at a propitious time for Kendall. Beginning to feel the effects of the Depression, the University of Illinois was starting to institute cutbacks, including slashing assistantships and instructorships awarded to its graduate students. In the Spring of 1932, as he was planning his Oxford odyssey, Kendall believed it doubtful that he could have retained his salaried position in Champaign-Urbana. He believed department authorities would keep him "first on the list" but thought money so tight that he would likely lose his position. This latter impression deepened in England when he heard from afar that Illinois was resorting to paying its teachers in scrip.[19] The Rhodes stipend, on the other hand, gave Kendall financial security, providing him with enough money to live in frugal comfort for the next three years.

On a less happy note, Kendall had to put off getting married to accept the Rhodes Scholarship. Even in his early teens Willmoore had shown considerable romantic interest in the opposite sex. At the University of Illinois he became involved with his star student Katherine Tuach, and they socialized happily together with the campus "bohemian crowd of young faculty members and graduate students." At age twenty-one, he was only a year older than she. They began to discuss marriage. Winning the Rhodes Scholarship excluded that possibility, for its recipients had to remain single for the duration of the award.[20]

The two Willmoores were at their closest in the summer of 1932, when Kendall, Jr., returned to Oklahoma in preparation for traveling to Oxford. Reverend Kendall played the piano accompanied by Willmoore on the flute. They sang songs together and engaged in intellectual "fencing." After this training in intellectual give and take at home, Kendall, Jr., never felt overawed when verbally sparring with anyone. Overcoming butterflies about leaving home, Kendall shipped out from Galveston on the SS *Tripp* on September 5, 1932. After almost a month at sea (described delightfully in his journal), Kendall disembarked in England on September 30. On October 6 after seeing the sights of London for a week, he made the short trip to Oxford. He had been assigned to Pembroke (one of the more obscure Oxford colleges). In letters home he described his new experiences. He told of coming upon "a barren and crumbling wall" whose "gate reminds you of nothing you've ever seen before." Passing "directly under Dr. [Samuel] Johnson's sometimes rooms," he knew instinctively not to carry his typewriter into his lodgings, for servants performed such tasks at Oxford.[21]

Pembroke College possessed a distinguished faculty. There Willmoore studied philosophy, economics, and politics, then a regular Oxford course of study known as "The Modern Greats." Kendall established friendly relations with his tutors, R. G. Collingwood for philosophy and political theory, R. B. McCallum in comparative government and history, and Russell Frederick Bretherton in economics. From these men, he received superb instruction. Collingwood was one of the most important philosophers of the twentieth century. He published his most important book, *An Essay on Philosophical Method*, in 1933 when Kendall was his student. McCallum was a prominent historian of British politics then working on a biography of H. H. Asquith. McCallum was also associated with the Inklings circle of C. S. Lewis and J. R. R. Tolkien (who taught at Pembroke). Bretherton, after Oxford, enjoyed a long and distinguished career as an economist in the British civil service. Of the three, McCallum "stood out in appreciating" Willmoore's intellectual gifts and originality.[22]

Collingwood challenged his new student, assigning him intensive reading of Berkeley, Locke, and Hume. He expected weekly essays which "simply must cover the ground and hang together." Kendall relished this challenge. Pleasing Collingwood, he admitted, required "the sort of discipline I have needed for years." When Collingwood congratulated his new American student for an "excellent essay" on Kant or complimented him during "Don's Rag," Kendall relished his praise. Later Kendall said that he could not "develop any fondness" for Collingwood but saw him as "the most superior dialectician I have ever known." Enthralled with Collingwood's "intellectual discipline," Kendall once sat "with open mouth" as his tutor explained intellectual problems inherent in Cartesian epistemology.[23]

Kendall regaled his father with tales of what he was learning. In economics, for example, one letter launched into a detailed analysis of current contemporary theories based on Frederick Soddy's *Wealth, Virtual Wealth and Debt*. In history, he provided details of his growing appreciation for Edmund Burke, and so forth. In his first year, Kendall expressed misgivings about the tutorial system, suggesting that he needed more regular interaction with his tutors. Collingwood, he knew, was "radiantly brilliant" and expressed willingness to "spend hours at his feet every day." He complained that in reality neither he nor other undergraduates got to spend much time with Collingwood or with their other tutors.[24]

At Oxford, despite occasional dissatisfaction, Kendall found himself at the center of the interwar intellectual world. There he found forces and ideas before strange to him and adopted some for himself. Much that he learned came through activities outside the regular course of instruction. In October 1932 Kendall went to hear a speech by H. G. Wells. Unimpressed with the author's speaking ability, he was sympathetic with his program to build "a better civilization" through globalized "oligarchy." The young American then stood amazed as fellow undergraduates savaged Wells. They called him a privileged elitist whose idiocy kept him from recognizing that class conflict necessitated violent revolution. Kendall at this point agreed with Wells that such needed social change could come without violence and expressed his own fear of Marxism. In Fall 1933 Kendall was able to hear a presentation by C. S. Lewis on "Objective Value in Poetry" at the 400th meeting of Pembroke's Beaumont Society. The next March—encouraged by Collingwood—Kendall himself delivered a talk on Henri Bergson's views on the freedom of the will at the Pembroke College Philosophical Society.[25]

At Oxford, Kendall witnessed events of global significance. He was present, for instance, at the famous King and Country Debate at the Oxford Union on February 9, 1933. The motion debated that evening was: "This House will under no circumstances fight for its King and Country." The eloquence of C. E. M. Joad—then a stalwart of the Labour Party—who came down from London to speak for the resolution, impressed the Rhodes Scholar. So moved was Kendall that he recorded Joad's address verbatim in a letter to his father. When put to a vote the motion passed by a margin of 2 to 1. This decision quickly became an international event, as Winston Churchill denounced Oxford's pacifism, and his son Randolph tried unsuccessfully to have the vote expunged from the records of the Union. Hitler cited the resolution as a sign of English weakness. American pacifists took inspiration from the "Oxford Oath" and adopted their own pacifist pledge. Willmoore, despite admiration for Joad's eloquence, had voted no. Reverend Kendall approved his son's stance, agreeing that the statement was extreme.[26]

Absence may make the heart grow fonder, but for Kendall's father, it also made the urge to give advice stronger. "I regret," said Reverend Kendall in early 1933, "to having you soak yourself in eighteenth-century philosophy and groping in benighted ignorance about the world you must live in." The minister suggested that his son get out from the university environs, lest he become a "pedantic donkey besotted with excess of philosophical learning." Reverend Kendall then wrote to John Buchan, a famous novelist, Christian evangelical, and member of Parliament (and later Governor General of Canada). Expressing admiration for Buchan's novels, the elder Kendall informed him that his son was lonely and urged Buchan to have Willmoore over for a talk. Buchan accepted the proposal and invited Willmoore to tea, who was confused at receiving the invitation. Kendall expressed appreciation to his father for arranging the visit. He spent an unforgettable Sunday afternoon with Buchan who was on a first name with Franklin Roosevelt, John J. Pershing, and other notable persons.[27]

Reverend Kendall also pushed his son to contact the up-and-coming Oxford Group. The organization aimed at spiritual reformation of individual lives. Based on the ideas of American missionary Frank Buchman, its approach focused on shared fellowship. Members engaged in frank discussions meant to help them lead lives of "absolute honesty" and "absolute purity." Willmoore heard about the organization—from which Alcoholics Anonymous later evolved—as soon as he arrived at Oxford. After attending several meetings Willmoore was unimpressed. He found the "public confessions" of "self-abuse" and "incipient dipsomania" disgusting. He admitted that the nondenominational group possessed spiritual power by sidestepping age-old theological disputes. Mostly, Kendall viewed the "Groupers" as "hopelessly immature" and self-righteous.[28]

Reverend Kendall wanted Willmoore to become an "international journalist" earning a good paycheck, using Walter Lippmann as his model. When his son hesitated, Kendall, Sr., called him a dillydallying "Hamlet" and discouraged him from becoming a "pedant" who earned "a bare living" as a teacher. For many years Kendall, Jr., shared this journalist dream. He admitted that he found "Spanish-professing" unappealing. Even though he wanted to marry Katherine Tuach, he had refused to do so if it that meant being tied to the "professing business." In Europe, however, the young man became increasingly annoyed with his father's advice-giving mania. In one response to complaints about his laggard writing career, Willmoore laid out his plan to obtain the best academic preparation possible at Oxford. Thus, he would have something worthwhile to write about as a journalist.[29]

In response to his father's torrent of advice, Kendall developed a habit of accounting for his time to another person whom he recognized as a higher authority. In April 1932, for example, still teaching at Illinois, he wrote home to his parents to let them know how diligently he was working. While preparing to turn in his midterm grades, he was spending "three or four hours a day over my short stories, always, and three or four hours over my books, and an hour and a half at the gymnasium." He sent similar epistles from Oxford which contained long self-justifying explanations of events if something happened to go wrong. Although his parents knew he smoked (and disliked the fact), his reports to them minimized his drinking. Recounting a meeting of Pembroke's Beaumont Society in January 1934, for example, Willmoore claimed that his "own libations" were limited to "the toast [of port wine] with which each meeting begins."[30]

Kendall made lasting friends among his English classmates, including Edward Grant (a fellow leftist) and Hong Kong-born George Apcar, both later successful financiers. Also important to him were friendships with other Oklahoma Rhodes scholars. Soon after his arrival he met Carl Albert from Bugtussle, Oklahoma. The two men socialized regularly, often playing chess or pitch, a card game popular in English pubs. In 1933 Kendall moved out of his Pembroke lodgings into a house across from Oriel College which he rented together with Albert. When Albert—who possessed well-developed "political ambitions"—returned to Oklahoma, Kendall introduced him to his father to help apprise Albert of the state's political situation. Years later Carl Albert recalled these years at Oxford with Kendall, especially the "bittersweet" academic year of 1933–1934 when he and Kendall lived together. Albert respected Kendall's intelligence and loved socializing with him. He also remembered Willmoore's "favorite phrase was, 'I beg to disagree with you.' He hardly talked to anyone without taking exception to something that was said—even though that person probably thought he was agreeing with Willmoore." Albert noted that Kendall and his other housemates partied so heartily that he had to retreat to an upstairs bedroom to find a quiet place to study.[31]

Jack Fischer, who arrived at Oxford in Fall 1933, also became Kendall's boon companion. A native of Amarillo, Fischer had graduated from the University of Oklahoma. He also boasted experience as a journalist, having worked as a reporter for the *Daily Oklahoman*. With Fischer, instead of chess, Kendall took up boxing. For a time he worked with Fischer at producing a series of small popular books on economics, like the Little Blue Books. The project fizzled out when, busy with their academic work, they failed to finish a single volume. Indeed, at Oxford, Kendall began a habit of starting book projects but failing to bring them to fruition. The same year as the failed Fischer scheme, for example, Kendall—impressed by G. D. H. Cole's *Intelligent Man's Review of Europe*—proposed to write something similar for Latin America. After getting the endorsement of his tutors, the warden of Rhodes House, and Cole himself to proceed, he soured upon and dropped the project.[32]

In June 1934 Kendall traveled to Spain with Oklahoma friends, including Fischer and George Milburn who had arrived in England. Milburn had received a Guggenheim Fellowship to further his efforts in creative writing and had come to England to work on a novel. He and his wife and daughter traveled with Fischer, Kendall (Ken to his closest friends), and Katherine Tuach (aka Katy) to Madrid. Milburn changed his residence to Spain at the suggestion of Willmoore who knew that the family could live cheaper there than in England. This advice proved fruitful as Milburn made significant progress in Madrid on his novel *Catalogue*. Yet another Oklahoma lad who ran in Kendall's circle was Daniel Boorstin of Tulsa who arrived at Oxford in 1934, to study law at Balliol College. Reverend Kendall and Samuel Boorstin, Daniel's father, were friends back home. Samuel Boorstin was a leader in Oklahoma's Jewish community, and the minister worked with him over the years to combat anti-Semitism in Oklahoma. Impressed by Daniel's intelligence and work ethic, Willmoore expressed conviction that his new friend was destined for greatness.[33]

Still Kendall, Jr., was often lonely, sometimes bemoaning his "isolation." Especially in his first year, he missed his family and Katherine Tuach. In the summer of 1933 he got a little less lonely when Katy, after graduating from Illinois in French, relocated to Europe. Putting her own ambitions on hold for a time, she lived with relatives in Scotland and England. Then she took a position as manager of a tea shop in London, before getting fired for attempting to organize a union. The couple spent weekends and vacations with one another, including a pleasant summer together in Spain in 1933 when both of them enjoyed lots of leisure, including lots of reading. She remained in Europe until 1936 when they both moved back to the United States—as a married couple. Katy and Ken married in London on June 22, 1935. It was a small, civil ceremony, with Edward Grant serving as the best man and

Daniel Boorstin in attendance. Afterward the couple traveled to Paris for their honeymoon.[34]

Given Kendall's later prominence as a political theorist and political activist, scholars have been interested in clarifying his political views during his Oxford years. Such clarification has proved difficult because the young scholar's views were inconsistent and evolving. The best way to conceptualize Willmoore's political orientation during these early years in Europe is to say that he was avidly seeking for answers. Intelligent but immature, Kendall found himself exposed to the highest levels of academic and political discourse. In response, he explored, with guidance from his tutors and fellow students, many ideas about politics, philosophy, and economics. He then sought to integrate what he learned in Europe with those values and beliefs which he already held. Willmoore's maturation as a human being required him to rebel against his father's advice. One key step on this journey was to break with his family's self-identification as Democrats. Allegiance to the Party had suffused the family's outlook for all Willmoore's life. As judged by his correspondence, party loyalty was more important to Reverend Kendall than fidelity to the southern Methodist Church (which he often toyed with leaving and whose theology he did not take seriously). But being a Democrat went deep down into the family bones. The Party connected the Kendalls to the heroes and villains of American history, linked them to their ancestors, provided a schematic for interpreting current events, and gave them jobs. By the time he arrived in England, Willmoore, Jr., had drunk fully from this Democratic trough.

In August 1933 an episode occurred in Spain which shed light on Kendall's family-based political convictions. Taking a page from his father's book, Willmoore introduced himself to American Ambassador Claude G. Bowers. Before serving in Madrid, Bowers had been a newspaper editor and prominent Indiana Democrat. Willmoore and his father became Bowers fans in 1928 when he delivered the keynote address at the Democratic Convention, blistering Republicans as privileged and corrupt. In 1932 Bowers backed Franklin Roosevelt early on and received appointment as ambassador to Spain as his reward. In the embassy Willmoore seemed to find a kindred spirit—a man interested in journalism and Democratic Party politics. He and Bowers had a long conversation about politicians and journalists. Bowers argued that neither should become "too blooming intellectual." This proposition—in regard to journalists—was the very one Kendall had denied in his Rhodes interview. Bowers also called Lippmann an indolent Easterner who loved Europe but knew zero about anything "west of Hoboken." Being "an Oxford man," Bowers assured Kendall, would open doors for him in journalism. He could "thumb his nose" at "the Jews" who dominated American journalism and who normally snubbed Midwesterners lacking Ivy League degrees. Kendall then told Bowers he had decided not to work in the State Department because of its elitism. The ambassador heartily approved. As a political appointee, he was already battling Harvard-educated bureaucrats in the embassy.[35]

In setting up this meeting, Kendall cited his high regard for the diplomat's bestselling book on Reconstruction, *The Tragic Era* (1929). Reconstruction to Bowers meant white southerners as victims, Yankees as avaricious plutocrats, and African Americans as pawns and primitives. Similar views were then dominant among professional historians, but Bowers was a journalist not a scholar. Aiming at "melodrama," he penned lurid and purple prose. Radical Republicans, he declared, had used the Constitution as a "doormat" and built "monstrosities" they called state constitutions. Moreover, *The Tragic Era* had a partisan purpose. Bowers wrote it as propaganda "to bring the South back into line" after its dalliance with Hoover in 1928. Party leaders, including Roosevelt, recognized that *The Tragic Era* had succeeded in this purpose. One reader who succumbed to its "lure" was Reverend Kendall. He called Bowers "his favorite historian" and used his ideas to rationalize never again voting Republican. He "commended" his son to "Claude Bowers' philosophy." Republicans, he agreed, worshipped financiers while Democrats helped the working class. Although Willmoore had sought out Bowers, Reverend Kendall decided to write the embassy directly to correct the ambassador's favorable opinion of Alfalfa Bill Murray.[36]

As his father's views on the New Deal grew more positive, Willmoore, from a distance, grew hostile to Roosevelt and to Bowers-style loyalty to the Democratic Party. He admitted the new president was good at politics but thought remaining popular his only positive attribute. In December 1934 Willmoore told his dad that the president "makes me sick." In general, he criticized the New Deal from the left, arguing that the federal government should intervene decisively to restructure the economy. At one point, he even argued for "sterilization of the state units." Knowing this viewpoint put him at odds with the traditional Jeffersonian position of the Democratic Party, Willmoore declared himself ready "to forego the pleasure" of belonging to that "great organization" (or to any political party). His view that Roosevelt was too cautious grew stronger over time. The New Deal, he proclaimed in 1935, meant rebuilding "a rotten and iniquitous system."[37]

Despite the leftward tilt of such critiques, the young scholar sometimes contended that the New Deal was unsuccessful not because it was too conservative but because it was an ad hoc program following presidential whims. Either a consistent program of free market economics or of genuine socialism, thought Kendall, would work better. Studying economics at Oxford when the ideas of John Maynard Keynes were in vogue, Kendall absorbed lots of Keynesian ideas. In 1934 he told his father that large-scale deficit spending and a massive program of public works would lead to a financial recovery. Roosevelt ought to apply actual Keynesian solutions rather than a politically palatable hodgepodge. In breaking from his father, the direction Willmoore chose sometimes seemed secondary. But it had to mean getting out of lockstep with the Democratic Party. He reminded his dad that progressive heroes Abraham Lincoln and Theodore Roosevelt had belonged to the Grand Old Party. Contra Bowers, he suggested that disliking Alexander Hamilton or Thaddeus Stevens gave no guidance for the present.[38]

Kendall was definitely not a communist when he left the United States in 1932. According to Carl Albert he possessed the typical views "of an Oklahoma Democrat." But at Oxford, Kendall came to identify as a Marxist. This process began to get serious in the summer of 1933 when, for the first time, he read Marx's *Capital*. Entranced by the author's empathy for working people, Kendall found *Capital* enthralling. On the other hand, he saw Marx's economics as completely false and was not ready to convert to communism. In October 1933, for example, he argued that workers deserved "a just wage" but that entrepreneurs also deserved to make reasonable profits. The next month he denied that communism provided an antidote for the difficulties of mankind. In early 1934 Kendall, after reading works by G. D. H. Cole, edged closer to a collectivist position. By summer's end, one may call Kendall a socialist, for he supported nationalization of American banks and railroads. In the bloody aftermath of the failed October Revolution of 1934 in Spain, Kendall said socialists should have seized power even if it required using violence against an unwilling populace. By January 1935 Kendall was convinced of the need for socialism and unapologetic in supporting it. He called private property "an enslaving convention" whose greatest stronghold was in the United States. He now regarded his mission in life to become "a Great Socialist Publicist" and preferred "bloody revolution" to none at all. When Willmoore visited Oklahoma in 1935, his father expressed dismay that his son had accepted communist dogma.[39]

Yet Willmoore's socialism remained intertwined with American principles of democracy. He saw capitalism as "founded on inequality" and socialism on "equality," but his solution was to make democracy real. Existing democracies, he claimed, were schemes to thwart the "popular will." Using an example designed to appeal to his father, Kendall argued that socialism and democracy were akin to prohibition, that is, they were good ideas which needed to be put into actual practice to see if they worked. In 1936 Kendall vowed to avoid all labels, asserting that he was neither "a Mason nor a Pythian nor a fraternity man nor a Catholic nor a Democrat nor a Republican." Nor was he much troubled about which socialist group to join, though he swore to avoid any Stalinist party. Many years later, R. B. McCallum contextualized Kendall's rather generic socialism of the mid-1930s. At Pembroke, he said, Willmoore had been "something of a socialist and a man of the Left as was frequent amongst Rhodes Scholars with political interests at that time."[40]

Even in this socialist phase, Kendall, like many interwar leftists, was as concerned with foreign policy as with proletarian rule. In 1934 he expressed distrust for American, British, and French diplomacy, declaring himself an isolationist. He argued that the United States should mind its own business and stay out of a Europe "hellbent for another war." He recognized that American voters would not support socialism. He believed, however, that socialists could tap into growing "pacifist sentiment" because both major parties sought to boost military spending. On balance, as regards Kendall's political views as a student in Europe, one must agree with political scientist M. Susan Power that he never became a committed communist. On the other hand, her view that Willmoore was a left-wing southern Democrat is inaccurate, for in Europe he also broke from the party of his ancestors. Rather he was an up-and-coming intellectual asking probing questions about politics and economics, finding many answers within the Marxist matrix, but keeping his eyes and options open. He remained "an eager debater and disputer on all subjects."[41]

Willmoore's break with his father also involved deciding what profession to follow—journalist or professor. If the former, the question was whether to be a partisan popularizer or a cerebral analyst. That is, should a journalist emulate Claude Bowers or Walter Lippmann? As his father urged him to follow the Bowers model, Kendall, Jr., became attracted to the academic life. He believed that, as a Rhodes Scholar, he could land a good-paying post at a prestigious university. He thus decided to pursue a third year at Oxford, hoping to achieve a "First" on his examinations. Even if he were to pursue journalism, he favored the balanced approach of Lippmann, which earned the younger man's admiration more than the crude partisanship of Bowers. The Rhodes Scholar had decided that it was his "destiny to do important things" and that he could best achieve that goal by learning all he could from his tutors. No one ought to waste valuable time in Europe merely at play.[42]

While blazing his path, Kendall sometimes yearned for American simplicities and verities, longing for steak and potatoes rather than elaborately prepared Spanish food. He missed the relative abundance of home with regular supplies of hot water and toilet paper. As he reported on Spain's "Great Red Day" of August 1, 1934, European politics appeared bewildering and frightening to him. He saw bitter tension building between Spanish left and right and was not optimistic about its end. He saw Hitler creeping closer to complete power in Germany. Kendall's sympathies lay with the left as these world-shaking events unfolded. He denounced the rightist government's repression of the Madrid General Strike of September 1934. Yet Kendall was also sometimes nostalgic for home-style politics. "Give me the state," he declared, "where they re-elect crooked politicians."[43]

By no means had the younger man given up his dream to be a famous and well-paid journalist. In January 1934, for example, he paid a visit to Clifford Day at the office of United Press International (UPI) in London. Day was a good friend of Victor Barnett, friend of Willmoore, and editor of the *Tulsa Tribune*. After some discussion, Kendall received an offer to work that summer at the UPI office in Madrid, translating articles from English that would appear in Latin America. Such experience, he hoped, would open employment opportunities for him in the United States. To please his father, Kendall pledged to work only on his writing and to forget his studies.[44]

Yet he found work at UPI Madrid tedious. The real reporting was left to Spaniards, while he did rewrites from the English. This experience did affirm his fluency in Spanish, as his work in that language needed no correction from editors. Despite the allure of international journalism, he expressed low regard for international journalists, none of whom were as "competent" or "intelligent" as Tulsa's Victor Barnett. Still, it was difficult for Kendall to turn down a permanent job with UPI when Madrid bureau chief Jean De Gandt offered him one in July 1934. The pay was adequate and the work easy, but Kendall thought it would be a betrayal of the Rhodes organization to leave Oxford without a degree. Moreover, he valued the training in economics he would receive in the upcoming year, and UPI promised him a job in Madrid in 1935 after he graduated. Kendall expressed misgivings about such work, a style of journalism which focused on getting out a story rather than getting to the truth. As a life vocation, it was not earnest or meaningful.[45]

While in Europe, the power dynamic between Willmoore and his father changed. Willmoore was living comfortably on his Rhodes monies and began to send funds home to help with family. He also began to offer unsolicited advice, particularly as regards the education plans of his brother Walter. Meanwhile his parents were barely able to pay their bills. Reverend Kendall expressed regret about his own life choices, hoping his son might avoid similar mistakes. Marriage, he assured Willmoore, would mean major new responsibilities. In meeting them he hoped Willmoore could avoid the constraints which his own decision to become a minister at age twenty had condemned him to.[46]

When the younger man began to contemplate staying in Madrid to work for UPI long term, his dad admitted that taking such a position might be a good financial move especially for a newly married man. But Reverend Kendall was facing professional burnout, financial difficulty, and had not seen his son for three years. He dreaded the prospect of a Spanish post for Willmoore. In making this admission, he confessed emotional dependence upon his eldest son. He feared a Madrid job would mean abandoning their "long and happy comradeship." Indeed, he continued, "I cannot write about it without crying like a woman. I have come to feel such desperate need to be with you and talk with you."[47]

Willmoore sometimes longed for a face-to-face talk with his dad. But he answered this missive cruelly. The younger man expected his wife to work for a living. Theirs would be a socialist marriage of giving by ability and receiving by need. Unlike his father going to Eufaula in 1907 to work for a pittance, he would be going to Madrid in 1935 for generous pay. His father had joined the ministry with few prospects for promotion. He, on the other hand, viewed UPI as a stepping stone to better things. Unlike his father, Willmoore had no intention of having children too quickly at the expense of his career. When Yvona berated him for these severe words and for his long absence, the younger man apologized for his brusqueness. Willmoore assured his parents that his stay in Madrid would be brief and that he would return to the United States. Madrid was an opportunity to write on an exciting political situation of global importance and more attractive than returning to Tulsa to write about the "doings of the Water Commissioner." Kendall, Jr., also strongly asserted that he wanted to maintain connections with his family.[48]

Amid this harsh exchange of letters, Kendall's grandmother, Jenny Kendall, had a massive stroke and for some weeks lay near death. This event reawakened Willmoore to his family responsibilities. In early 1935 he returned home for his first visit since departing almost three years before, arriving hours before his grandmother's death on March 14. He stayed in Oklahoma for three weeks. Though distraught over his mother's death, Reverend Kendall expressed great joy over weeks visiting with his son. Willmoore, meanwhile, admitted his own sadness when he had to go back to Europe. In a sense, he had grown too big for Oklahoma. Paying a visit to Walter M. Harrison, managing editor of the *Daily Oklahoman*, he left a vivid impression. "He breezed in," said Harrison, "big and tweedy . . . but still as simple as the Oklahoma soil from whence he came." Ambitious, idealistic, talented, superbly educated, Kendall had a great future ahead. The visit made Harrison, "poking over a dusty desk," ask himself: "Am I the man who stood still?"[49]

Kendall had focused most of his energy on career prospects and on global politics for months, working less intently on his studies. Now he knew it was time to prepare seriously for his exams, the ultimate measure of how well one had done at Oxford. He doubted he would get a "First" but came to realize there were "several classes below a second." He buckled down to his studies over the next several weeks because he did not want to let down his teachers, family, and friends. In the end, he did well, scoring better in history than he had expected but worse in philosophy and economics, getting a "Second" overall. Tellingly—though Willmoore fancied himself an expert in economics—he got his highest score, "an outright alpha," in the test on political institutions.[50]

NOTES

1. WK to WKS, October 25, 1931, in *OxY*, 1–3.
2. WKS to WK, November 19, 1931, December 13, 1931, and October 30, 1932, in *OxY*, 3–5, 9; "Letters and Arts Club Meets," *Miami Daily News-Record*, March 5, 1933, p. 3.
3. WK to WKS, December 15, 1931 and [March] 1932, in *OxY*, 6–7, 16–17.
4. WK to WKS, July 1, 1931, B2F3, KP; WK to WKS, April 19, 1929, B2F1, KP; WK to WKS, March 19, 1930 and August 1930, B2F2, KP.
5. Year: 1930; Census Place: Miami, Ottawa, Oklahoma; Roll: 1923; Page: 14B; Enumeration District: 0016; Image: 847.0; FHL microfilm: 2341657 (Provo: Ancestry.com, 2002); YM, Biography, 155–56, B10F1, KP; WK to WKS, Several Letters from September 1932, January 14, 1933, December 22, 1934, and WKS to WK, February 28, 1934, in *OxY*, 21–45, 120–21, 333, 440–43.
6. WK to WKS, October 16, 1933, in *OxY*, 272; WK to WKS, Summer 1930, October 6, 1930, and Fall 1930, B2F2, KP.
7. WK to WKS, October 6, 1930 (two separate letters), WK to WKS, December 7, 1930, B2F2, WK to WKS, Fall 1930, B2F2, KP; *Passenger Lists, 1865–1935*. Microfilm Publications T-479 to T-520, T-4689 to T-4874, T-14700 to T-14938, C-4511 to C-4542. Library and Archives Canada, n.d. RG 76-C. Department of Employment and Immigration. Library and Archives Canada Ottawa, Ontario, Canada; Ruth A. Brandwein, "Katherine Kendall: A Social Work Institution," *Affilia* 20, no. 1 (Spring 2005): 104.
8. "Locals," *Miami Daily News-Record*, June 19, 1931, p. 6; WK to WKS, June 25, 1931, B2F3, KP.
9. WK to WKS, June 25, 1931, B2F3, KP.
10. WK to WKS, Summer 1931, B2F3, KP.
11. YM, Biography, 159–60, 188, B10F1 and B10F2, KP; WK to WKS, June 24, 1931, July 1931, Summer 1931, and July 8, 1931, B2F3, KP.
12. WK to WKS, July 1, 1931 and July 6, 1931, B2F3, KP; "Locals," *Miami Daily News- Record*, June 19, 1931, p. 6.
13. WK to WKS, Summer 1931, B2F3, KP; WK to WKS, March 21, 1932, B2F5, KP.
14. Jack S. Richards and Theodore S. Rogers, *Approaches and Methods in Language Teaching*, 3d ed. (Cambridge, UK: Cambridge University Press, 2014), 11–13; WK to WKS, 1931 and May 1931, B2F3; WK to WKS, 1932, B2F5, KP.
15. WK to WKS, July 1 1931, July 11, 1931, August 11, 1931, September 28, 1931, B2F3, KP; WK to WKS, March 1932, March 5, 1932, March 21, 1932, B2F5, KP.
16. GWC, Prologue to *OxY*, xix; WK to WKS, Spring 1932, in *OxY*, 11–13; WK to WKS, April 4, 1932, B2F5, KP; WK to WKS, January 1932, in *OxY*, 11–13; WK

to Charles Hyneman (hereafter CH), August 7, 1937, Charles S. Hyneman Papers (hereafter CHP), Collection C2, Indiana University Archives, Bloomington.

17. WK to WKS, October 4, 1932, November 19, 1932, October 16, 1933, and September 17, 1934, in *OxY*, 51, 96–97, 273–75, 410.

18. "City Youth," *Daily Oklahoman*, December 13, 1931, p. 9.

19. WK to WKS, April 4, 1932, B2F5, KP; WK to WKS, January 21, 1933, in *OxY*, 126.

20. WK to WKS, April 20, 1933 and May 2, 1933, in *OxY*, 176, 187; Brandwein, "Katherine," 104–05.

21. Mason, *OxY*, 19; WK, Journal Entries, September 1932, WK to WKS, October 4, 1932 and October 11, 1932, in *OxY*, 19–45, 51–53, 55–58.

22. Carl Albert to George H. Nash, March 3, 1972, B2F27, Biographical, CAC; "R.B. McCallum" and "J.R.R. Tolkien," *Pembroke College Record: 1973*, 13–18, 20; WK to WKS, October 11, 1932, May 17, 1933, September 1, 1933, and October 16, 1933, in *OxY*, 60–62, 204, 247, 282.

23. WK to WKS, November 2, 1932, November 19, 1932, October 16, 1933, and November 25, 1933, in *OxY*, 82–83, 97, 100, 264–65, 304.

24. WK to WKS, January 29, 1933, March 10, 1933, and May 17, 1933, in *OxY*, 126–29, 161–64, 203.

25. WK to WKS, October 27, 1932 and March 5, 1934, in *OxY*, 78–79, 334; "Beaumont Society," *Pembroke College Record: 1933–34*, 35.

26. WK to WKS, February 16, 1933, February 25, 1933, March 5, 1933 and WKS to WK, March 4, 1933, in *OxY*, 136–44, 148–49, 156, 159.

27. WKS to WK, December 26, 1932, January 10, 1933, and January 14, 1933, in *OxY*, 109–110, 119; WK to WKS, January 14, 1933 and September 1, 1933, in *OxY*, 121–24, 134, 246.

28. WKS to WK, April 5, 1933 and WK to WKS, May 17, 1933 and June 2, 1933, in *OxY*, 173, 192–98, 205–08.

29. YM to Savoie Lottinville, October 8, 1972, B92F26, General Correspondence, CAC; Nash, 227; GWC, Prologue, xvii–xviii; Wills, 19–20; WKS to WK, January 14, 1933, March 4, 1933, March 29, 1933, May 5, 1933, October 4, 1933, October 27, 1933, December 23, 1933, January 29, 1934, February 28, 1934, August 2, 1934, August 17, 1934, December 23, 1934, and July 26, 1935, in *OxY*, *passim*; WK to WKS, April 20, 1933 and May 17, 1933, in *OxY*, 173–76, 201–03.

30. WK to WKS, April 4, 1932, B25 and December 15, 1936, B3F3, KP; WKS to WK, February 8, 1936 and March 27, 1936, B4F3, KP; WK to WKS, January 18, 1934 and June 26, 1934, in *OxY*, 315, 367–68; WK to YM, [Fall 1961], B6F3, KP.

31. "E.A. Grant," *Pembroke College Record: 1988*, 36–37; WKS to WK, March 16, 1936, B4F3, KP; Carl Albert to Robert S. McNamara, November 9, 1976, B12F7, Office, CAC; WK to Albert, January 30, 1967 and Albert to WK, February 2, 1967, B43F9, General, CAC; WK to WKS, October 18, 1932, January 14, 1933, December 23, 1933, and May 10, 1934, in *OxY*, 71–72, 121, 308, 360–61; Carl Albert to YM, February 5, 1975, B92F26, General Correspondence, CAC; Albert to George H. Nash, February 17 1972 and March 3, 1972, B2F27, Biographical, CAC; Albert to

Paul Berman, October 12, 1972, B92F26, General Correspondence, CAC; Albert *Little Giant*, 109.

32. "Jack Fischer, Amarillo," *Amarillo Daily News*, September 4, 1934, p. 5; Carl Albert to George H. Nash, March 3, 1972, B 2, F 27, Biographical, CAC; WK to WKS, February 4, 1934, February 5, 1934, February 10, 1934, March 21, 1934, April 6, 1934, April 28, 1934, May 2, 1934, May 10, 1934, June 26, 1934, August 3, 1934, August 28, 1934, and October 14, 1934, in *OxY*, 325–26, 337–39, 340–347, 350–53, 356, 367, 383, 399–400, 425.

33. Ancestry.com. *UK and Ireland, Outward Passenger Lists, 1890–1960* [database on-line]. Provo, UT, USA: Ancestry.com Operations, Inc., 2012; WKS to WK, February 16, 1934, B4F2, KP; "Lines from Spain," *Coweta Times-Star*, July 1, 1934, pp. 1, 3; WK to WKS, June 26, 1935, WKS to WK, November 27, 1934 and WK to WKS, January 25, 1935,in *OxY*, 436–37, 471; WKS to WK, Spring 1940 [2 Letters], B4F3, KP.

34. WK to WKS, [Late June] 1933, June 28, 1933, July 13, 1933, January 18, 1934, February 5, 1934, June 23, 1935, in *OxY*, 220–26, 318–19, 324, 334, 492–93; WK to YM, [Fall 1961], B6F3, KP; Brandwein, "Katherine," 105; *"U.S., School Yearbooks, 1880–2012"; University of Illinois;* 1933; "Marriage Announcement," *Sooner State Press*, July 20, 1935, p. 3.

35. YM, Biography, 234–37, B10F2, KP; WK to WKS, August 10, 1933 and October 16, 1933, in *OxY*, 231–34, 277; Peter J. Sehlinger and Hamilton Holman, *Claude G. Bowers: Spokesman for Democracy* (Indianapolis: Indiana Historical Society, 2000), 166–68.

36. Claude G. Bowers, *The Tragic Era: The Revolution After Lincoln* (Cambridge, MA: Houghton-Mifflin, 1929), v, 217; Sehlinger, *Bowers*, 120–22; Claude G. Bowers, *My Life: The Memoirs of Claude Bowers* (New York: Simon and Schuster, 1962), 210, 249; WKS to WK, September 9, 1932, January 31, 1933, August 29, 1933, September 28, 1933, October 27, 1933, January 29, 1934, May 19, 1934, August 2, 1934, August 20, 1934, September 3, 1934, September 30, 1934, January 11, 1935, and May 28, 1935 and WK to WKS, January 29, 1933, August 10, 1933, and August 17, 1934, in *OxY*, 47, 130–34, 231 240–41, 261–62, 291–95, 320–21, 341–43, 354–55, 380–81, 394–97, 404–05, 417–18, 460–61, 486; "Recovery Road," p. 6.

37. WK to WKS, January 18, 1934, August 14, 1934, September 17, 1934, December 22, 1934, and January 25, 1935, in *OxY*, 316–17, 393–96, 411–15, 444–45, 470.

38. WK to WKS, [1936], B3F3, KP; WK to WKS, August 10, 1933, September 1, 1933, October 16, 1933, November 25, 1933, May 22, 1934, August 10, 1934, August 28, 1934, January 25, 1935, and August 18, 1935, in *OxY*, 239, 245–46, 277–81, 304–05, 361–65, 385–90, 400, 470–71, 507.

39. Carl Albert to George H. Nash, February 17, 1972, B92F26, General Correspondence, CAC; WK to WKS, September 22, 1933, October 16, 1933 and November 24, 1933, March 21, 1934, September 22, 1933, October 16, 1933, November 24, 1933, August 17, 1934, October 12, 1934, November 7, 1934, January 8, 1935, January 25, 1935, and WKS to KK, April 13, 1935, in *OxY*, 256–58, 280,

302, 337–38, 393–95, 420–24, 434, 457–59, 470, 477–78; "Jack Fischer, Amarillo," p. 5; Brandwein, "Katherine," 105.

40. WK to WKS, February 5, 1935, B3F2, KP; WK to WKS, [1936], B2F3, KP; R.B. McCallum, "Willmoore Kendall, 1932–35," *Pembroke College Record: 1966–67*, 33.

41. WK to WKS, October 1933, B3F1, KP; WK to WKS, January 25, 1935, in *OxY*, 470; WK to WKS, November 27, 1935, B3F3, KP; M. Susan Power, "Willmoore Kendall: The Early Years," *Modern Age* 38 (Fall 1995): 82–87; McCallum, "Kendall," 33.

42. WKS to WK, October 4, 1933, October 27, 1933, December 9, 1933 and WK to WKS, October 16, 1933, November 24, 1933, and February 10, 1934, in *OxY*, 263–95, 300–301, 328–32.

43. WK to WKS, August 1, 1934, August 3, 1934, and September 9, 1934, in *OxY*, 376–77, 381–83, 405–08.

44. WK to WKS, January 7, 1934 and May 2, 1934, in *OxY*, 310–11, 349–50.

45. WK to WKS, May 2, 1934, June 26, 1934, Early July 1934, July 28, 1934, and August 1, 1934, in *OxY*, 349–50, 368–78.

46. WK to WKS, August 8, 1934 and September 17, 1934, and WKS to WK, January 29, 1934, August 14, 1934, and December 23, 1934, in *OxY*, 321, 383–84, 390–91, 408–410, 446.

47. WKS to WK, December 23, 1934, in *OxY*, 446–47.

48. WK to WKS, May 10, 1934, January 8, 1935, and January 25, 1935, in *OxY*, 361, 453–60, 466–70; Brandwein, "Katherine," 108–9.

49. Mason, *OxY*, 476; WKS to KK, April 13, 1935 and WK to WKS, April 15, 1935, in *OxY*, 476–77, 480; "Rhodes Scholar," *Sooner State Press*, April 6, 1935, p. 2.

50. WK to WKS, May 17, 1935, May 29, 1935, and August 18, 1935, in *OxY*, 482–82, 487, 507–08; R.B. McCallum to WK, July 29, 1935, B30F12, KP.

Chapter 3

1935–1942
"A Great Creature of the Earth"

Now broadly educated from his years at Oxford, Kendall relocated to Spain. There he received a baptism of fire in political journalism. Before graduation he had considered several possibilities for employment but decided to return to Madrid to work as a reporter for UPI. Together with Katherine, he moved to Spain in June 1935 and worked there until March 1936. Kendall already knew Spanish politics were careening dangerously between left and right. When Kendall worked at the Madrid Bureau, Spain had a center-right coalition government which regularly threatened to collapse. Mounting social disorder—large-scale strikes, vicious parliamentary infighting, and political murders—plagued the country. Spain exhibited a menagerie of competing political factions. On the left were radicals, democratic socialists, revolutionary socialists, Stalinists, Trotskyists, anarchists, syndicalists, and powerful, politicized labor unions. On the right were conservative republicans, several sorts of monarchists, fascistic Falangists, Catholic conservatives, frightened farming interests, and a powerful, politicized army. Also on display were business friendly moderates together with Basque and Catalan nationalists. These complex political rivalries played out in mass demonstrations and acts of violence, especially in Madrid and Barcelona but also in rural areas.[1]

At UPI, Kendall stood out as the resident leftist scribe in a right-leaning office. He reported positively about the Spanish left and suggested that it had an excellent chance to win forthcoming elections. In Madrid he associated with left-wing friends, some of whom he had met on previous stays in the city. One was Maria Teresa Andrade, another left-leaning reporter at UPI Madrid. After hours Ken and Katy socialized happily with Maria Teresa and her husband Juan Andrade, a key founder of Spanish communism. A former member of the central committee of the Communist Party of Spain, Juan Andrade was expelled in 1927 for Trotskyist sympathies. Over drinks the two couples enthusiastically discussed politics. Willmoore disagreed with the Andrades about how to interpret American politics, but he endorsed the cause of the Spanish left. These experiences in Spain deepened Katherine's leftist convictions for life.[2]

Willmoore called himself a communist before returning to Spain in 1935 but remained uncommitted to any particular faction. He embraced the controversial label because he viewed socialists as an unserious lot who cared little about actually remaking society. In one letter home, Kendall laid out his political commitments. He believed that (1) "the profit system" was corrupt, (2) the economic and social problems of the United States would improve only if the proletariat seized power, (3) liberal pseudo-reforms were misleading, and (4) one must maintain "unshakeable faith in democracy." From Spain, he tried to convince his father that the Democratic Party was no more socialistic than the Republican Party and that there was no "mediate position between Capitalism and Communism."[3]

In Madrid, no longer a mere assistant, Kendall was able to do some real reporting in 1935 and 1936, drawing upon skills developed in Tulsa and Chicago. Working the night shift, for example, he rode the subway home as Madrid's factory workers headed to work. In his seat he would unfold a copy of *El Debate*, the main newspaper of conservative Catholic opinion in Spain. Based on hostile glares he received, Kendall concluded that the right-wing government was extremely unpopular with the masses. His reports therefore contradicted those of UPI colleagues Jean De Gandt (who soft-pedaled his leftist sympathies to please UPI headquarters) and Lester Ziffren, an American who, said Juan Andrade, was an ultra-reactionary.[4]

In the election of February 16, 1936, held shortly before Kendall left Spain, the left-wing Popular Front achieved decisive victory, winning a plurality of the popular vote but a large majority in parliament. This result vindicated Willmoore's prediction about how the vote would go. In the streets and cafés of Madrid, the Kendalls—together with their left-wing friends—jubilantly celebrated this electoral triumph. Shortly thereafter, thinking the excitement was over, they left for the United States. Kendall was frustrated that UPI would not allow him to do "deep coverage" rather than report daily ephemera. By leaving he missed the drama and blood of the ensuing Civil War (which broke out in mid-July and which he did not see coming). Kendall's decision to return to the United States came neither from fear nor politics. Rather he had grown disillusioned with journalism practiced "on a plane where thought is not only impossible but forbidden." Kendall's political convictions had been shaken in Madrid by acts of terrorism committed by communists (assassinating delivery boys of right-wing newspapers), but he left Spain committed to the left. That fall Willmoore wrote Juan Andrade offering to return to Spain to fight for the Republic but Andrade warned him off. Kendall's leftist friends soon suffered grave hardships. In 1937 Juan Andrade, who served on the central committee of the semi-Trotskyist Workers Party of Marxist Unification (POUM), was imprisoned by Spanish Stalinists. Later the Andrades went into hiding, then fled to France to avoid reprisals from the Francoists. Had Kendall fought for POUM, perhaps he—like George Orwell, another POUM sympathizer—would have been shot through the lungs, or worse. Kendall attempted to help the Andrades migrate from France to the United States, but World War II overtook these efforts.[5]

Once he returned to the United States, Kendall pursued an academic—not an activist or journalistic—path. Despite comparative political stability, the United States remained bogged down in the Depression. Unemployment had declined and New Deal programs had given relief to millions, but severe problems persisted. Oklahoma, for example, was suffering from the Dust Bowl and experiencing massive out-migration caused by low agricultural prices and the consequences of federal farm policy. Even for a new Oxford graduate, finding a decent job proved difficult. For a time, Willmoore considered teaching at a university in his home state. Because of his son's left-wing political convictions, Reverend Kendall suggested that he would find Illinois "more genial." Willmoore thought he could get his old job back as an instructor in Romance languages at Illinois but did not want to do so. Then the university offered him a fellowship to pursue his PhD in political science, and he decided to return to Champaign-Urbana.[6]

There he had to adjust to an American-style graduate school. Its approach to educating students was quite different from that at Oxford. The Illinois political science department, he said, "lays great emphasis upon detailed mastery of the subject, does not encourage criticism or original thinking as such, and attempts to place its 'stamp' on the men who pass through it." This approach was less suited to Kendall's own intellectual gifts and contradicted his pedagogical beliefs. Kendall assured his parents that he had "never before had so many brutal facts at [his] fingertips" and that "by next June" he would be "lousy with 'em." Because of this departmental approach, Kendall also had to adjust to teaching his classes in a lecture format.[7]

Dr. James Wilford Garner served as his advisor and major professor at Illinois. Garner earned his doctorate at Columbia as a student of William H. Dunning in 1902. He was nearing retirement and his energy level had faded by the time of Kendall's arrival. Garner's lectures had a reputation for being "tedious." Working with Garner, Kendall struggled to find a proper subject for his dissertation. He rejected his advisor's suggestion to pursue study of the sixteenth-century Monarchomachs because the project would have required him to relearn Latin. He also considered writing a comparative study of American and Mexican governmental institutions, a plan which enthused

Garner because it could open up professional opportunities for Kendall at prestigious American universities.[8]

In June 1937 the department erected a roadblock in Kendall's academic path, unexpectedly urging him to take written examinations before proceeding with his orals. The department took this step because of Kendall's unorthodox qualifications, an MA in Spanish literature and an Oxford degree in "modern greats." Given only a week to prepare, Kendall at first agreed to the written exams but then decided to delay for a year. He called Garner "very selfish" for going along with the departmental demand while offering him little guidance. Shortly thereafter, Kendall claimed to be "thoroughly glad" about what happened, as the delay would aid his "vocation" as a political scientist. For the sake of his career, Kendall said he wanted to excel on the exams. He decided that more familiarity with the nuts and bolts of the American political science profession would help him become a better teacher.[9]

Reverend Kendall was predictably unhappy with his son's choice to focus on an academic career and with his views on politics. In March 1936, for example, he compared Willmoore to George Milburn, then finding critical success as a novelist. He told his son that he wanted him to do greater things "with the gifts" he possessed. Receiving the Rhodes gave Willmoore a moral responsibility to use his talents to benefit society. He accused his son of "living in a vacuum" and suggested that if he felt unable to write prose for a popular audience, such fact was due to laziness. Reverend Kendall then berated Willmoore as "a propagandist for an 'ism'" who hardly spoke "of anything else."[10]

And Kendall, Jr., was promoting communism at Champaign-Urbana. In the Spring Semester of 1937, for example, he took time out from his academic duties to lecture on Marxist economic theory to undergraduates. However, he was neither consistent in his communist principles nor a committed activist. As a creature of the 1920s, for example, Kendall continued to be intrigued by the stock market, giving and receiving stock tips. Nor did socialism interfere with socializing. In March 1937, for example, he "swallowed enough of [his] proletarian pride" to attend a "dance in a monkey suit and a stuffed shirt." He and Katherine were "getting along as well as good bourgeois can without a six cylinder automobile to drive back & forth to work." Katherine was working at an Urbana newspaper to supplement their income. The couple also started to spend lots of time apart, months at a stretch, because of professional responsibilities.[11]

Disenchanted with his less than ideal academic year, Kendall began to explore other options. An attractive one soon appeared. At Illinois, Kendall had become fast friends with Charles S. Hyneman, then an assistant professor of political science. In the fall of 1937 Louisiana State University hired

Hyneman to chair its Department of Government. He enticed Willmoore to Baton Rouge as an instructor on a two-year appointment, teaching both senior-level and graduate students. When the Kendalls relocated to Louisiana, they found an oasis. Even as the economy was cratering, LSU and Baton Rouge were awash in money, booming because of large-scale spending by the state government. Housing was hard to find because so many new people were moving to town. Huey Long, the Louisiana Kingfish, had been dead for two years. But his political machine continued to pump money into the state's flagship university and capital city, purchasing brainpower for the one and infrastructure for the other. These years in Baton Rouge—spent in relative prosperity within an intellectually stimulating environment—were exciting for Ken and Katy and formative for their future careers. Decades later, Katherine Kendall, though gimlet eyed about her former spouse's faults, fondly recalled the couple's "Cajun Camelot."[12]

Willmoore cut loose as a teacher at LSU, revealing himself a Socratic virtuoso. Certain that American students could achieve at the highest intellectual levels, his classes overflowed "with intelligent inquiry and passionate debate." He succeeded in attracting bright students to his "exciting and noisy" classes. In a course called "Social Policy," Kendall explored "man's concerns, his perplexities, his worries, his aspirations" to discern what molded "a people's institutions." He assigned challenging readings to students, then began class by making "some outrageous statement" just plausible enough to stimulate discussion. Reasoning together with his students, he pushed them to state their ideas precisely. He once horrified his class by contending that women should not be able to vote. After three weeks he switched sides, claimed student counterarguments had convinced him of his error, and suggested their arguments demanded immediate repeal of all barriers against black voting in Louisiana. In a firmly segregated state, this tack created a lively stir. According to Hyneman, Kendall's teaching shook "those kids up," and his students continued to talk "about him all the rest of their lives." Among these students were future Vice President Hubert Humphrey and future U.S. Senator Russell Long. Kendall's later achievements in the classroom were incredibly influential, but Hyneman believed his friend never "made a deeper impression or worked a greater transformation on young men than he brought off during that brief stand in Baton Rouge."[13]

In accepting the appointment Kendall committed to an academic career, but his research focus remained unclear. In 1937 he was considering four topics for his dissertation: (1) a study of protest literature on judicial supremacy, (2) the application of American federalist principles to international organizations, (3) a comparative study of Mexican and American federalism, and (4) explication of the ideas of the Spanish thinker José Ortega y Gasset.[14] Despite this indecision, Kendall began to come into his own as a political theorist at LSU. Professors of Literature Robert Penn Warren and Cleanth Brooks, both former Rhodes scholars, became good friends. They were doing some of their finest work at the time. The first edition of their influential textbook *Understanding Poetry* came out in 1938. The novelist Katherine Anne Porter also lived in Baton Rouge and grew close to the Kendalls. For his part, Kendall—in Louisiana as elsewhere—loved to "argue, argue, endlessly, endlessly, endlessly." Amid a "comfortable pluralism" he discovered lots of fascinating, learned, serious, and nondoctrinaire people—liberals, conservatives, and communists—with whom to engage in verbal jousts. Kendall dropped his Trotskyism at LSU. Still focused on practical political solutions and wary of "cultural elitism," he remained a leftist.[15]

In the summer of 1938 Kendall returned to the University of Illinois to face his oral doctoral exams (with written exams not required after all). The committee consisted of economist Horace M. Gray and three political scientists: James Wilford Garner, John Fairlie, and Clarence Berdahl. The experience initially went well, with Kendall breezing through questions about English economists. He made Fairlie laugh by telling Gray that economists were not really scientists. Then Berdahl grilled Kendall for 45 minutes, trying to get him to admit that the federal government had intruded upon the powers of the states. Kendall instead argued that the federal government had always possessed adequate power to do its job, that it had exercised decisive power more frequently than states, and that such exercise was appropriate. Garner asked only a few questions and ended the exams. After some disagreement, the committee declared that Kendall passed. Willmoore believed he could have done as well on the exams a year before and that much of the reading he had done in preparation had been wasted. He joked that he now had "special reasons" to support "the majority principle" because there had been "some disagreement in the committee about whether or not to pass me."[16]

Kendall then left for Chicago to relax with friends. There he regaled his "Stalinist host" with tales of "my friends the Southern Agrarians, whose hearts remain in the right place no matter how much they allow themselves to be misled as Minds." Kendall again took up his post at LSU as the Fall Semester began. In these Baton Rouge years, Charles Hyneman later recalled, Willmoore was "a great creature of the earth," a man who understood and empathized with the yearnings of the American people. Partly for this reason, Kendall always remained friends with Hyneman whom he in turn believed remained in touch with the pulse of the people because of roots in rural Indiana. On the other hand, Kendall disliked LSU department colleague Alex Daspit as "an unadulterated southern aristocratic snob." According to Hyneman, Kendall possessed considerable firsthand experience of associating as an equal with working-class Americans so had "high regard for the common man." In exhibiting "genuine respect" for ordinary people, Willmoore sometimes estranged his colleagues, especially those without such connections. When Hyneman wanted someone to prepare a paper on state and local government for a scholarly conference in Texas, an annoyed Daspit refused the task as inappropriate for a political theorist. When Hyneman suggested to Willmoore that the project would help him understand "the problem of government right where the people live," Kendall energetically took on the task.[17]

Preparing this paper led to Kendall's first scholarly publication as a political scientist. It appeared in the summer of 1939 as an article in LSU's new, but already prestigious, *Southern Review* (coedited by Brooks and Warren). This first foray into political theory was entitled: "On the Preservation of Democracy for America." In it Kendall adopted a progressive rubric to suggest that the American Constitution was a Machiavellian mechanism designed to thwart the people's ability to rule. Lauding the wisdom of the "common man," Kendall attacked judicial review, portrayed freedom of the press as an illusion meant to protect the powerful few, and repudiated attempts "to equate democracy with a particular set of 'natural rights.'" Moreover, Kendall criticized the Bill of Rights, the Constitution's "fantastically difficult amending process," and "separation of powers" as devices to perpetuate elite power. Congress frequently thwarted the popular will, he argued, while the presidency, except on foreign policy, remained more attuned to popular desires. He also decried the tradition of teaching the people to view the Constitution as a "*symbol*" of their values. Viewed this way, the LSU instructor argued, the document became almost unchangeable and frustrated popular desires for change.[18]

Meanwhile, Kendall maintained that democracy worked best at the local level where "deeply felt group relations" existed. In what became a lifelong fascination, he looked to Rousseau's ideas as a rubric for understanding contemporary democracy. As part of this analysis, Kendall started to ponder the question of how minorities in a democracy could come to accept the will of the majority. He argued that "boss and machine rule" facilitated "oligarchic political control" of local government. Weakness and corruption in local government resulted from lack of voter interest. Such apathy stemmed from the fact that most important political decisions in the United States happened at the state or federal level. Where individual votes mattered most, voters were not interested because local elections only affected trivial matters.[19]

In the winter of 1939 Kendall published another article in *Southern Review*, this one entitled: "The Majority Principle and the Scientific Elite." Here Kendall argued for a fundamentalist version of majoritarianism: "that in any decision-making group one half of the members, plus one, have a *right* to commit one half of the members, minus one, to any policy they see fit to support." He denounced a system "in which ultimate power is entrusted to an unremovable judiciary." In "Majority Principle" Kendall maintained that political decisions are ethical in nature and accessible to uneducated citizens. Politics, he said, involves value judgments—decisions about what ought to be—and does not require specialized, "scientific" knowledge. Yet, conflict between the "small minority" of scientifically literate elites and the masses is inevitable because the former confuse their knowledge of means—*how* to achieve goals—with the political/ethical process of deciding *what* goals to pursue. Kendall then proclaimed "that between those who accept the majority principle as the differentia of democratic government, and those who repudiate it, a wider gulf is fixed than that which separates the latter from the defenders of Fascism." At this stage in his career, then, Kendall (1) wrote from a leftist perspective, (2) was a maximalist regarding popular sovereignty, and (3) distrusted elites who might interfere with the people's right to rule. In "Preservation," for example, Kendall relied on the insights of leftist scholars, including Charles A. Beard, J. Allen Smith, and Louis B. Boudin. In "Majority Principle" he staked out theoretical ground as an "absolute majoritarian" who valorized popular rule above all else.[20]

Within his department, Kendall received criticism for these articles because they were too literary, not carefully documented with the latest findings of contemporary political science. When read closely, however, these early articles reveal flashes of Kendall's brilliance, heralding his later intricately constructed and inquisitorial style of scholarship. He already evinced determination to get at the most vital questions of democratic governance. He possessed a cosmopolitan erudition, rare among American political scientists. He was not interested in piling footnote upon footnote to make his arguments. No one else, thought Hyneman, would have approached a pedestrian assignment on local government by delving into the deepest meanings of democracy as elucidated by Rousseau. In embryonic form, several ideas appear in these articles which Kendall developed more fully as a conservative. His tributes to Smith and Boudin, for example, were not pro forma. He absorbed and agreed with many of their ideas, but chided them for neglecting local politics where the heart of democracy lay. Impressed with the articles, Kendall's father hoped they would "hasten" his son finding "recognition in [his] chosen field of scholarly research." Picking up an old refrain, however, he criticized Willmoore's "long and involved sentences." With some reservations, he deferred to Brooks and Warren who, Willmoore told his father, praised his prose. Kendall also was receiving useful guidance from Hyneman to keep his focus on American political theory. In the summer of 1938, for example, the department chair discouraged Kendall from going to Mexico and "scatter [his] intellectual interests." Reverend Kendall seconded this advice, admitting that his son was "becoming an outstanding authority on American government."[21]

Kendall saw majoritarianism as applicable to political problems of his day, including foreign policy. By March 1937 Willmoore had, according to his father, become a pacifist who held to "a doctrine of absolute non-resistance." The younger man defended his stance by claiming it helped defend American democracy from both foreign and domestic foes. He supported "a policy of Isolation" as a way to strike at "Poverty and Inequality in our democracy." Widespread prosperity, he thought, was the best antidote for fascist propaganda. He castigated Reverend Kendall for arguing that Franklin Roosevelt had the "right" to pursue his own foreign policy. Such a position, said Kendall, Jr., missed the main point of democracy, that political leaders should carry out the people's will. If the American people opposed closer cooperation with Britain and the president pursued it, then "Mr. Roosevelt is simply setting himself up as better able to do their thinking for them than they are able to do it for themselves." Moreover, if politicians claimed to know better than the people on foreign policy, they might try to do the people's thinking on "other problems as well."[22]

Katherine Kendall also started on her career path at LSU, when she entered graduate school in social work. She made this decision partly because she could make as much money with a fellowship as with a regular nine-to-five job. She had no real background in social work but as a faculty wife and member of Phi Beta Kappa was accepted into the program. By this time Katherine had also developed hearing trouble severe enough to warrant obtaining a hearing aid. Nervous about teaching classes with a hearing deficit, she pushed forward to become a successful teacher. She received some pushback because of her left-wing political opinions but was able to make peace with her teachers. In 1939 she received her Master's of Social Work from LSU. She did so well that the faculty urged her to pursue a doctorate at the University of Chicago, from which many of them had graduated.[23]

For the Kendalls the beginning of the end of *les bon temps* in Baton Rouge came on June 26, 1939. An unsuspecting university community woke up to discover that LSU president James Monroe Smith had absconded. It soon became clear that Smith had resigned his office and then flown out of the country on a university plane. The next day the governor of Louisiana resigned. "Jingle Money" Smith had escaped north to Canada because his speculations in the commodities market had gone south. He had lost several hundred thousand dollars using expired university bonds as collateral for his shenanigans. Monroe would eventually be convicted of forgery, embezzlement, and mail fraud and sentenced to a long stretch in prison. Faced with a fiscal crisis LSU had to make drastic financial readjustments. The scandal's impact on the political science department was immediate. Kendall was away for the summer when the crisis struck. Over the next several years LSU's academic prestige declined as illustrious professors sought jobs elsewhere. Untenured faculty were especially vulnerable. Partly for that reason Kendall's head appeared on the academic chopping block. Before the scandal hit, he was to receive a regular contract for the academic year 1939–1940 (i.e., over and beyond the initial promise of a two-year stint). The crisis changed this calculus so that by August 1939 he appeared unlikely to get a contract for the upcoming year.[24]

With Hyneman's support, however, Kendall obtained an assignment with the university extension department. He was to hold forums around the state on political issues of the day, rather than serving as a regular member of the political science faculty. Well into the semester, Willmoore discovered himself drawing a salary for this position but without any duties to perform. At that point, it became clear that factors other than the scandal were jeopardizing his employment. In October 1939, in fact, the political science faculty, by a vote of 4–1, asked for Kendall's removal. Kendall received support from Dean Charles Pipkin, but even Hyneman, aka "the Chief," voted with the majority to purge Willmoore. Hyneman claimed he took this step to maintain harmony in the department and to push Kendall to pursue better opportunities. Vague charges against Willmoore's teaching and research supported this move. Given Hyneman's awe at Kendall's teaching prowess and that he had published more than other junior members of the department, these claims served as window dressing to disguise the real issue: Kendall's "uncooperative" attitude. Endlessly arguing Willmoore intrigued Hyneman and Pipkin but annoyed others enough that they insisted on his ouster. Ultimately, LSU gave Kendall a leave of absence with full pay for the Spring Semester of 1940 to finish his dissertation at Illinois. This time LSU stipulated that his contract would not be renewed.[25]

In February 1940, Katy and Ken, both downhearted about his dismissal, moved to Chicago. For months Willmoore made little progress. He spent time socializing with Revilo Oliver (successfully encouraging Oliver to finish his PhD) and with a new friend, the writer Saul Bellow. After exploring the job market for a time, he accepted an offer from Hobart College in Geneva, New York. Having promised Hobart to complete the dissertation, Kendall worked hard to finish it. By spring 1939 he had decided to work on majority rule. That summer he narrowed the focus to John Locke's *Second Treatise of Government*, completing two chapters before returning to Baton Rouge in the fall. Garner died in 1938 so Kendall was now working with John Fairlie, the new department head. In 1940 Fairlie turned supervision of Willmoore over to a junior professor, Francis Graham Wilson. A conservative political theorist, he was more sympathetic to Kendall's academic style. When Kendall got back to writing in the spring of 1940, most of his guidance came from Wilson. Writing for months, Kendall completed the dissertation, "John Locke and the Doctrine of Majority Rule," in August. Awarded his PhD that same month, he telegrammed home: "Call me Rabbi."[26]

A year later the University of Illinois Press published this work verbatim as *John Locke and the Doctrine of Majority Rule*. In the dedication, Willmoore acknowledged his father's influence in pushing him toward intellectual excellence. This book made Kendall's reputation. It was an expository tour de force in which the author revealed his unique approach to scholarship. Most importantly, he focused on reading Locke rather than relying on authorities. Kendall often suggested that he adopted this style of scholarship from R. G. Collingwood. In Locke he followed Collingwood's ideas about identifying the key question for an enquiry then examining his subject in pursuit of that question, as a detective might do in a murder investigation. The book showed obvious influence from the formalist approach to literary criticism, the "New Criticism," then coming into vogue in the United States and championed at LSU by Brooks and Warren. Like the New Critics, Kendall focused on closely reading a text to tease out its deepest meaning, while putting aside, for purpose of analysis, questions of historical context. Kendall first used this method of scholarship in his *Locke*. He had to have picked it up from the LSU New Critics because his previous work showed little evidence of formalism. For the rest of his career Kendall combined Collingwood's inquisitorial focus on asking the right question with the close reading and careful textual analysis of the New Critics.[27]

Kendall's purpose remained much the same as in his *Southern Review* articles, that is, to understand and to strengthen the intellectual foundations of democratic majoritarianism. Part I was prefatory. It contained an exhaustive survey of how political philosophers—from Plato through Pufendorf, Althusius, and Spinoza to Hobbes—had addressed majority rule. After this review, Kendall opined that "if Locke espoused the doctrine of majority rule, he was the earliest writer to deal with it on a scale sufficiently ambitious to merit our attention." Locke's expositor then argued that his subject, contrary to previous claims, advocated political "collectivism" not individualism based on natural rights. Meticulous reading of Locke, Kendall claimed, necessitated "reassessment of Locke's position in the history of political philosophy," overthrowing him as "a symbol in the continuing struggle for power under the American constitution . . . [who] has been extremely useful to those who prefer government by judiciary to majority-rule." Kendall concluded the first part of the book by proclaiming that he meant to elucidate "whether or not that doctrine [majority-rule] can be defended on rational grounds."[28]

After this introductory material, one can see Kendall's analytical genius come into its own. From the get-go, Kendall showed that Locke's analysis did not in fact begin with the "state of nature" (chapter 2 of the *Second Treatise of Government*) as per what everyone else said, but rather that it commenced with a strong defense of the community's ability to exercise political power up to and including imposition of the death penalty (chapter 1 of the *Second*

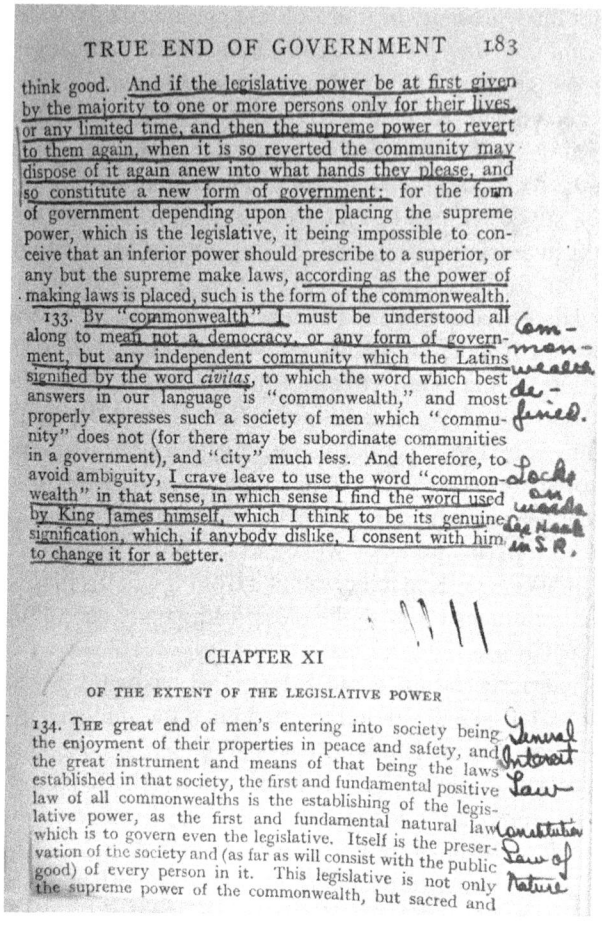

Figure 3.1 Close Reading, Kendall Marginalia in the *Second Treatise*. *Source:* Photo By the Author. Willmoore Kendall Memorial Library, University of Dallas.

Treatise). Kendall demonstrated that Locke knew that individual rights were "not inalienable," understood that individuals could not exist except as "*community members*," and used the state of nature merely as an "expository device." Thus, Locke was in the camp of "*the majority rule democrats.*"[29]

Kendall then subjected Locke to withering criticism, exposing serious contradictions in the *Second Treatise*. Most basically, he showed that Locke's analysis of the relationship between liberty (individual freedom based on natural rights) and democracy (binding rules established by the community) was confused. Locke argued, as summarized by Kendall, that: "The individual owes to the commonwealth ... a duty of obedience which is absolute and perpetual and *must* be absolute and perpetual because the alternative is the anarchy of the state of nature." Yet such a position, Kendall noted, was logically incompatible with defining the individual as obligated to preserve "his life, liberty, and estate." The English thinker "was trying to have it more ways than one with his law of nature."[30]

Locke went on to argue that the majority had the right to rule and the minority a duty to accept "political subjection." Then Locke, again as paraphrased by Kendall, stated that the majority "may if it chooses, act to prevent the exercise of power by future majorities." Such delegation might be permanent and could include cession of political power to "an *hereditary* monarchy." This argument was a nonsequitur, thought Kendall. Locke's previously stated principles had excluded "a duty of obedience to any decrees save those of the majority (or its indisputable agent)." Should the majority be oppressed, its chief, or only, remedy was, as expressed by Locke, "an appeal to heaven," that is, resort to revolution. This position appeared absurd to Kendall. The "logical corollary of Locke's doctrine of majority-rule" demanded that "the people as a matter of course are invited, from time to time, to express (by majority vote) their preferences regarding future government policy and personnel." To resolve this logical incompatibility between absolute liberty and absolute democracy, Kendall concluded that Locke's political theory must contain a "latent premise." He argued that Locke certainly believed in moral principles and so could not have meant to define as right whatever the majority willed. Instead, Kendall maintained that Locke could "argue both for individual rights and for a right of the majority to define individual rights" because he thought the people "rational and just" enough "never to withdraw a right which the individual ought to have."[31] Kendall ended his book with this clever argument, but his readers might well have surmised that the latent premise was his own rather than Locke's.

Meanwhile, Kendall, new PhD in hand, went off to teach in Geneva, New York. Hobart College hired him as part of an initiative by President William A. Eddy to create a program in "Democratic Citizenship." Kendall believed the new program mirrored his own ideas about fashioning an informed citizenry. Such programs were vital in a democracy, where citizens were to make the most important political decisions. Eddy had already hired J. Raymond Walsh—a left-leaning economist recently released from Harvard— as Hobart's "Director of Citizenship." Looking for a political scientist to staff the program, Walsh had a conversation with the liberal journalist Max Lerner. Lerner had read Kendall's *Southern Review* articles and recommended him as well suited for the position in Geneva.[32]

When he accepted the post Kendall envisioned a long career at Hobart but was aware of potential conflict ahead. Hobart hired him as "an independent member of the faculty responsible to the president." As Kendall arrived, the president and the faculty were engaged in a struggle about the citizenship program. Kendall made no attempt to disguise his left-wing convictions. But he knew that Hobart faculty had expressed concern that the "citizenship course was a discipline in the ethics of socialism." Kendall believed he would bring diversity to the program because—unlike Walsh and the program's other faculty—he did not believe in economic determinism. His duties included teaching classes for undergraduates, holding faculty seminars, and setting up political debates at public venues around the state. At one such debate in October 1940 Kendall voiced support for Republican Wendell Willkie for president. He said that the Democratic president, now running for an unprecedented third term, possessed "a temperamental incapacity for high office in a democracy." The spending priorities of the New Deal, he went on, were based on "political principles best understood by ward heelers."[33]

Kendall quickly got embroiled in controversy. He found the intellectual climate at Hobart less exciting than at Illinois or LSU but continued to be "a highly stimulating and able teacher." However, in February 1941, Hobart College erupted into a full-blown crisis. As Eddy came under attack, Kendall found himself vulnerable because he was directly responsible to the president. In the end, a revolt of conservative faculty forced the resignations of Eddy and Walsh. Kendall also resigned because of his sympathy for Walsh and the aims of the citizenship program. Sympathetic student protesters "hung an effigy bearing a placard, 'Citizenship'" at Coxe Hall, the ornate Jacobean edifice which housed the college administration. President Eddy, disgusted at the faculty response to his initiative, vowed to leave higher education and return to military service. Fluent in Arabic, he soon became American naval attaché in Egypt. On the way out, Eddy denied "rumors" that instructors in the program had been inculcating "liberal political views." Ironically, given his future views, Willmoore Kendall had become the victim of a red scare.[34]

After the dénouement of this well-publicized fiasco, Reverend Kendall lauded his son for standing up like Luther did at the Diet of Worms. Strong words, but Kendall, Sr., had applied the same trope to himself during World War I. Reverend Kendall did remain consistent in his stance on academic freedom and leftist influence in the academy. In 1939 he had a long meeting with Governor Leon C. Phillips. He advised the governor not to oust suspected communists from Oklahoma universities. As Hobart's semester ended, Willmoore, Jr., planned an extended debating tour with Walsh on issues of war and peace. Though leftists, both men so strongly believed in isolationism that they became admirers of Lawrence Dennis, "America's No. 1 Intellectual Fascist." The planned tour included events in Oklahoma but fell through when Walsh got a good job offer. Kendall's published work from this period continued to show a leftist, majoritarian perspective. He suggested that private property existed only because of acquiescence of the majority. He belittled John Stuart Mill for promoting individual "diversity" by restricting majority rule. He also began to question whether majoritarianism led inexorably to socialism, noting that the richest 51 percent of society was a majority as well as the poorest 51 percent.[35]

Katherine Kendall had begun taking doctoral classes in social work. She was also teaching at the University of Chicago and remained in Illinois when her husband went east. So Katy and Ken would experience a commuter marriage over the next several months. As the newly minted Dr. Kendall tried to establish himself in upstate New York, Mrs. Kendall grew lonely and depressed by her husband's absence. She complained that her teaching duties seemed pointless and told friends she longed to do actual "relief work" instead. "Completely demoralized," she looked forward to Willmoore coming home to visit her at Thanksgiving. "I desperately need," she told Cleanth and Tinkum Brooks in November 1940, "the tonic effect of his masterful presence. He'll know all the answers."[36]

In September 1941 Willmoore obtained a position as assistant professor of government and political science at the University of Richmond. Katherine got a job at the Southern Baptist institution first, hired by one of her former teachers from LSU to replace a member of the social work faculty on sabbatical. Willmoore was glad "to return to the South" and excited "at the prospect of a year—at least—of normal and respectable married life." Soon, however, he "hated" Richmond where he labored under "a sweatshop teaching load" of 15 hours per term. He resigned his post there on February 1, 1942, just as the second semester began. Kendall knew that he was about to be put in charge of "morale-building activities" involving "a college-wide program of seminars on why we are fighting the war." He could not stomach being a cheerleader for World War II, American entry into which he had passionately opposed. He also found no intellectual "stimulation" in Richmond and rejected demands to teach public administration. Willmoore then set out to find a position in government service, but found it difficult to find a job. He feared the FBI was blocking his efforts for government employment because of his radical past. Yet the budding scholar had never committed to any communist organization. Rather he had remained a fellow traveler, a "radical" intellectual committed loosely to the cause. Looking backward in 1942, Kendall told Hyneman that: "I was never a member of any radical organization although my name must have been on the name of every Fourth International mailing list at the time."[37]

Kendall's left-oriented isolationism lasted beyond Pearl Harbor. Over Christmas 1941 his father expressed hope to his son that he would not be drafted to fight "for a cause which fails to claim your faith and enthusiasm." Were he himself able to fight, Reverend Kendall proclaimed he would gladly give his life "to further the ultimate triumph of free governments in the world." The younger man denied that he was a "Pacifist." But he did blame the Japanese attack on previous provocations by Roosevelt. Reverend Kendall wondered if his son's Trotskyist "sympathies against Stalin" made him reluctant to embrace the war. He suggested that his son's track record of teaching Marxist theory might preclude him from federal service.[38]

Meanwhile, the younger Kendall was considering several possible opportunities for wartime employment. He quickly rejected an offer from his old Oxford companion Jack Fischer to risk his life as a spy in Europe. He grew excited for a time at the chance to be a Social Science Analyst in the Department of Agriculture. Then he believed he had secured a commission in the Army Air Force, but failed his physical due to a slow heartbeat. At that point Kendall got "an extremely attractive offer" from the Office of the Coordinator of Inter-American Affairs (CIAA), headed by Nelson A. Rockefeller. Irving Pflaum, a UPI colleague from his days in Spain, recommended him for the position. Kendall's fluency in Spanish and journalistic experience convinced the Rockefeller organization that he "was a guy they ought to have."[39]

Before receiving this offer of employment, Kendall regretted resigning his post at Richmond. He feared the draft board in Stillwater, Oklahoma (where he was registered) would require him to enter military service as an enlisted man. As various government employment opportunities fell through one after another, he also grew frustrated that no first-rate university wanted to hire him. Most immediately worrying to him was that he suspected he was about to "acquire a couple of dependents." Reverend Kendall, that is, had experienced a drastic decline in health and would likely have "to retire from the ministry." In May and June of 1942 Willmoore, still unemployed, traveled to Oklahoma three times to deal with these family concerns.[40]

Reverend Kendall's career had entered a tailspin in 1939. When the northern and southern Methodist churches in Stillwater merged, he had to leave his attractive position in this college town, where he had served for years. Soon thereafter he began to experience serious health problems. In July 1940 he had begun a new pastorate in Shawnee, Oklahoma. Arising to speak from the pulpit of his new charge, the minister found himself unable to talk. Without fainting, he stood mute, as if paralyzed, for many minutes as a concerned and puzzled congregation looked on. Faced with this malady (and perhaps from impairment of his reason), Reverend Kendall came to notice "something positively demonic in the atmosphere" of his Shawnee congregation. In October 1940 Reverend Kendall was therefore thrilled to be appointed vice president of Oklahoma City University. Here he immediately went to work trying to raise funds for the Methodist institution. Reverend and Mrs. Kendall were ecstatic about the move. Willmoore, Sr., said it released him from "the most hopeless impasse of my lifetime" and revealed "appreciation for my long disprized gifts."[41]

Kendall, Sr., retained an ability to move audiences. In a March 1941 speech, for example, he had four hundred student delegates of the (Methodist) Epworth League "almost in the aisles" with laughter. In June, Northwestern University awarded him its order of merit, an honor given only to a handful of its theological alumni each year. In October he received an honorary doctorate from a seminary in Colorado. He continued to promote "cooperation between all faiths and races," giving, for example, two presentations in Waxahachie, Texas, in November 1941 sponsored by the National Conference of Christians and Jews. However, he found it difficult to translate his ability to move audiences into an ability to raise money. Hence, his position at the university was soon "precarious." After having had another seizure in the pulpit, he resigned from the college in August 1941, returning to Miami, Oklahoma, to serve as a replacement pastor. Then came an unexpected blow, the "ultimate tragedy" he called it, with an assignment to Poteau. Placement in this small-town backwater left the blind minister "crushed and heartbroken." Pearl Kendall contacted her eldest son asking him to write a note to cheer up her now "utterly hopeless" husband, whose health was in severe decline and whose career had collapsed.[42]

Worse was coming. "Dreadfully frightened" about his health, Reverend Kendall sought medical attention. First he received diagnosis of a digestive disorder, then diabetes. His health, however, continued to deteriorate. From Poteau in early 1942, he admitted to Willmoore and Katherine "that something too terrible for words is happening to me. Both my body and my mind are disintegrating." The family soon received news that its paterfamilias had a brain tumor. Reverend Kendall's ability to think deeply and to speak well had always provided much of his sense of self-worth. Therefore, the fear of losing these capacities was especially frightening, probably even more acute for him than so grave a diagnosis would have been for another.[43]

Consequently, Reverend Kendall decided to undergo extremely risky surgery to remove the tumor. Given only a 1 percent possibility of surviving the operation, he took the chance. He did not die on the operating table, but the expected complications soon set in. On June 6, 1942, Reverend Kendall died at St. Anthony's Hospital in Oklahoma City, aged fifty-five. Numerous obituaries appeared for him, especially in cities where he had served. These notices all praised his thirty-eight years of service to Sooner State Methodism. According to the local bishop, for example, Reverend Kendall had been "a real leader of men." He had "kept abreast of the best thought of his time" and "was one of our most distinguished and most useful ministers." Inevitably, of course, such summaries of Reverend Kendall's achievements ended with some version of: "despite the handicap of blindness since birth."[44]

The sudden and dramatic demise of his father marked a major turning point in Willmoore's life. For thirty years the "special relationship" between the two men had profoundly—though not always positively—shaped them both. Suddenly, this larger-than-life persona was no more. Of course, Reverend Kendall's effects on his son's psyche and way of life long survived the minister's physical demise. Willmoore the Younger now had to deal with his mother, who had become almost paralyzed with grief and anxiety about the future. Meanwhile, Kendall was launching into a new phase of his career with Rockefeller's CIAA. This new post would challenge the professional political scientist to marshal his talents for the war effort, shore up his financial situation, and open up a new world for him in intelligence work.

NOTES

1. Stanley G. Payne, *Spain's First Democracy: The Second Republic, 1931–1936* (Madison: University of Wisconsin Press, 1993), *passim*; Hugh Thomas, *The Spanish Civil War* (New York: Harper and Brothers, 1961), 64–94.

2. Juan Andrade to George H. Nash, "About Willmoore Kendall," January 8, 1974, B4F18, KKP; Brandwein, "Katherine," 105.

3. Mason, Biography, 1293, B11F2, KP; WK to WKS, [Spring 1936], B3F3, KP; Andrade to Nash, January 8, 1974, KKP.

4. WKS to WK, January 22, 1936, B4F3, KP; Andrade to Nash, January 8, 1974, KKP.

5. American Political Science Association, Oral History Project, Transcripts of Tapes Recording Conversations with CH, 1978–79, p. 34, B4F18, KKP; Nash, "Iconoclast I," 134; WKS to WK, March 16, 1936, B4F3, KP; WK to CH, August 7, 1937, B7, CHP; Brandwein, "Katherine," 105; Andrade to Nash, January 8, 1974, KKP; WK to Henry Regnery (hereafter HR), [1964?], B38F2, Henry Regnery Papers (hereafter HRP), KP; Kenan Heise, "Irving P. Pflaum," *Chicago Tribune*, April 25, 1985, chicagotribune.com.

6. WKS to WK, January 22, 1936 and February 8, 1936, B4F3, KP; WK to WKS, [1936], B3F3, KP; Brandwein, "Katherine," 105.

7. WK to WKS, December 25, 1936, B3F2, KP; WK to WKS, March 25, 1937, B3F4, KP.

8. WKS to WK, December 8, 1936, and WK to WKS, December 15, 1936, B3F3, KP.

9. WK to WKS, June 14, 1937, B3F4 and WKS to WK, September 13, 1937, B4F3, KP.

10. WKS to WK, January 22, 1936, February 8, 1936, March 16, 1936, December 21, 1936, B4F3, KP.

11. WK to WKS, November 27, 1935, B3F3, KP; WK to WKS, September 1937, B3F4, KP; WK to WKS, March 25, 1937, July 1937, B3F4, KP; WK to WKS, [Fall] 1938, B3F5, KP; Brandwein, "Katherine," 105.

12. WKS to WK, September 13, 1937, B4F3, KP; WK to R.B. McCallum, January 5, 1937 and R.B. McCallum to WK, November 11, 1937, B30F12, KP; WK to WKS, December 15, 1936, B3F3, KP; CH to WK, August 6, 1937, WK to CH, August 7,

1937, CH to Fred C. Frey, October 31, 1939, CH to WK, August 26, 1937, B7, CHP; WK to WKS, [August] 1937 and September 1937, B3F4, KP; KK to John W. Fiser, January 21, 1982, B4F18, KKP.

13. "Excerpts from the 'Last Will and Testament of Charles S. Hyneman' . . . ., Chicago, May 2, 1970," B4F18, KKP; Wills, *Confessions*, 20–21; Conversations with Hyneman, 33–37; "Willmoore K. of Idabelle," B7, CHP; GWC, Epilogue to *OxY*, 514; William Wingfield, "Educator With Optimism," Newspaper Clipping, 1963, B26, BP.

14. WK to CH, August 7, 1937, CHP.

15. Robert B. Heilman, "The State of Letters: Baton Rouge and LSU Forty Years Later," *Sewanee Review* 88, no. 1 (1980): 126–43; Cleanth Brooks (hereafter CB), Robert Penn Warren, and WK to Fred Aydelotte, October 1, 1938, B6F147, Cleanth Brooks Papers (hereafter CBP), Yale Collection of American Literature, Beinecke Rare Book and Manuscript Library; Conversations with Hyneman, 1978–79, 26–36; Brandwein, "Katherine," 105; Mason, Biography, 1432, B11F4, KP; Nash, "Iconoclast I," 134; Mark Royden Winchell, "An Extended Family," *Southern Review* 31, no. 2 (Spring 1995): 197–218.

16. WK to CH, [June 1941] and WK to CB, [June 1941], B6F148, CBP.

17. Conversations with Hyneman, 1978–79, pp. 34–35, 41, B4F18, KKP.

18. WK, "On the Preservation of Democracy for America," *Southern Review* (Summer 1939): 53–58; Christopher H. Owen, "Pondering the People: Willmoore Kendall's Path from Progressive to Conservative Populism." In *Walk Away: When the Political Left Turns Right*, ed. Lee Trepanier and Grant Havers. Lanham, MD: Lexington Books, 2019), 15–34.

19. Ibid., 59–68.

20. WK, "The Majority Principle and the Scientific Elite," *Southern Review* (Winter 1939): 463–73; WK, "Preservation," *passim*.

21. "Willmoore K. of Idabelle" and WK to Fred C. Frey, October 28, 1939, B7, CHP; Conversations with Hyneman, 38–39; WKS to KK/WK, April 29, 1939 and WKS to WK, July 4, 1939, B4F3, KP; WKS to WK, March 17, 1938, B4F3, KP.

22. WKS to WK, March 30, 1937, 1938 (n.d.), and March 17, 1938, B4F3 and WK to WKS, [Spring 1938?], B3F4, KP.

23. WK to WKS, July 1937, B3F4, KP; Brandwein, "Katherine," 106–08.

24. Harnett T. Kane, *Huey Long's Louisiana Hayride: The American Rehearsal for Dictatorship, 1928–1940* (New Orleans: Pelican Publishing, 1971), 299–301; Allan C. Michie and Frank Ryhlick, *Dixie Demagogues* (New York: Vanguard Press, 1939), 138–39; CH to Evron Kirkpatrick, July 28, 1939, CH to WK, June 30, 1939, "Stipulation Concerning the Hiring of Willmoore Kendall," [1939], CH to Kirkpatrick, July 28, 1939, CH to WK, June 30, 1939, and CH to WK, August 9, 1939, B7, CHP.

25. YM, Biography, 1453, B11F4, KP; WKS to WK, July 4, 1939 and WKS to WK, January 1940, B4F3, KP; WK to Fred C. Frey, October 28, 1939, CH to Frey, October 31, 1939, CH to Fred C. Frey, November 4, 1939, and Paul M. Hebert to WK, December 19, 1939, B7, CHP.

26. YM, Biography, 1435–36, 1459, 1479–89, B11F4, KP; Saul Bellow to NK, October 2, 1970, B18F3, KP; WK to CB and Tinkum Brooks, May 28, 1940, B6F147,

CBP; WK to FGW, December 22, 1938 and August 11, 1940, B2, Francis Graham Wilson Papers, University of Illinois Archives (hereafter WP).

27. Pemantle, *Contrasting*, ch. 10.

28. WK, *John Locke and the Doctrine of Majority Rule* (Urbana: University of Illinois Press, 1941), 33, 37–38, ch. II, 52–59.

29. Ibid., 66–67, 69, 74–75.

30. Ibid., ch. V, 103–107.

31. Ibid., 122–36.

32. WK to CB, May 28, 1940, B6F147, CBP; Nathan Godfried, "Fellow Traveler, Organic Intellectual: J. Raymond Walsh and Radio News Commentary in the 1940s," *Democratic Communiqué* 22, no. 2 (Fall 2008): 23–24.

33. WK to Brooks/Brooks, May 28, 1940 and WK to CH, Mary 28, 1940, B6F147, CBP; Mason, Biography, 1492–93, B11F4, KP; "Hobart Aide Hits Program of FDR," *Democrat and Chronicle*, October 25, 1940, p. 45.

34. Walter H. Durfee to FGW, July 11, 1941 and WK to FGW, July 20, 1941, B2, WP; "Dr. Eddy Hints," *Democrat and Chronicle*, February 26, 1941, p. 7; "Leader Backs," *Democrat and Chronicle*, February 26, 1941, p. 30; "Hobart Faculty," *Star-Gazette* (Elmira, New York), February 26, 1941, p. 7; "Students at Hobart," *Democrat and Chronicle*, March 1, 1941, p. 21; WKS to WK, [February 1941], B5F1, KP; WK to FGW, July 20, 1941, B2, FGWP; R. Harris Smith, *OSS: The Secret History of America's First Central Intelligence Agency* (New York: Lyons Press, 2005), 42.

35. WKS to WK, February 1941, B5F1, KP; WKS to WK, 1939, B4F3, KP; WKS to WK, May 19, 1941, B5F1, KP; WK to Lawrence Dennis, October 26, 1941, B4F3, Lawrence Dennis Papers, Hoover Institution, Library and Archives; WK to CB, [June 1941] and WK to Tinkum Brooks [Summer 1941] , B6F148, CBP; Godfried, "Traveler," 24; WK, "Review of Parliamentary Government in England, by Harold Laski," *Journal of Politics* 1, no. 2 (April 1939): 220–22; WK, "Men on the Job," New Republic, August 18, 1941, pp. 226–27; WK, "Summons to Revolution," *New Republic*, June 30, 1941, pp. 895–96.

36. WK to CB, May 28, 1940, September 13, 1941, and KK to CB, November 16, 1940, B6F147, CBP.

37. "U. of R. Faculty Members," *Richmond Times-Dispatch*, September 17, 1941, p. 7; Brandwein, "Katherine," 106; WK to CB, September 13, 1941, B6F147, CBP; WK to FGW, September 14, 1941, B2, FGWP; WK to CH, February 11, 1942 and WK to CH, April 14, 1942, B7, CHP; WK to FGW, March 25, 1942, B2, WP; WKS to WK, July 1941, B5F1, KP; WK to WKS, June 2, 1933, *OxY*, 208–09; WK to CH, February 11, 1942, B7, CHP.

38. WKS to WK/KK, December 22, 1941, B5F1, KP.

39. WK to CH, Spring 1942 (2 letters), B7, CHP; Heise, "Pflaum;" WK to FGW, [1942], B2, FGWP.

40. WK to FGW, March 25, 1942, May 3, 1942, and FGW to WK, July 27, 1942, B2, FGWP.

41. "Kendall Will Take," *Daily Oklahoman*, October 27, 1940, p. 18; "Endorse Kendall," *Daily Oklahoman*, December 12, 1940, p. 6; WKS to KK, October 1941, B5F1, KP.

42. WKS to WK, Spring 1939, B4F3, KP; "Methodists Agree," *Miami Daily News-Record*, April 19, 1939, p. 2; WKS to WK, November 1940, B5F1, KP; "Epworth Leaguers," *Glencoe Mirror*, March 14, 1941, p. 1; "Honorary Degree," *Miami Daily News-Record*, June 16, 1941, p. 3; "Oklahoman Coming," p. 1; "Nov. 11 Speaker," p. 1; "Death Claims Rev.," p. 2; WKS to WK, February 1941, B5F1, KP; WKS to WK, July 1940 and Spring 1941, B5F1, KP; "Farewell Sermon," *Miami Daily News-Record*, October 19, 1941, p. 7; WKS to WK, October 26, 1941, October 1941 and PGK to WK, October 1941, B5F1, KP.

43. WKS to WK, July 1940 and May 19, 1941, B5F1, KP; WK to WK/KK, [1942], B5F1, KP; KK to Tinkum Brooks, September 24, 1943, B6F147, CBP; WK to WKS, May 22, 1934, in *OxY*, 361–62.

44. "Eufaula Pastor," *Indian Journal*, June 11, 1942, p. 1; "Rev. Willmoore Kendall," *Daily Oklahoman*, June 7, 1942, p. 25; "Death Claims Rev.," pp. 1–2.

Chapter 4

1942–1947

"Spreading Like the Green Bay Tree"

When his opinions were unpopular, Willmoore Kendall usually upheld them all the more. Given his opposition to American entry into World War II, it was predictable that he would continue to champion isolationist ideas. He might have chosen this path as an alternative academic career. If an established isolationist intellectual, Kendall would have found it psychologically difficult to sound academic retreat. For inspiration, he might have drawn inspiration from renowned scholars Charles A. Beard and Harry Elmer Barnes. Both stuck stoutly to their noninterventionist views, deriding Roosevelt's foreign policy even in wartime. With his combative persona, Kendall—with the prominence of a Beard or a Barnes—would have been tempted to dig in to defend his views.

If *John Locke and the Doctrine of Majority Rule* had come out a year earlier, Willmoore might have possessed sufficient scholarly stature to have taken this stand. Appearing in 1941, the book had attracted favorable notice. In *Social Forces* James Godfrey of the University of North Carolina praised Kendall's "minute examination" of Locke. Finding that the English philosopher advocated majority rule more than individual rights, said Godfrey, amounted to a "revolution" in Locke studies. In November 1941 budding political theorist Eric Voegelin wrote Kendall seeking advice about Locke's views on religion. Kendall, he said, was "the only expert on Locke I know in this country." Kendall sent back a textual analysis of Voegelin's article, with 165 suggested corrections. Though stunned, Voegelin made many of the revisions. Charles Hyneman called critics of Kendall's *Locke* less imaginative than its admirers.[1]

Had Kendall proclaimed his antiwar position longer than he did, his stance would have come at great cost. As his father had come to understand (during World War I) and as Willmoore surely remembered, the United States treated wartime dissidents harshly. If famous enough, even isolationists who tried to get behind the American war effort suffered Roosevelt's wrath. Charles Lindbergh—banned from military service—and Lawrence Dennis—tried for sedition—provided examples of the administration's vindictiveness. Despite their fame, Beard and Barnes became personae non gratae in academia. Kendall was obscure enough that his isolationism remained under the radar. He was able to shift careers to join the "cloak and gown" world of American intelligence work. And he would remain part of this world for more than a decade.[2]

To be sure, many other isolationists of Kendall's ilk also navigated this wartime transition. Raymond Walsh happily went to work doing public relations for the CIO, becoming an avid supporter of FDR and his policies, foreign and domestic. When William Eddy left academia, he became a major player in the rapidly expanding American intelligence apparatus. Charles Hyneman, also an isolationist, slid successfully into wartime military service. Revilo Oliver, Kendall's anti-New Deal friend from Illinois, used his linguistic skills to lead a large government cryptography effort at Arlington Hall, part of the United States Army Signal Corps.[3] One notable exception to this accommodation to war was Mulford Sibley. As a Quaker convert from Methodism, Sibley declared as a conscientious objector.

When Kendall joined the CIAA in June 1942, he entered a bureaucratic arena in which lines of engagement between competing agencies had already been drawn. The CIAA was established (under a different name) in August 1940. Through the efforts of its chief, Nelson A. Rockefeller, it became the chief intelligence agency for the Western Hemisphere. By the time Willmoore joined the CIAA in June 1942, the organization—drawing on Rockefeller's fame, wealth, connections, and energy—had carved out a significant niche in intelligence circles. Rockefeller disliked William Donovan, head of the Office of Strategic Services (OSS) and convinced President Roosevelt to order the OSS out of Latin America. The Federal Bureau of Investigation did any needed clandestine work there. The CIAA retained control of American propaganda for the Western Hemisphere for the duration of the war. The main CIAA charge, of course, was to combat Axis influence.[4]

Kendall's skill set proved ideal for this work. He was fluent in Spanish and French, read German and Italian, had experience as a newspaper reporter, and possessed understanding of radio and advertising. With this background he could, on demand, write prose rapidly for various required reports and press releases. Kendall had spent lots of time abroad, had knowledge of contemporary world politics, possessed two degrees from Oxford, and a PhD in political science from Illinois. His "imaginative and inventive mind" gave Kendall "an extraordinary capacity to read and extract essentials." According to Charles S. Hyneman, Willmoore was "in the fullest sense loyal to the

American people and the government and other institutions which they establish."[5] Not all of Kendall's coworkers shared this last attribute.

After obtaining his new position in June 1942, Willmoore worked for a year with the "content committee" of the CIAA. Working 14 hours a day, he prepared two daily radio scripts, each of which he authored, translated, and readied for transmission. This work included typing and proofreading the final Spanish and Portuguese drafts. After an early promotion, Willmoore found himself leading a staff of eight "extremely able writers" tasked with promoting U.S. interests in Latin America via shortwave. Essentially, Kendall oversaw the production of propaganda for Latin America and found the post "the most interesting job that has ever fallen into my hands." He did some ghostwriting, including an article in 1943 for Francis Jamieson, chief of the CIAA's press division, within a large volume entitled *Journalism and the War*. From December 1942 until May 1943, Willmoore mostly lived in New York where both CBS and NBC partnered with the CIAA on producing broadcasts. His professional duties again separated him from Katherine whose job required her to be in Washington. Receiving a salary "out of the sphere of the rational," Willmoore "went up like a shot" in the organization. In 1943 he received an important promotion with an assignment as the CIAA Press Representative for Colombia.[6]

By late 1942, after he had become well settled in the organization, Kendall wrote glowingly to friends about his job. Addressing Francis Wilson, for example, he said he had taken "to the work like a fish to water." Expanding on this point (and mixing metaphors), Kendall continued that he "was spreading myself like the green bay tree."[7] As a preacher's kid, Bible verses came readily to Willmoore's mind. He took this line from Psalm 37:35 which, in good King James prose, reads in full, as follows: "I have seen the wicked in great power, and spreading himself like a green bay tree." From the context of the letter, Kendall meant that he was excited about his work and thriving in it, for he already knew himself to be an effective and innovative intelligence officer. With promotions and a growing salary, he was finding greater financial security than he had ever known. Kendall, then, did not mean to identify himself with "the wicked" referenced in the psalm. Yet his citation of the verse revealed the perils of his new course. Intelligence work allowed Willmoore to put his expertise to good use, but it was full of moral dilemmas and professional pitfalls, including a focus on secrecy and studied manipulation of the masses. The new job also drew him away from scholarly work. Political theory remained Kendall's passion, but intelligence work gave him little time for intellectual pursuits. Intelligence work also pushed him away from the left, for it was as an intelligence officer that Kendall made his rightward turn. This transformation would have major implications for his own career and, ultimately, for the future of American conservatism. World War

II meant the loss of isolationist innocence for Kendall but also for the United States more generally.

Meanwhile, the war threw Willmoore's personal life into disarray. In the Fall of 1942, the Kendall household in Richmond was crowded. Pearl Kendall, together with Walter, his wife Helen and their two children, lived there with Katherine. Close conditions made for "a harrowing experience" which was unpleasant for all concerned. The newly widowed Mrs. Kendall had a hard time getting over her husband's death, remaining despondent for months. She became "an almost pathological case," according to Katherine, as her grief deepened and her adjustment to widowhood worsened. For much of this time, Willmoore was living in New York. Trying to hold down the fort proved challenging for Katherine, as she found herself "with a house full of Kendalls, of all ages & sizes & temperaments."[8]

In the Spring of 1943 Kendall experienced a "violent reaction" after receiving shots for typhus and typhoid which were required before he could travel to Bogotá. Kendall looked forward to the upcoming assignment where, he told his sister, he was "down for very important tasks." In his job he would "mainly exercise a counter-propaganda function." At the end of May he left to take his new assignment which again separated him from Katherine who remained in the United States. She planned to travel to Colombia to live with him, but the couple did not come together again until Willmoore returned from South America. In fact, after their time together in Richmond in 1941 and 1942, Katy and Ken seldom lived together for long. The war opened up major career opportunities for both of them and deepened preexisting rifts in their relationship. When he went to work for the CIAA, she stayed in Richmond to finish her job there. Later she obtained employment with the Red Cross in Washington. There she experienced "a meteoric rise," then got a job with the United States Children's Bureau working with teachers and social workers from Latin America. These professional obligations forced them into separate domiciles. Even when living together, Katherine and Willmoore spoke of how busy they were. Many of their friends, including Charles Hyneman, lived in the Washington area, but it was difficult to socialize, as war work left little free time. Anyway, said Katherine, there was "a liquor shortage and how can you be convivial without a high ball."[9]

Kendall served as CIAA press agent in Colombia for several months. Stationed in Bogotá, he traveled throughout the country. Much of this work concerned mundane matters, such as how to design, print, place, and market American brochures, posters, press releases, and magazine subscriptions to appeal effectively to the country's many different social classes. The purpose was to use publicity to put the United States in the best light possible and its Axis enemies in the poorest. The means was to portray the United States as more democratic, humane, rich, powerful, and sophisticated than its Axis enemies. Part of this effort was to promote a pictorial magazine for Latin America, *En Guardia*, produced by the CIAA. This publication imitated such civilian magazines as *Life* from the United States and *El Hogar* of Argentina. It attained a circulation of a million readers by war's end.[10]

Kendall made good use of his knowledge, experience, and talents in Colombia. With broad knowledge of global alternatives to capitalism, he noticed "enormous interest" in consumer cooperatives in the country. He persuaded his CIAA superiors to emphasize Axis suppression of such groups and their vitality in Allied countries. He also promoted a pamphlet called "The Nazi War Against the Catholic Church." Designed to appeal to "a wide and select audience" of Colombians, it countered Axis propaganda about the Vatican. To "avoid offending the sensibilities of Colombian neutrals," he thought it unwise to picture the Nazis as Neanderthals. Relying "exclusively on positive themes" was more effective. Such themes included posters about Roosevelt's "Four Freedoms" and books of "cartoons and jokes."[11] Providing propaganda posters praising President Roosevelt, whom he still despised, must have stuck in Kendall's craw.

To his superiors Kendall stressed the need for cultivating the Colombian press. To do so he provided "exclusive" placements of CIAA material with *El Tiempo* and *El Espectador*, the widely circulated Bogotá dailies. He prized connections with these newspapers but placed materials they did not print elsewhere. In this effort, his knowledge of newspaper work and small-town life came in handy. He opposed the purchase of UPI or AP wire service subscriptions for local papers but came up with clever ways to share information with small-town weeklies. The CIAA provided them information more cheaply than they could get it from the wire services. He recognized that such outlets practiced a type of journalism almost entirely devoted "to strictly local events." Because the papers had lots of "cover-to-cover readers," however, he knew the CIAA might obtain "more careful attention" for U.S. publicity efforts than through other media venues. Cumulatively, these weeklies had a larger circulation in the hinterlands than did the big Bogotá dailies. Struggling financially, they would welcome free stories from the CIAA. As press agent, Kendall also tried to help friendly Colombian newspapers obtain newer printing presses made in the USA.[12]

Kendall pushed successfully for creation of a nationwide "daily radio news show." This program would "supplement" shortwave broadcasts from Washington, partnering with local radio stations. In the Fall of 1943, for example, Kendall promoted U.S. radio broadcasts saluting Cartagena's independence day. He also facilitated the request of the Colombian owner of a local radio station to air a program about this milestone in the United States. These radio programs rebroadcast or produced locally by the CIAA became among the most popular programs in Cartagena by 1944. Willmoore thought it important to travel throughout the country to cultivate "influential writers both on Bogotá and in the provincial capitals." He wanted such contacts to provide these intellectuals a nuanced view "of controversial questions." As regards radio, Kendall focused serious attention on quality control. He contacted Rockefeller, for example, to inform him that a particular Washington newscaster was unpopular with Colombian listeners. "San Francisco newscasters" he added, needed to learn to "pronounce correctly the names of Latin American personages and places."[13]

Kendall had to make sure that his country's message in Colombia was coherent and consistent with official American policy. In many respects he was a model press agent. In July 1943, for instance, he urged the CIAA chairman in Cartagena to trace and destroy posters with recruiting slogans for the U.S. Marines. The "armed forces of the United States," he said, "do not seek recruits in Latin America." When controversial topics arose, such as the Allied bombing of Rome, Kendall penned communiqués for release to the local papers. To superiors back home, he also reported Colombian local reactions to war news and to American propaganda efforts. CIAA efforts in Colombia were quite successful. Actual Axis initiatives in the region were few. But the war helped the United States expand its cultural and economic influence in South America. Kendall worked with bureaucrats, ambitious local politicians, American oilmen, embassy personnel, Allied intelligence agents, military officers, visiting journalists, CIAA representatives in other Colombian cities, and intellectuals hired to promote U.S. aims. He translated important newspaper articles and sent them to Rockefeller so the boss might react quickly to events. He sent cultural information on Colombia back home. For example, he provided local newspaper clippings on "feminism in Colombia" to journalist Ruby Black, first biographer of Eleanor Roosevelt. Kendall promoted cultural and economic exchanges between the two countries. He publicized in Colombia, for example, an exhibit of Latin American artists at the Museum of Modern Art in New York and gave American businessmen news about "an industrial exposition in Medellín." He also gave assistance to Colombian writers wanting their work to appear in the United States.[14]

By late 1943 Kendall was back in the United States. Impressed by his performance in Bogotá, the CIAA gave him a promotion and a pay raise. The organization also promised further moves upward if he stayed on. But Willmoore continued to fear being conscripted into military service. As he had prepared to fly to Colombia in May 1943, for example, Kendall had remained in a "disastrous" state of uncertainty. He believed the draft board back home in Oklahoma might not let him leave the United States. Feeling "the hot breath of the Stillwater board on the back of my wretched neck," he decided to enlist. He would have preferred to remain a civilian. The new military position promised to be tedious, but he did not regret his decision, for it ended a long "war of nerves" on his psyche. In making the formal shift into military service, Kendall received an "overnight commission." In March 1944 he wrote his sister that he would get "a two-weeks 'special' basic training course, at a camp near Washington." This arrangement would, he noted, "confirm my captaincy with an absolute minimum of discomfort."[15]

Kendall entered the army on February 14, 1944, was soon promoted to captain, and by 1946 had attained the rank of major in the Army of the United States. All along he knew that he would be assigned as an "Officer of the Secretariat" for the Inter-American Defense Board (IADB). This organization was established in January 1942 by the members of the Pan-American Union and based in Washington. Kendall continued to travel frequently to South America, mostly, he told his sister, "to Bolivia, Colombia, and Argentina." The IADB's purpose was to bring together technical specialists from the twenty-one Union republics to help plan defense of the hemisphere. Kendall found his IADB tasks of translating, editing, and writing official documents "tiresome." He often went through already translated documents "to certify them as absolutely correct." He served as an interpreter for U.S. military specialists who traveled on junkets to meet their Latin American counterparts and to show off U.S. military technology to its Western Hemisphere friends. In his position, Kendall had to attend "diplomatic cocktail parties" three times a week. The job required him to drink, make small talk, interpret for "fat Latin American generals," and push their wives "around the dance floor." Year later, as he struggled with alcoholism, Kendall pinpointed the onset of his drinking problem to this time. To his sister he complained in 1944 about "the pointlessness" of his job at the IADB.[16]

In November 1944 Willmoore looked back on his two and a half years in government service. He considered the experience to have been a "distressing phase" of his life. "Interminable" days at the office left him little time to do what he loved best, that is, to read good books and to engage in intelligent conversation. Long hours on the job and difficult commutes left him "much too tired to attempt anything likely to make demands upon the intellect." In Bogotá he had possessed more leisure time but confided to his sister that the "nervous strain" which he felt from making "the fight I was sent there to make left me little inclination for serious reading." He feared that he would come out "of wartime Washington with a mind dulled beyond all possibility of resharpening."[17]

At this point Kendall retained his left-wing political convictions but did not regard himself as a "liberal." In March 1944, for instance, Kendall still described himself as "a good socialist" in private correspondence. He considered liberals to be dishonest phonies not serious about social change. Just before the presidential election of 1944, he said that "everything I am interested in seeing accomplished in politics depends . . . upon getting Mr. Roosevelt out of the way, where he cannot claim the allegiance of the people most likely to get together, some day, to form a leftwing third party." Willmoore cast an absentee ballot in Oklahoma for Republican candidate Thomas Dewey. He had no real confidence in Dewey either whom, he said, "had become a New Dealer himself in the course of the campaign." When Roosevelt handily won a fourth term in office (and carried the Sooner State by eleven points), Kendall expressed chagrin. He wondered gloomily if FDR would run for a fifth time in 1948.[18]

In late 1944 Willmoore received a letter from Juan and Maria Theresa Andrade. The couple, almost miraculously, had survived in German-occupied France. Imprisoned, Juan had escaped in a daring rescue operation led by an old POUM colleague. The Andrades wrote that they were experiencing dire economic difficulties. Willmoore, who now had many useful government contacts, provided help. He sent generous, regular shipments to his old friends. Drawing upon the largesse of the United States government, the shipments included rice, sugar, flour, corned beef, honey, powdered milk, blankets, and clothes. There were enough supplies to provision not only the Andrades but also many of their refugee colleagues. Kendall also sent the Andrades boxes of Camel cigarettes—which he knew could be exchanged for cash—and sent similar packages to other old comrades from his days in pre-Civil War Spain. Kendall continued to send such help for more than a year until the economic situation of the Andrades improved. Tellingly, he did not get into politics in his letters with his friends, even though they were eager to engage in political discussion.[19] Aside from satisfaction at helping old associates, one suspects Kendall knew the Andrades could provide valuable information about politics in postwar Europe.

"Sick at heart" in 1944 about his IADB work, Willmoore grew depressed about his personal life. The death of his father and separation from Katherine strongly affected his psyche. In October 1943 he wrote Cleanth Brooks, also the son of a Methodist minister, that he had been dealing with "moral problems" for the previous two years. He longed for a chat with Brooks, "the best guy in the world to talk oneself out to." Often living apart, Willmoore and Katherine tried to keep in touch with long letters. Katherine told Tinkum Brooks in September 1943, that despite the couple's frequent separations, it was not "as if we didn't like to live together." But Katherine was making a mark in international social work and found her career "terribly interesting." Experiencing "great emotional disturbance" when Katy's career took her to Chicago and Mexico, Ken engaged in "great meditations about what to do and how to do it." By early 1944 the Kendalls were seriously contemplating divorce. Willmoore said his "heart" was "heavy" but that the couple remained "good friends" and "perhaps more in love with one another than ever." The prospect of divorce had arisen, according to Willmoore because of "our careers and long-term objectives." Divorce was not inevitable, but "reconciliation" not possible "because we did not quarrel." In November 1944, he said, the couple had decided "to go forward with our marriage," but he dreaded "another year of week-ending together on occasion."[20]

That Christmas, however, the couple, "overwhelmed with sadness," announced their formal separation. The on-again, off-again marriage saga of Katy and Ken would last several more years. Only in 1951 would the couple actually finalize their divorce. As he transitioned out of the war, however, Willmoore continued to experience "endless fits of depression." Kendall had already begun to see a therapist for "analysis" of his "feeling of hopelessness." By the summer of 1946 he claimed therapy had made him "a new man," not perhaps a "better" person but "a much happier one." On a visit to Minneapolis, however, Willmoore had a "difficult time," experiencing some "old-old problems." Such "problems" likely involved Kendall's penchant for extramarital sexual relationships. At the end of 1944, for example, Kendall had an affair with Anne Crutcher, while her husband Leon was in combat in Europe. By this time, he had developed a reputation as a womanizer which endured for years afterward. This reputation (partly explained by long separations from his wife), he admitted was earned, if perhaps exaggerated.[21]

These wartime travails wrung any remaining vestiges of romanticism out of Willmoore Kendall. His taste in fiction, for example, became decidedly hard-boiled. He loved the gritty, noir detective novels of James M. Cain, including *The Postman Always Rings Twice*, *Serenade*, and *The Embezzler*. And in early 1944 he expressed admiration for the unblinking look at alcoholism which Charles Jackson took in his novel *The Lost Weekend*. Given that these books were best sellers, such tastes were partly generational. Disillusioned by World War I, the Depression, and the Nazi-Soviet Pact, many intellectuals of Willmoore's age became skeptical of easy answers to complex problems.[22] For Kendall, these reading preferences also represented an ongoing emotional revolt against his deceased father—an extreme romantic. Additionally, these choices revealed Kendall's increasingly jaded attitude to working in a federal bureaucracy which he mostly did not respect and to being in a crumbling marriage with a successful professional woman whom he seldom saw. Then, as he was reaching an emotional low point in his life, Willmoore Kendall's career began to take off again, and within two years reached new heights.

As the war wound down Kendall feared that he would have to serve in the IADB for years, even after the fighting had ended. In his work with the board he had honed his language skills so that his command of Spanish was "pretty fancy." When the IADB sent him to Portuguese language school, he thought the move "insanity" because it might weaken his fluency in Spanish. He vowed to forget any Portuguese he learned as soon as possible.

In November 1944 Kendall began to see light at the end of his professional tunnel. He informed his sister that he would soon again be "going back to . . . [his] old job of writing and preparing transcripts for radio broadcasts to South America." Willmoore was "looking forward to the change with great eagerness" in which he would remain in the army but only loosely connected to it. In this new assignment he would "be more my own boss than the average colonel."[23]

Technically, Kendall remained in the army, under the aegis of the IADB until May 1946. In a sense, he was going back to his "old job" coordinating with the CIAA (soon renamed the Office of Inter-American Affairs). He worked again with that organization for a little over a year. As he contemplated his postwar career, Willmoore decided to apply for a Guggenheim Fellowship to have a full year to complete his "book on Rousseau and majority-rule." In December 1945 Kendall heard that his application for the Guggenheim had been successful. His reputation as a scholar, based largely on his Locke book, had survived the war. At the end of 1945, he claimed "great eagerness" to leave federal service. "I'm really sick of Washington," he told his sister, "and pretty much all the memories which attach to it."[24]

In early 1946 Kendall was pleased to "find himself flooded with generous offers." His "professional situation" had improved "since those difficult years just before the war." He turned down a well-paid position as American cultural attaché in Lima, Peru. Instead he accepted a teaching position at the University of Minnesota with plans to start teaching in the Fall Semester of 1946. In July the university announced it had hired Kendall as an associate professor of political science. The previous March, however, Kendall had agreed to serve as acting head of the Latin American Division of the State Department's Office of Research and Intelligence. Here he led "a staff of 17 economists, geographers, and political scientists." Upon obtaining the post, he told his sister that he was "real excited" about the opportunity.[25]

This professional progress came about because of the drastic restructuring of American intelligence. When Harry Truman took office in April 1945 he decided to reduce the influence of the Organization of Strategic Services. A major factor in this decision was "bumbling and lax security" in the OSS, as detailed in a "scathing report" by Colonel Richard Park, Jr., of U.S. Army Intelligence. Park finished this report in March 1945, intending to present it to President Roosevelt. But FDR never read it (perhaps because Park's superior was wary of its anti-Soviet perspective). Upon FDR's demise, Park reached Truman with his concerns. His report cited many problems with the OSS. It included several instances of extraordinary naiveté, incompetence, or worse regarding the Soviet Union. As one example, the OSS head in Bulgaria broke his cover after the Russians moved in. He provided the USSR with a complete list of OSS agents at work in the country. Park also noted that the "Communist element in O.S.S. is believed to be of dangerously large proportions."[26]

Taking such information under consideration, President Truman, a few weeks after VJ Day, abolished the OSS on October 1, 1945. This step resulted in bureaucratic chaos, with the tasks of the OSS farmed out to different federal agencies. The CIAA took over some of its functions, especially in research and analysis, that is, the areas in which Willmoore Kendall operated. Destruction of the OSS meant the transfer of its research and analysis functions to the State Department. Its clandestine operations went to military intelligence. Bureaucratic disorder continued for two years until the National Security Act—which created the CIA and National Security Agency—went into effect in September 1947.[27] It was during this transitional and chaotic period in the American intelligence world that Willmoore Kendall achieved his highest government position.

In the Spring of 1946 Kendall entered the big leagues of the American intelligence establishment. In March he received appointment as assistant director, Special Projects Staff, in the United States Department of State. Technically Major Kendall remained in the Army of the United States until he received his honorable discharge in May. Six weeks later he became branch editor and distribution officer at his State Department job. In August 1946 he was appointed chief of the Latin American Division of the Office of Reports and Estimates (ORE) for the Central Intelligence Group (CIG). Established as something of an interagency makeshift on January 22, 1946, the CIG was the embryonic form of the CIA. Soon a consensus developed among policy-makers that the Cold War required a more centralized setup. By the time the CIA came formally into existence, however, Kendall was teaching at Yale. The CIG focused on gathering information, rather than on covert action. That focus allied well with Kendall's views on intelligence work. Kendall took a year's leave of absence from Minnesota to work for the CIG. Washington insiders smoothed this career path for Kendall, making sure Minnesota would keep his position open. Even as he made this transition, however, Kendall "deep within" almost hoped something would happen to send him to the academic post in Minneapolis. In taking up this new "big job" at the CIG, Kendall claimed that for "all intents and purposes" he had "been drafted." He feared the position would cost him as a scholar, losing prime years as a writer and researcher. He "spent the better part of a week sweating over" this key career move. Taking "the national point of view," however, he believed it "of first importance that the CIG, through the difficult months and years ahead, have the personnel it needs for the indispensable function it is charged with."[28]

Kendall thus took a huge step up the professional ladder. He accepted the position because he could "have an impact on the nation's business far beyond any job I've had, or been mentioned for." He found himself near the center of the burgeoning postwar American intelligence community. He came into the CIG as part a purge of "dead wood" and lingering OSS influences from the organization. The new Director of Central Intelligence was Lieutenant General Hoyt Vandenberg. Previously head of Army Intelligence, Vandenberg brought in a coterie of "colonels" to fix the CIG. Kendall became part of this makeover, but he came in as a protégé of William Langer, Harvard historian. Langer had been chief of Research and Analysis in the OSS and continued to serve in this capacity as this division transferred to the State Department. Vandenberg and Langer worked to "refocus" American intelligence and make it more efficient. Thus, Kendall chose to put his academic career on hold for this "big promotion."[29]

Willmoore found the new job fascinating. He was in charge of about thirty-five employees whom he said were "pretty good people." He was an important liaison between his ORE and other intelligence agencies. Given a "free hand" to make changes, he reorganized the personnel in an office which he believed had suffered from poor leadership. Much of his job consisted of compiling daily intelligence reports from Latin America to provide to his superiors so that they might present the president "a daily summary of important information." At least initially, such information was what Truman mainly wanted from the intelligence services. Kendall was responsible for gathering, sifting, compiling, and presenting pertinent information from Latin America, much as he had done, on a smaller scale with lower stakes, when reporting to Coordinator Rockefeller. Kendall's reports went to the Assistant Director for Research and Evaluation, then passed through more bureaucratic hoops before reaching the president's desk. His superiors decided how to move forward with information Kendall had compiled. Sometimes they left out material which they believed did not merit presidential attention. Thus, Kendall was not in the inner circle of decision-makers and never actually met the president. Even as this work proceeded, Kendall was contemplating a return to academia. He thought at first that he would take up the post which he had left off at the University of Minnesota.[30]

He came into this position in the intelligence community because of his strong anti-Stalinist credentials and because of his stellar performance in previous jobs. Kendall's friend, the political scientist Evron Kirkpatrick, had joined the OSS in 1945 and voiced his concern to William Donovan that its Latin American research and analysis branch was chock full of Communists. Other intelligence personnel had shared this concern. Kirkpatrick had recommended to Donovan that Kendall "be brought in to clean out the division."[31] Apparently, this cleansing of communists was the "special project" to which Kendall was assigned in March 1946 in the State Department as it was taking over the research and analysis functions of the OSS. In this task, Kendall ran into some old Oklahoma comrades.

Writing privately in 1960, Kendall provided one key reason for his quick rise up the intelligence ladder. "I'm the guy who 'busted' the Maurice Halperin operation at OSS and State," he confided to ex-communist Nathaniel Weyl, "and because of that was named his successor." Halperin had joined the OSS after expulsion from the University of Oklahoma, where he had worked as a professor for fourteen years. Oklahoma governor Leon Phillips, ignoring Reverend Kendall's advice, sought to purge communists from the university. In 1941 the "Little Dies Committee" of the Oklahoma State Legislature took up the governor's plan. It demanded the firing of Halperin, a professor of Romance languages. Halperin lied by denying that that he was a member of the Communist Party. University authorities were skeptical of the charges and so helped arrange a "soft landing" for Halperin with the OSS.[32]

Halperin became one of "the most productive" Soviet agents within American intelligence agencies. He led OSS research and analysis efforts for Latin America, even as Kendall was working in the same region for the CIAA and IADB. In 1945—after he received warnings from Duncan Lee (advisor to William Donovan and himself a Soviet agent) that the FBI was closing in on him—Halperin left the OSS. He went to work for State Department intelligence, resigning this office in early 1946, to be replaced by Willmoore Kendall. Halperin, following the line of the *Daily Worker*, had been quite effective at spreading fake news, including reports which denounced and slandered Trotskyists (which surely annoyed Willmoore). In 1953 he fled the United States to avoid prosecution, and the KGB later helped him move to the USSR. Willard Z. Park, who worked for the CIAA and once led the Anthropology Department at the University of Oklahoma (and who had also been denounced the state's Little Dies Committee), turned out to be a Soviet spy too. Kendall's intelligence career, then, was built over the professional corpse of Soviet spy (and fellow Oklahoman) Maurice Halperin. Halperin's disloyalty had been an open secret for years, but when information from the ultra-secret Venona Project confirmed his guilt, Kendall was on hand to deliver the bureaucratic coup de grâce. Perhaps Kendall's most important achievement in his new post was advocating to work with the Perón regime in Argentina, not overthrow it, as some American experts, including Halperin, wanted to do.[33]

Despite his intelligence work, Kendall kept a hand in the academic world by teaching a political theory class at the University of Minnesota. He did much of this work from a distance, but he also made periodic visits to the Minneapolis campus. He spent lots of time in the Fall of 1946 on preparing his classwork, noting that it was the one part of his 70-hour "work week which I truly enjoy." He strongly desired to return to academia in 1947 after a "year of money-making" in intelligence work. Had Kendall ended up at the University of Minnesota as planned, he would likely have joined the

"Minnesota Mafia," a group of anticommunist, Democratic Party liberals which over the years included several friends and former colleagues—Hubert Humphrey, Evron Kirkpatrick (and his new wife Jeane Kirkpatrick), Leon and Anne Crutcher, and Howard Penniman. With Evron Kirkpatrick in particular, Kendall had a close but competitive relationship. By January 1947, however, Kendall had started to have second thoughts about taking up his post in Minnesota. He was "getting quite a bang" out of his work with the CIG. With his office becoming "a pilot plant as regards the intelligence problem in general," he considered remaining in federal service.[34]

By the Spring of 1947 Kendall had made his conservative turn, and ever after viewed himself as a man of the right. Working closely with a strong group of liberal political scientists was not attractive to him, however anticommunist they might be. His work in exposing disloyalty within American intelligence circles contributed to this turn. Liberals who complained about loyalty oaths or suggested protecting the civil liberties of spies were, in his view, a big part of the problem. In an April 1947 letter to Charles Hyneman, Kendall suggested that the founding fathers, if necessary, would been have required "tests" to hold political office. He added that the American revolutionaries had exiled their own Loyalist opponents, "the then-equivalent of the modern Communists." Later that year, he told Francis Wilson, well known as a conservative, that he too was now "thinking along the same lines." Then he continued that: "We've had a common enemy (though of course not a common quarrel) for many years—the Liberals."[35]

Then something good turned up. Kendall discovered that Yale University was hiring, put in his application, and was offered a job. Strong letters of recommendation from intelligence colleagues and fellow political scientists helped Kendall secure the position. On March 24, 1947, Professor P. E. Corbett wrote to Kendall offering him a post as tenured associate professor of political science "in the fields of political theory and comparative government." Corbett noted that the department, "with rare unanimity," believed Kendall "would add greatly to the scope and quality of our work." The minimum salary for Yale associate professors was $5,000, but the university offered Kendall $6,000 (more than Minnesota paid but less than Kendall was making as an intelligence officer). As he prepared for Yale, Kendall told his sister that he was looking forward to the job as "the ideal solution to most of my problems." He expressed regret about leaving the organization which he had built at the CIG. His office was "jelling wonderfully" after a rough start and would now "be fun to run." In accepting the new job, Kendall expressed gratification that would be "able to teach a course at Yale on the intelligence problem." He left the CIG in "clear conscience" because he could "be instrumental in focusing the attention of a major university upon professional training for intelligence work."[36]

Kendall experienced a sense of vindication in getting the political science job at Yale. He beat out both Evron Kirkpatrick and Francis Wilson for the post. He told Hyneman how impressed his former professors at Illinois (including Wilson) were with his success. He mentioned his annoyance that Wilson, Clarence Berdahl, and their "little clique" had been keeping "the theory panels . . . sewed up in recent years" at the meetings of the American Political Science Association. Then he suggested that Wilson's own chances of getting a job at Yale were now slim. He was angry at Wilson and the other Illinois faculty for not having helped him secure a decent academic position.[37]

Kendall knew that he would have enemies in the political science department (which even in 1947 was no conservative bastion). "This guy [Cecil] Driver is full of venom," he told Hyneman, "as no man I have ever known," to whom Berdahl, his old nemesis at Illinois, was "positively Christ-like." Kendall decided, however, that Driver had little influence in the department and would not hamper his career. Kendall also believed he had strong allies in New Haven and thought he was well prepared for any departmental "infighting."[38] Kendall had emerged victorious from high-stakes battles in the American intelligence establishment. Perhaps he assumed that any struggles within a university political science department would be easily manageable. If so, he was dead wrong.

Meanwhile, Yale hired Kendall knowing about his quarrelsome reputation. Willmoore's faults were "an exaggeration of his virtues," Hyneman told Yale professor Francis Coker. Caring deeply about issues, Kendall "irritates people who would like to ignore or brush aside things that ultimately have to be faced up to." Receiving "friendly counsel on these matters" would turn him into "a tower of strength" for Yale's political science department. Hiring Kendall had an enormous upside for Yale, thought Hyneman. Quoting James Wilford Garner, he said: "That Man Kendall has read everything, and if you name a book he hasn't read, he will read it while you wait." Ultimately, Hyneman opined, Kendall would be one of "very few *American* political theorists . . . likely to make a very important contribution to political theory in the next two or three decades."[39] In hiring Kendall, then, Yale knew of his scholarly gifts but also understood that it was taking a risk. Apparently, the university believed it could tame Kendall's wildness. If so, the university was dead wrong.

NOTES

1. WK to FGW, [1942], B2, WP; James L. Godfrey, Review of *John Locke and the Doctrine of Majority Rule*, by WK, *Social Forces* 20, no. 3 (March 1942): 417; Steven D. Ealy and Gordon Lloyd, eds., "The Eric Voegelin-Willmoore Kendall

Correspondence" (hereafter "VK") *Political Science Reviewer* 33 (2004): 358–59; Eric Voegelin (hereafter EV) to WK, November 23, 1941 and December 5, 1941, B15F1, KP; EV to WK, March 15, 1948, in "VK," 367; CH, Guggenheim Fellowship Letter of Reference for WK, January 16, 1945, B7, CHP.

2. Robin W. Winks, *Cloak and Gown: Scholars in the Secret War, 1939–1961* (New York: Collins-Harvill, 1987); United States Air Force, Honorable Discharge, Lieutenant-Colonel Willmoore C. [*sic*] Kendall, March 28, 1962, B20, KP.

3. Godfried, "Fellow Traveler," 24; Kermit Roosevelt, Introduction to *War Report of the O.S.S.* (New York: Walker, 1976), ix; Smith, *OSS*, 42–46; WK to CH, February 11, 1942, CH, Job Reference Letter for WK, March 23, 1943 and CH to George Pettee, August 21, 1950, B7, CHP; RPO, *The Jewish Strategy* (Earlysville, VA: Strom, 2005), vi–vii; "Testimony of Professor Revilo Pendleton Oliver before the Warren Commission," September 9, 1964, RPO Online Papers.

4. Donald Rowland, *History of the Office of the Coordinator of Inter-American Affairs: Historical Reports on War Administration* (Washington, DC: GPO, 1947), 1–7, 59–60, 204; Smith, *OSS*, 16, 20; Thomas F. Troy, *Donovan and the CIA: A History of the Establishment of the Central Intelligence Agency* (Frederick, MD: University Publications of America, 1981), 120–21; Luis Eduardo Bosemberg, "The U.S., Nazi Germany, and the CIAA in Latin America during WW II," https://core.ac.uk/download/pdf/86445397.pdf.

5. Curriculum Vita of Willmoore Kendall, March 5, 1909—June 30, 1967," B13, KP; CH, Job Reference Letter for WK, March 23, 1943, CHP.

6. WK to FGW, [1942], B2, WP; WK to CB, October 4, 1942, B6F147, CCBP; WK to YM, April 1943 and October 21, 1942, B5F2, KP; KK to Tinkum Brooks, September 24, 1943 and WK to Cleanth Brooks, October 4, 1943, B6F147, CBP; Rowland, *History*, ch. V.

7. WK to FGW, [1942], B2, WP.

8. WK to YM, June 1942, KK to YM, September 12, 1942 and December 31, 1942, B5F2, 1942, KP; KK to Tinkum Brooks, September 24, 1943, B6F147, CBP.

9. WK to FGW, May 28, 1943, B2, WP; KK to Tinkum Brooks, September 24, 1943 and WK to CB, October 4, 1943, B6F147, CBP; WK to Nelson A. Rockefeller, October 5, 1943, COR-1226, Coordination Committee for Colombia Records, 1941–45, (hereafter CCR); Brandwein, "Katherine," 106.

10. WK to YM, April 1943, B5F2, KP; WK to FGW, May 28, 1943, B2, WP; KK to Tinkum Brooks, September 24, 1943 and WK to CB, October 4, 1943, B6F147, CBP; WK to Rockefeller, June 16, 1943, COR-859, June 22, 1943, COR-874, June 23, 1943, COR-878, July 5, 1943, COR-899, July 6, 1943, COR-904/905/906/907/909, August 10, 1943, COR-998/1000, August 23, 1943, COR-991, September 20, 1943, COR-1169/1170, September 21, 1943, COR-1174, and October 5, 1943, COR-1226, B1F2, CCR; WK to David Lindquist, August 17, 1943, R-70, WK to Manuel Salas, August 24, 1943, and WK, AirGram to Rockefeller and Francis Jamieson, September 20, 1943, CCR; Carlos Roberto de Souza, "Para la defensa de las Americas: The Pictorial Magazine *En Guardia* in Nelson A. Rockefeller's Propaganda Campaign for Latin America during World War II," 2011, pp. 1–3, 17–18, https://core.ac.uk/reader/86445257.

11. WK to NR, June 7, 1943, July 8, 1943, August 5, 1943, and September 22, 1943, COR-836/921/923/990/1180, WK to Clarence Jones, June 16, 1943, [WK?] to Manuel A. Blanco, October 5, 1943, WK to Henry Vicinus, July 5, 1943, WK to David Lindquist, July 16, 1943, and WK to Edwin Sours, October 4, 1943, B1F2, CCR.

12. WK to Rockefeller, June 7, 1943, COR-836, June 22, 1943, July 8, 1943, July 10, 1943, July 27, 1943, July 29, 1943, August 19, 1943, September 8, 1943, COR-870/871/919/942/970/972/1046/1126, WK Cable, August 10, 1943, B1F2, CCR.

13. WK to Rockefeller, July 12, 1943, August 6, 1943, September 22, 1943, and October 7, 1943, COR-911/994/1182/1237, WK, Memorandum to Forney A. Rankin, October 6, 1943, CCR; Bosemberg, 8.

14. WK to St. Clair Baumgartner, July 10, 1943, CCR, Cordell Hull, Circular, "US Urgent: For Coordination Committee From Rockefeller," July 19, 1943, WK, Press Division Cable, July 20, 1943, WK to Francis A. Jamieson, August 14, 1943, WK to Rockefeller, July 14, 1943, July 24, 1943, July 29, 1943, August 5, 1943, August 10, 1943, August 24, 1943, August 27, 1943, October 4, 1943, October 6, 1943, COR-946/964/979/988/1001/1060/1070/1089/

220/1222/1233, WK to Frank Plaza, July 13, 1943 and July 21, 1943, WK to Herschel Brickell, July 13, 1943, WK to Ralph Hilton, July 13, 1943, WK to Frank Bradley, Jr., August 4, 1943, WK to Arthur H. Dewey, August 20, WK to Plinio Neira, August 10, 1943, WK to Frank Bradley, August 19, 1943, CCR, WK to Antonio Alvarez Restrepo, August 20, 1943 WK to Edwin Sours, August 23, 1943, CCR.

15. WK to YM, October 21, 1942, April 1943, March 13, 1944, March 17, 1944 March 26, 1944, WK to YM, October 21, 1942 and KK to YM, September 12, 1942, B5F2.

16. WK Vita, B13, KP; *U.S. Government Manual, Summer 1944* (Washington, DC: Office of War Information, 1944), 177; *U.S. Government Manual, 1945*, 2nd ed. (Washington, DC: Government Information Service, 1945), 172; Army of the United States, Certificate of Service for Major Willmoore Kendall, May 1, 1946, B20F3, KP; WK to YM, March 17, 1944 and November 1, 1944, B5F2 and WK to YM, November 22, 1960, B6F2, KP; YM to George H. Nash, April 20, 1972, B21F13, KP; "Latin Airmen," *The Evening Courier*, May 21, 1945, p. 3; CH, Guggenheim Reference Letter for WK, January 16, 1945, B7, CHP.

17. WK to YM, November 17, 1944, B5F2, KP.

18. WK to YM, March 17, 1944, November 1, 1944 and November 17, 1944, B5F2, KP.

19. Juan and Maria Theresa Andrade to George H. Nash, January 8, 1974, B4F18, KKP.

20. WK to YM, March 13, 1944, November 1, 1944, and November 17, 1944, 1947, B5F2, KP; WK to CB, October 4, 1943 and KK to Tinkum Brooks, September 24, 1943 and April 24, 1946, B6F147, CBP.

21. KK to YM, January 5, 1945, B5F2, WK to YM, [Summer 1946], B5F2, KP; WK to YM, [1947], B5F3, KP; Peter Collier, *Political Woman: The Little Big Life of Jeane Kirkpatrick* (New York: Encounter, 2012), 55; Judis, *Buckley*, 61.

22. WK to YM, March 17, 1944, November 1, 1944, and November 17, 1944, B5F2, KP; Daniel Bell, *The End of Ideology: On the Exhaustion of Political Ideas in the Fifties* (New York: Collier, 1961), 300–01.

23. WK to YM, November 1, 1944, November 17, 1944, 1945, and KK to YM, November 15, 1944, B5F2, KP.

24. WK to YM, December 1944, WK to YM, [1945], WK to YM, December 1945, B5F2, KP.

25. "Regents Name Six," *Minneapolis Star*, July 12, 1946, p. 9; WK to YM, [Early 1946], B5F2, KP.

26. Michael Warner, "Salvage and Liquidation: Creation of the Central Intelligence Group," [1996], cia.gov.; Richard Park, Jr., "Memorandum for the President," March 12, 1945; https://www.futile.work/uploads/1/5/0/1/15012114/284321062-park-report-memorandum-for-the-record-colonel-park-s-comments-on-oss-declassified-top-secret-report-12-march-1945.pdf.

27. Troy, *Donovan*, 463; Jan Goldman, ed. *The Central Intelligence Agency: An Encyclopedia of Covert Ops, Intelligence Gathering, and Spies* (Santa Barbara: ABC-CLIO, 2016), I: 62; John Patrick Finnegan, *Military Intelligence* (Washington, DC: Center of Military History United States Army, 1998), 103–05.

28. Jack Davis, "The Kent-Kendall Debate of 1949," *Studies in Intelligence* 35, no. 2 (June 1992); 94; WK Vita, B13, KP; Kendall, "Willmoore," *US State Department Register*, December 1, 1946, (Washington, DC: Government Printing Office, 1947), 293; *Government Manual, Summer 1944*, 177; *Government Manual, 1945*, 172; Army of the United States, Certificate of Service for Major Willmoore Kendall, May 1, 1946, B20, KP; David Wise and Thomas P. Ross, *The Espionage Establishment* (New York: Random House, 1967), 62; Troy, *Donovan*, 464–65; David P. Hadley, *The Rising Clamor: The American Press, the Central Intelligence Agency, and the Cold War* (Lexington: University Press of Kentucky, 2019), 8. "Sooner Named," *Daily Oklahoman*, April 15, 1946, p. 21; WK to YM, [June 1946] and WK to YM, [Summer 1946], B5F2, KP.

29. WK to YM, [June 1946], B5F2, KP; Troy, *Donovan*, 359–61.

30. Central Intelligence Group, Memorandum for the Central Director of Collection and Dissemination, November 19, 1946, cia.gov; Troy, *Donovan*, 365; WK to YM, 1946, B5F2.

31. Collier, *Political Woman*, 33; Smith, *OSS*, 14.

32. Don S. Kirschner, *Cold War Exile: The Unclosed Case of Maurice Halperin* (Colombia: University of Missouri Press, 1995), 59–64; WK to Nathaniel Weyl, November 20, 1960, B7F7, Nathaniel Weyl Papers, Hoover Institution, Library and Archives; Landry Brewer, "Maurice Halperin: From Sooner Subversive to Soviet Spy," *Chronicles of Oklahoma* 96:2 (Summer 2018): 156–68; John Earl Haynes and Alexander Vassilev, *Spies: The Rise and Fall of the KGB in America* (New Haven: Yale University Press, 2010), 312.

33. Kirschner, *Halperin*, 88–92, 100–05, 112–13; John Earl Haynes and Harvey Klehr, *The Venona Project: Decoding Soviet Espionage in America*, new ed., (New Haven: Yale University Press, 2011), 10, 100–03, 106–07, 351; Haynes, *Spies*, 270, 312–14, 443–44; Harvey Klehr and John Earl Haynes, *The Early Cold War Spies:*

The Espionage Trials That Shaped American Politics (Cambridge, UK: Cambridge University Press, 2006), 81, 84; Brewer, "Halperin," 165–75.

34. WK to YM, November 11, 1946, B5F2, KP; William Anderson to CH, June 17, 1946, B7, CHP; Julius Paul to CH, April 1968, B16F9, KP; Collier, *Little Big*, 31–36; WK to CH, January 28, 1947, B7, CHP.

35. WK to CH, April 17, 1947, B7, CHP; WK to YM, 1952, B5F3, KP; WK to FGW, [1947], B2, WP.

36. P.E. Corbett to WK, March 26, 1947 and WK to P.E. Corbett, April 2, 1947, B39F14, KP; *U.S. Government Manual, 1945*, 172; WK to YMK, 1947, B5F2, KP.

37. WK to CH, May 16, 1947, B7, CHP.

38. WK to CH, April 17, 1947, B7, CHP.

39. CH, Guggenheim Reference Letter for WK, January 16, 1945 and CH to Francis Coker, April 7, 1947, B7, CHP.

Chapter 5

1947–1954
"It Sure Is a Hard World"

In the Spring of 1950 William F. Buckley, Jr., was a senior at Yale. Champion debater, chairman of the *Yale Daily News*, member of the elite Skull and Bones fraternity, and general big man on campus he was looking forward to graduation at the end of the semester. Then a "dark mood" descended on the university. The origin of this gloomy cloud was Senator Joseph McCarthy. In a recent appearance before a subcommittee of the Senate Foreign Relations Committee (the Tydings Committee) he called a liberal judge disloyal for belonging to several Communist front organizations which a government agency had declared subversive. Still smarting from the recent conviction of Alger Hiss—whom they had strongly but wrongly defended—the Yale faculty fumed at these accusations. "By intuition and experience alone," recalled Buckley, they *knew* such charges were bogus, with one comparing them to investigating the Loch Ness monster. If the word had been invented, Buckley declared, the faculty would have proclaimed that "'McCarthyism' had arrived."

That semester, however, Buckley was sitting in a political theory class "conducted by a man whose frustration" surpassed that of his downhearted colleagues. This professor "was shocked" by McCarthy's charges but also appalled by how "the Liberal Intelligentsia" had responded to them. He noted that McCarthy had begun to focus on "*loyalty risks*" rather than trying to ferret out actual members of the Communist Party. A wise change, the theorist thought. He then labeled the liberal response as unserious because few spies would openly join the party. Wishing the committee to "stop acting like a chastity belt for the State Department," Buckley's teacher hoped it would stop obsessing over "McCarthy's personality." The real issue was to find the "possible traitor" at work in government by ending lax enforcement of the loyalty regimen instituted by President Truman. The instructor predicted, however, that the committee, "with the hearty consent of the nation's press and intellectuals," would obscure this key issue—one central to American national security—by focusing on who did or did not belong to the Party. Although Buckley's recollection—written about 1955—did not specify the professor who held these views, the man, of course, was Willmoore Kendall.[1]

To a great extent, Kendall's name, if noticed at all by historians, is linked to that of his most famous student, who, within a year of graduation, had become a well-known spokesman for American conservatism. Quite a few scholars date the start of the late-twentieth-century American conservative resurgence to publication of Buckley's *God and Man at Yale* in 1951. Kendall had a profound effect on young man Buckley (and on his early books). The interplay of their ideas helped shape American politics, and, for that reason alone, Kendall's life and thought merit historical scrutiny. On the other hand, a would-be biographer ought not overstate Kendall's influence on Buckley. Nor should one subsume Kendall's teaching under the umbrella of conservatism as later delimited by Buckley and *National Review*. Their relationship was of great consequence for both men, but it was complex, intimate, and messy.

At Yale, Kendall's anticommunism never wavered. He arrived committed to an "absolute majoritarian" position in political theory. He believed, for example, that parliamentary supremacy in Britain left its people freer than Americans whose rights the courts supposedly protected. He defended his notions about majority rule from all comers, taught these ideas to his students, and propounded them in his writing. His political theory was entwined with Cold War politics, lying "under the shadow," he said, of the federal government's loyalty program and reflecting his own experiences in academia and government.[2] Despite changes in emphasis which reflected his new personal circumstances and changes in the global political situation, Kendall's postwar ideas demonstrated continuity with his prewar positions. Few would regard Kendall's academic output from this period as his best work. His later works on democracy were more nuanced and less harsh. Yet his scholarship from these years was meticulously constructed, coherent, and insightful. He also remained a successful, influential, and controversial teacher.

As he returned to academia after the war, Kendall remained focused on democracy and enamored with Rousseau. In 1945, for example, Hyneman declared Willmoore "devoted to the proposition that political power ought to vest finally with the people, and that political institutions and processes ought to effectuate ultimate control by the people." Kendall, he continued, was certain to continue in pursuit of this "fundamental proposal" in upcoming years. As always, Kendall integrated this scholarly concern about democratic governance into his teaching. He believed, for example, that he could use his "theory lectures" to produce future articles on Thoreau, Locke, and Milton.

He was optimistic about his teaching and scholarship as he transitioned into university life. "I've brought a better point of view than my prewar one away from Washington," he said, "and a mind a little less dulled than I had feared."³

On June 16, 1947, Kendall was appointed a resident fellow of Pierson College at Yale. For three years he lived in close contact with Yale undergraduates, then all male. His first order of business was to prepare himself for the classroom. At Yale, Kendall confided to friends, he "never faced my seminar in theory with less than thirty hours' preparation." New classes meant considerable work in familiarizing himself with key works. His reading assignments provided him "a valuable education," Kendall added, because in his classes he covered "things I greatly wish to know well." He discovered that undergraduates at New Haven were, "because of their abilities, their inherited position, and their prestige as Yale men, . . . a real challenge." Many students, he found, possessed "a proprietary view of the instructor." A teacher can show them that "they don't own you," but that means "you kiss your effectiveness goodbye."⁴

Kendall had requested to teach a course in local government. He wanted to teach political theory too but knew that Yale already had a theorist with Cecil Driver. Robert Dahl, who taught local government, was ready to cede responsibility for it to Kendall. Explaining his interest in this class to P. E. Corbett, Kendall said "his thoughts and interests in politics has carried me more and more in recent years to the local government level as the best remaining bet for the rehabilitation of the democratic process." Willmoore assigned Herman Finer's work on local government in Britain as a key text for this course. Thus, Kendall showed that, even after his conservative turn, he had not become an advocate of free-market economics. Finer was the author of *Road to Reaction* (1945), a major refutation of F. A. Hayek's *Road to Serfdom*, the free-market bible. Kendall had been entranced for years with Finer's scholarship, which expounded upon social democratic ideas—linked to the British Labour Party—by which the people, using democratic processes, controlled the economy. Kendall retained this perspective on economics to the end. He "held," said one later colleague, "that if capitalism worked in a society, O.K., but if it didn't work in a society, he had no objections whatsoever to a planned economy." In future Kendall often had to disguise these economic views from laissez-faire-loving allies.⁵

In the classroom Willmoore challenged and puzzled his students. As early as his Oxford days, Kendall had learned that "good Oklahoma idiom" appeared exotic to those unused to it. He therefore deployed down-home turns of phrase to gain the attention of listeners. Kendall seldom lectured but continued using the Socratic techniques he had pioneered at LSU. He disliked flashy lecturing. Driver's classroom, he said, was a "circus with all the trappings (including the crowd) except the big top and the peanuts."

Kendall soon won a reputation at Yale as a "wow" in the classroom. Even his critics admitted that his classes aroused "thought." Kendall sometimes let students vote about what "subjects of inquiry" to pursue, and his students could always expect "a heavy budget of reading." Weekly assignments might include Thoreau, Calhoun, and Ortega y Gasset. Using notions picked up from Collingwood, Kendall and students "interrogated" these authors. They tried to clarify and understand their meaning by putting them "in the witness box." Kendall's students, to the discomfort of some, became aware of "his own political theory" as they worked with their instructor to free themselves from "notions currently a la mode." Kendall loved to entertain "heated and varied" objections from students. His classes were therefore among "the most stimulating" at Yale.[6]

Kendall sometimes pursued "tangents" in his classes. These forays were often "quite stimulating," revealed his personal views, and inspired some students to think along similar lines. Buckley, for instance, once asked Kendall's thoughts on a review "in this morning's *Times*" of Basil Rauch's *From Munich to Pearl Harbor*. The reviewer claimed the book "once and for all discredited Charles Beard." Simple, said Kendall: "the greatest American historian of our time has challenged the greatest American politician of our time. There's no doubt about who's going to win." Buckley then wrote a paper reflecting and expanding upon Kendall's ideas by the device of grading the American professoriate. If the people were to grade professors, they should give them "a resounding flunk." Academics, argued the paper, had built an "iron curtain" to defend FDR's foreign policy. By challenging this consensus, Beard had provoked "the concentrated wrath of the Ph.D. apologists for the New Deal." Naming names—Arthur Schlesinger, Jr., Allan Nevins, Lewis Mumford—the paper suggested that the "ruling cadre of historians and publicists in the U.S.—can always be counted on to step in and save Franklin Roosevelt from detached historical scrutiny." Sensitive documents were available "only to hired hands" supporting "the Court Interpretation of history." Bowing to "prevailing political historical orthodoxy," Buckley concluded, the reigning "academicians" have either "lost their perspicacity" or "their appetite for truth and integrity." Kendall also exercised influence at New Haven outside these stimulating classes. He socialized uproariously with his students (who called him Ken), seeking friends and acolytes and impressing many with his larger-than-life personality.[7]

As always, then, Willmoore excelled as a teacher at Yale. Outside class, in the Spring of 1948, he began to blow through Yale like an F5 tornado, complete with figuratively flying debris. In February Kendall spoke positively about his situation but with some misgivings. "Yale distrusts strong opinions," he said. He thought his colleagues focused too little on theory and that the curriculum leaned too much "towards heterodoxy." By working with colleagues Robert Dahl, Howard Penniman, and Henry Wells, he hoped to make Yale "the standout department of the country." When this "caucus" tried to get the department to hire Eric Voegelin and Herman Finer, all hell broke loose. Cecil Driver and Arnold Wolfers opposed both appointments. Kendall's group responded with a letter of no confidence in the full professors. In the end, the full professors squashed the revolt at a decisive meeting. After "hard words" Corbett said the senior faculty would impose their own choices, whatever the assistant and associate professors might think. Rejecting Voegelin and Finer, they brought in V. O. Key from Johns Hopkins for an endowed chair. Kendall had led the opposition, but Wells and Penniman also considered resignation rather than submit to this power play. Dahl remained silent. "I predict," said Willmoore, "an early rise to a full professorship for him." Quizzed by Corbett, Kendall sarcastically acknowledged some advantages to bringing in Key. Hiring him would help build "a good department" at Johns Hopkins, he said, and give Yale "what it deserved." In an understatement, Kendall admitted that "things were a little tense by the end of the evening." Having suffered a comprehensive defeat in this "fiasco," Kendall later dated his pariah status at Yale to Spring 1948 when the departmental "colonels" crushed the younger faculty's attempt "to carry through a revolution." Exhausted, Kendall told Hyneman: "From now on I teach my classes and don't get close enough to my senior colleagues to see the whites of their eyes." Then he confessed that: "It sure is a hard world."[8]

This academic brawl had occurred outside the public eye, but Kendall soon got into an awkward public confrontation. On April 18, 1948, Kendall stated over radio station WAVZ that supporters of Henry Wallace's campaign for president "had in effect transferred their loyalty to the Soviet Union." After the broadcast and "in the presence of others," he suggested to Nathaniel S. Colley, an African American law student who had provided a pro-Wallace perspective, that the accusation "had specific reference to and included him." Threatened with a lawsuit and lacking funds to defend himself, Kendall apologized to Colley and publicly retracted his statement on May 14. He admitted having no actual knowledge that "a majority of Mr. Wallace's followers" were loyal to the USSR and "no reason to believe that Mr. Colley is other than fully loyal exclusively to the United States of America." Kendall's friends in the department—Wells, Penniman, and Dahl—came to his defense. They suggested that if Kendall's words were libelous, then "the freedom of everyone of us to speak without fear of reprisal on the radio and in the classroom has been placed in jeopardy." Buckley, Kendall's debate partner for the broadcast, defended the Yale professor more strongly. He said no one listening believed Kendall thought all Wallace supporters were communists. Buckley condemned their adversaries in the debate for using "legal chicanery" to force the apology. Unlike Kendall, Buckley had plenty of money to defend a potential lawsuit. So he double-downed, affirming in print that Kendall's "fundamental assertions" about the Wallace camp were true. As part of that camp, he added, Colley was "furthering the ends of the Soviet Union."[9]

Over the next couple of years Kendall returned this favor by supporting Buckley in various campus controversies. In the fall of 1949, for example, the FBI visited New Haven in response to charges that Yale professors were living in fear because of FBI spies on campus. The most important case involved Robert S. Cohen whose employment in the philosophy department in 1948 was held up when a campus informant told university authorities that Cohen had strong links to the American Communist Party. Yale had a policy of hiring no communists. When Cohen denied being a communist and gathered testimonials, Yale hired him. To clarify the situation, the *Daily News*, chaired by Buckley, invited the FBI to a campus symposium to discuss its actions at Yale. Law professors Fred Rodell and Fowler Harper were recruited to criticize the FBI with the conservative response to be led by Kendall and Cleanth Brooks. Buckley moderated while two students, one liberal and one conservative, also participated. In the end, Kendall stood as the bureau's lone faculty defender when Brooks failed to show. On Monday, October 24, 1949, an overflow audience filled Sterling Law Auditorium for the debate. The FBI men did most of the talking, denying there were agents on campus and refusing to apologize for anything the bureau had done. Afterward, Cohen asserted that the FBI and Yale had violated his due process rights. Kendall replied that Cohen was incorrectly asserting a criminal trial standard of innocent until proven guilty while the correct standard for hiring an employee was "unacceptable until proved acceptable." American voters had charged the FBI with finding the nation's Soviet-sympathizing "internal enemies," whereas FBI critics were self-appointed busybodies. Cohen left Yale the next year, later making his way to Boston University where he enjoyed a long career as an avowed Marxist.[10]

About the same time, on October 17, 1949, a *Yale Daily News* editorial, presumably penned by Buckley, praised a federal court verdict in New York. Twelve American Communist Party leaders had received prison terms for violating the Smith Act (which made advocating the violent overthrow of the United States government felonious). Law School professors Thomas Emerson and Fowler Harper condemned the verdict. Harper suggested that freedom of speech included the right to such advocacy if not a "clear and present" danger to the government. The *News* objected to this view, arguing that Congress could pass any law unless it was clearly unconstitutional. The best comment, opined the *News*, came from Kendall. He said: "Yes, things have come to a hell of a pass when you can't conspire against your own country and get away with it." In March 1950, as appeals continued, Kendall again took on Harper in the university paper. It was not possible "to resume the good old American way of life," he told Harper. One could no longer assume that "your next door neighbor, or the man in the next desk in your Washington agency, was not engaged in espionage for a potential enemy power." Kendall defended prosecuting Communists "for their beliefs." Certainly, by limiting what they might say, such persons sacrificed some freedom. Indeed, that was the point of the Smith Act. Harper responded that Kendall's principles would "make the Bill of Rights obsolete."[11] Here Harper misconstrued his opponent's point. Kendall did not think the Bill of Rights obsolete but that it should never have been adopted in the first place.

For Kendall, the sovereign right of the American people to protect itself from all enemies took precedence over individual liberties. In April 1950 Kendall was one of two members of the Yale political science department to support the "Mundt Bill," which called for deporting communists from the United States. He took this position not because communists were a "clear and present" danger to the country but because, he said, they were "incapable of participating in democratic government." Kendall's views were widely known on campus, both by enemies and allies. That May one critic wrote to the *Daily News* to call Kendall "naïve" for supporting absolute majoritarianism. He said this view disregarded morality and ignored the possibility that majorities might mistreat minorities. Rushing to Kendall's defense was F. Reid Buckley, Bill's younger brother. Kendall was neither too authoritarian nor too democratic, he said. Rather, the political theorist sought to build "Rousseau's homogeneous society." The majority would set limits on toleration and—within these limits—provide "ample room for minority agitation." For society to be "harmonious," he added, its members needed "common principles and ends."[12]

Another Kendall student and ally was L. Brent Bozell, Jr., who was Bill Buckley's debate partner and would soon marry his sister Patricia. An accomplished debater and public speaker, he joined Buckley and Kendall in the struggle against campus Marxists. In January 1948, for instance, Bozell got crossways with Pasquale J. Vecchione, student leader of Yale's Progressive Citizens of America (PCA). At a meeting of this organization, Bozell grew angry when Vecchione refused to let him ask questions. He then proposed to debate whether the PCA was "dominated by communists." After considerable back and forth, the two men held a dramatic public debate on February 25. Vecchione talked only about PCA support for Henry Wallace's presidential platform. Bozell was annoyed that his opponent would not discuss communist influence in the PCA. He charged that the organization consistently followed the Stalinist line and urged liberals to shun Wallace to avoid throwing the election to the Republicans. A couple of months later, thirty Wallace supporters led by Vecchione held a "Save the Peace" rally to denounce the

Truman Doctrine. Several hundred Yale students pelted them with eggs and drove them off campus.[13] The Kendall-Colley radio face-off happened the next day.

In October 1948 Bozell, who had previously described himself as a liberal, joined the Conservative Party of the Yale Political Union. Later he served as president of the Union. In Bozell's debates and speeches, one could often see Kendallian themes. In January 1950, for example, he delivered a speech against bipartisanship in foreign policy about a month before Kendall's own article against bipartisan foreign policy appeared in print. In May 1949 Bozell and Buckley, taking the affirmative, lost a debate to Princeton, with Bozell arguing, a la Kendall, that the Communist Party of the USA "takes its orders from the Kremlin." In Yale law school, which he entered in 1950, Bozell continued to give Kendall-tinged speeches favoring censorship and suggesting the perils of federal civil rights legislation getting ahead of public opinion in the South.[14]

These public disputes cemented the Buckley-Bozell-Kendall bond but weakened Willmoore with the faculty. Various colleagues at Yale, led by Driver, came to hate Kendall as a "Fascist" and "War-monger." In 1950 department members informed Kendall that he was not welcome in their midst. V. O. Key told him in July that he would never receive promotion and that he could either resign or serve permanently as an associate professor. This determination, said Key, stemmed from a desire for "peace" in the department. Kendall also feared that his popularity at Yale as a teacher was waning. Enrollment in his classes was dropping perhaps because of his notoriety. Students did not think him dull, he claimed, but they "just don't like what I have to say." For the coming year, he therefore planned to teach intensively for three days a week, "claim the other four days for me & let Key and Driver go to hell at sunset." By mid-1950 Willmoore regarded his situation as increasingly unpleasant. He began to look for other opportunities, eventually deciding to reenter intelligence work.[15]

During these years Kendall—before Senator Joseph McCarthy came into national prominence—forcefully articulated devotion to majority rule in his scholarship. This vision included the people's right to exclude communists and to restrict free speech. In 1949 he set up a panel at the American Political Science Association to reexamine commonly held notions of free speech. He recognized that most Americans thought free speech meant the right "to think and say and write what they bloody well please." They also believed "no standard of orthodoxy" existed to judge which ideas were "beyond the pale" and that only when "a clear and present danger" arose should society repress expression. Kendall told Eric Voegelin that he was "no great admirer of the kind of thinking that has gone into all of that." He wanted to examine the theoretical underpinnings of these commonly accepted ideas. One proposed speaker was Lawrence Dennis, who had spoken in Kendall's classes at Yale. In 1944 Dennis, denounced as a fascist, had been charged under the Smith Act with sedition based on his writings. When he, together with thirty-two codefendants, was released after a mistrial, liberals reacted with dismay. Himself ready to prosecute fascists under the Smith Act, Kendall saw liberals as inconsistent for unwillingness to apply the same law to left-wing radicals.[16]

Then in 1950 Kendall published an article in the *Journal of Politics*. Here he used the scalpel of close reading to vivisect an antimajoritarian work by Minnesota political scientist Herbert McClosky. McClosky, said Kendall, favored "limits" on majorities but did not specify whether such limits were voluntary or embodied in "constitutional checks" on majority will. In suggesting that majoritarians had to agree to any vote in favor of dictatorship, McClosky was playing a cheap parlor trick. Sure, a democracy could "*commit suicide*." Once it reinvented itself as dictatorship, it was no longer a democracy and could not serve as an example of majority rule. Kendall argued that McClosky confused the question of what was good for society with the distinct question of who should specify and maintain that good. Perhaps individual rights were a positive thing, but the question remained of who would decide their nature, extent, and application. For a democrat the answer could only be the majority, which, Kendall argued, ought to judge all political questions. McClosky's prescriptions meant that the community must always accept the "traditional interpretation" of "political rights." This position left the nation "impotent vis-à-vis its internal enemies," forcing it to tolerate those "openly waging war" against it. For Kendall, the community itself, through majority rule, should decide the limits of its "claim to obedience," what liberties to permit and which to restrict.[17]

Kendall's absolute majoritarianism hampered his academic career. It also hurt him with the CIA. Kendall's article "The Function of Intelligence" appeared in the journal *World Politics* in 1949. It contained majoritarian elements which offended powerful people in the intelligence community. In it he reviewed *Strategic Intelligence*, a book by Sherman Kent, a Yale historian who was an important player in the CIA. The article contained an admixture of Kendall's ideas on intelligence work, political theory, and teaching. In intelligence circles, this article has remained a landmark. Kendall thought intelligence officers—contra Kent—should not merely gather information but ought to interpret complex political realities to shape and clarify the views of decision-makers. The article tapped into Kendall's larger, theoretical concerns about politics. He disparaged covert operations as less effective and more expensive than open-source intelligence and also as undemocratic. The "big job" for operatives was to integrate world events into a coherent pattern for "elected officials." They should not serve as "research assistants" to bureaucratic "policy planners." Fulfilling this function, he thought, would let the United States shape its global "destiny." Sadly, said Kendall, Kent's book took the "crassly empirical" approach of historians. Theoretically naïve, this method was detrimental to intelligence work. Any improvement in the intelligence enterprise achieved by following Kent's suggestions, Kendall concluded, would "be very small."[18]

The review outraged Kent. Circa 1947, Kent had considered Willmoore a model intelligence officer. He was, Kendall admitted, "in large part responsible for my appointment at Yale." By 1951 Kent, as he was growing more powerful in the CIA, had become Kendall's inveterate foe. His views about the role of intelligence officers would prevail, Kendall's ideas surviving as an intriguing example of a road not taken. Moreover, Yale political scientist Arnold Wolfers, perhaps Kent's closest friend, was Kendall's enemy, both because of departmental struggles and because of Willmoore's public views "on loyalty programs." Years earlier Kendall noted that he had caught "the intelligence bug," and by 1950 he longed to lead the newly established Office of National Estimates—charged with medium-term and long-term planning at the CIA. Its initial head, William Langer, was a friend, but Kent stood second in command. Replacing Langer as its chief in January 1952, Kent provided a powerful roadblock to any plans Kendall had for a position of influence in the CIA.[19]

Kendall's scholarship was calculated to annoy powerful figures in the foreign policy establishment. In 1949, for example, Yale University Press published *A Communist Party in Action*, written by former communist Angelo Tasca—as edited, abridged, and translated by Kendall. Kendall called its introduction "an attack" on George Kennan, whose policy of containment was becoming the cornerstone of American Cold War policy. He argued that people became communists because their own nations failed "to infuse *meaning* into their members' lives." He thought creating powerful counter-narratives more important than using money to prop up Western Europe (as with the Marshall Plan). Tasca's tale bore witness to communism's ideological appeal and ruthlessness. To counter it Americans must not be squeamish about political "surgery" to remove this social "cancer" from their own body politic. In 1950 Kendall followed up with an article attacking "bipartisan" foreign policy. This increasingly popular idea, including Walter Lippmann's 1948 statement that partisanship should "stop at the water's edge," said Kendall, reinforced "the most undemocratic features of our political system." To illustrate, he cited Senator Arthur Vandenberg of Michigan, a powerful Republican voice for bipartisanship who suggested questioning Truman on the Berlin Crisis was "treason." Kendall claimed this elitist vision championed by experts was alien to American tradition. Instead, there should be democratic debates on "real issues." Such dialogue would channel "into American foreign policy the native good sense of the American electorate."[20]

Kendall had kept his hand in intelligence when he went to Yale. In the Fall Semester of 1947, for instance, he worked a day and a half each week for the CIA. In those early days, he told Hyneman, it would have been "pleasanter" to have "settle[d] down for the long pull at the CIA." By 1950, however, Kendall had made powerful enemies both at CIA and in the State Department. When searching for a way out of Yale, he therefore looked toward military intelligence. In the summer of 1950 he applied to work for the U.S. Army-led Operations Research Office (ORO) doing "research in psychological warfare." In August 1950 George Pettee—in charge of hiring at ORO—wrote Cleanth Brooks and Charles Hyneman, whom Willmoore had supplied as references. Pettee said he was looking for someone versed in psychology, ideology, and communications, "a man of high competence on at least one side of the problem and with real ability as generalist." The position required someone with "mental energy and imagination" possessing the analytical ability to "solve a problem that does not fit any regular compartment." The capacity "to conduct executive business," Pettee added, was "also important."[21]

Brooks and Hyneman responded with gushing letters of praise. Kendall, said Brooks, "would fit better than anyone I know the qualifications you outline in your letter" to head up a project in psychological warfare. Kendall loved to argue, Brooks told Pettee, but he was "one of the most brilliant minds I have ever known, admirably trained, and filled with a real passion for ideas." Kendall was "tremendously skilled in dialectic" and his "convictions are real and deep." Kendall was "one of the shrewdest masters of a text that I know of, alive to every gradation of connotation and implication." Hyneman focused on Willmoore's "devotion to ideals of democratic government." Hyneman could imagine few people "better equipped than Kendall" for the proposed position. If "running" the USA, Hyneman added, he would place "Kendall in Moscow right now . . . watching what Soviet leaders are doing and countering their influences."[22]

Kendall got the job, received a leave of absence from Yale, and took up a new post as chairman of Project POWOW. Its mission was to discover how best to wage psychological warfare (psywar). At ORO—based in Washington, DC, before relocating to Baltimore—Kendall soon had squabbles with his new boss "about what Project POWOW ought to do, and how it ought to do it." Kendall's relationship with Pettee grew strained but never quite hostile, as the men had similar views about the proper role of analysts. The project's mission was global. It centered on the USSR, including studies of Soviet radio broadcasts and historical analysis of Nazi propaganda in Eastern Europe. In the fall of 1950, however, not long after Kendall arrived at ORO, Pettee sent him to Korea (where war had broken out in June). Kendall initially served a three-month stint. With his staff, he put the principles of psywar into practice and analyzed their effectiveness. By November he was working near the front lines with American forces at Pusan and Seoul. He was present during the brief occupation of Pyongyang. After spending three days in the enemy capital, he evacuated to Tokyo, experiencing his "first air raid," but coming out *"sain et sauf."*[23]

For the rest of the war Kendall shuttled back and forth between East Asia and the United States. As POWOW chair he saw Korea as "a laboratory of operational experience in which every opportunity should be seized for operations research in psywar." With associates, many of whom he worked to recruit from American universities, he crafted sophisticated propaganda. Much of it was contained in leaflets dropped by air behind enemy lines. These pamphlets, produced by the billion to distribute to enemy citizens and soldiers, appealed to communal themes of solidarity and to individual desires for safety and prosperity. To be effective, the flyers had to be believable, had to address real concerns of enemy soldiers, and had to suggest a safe way to switch sides. One leaflet, for example, suggested that Kim Il Sung was an imposter put in place by the Soviets after the real Kim died in Siberia. This story was plausible enough to be believed by Koreans decades later. Propaganda which worked for Koreans, however, differed from what was effective with Chinese soldiers, so two sets of leaflets were necessary. These leaflet bombs had considerable success, convincing a hundred thousand enemy soldiers to surrender. Propaganda broadcasts via loudspeaker proved less effective. Meanwhile, Kendall helped pioneer new interrogation methods in Korea. Most important was the use of polygraph tests. Kendall prepared questions for captured enemy soldiers and helped analyze the effectiveness of the tests. Project POWOW also studied "fear reactions" evoked by certain weapons. One study noted that napalm inflicted psychological damage far beyond its physical destructiveness. Kendall had high regard for General Douglas MacArthur. Intelligence chief General Charles A. Willoughby, whose daily briefings he attended in Tokyo, was another matter. Willoughby had utterly failed to predict Chinese intervention. Poorly versed in political theory, said Kendall, he never learned to apply military intelligence to political problems.[24]

Working with the ORO Kendall attempted to improve this relatively amateurish work. In April 1952 he apparently helped establish Japan's own Research Office, modeled on the ORO and later regarded as the Japanese version of the CIA. Kendall, then, was an effective theorist and practitioner of psywar. He considered taking up an "attractive" post in Japan, but for the most part he did not like serving in Asia which he saw as a backwater. As an intelligence officer Kendall always had the great global game in mind. In the early 1950s he believed "hot war" with the Soviet Union was imminent and that when it came psywar would play a key role. Kendall thought the United States, because of its rapid demobilization after World War II, might lose that war. He claimed at times to favor temporary "appeasement" until the country rebuilt its military strength. Less than "fifty people in Washington," he told Hyneman, appreciated the magnitude of the Soviet threat. As part of this big picture, Kendall prioritized the need for effective propaganda in Russian and began to study the language. As Project POWOW chairman, he sought to avoid Kent's "crassly empirical" approach by focusing on the "theory and nature" of psywar. In this effort, he drew on the skills of his academic friends. He recruited Cleanth Brooks and Robert Penn Warren from Yale, for example, to produce and evaluate propaganda leaflets. He hired former Hobart and Yale student John Ponturo as a member of his staff. And he recruited Charles Hyneman to work as a consultant on military government.[25]

In March 1951, now enmeshed in the psywar world, Kendall requested Yale to extend his leave of absence for a year. Provost Edgar S. Furniss granted his approval "quite willingly." Furniss told Willmoore that he had "encountered people who commented most emphatically upon the importance of the services you are now rendering the Government in this national Emergency." A year later Kendall wrote to James W. Fesler, the new chair of the political science department, sounding him out on another extension. Fesler quickly agreed to Kendall's request, granting him a leave absence for the 1952–1953 academic year, which Yale ultimately extended for yet another year.[26] Kendall later joked that he was offended that Yale gave him leaves of absence so willingly. But for a time this arrangement satisfied him and the university. It also allowed Willmoore to deploy his considerable talents in service to his country.

During his time at ORO, Kendall and his unit translated, composed, and edited numerous (mostly classified) studies regarding psychological warfare and the Cold War. Project POWOW had lots of ventures going on. They ranged from analysis of Soviet "printed media" to clarifying the psywar needs of American combat divisions. The organization produced some sixty publications in Kendall's years there ranging from ten to hundreds of pages. He worked on many team-written publications, only sometimes receiving credit as author or editor. One such task, he noted, meant taking "1800 pages of completed research, done by a sub-project at Yale," then revising it "down to 550 pp. or such matter, and fancied and sharpened-up in the process." Kendall, said George Pettee, carried out "the central fundamentals" of POWOW with great "intensity and depth," guiding and structuring a "very high quality program."[27]

Two larger works from these years stand out. First was *China: An Area Manual*, in three volumes, which appeared in 1953. Its lead editor was David Rowe, a Yale political scientist friendly to Kendall, with Willmoore listed as coeditor. Others wrote most of the narrative, consisting of geographical and historical background. But Kendall's fingerprints, including characteristic turns of phrase, appeared in key parts of the book. Most importantly, the *Area Manual* strongly reflected Kendall's radical anticommunism. The book concluded, in bland bureaucratic language, that communism had triumphed in China because of U.S. policy blunders. In the late 1940s the United States had promoted a coalition government, negotiated with Mao Zedong, and embargoed arms to Chiang Kai-shek at a crucial time. The Communists kept talking while preparing for military victory. Thus, the book inferred that President Truman had stupidly sacrificed the world's most populous country to communism. The other big book was *The Nature of Psychological Warfare* (1954), authored by Wilbur Schramm (with Kendall and two other assistant authors). This book laid out the theory and practice of psywar. Much of it focused on psywar as communication—Schramm's specialty—with Kendall editing Schramm's prose. The introduction, however, reflected Kendall's cherished theme of scientific skepticism. It claimed that psywar was not a science but an art which used scientific findings.[28]

As he returned from his first assignment in Korea at the end of 1950, Willmoore took steps to complete his divorce from Katherine. Their final breakup occurred partly because both were following high-powered careers in different parts of the world, making it difficult to live together. Another dividing point was political, for Katy remained a staunch leftist. The divorce, finalized in Oklahoma in early 1951, was relatively cordial. The ex-spouses remained on speaking terms, though with some lingering bitterness. Katy and Ken did not reside together after 1947, but they continued to share weekends and holidays until January 1950, when their separation became definitive. Until then Willmoore sometimes traveled to Katherine's apartment in Jamaica, New York, to escape Yale's hothouse. Meanwhile he found a new love interest in graduate student Anne Brunsdale, who had worked for him at the CIA.[29]

Anne had given Kendall considerable help in translating the Tasca book from French. By early 1951 she was traveling with Willmoore as his companion. She came from a more privileged place than did the earthy Katherine, with tastes running to expensive jewelry and fancy clothes. High spirited and strongly opinionated, her relationship with Willmoore, almost from the beginning, was tempestuous. Kendall confessed to his sister that Anne was not his ideal woman, who would be wealthy, good-looking, "*not* a career woman and not an intellectual." Anne was both a career woman and an intellectual, but on June 7, 1952 she and Willmoore got married anyway. The wedding took place in Minneapolis. Kendall's groomsman was Revilo Oliver with Bill Buckley serving as an usher. Kendall's mother and sister attended, as did Norman Brunsdale, the Republican governor of North Dakota, who was Anne's uncle. As Anne worked for the CIA, like several other Kendall students, she was authorized to view classified information. She sometimes helped Ken with his "rockpile," that is, his efforts to recast poorly conceived, turgidly written ORO drafts into "consistently good" prose.[30]

Intelligence work paid Kendall considerably more than he made at Yale, especially as he continued to receive regular raises at ORO. By 1954 his annual pay had increased to $13,000, roughly twice his salary at Yale. By 1952, however, he was coming to see his professional situation as "hopeless" at ORO. He believed the organization was using his "energies" but not his "abilities." He now "had so many enemies who occupy strategic positions in the activities I am most interested in that I just can't hope to beat the game, no matter how I slice it." Through his unpopular "intellectual and political positions" and from "expressing too freely my opinions about incompetence, dishonesty, and laziness in high places," Kendall knew he had developed a reputation as a "trouble-maker." In 1953, when Kendall was turned down for a post he desired in the State Department, he believed the reason was his "support of Senator McCarthy." Having his position at Yale to fall back on did give Willmoore more "freedom of speech" than his fellow bureaucrats enjoyed. But he knew pushing forward with the unpopular themes of his scholarship would create "more enemies in strategic places, and more friends in unstrategic ones."[31]

In the fall of 1953 Kendall took the "worst licking of my entire career" and was removed as chairman of Project POWOW. He became "what we euphemistically call a senior analyst." He described this move as a "rebellion against me by rank and file members of the project angry, in large part, about things outside my control." When George Pettee "removed" him as POWOW chairman and replaced him with the revolt's "ringleader," Kendall considered the decision unjust. He also understood that he was powerless to change the decision. Kendall admitted that he preferred the more "congenial" role of analyst and that his removal from management was something of a blessing, especially as he received no reduction in salary. When in a leadership position, at ORO and elsewhere, Kendall was a demanding boss. He was not a good listener and often unsympathetic to the viewpoints and needs of subordinates. As an analyst, however, his talents were undeniable. In time, Kendall decided to leave the ORO, even with a major reduction in salary, because staying involved "a psychic cost beyond bearing."[32]

He explored many possibilities for post-ORO employment. In 1952 he had declared to Charles Hyneman that he was "not going back to Yale," but in the end he decided to return to New Haven for the Fall Semester of 1954. There had been changes since he left. When Key went to Harvard, James W. Fesler became the new department chair. In late October 1951 Fesler wrote to Kendall to assure him that he valued his contributions to the university and hoped the department could "start off afresh." He went on to suggest that Willmoore had "a quite individual approach verging on a Kendallian school" and that Yale students needed exposure to many political theory approaches. Kendall replied positively but denied creating his own school of political theory. He admitted that he was not a liberal, that his teaching stressed theory, and that his approach was more "critical" than "historical." As all good teachers do, he influenced his students. He did not, he informed Fesler, have the "hypnotic and/or chauvinistic" powers over students attributed to him at Yale.[33]

Meanwhile, larger events were afoot. On October 15, 1951, Henry Regnery and Company released William F. Buckley, Jr.'s *God and Man at Yale: The Superstitions of "Academic Freedom."* The university had seen "Bill's book" coming. Faced with a multipronged indictment of the university's liberal proclivities, Yale launched a well-coordinated anti-Buckley publicity campaign. The *Yale Daily News*, for example, printed a caustic student editorial and two thoroughly prepared faculty refutations on the very day the book appeared in print. Two more faculty rebuttals and a lengthy attack by a Yale undergraduate appeared in the next day's edition. Denunciations in *The Atlantic*, *The New York Times Book Review*, and other prestigious publications soon followed. These tactics backfired, with the obviously orchestrated crescendo turning *God and Man at Yale* into a best seller. The book vaulted Buckley into a spot in the national limelight and helped kickstart conservatism to challenge the postwar neo-New Deal consensus. *God and Man at Yale* thus earned its status as an historical landmark: "ALL-TIME 100 Nonfiction Books," and so forth.[34]

Focusing on undergraduate instruction, Buckley's book argued that the Yale faculty had abandoned Christian orthodoxy for agnosticism and free-market economics for collectivism. The faculty thus undermined the values Yale freshman brought to campus and denied the ideals of most Yale alumni. Yale's administration protected these views by misapplying principles of academic freedom. Though not mentioned by name in the iconic volume, Kendall's presence looms large in the background. Buckley never disguised getting help from his former politics professor. He later explicitly acknowledged that Kendall carefully "went over" the prepublication manuscript. He also noted that the book's most "provocative" sentence came verbatim from a suggestion made in Willmoore's signature green ink. "*I believe*," read the statement from the original preface, "*that the duel between Christianity and atheism is the most important in the world. I further believe that the struggle between individualism and collectivism is the same struggle reproduced on another level.*"[35]

By focusing on this statement, a reader will misunderstand Kendall's influence on *God and Man*. Kendall, if a Christian believer in 1951, was not a devout or orthodox one. He also supported the Keynesian economics which the book condemned. In questioning religious heterodoxy, Buckley's critique drew on his own family's vigorous Catholicism, not on Kendall. In defending economic "individualism," Buckley's inspiration came from Frank Chodorov, the old school libertarian, who also read and critiqued the manuscript before publication. Willmoore's influence was subtler but deeper. Four of his ideas not only permeated but actually provided the conceptual framework for *God and Man at Yale*. At the heart of the book, an attentive reader will notice: (1) distrust of experts, (2) belief that freedom must have limits, (3) an argument for institutional orthodoxy, and (4) support for a more democratic style of university governance. Loving Yale and knowing it more intimately than Kendall did, Buckley's popular style remained dominant throughout the narrative. Kendall long paid homage to his student's "remarkable achievement" in authoring *God and Man*. He did not ghostwrite and—given his often convoluted prose—could not have written *God and Man*.[36] Rather the point is that, as of 1951, Buckley had so thoroughly absorbed Kendall's ideas that—to a degree neither man fully recognized—these ideas had become his own.

Author and mentor knew that Kendall's name was toxic at Yale and that alluding to him as editing the book might damage its prospects. Kendall had come to understand "the incredible efficacy of the Yale propaganda machine, and the determination with which it has gone to work on me." He told his sister that by supporting majority rule he actually weakened its popularity. Academics rushed to reject ideas championed by "that bastard Kendall."[37] So there was no explicit mention of the controversial political theorist's contributions to *God and Man*. But each of the four ideas above was Kendallian. The book's distrust of experts (professors and administrators) echoed Kendall writings from the 1930s and 1940s. To apply majority rule (Kendall's obsession) to a private university had to mean appealing to other stakeholders to rein in the faculty and administration. *God and Man* did that. That Yale should stand for certain principles and unapologetically reject others, that is, ought to adopt an institutional orthodoxy, is also traceable to Kendall's teaching. Buckley later wondered whether Kendall's association with *God and Man* was what made Yale so intransigent in denying him promotion. But the political science department made that determination long before the book came out and never wavered on it.

Kendall was not on campus when *God and Man* came out. At ORO he remained mostly cut off from academia but did occasional work in political theory. He coauthored an article on democracy in 1952 with Illinois political scientist Austin Ranney, which a few years later grew into a textbook. In 1954 Kendall's translation of Rousseau's *The Social Contract* appeared in an edition published by Regnery. In his introduction, Kendall contended that it was important to read Rousseau's most famous work carefully. Some saw Jean-Jacques as the father of democracy and others as the founder of "contemporary dictatorship." Much of this confusion came from *The Social Contract*. It encompassed democratic, authoritarian, and anarchist elements and never molded them "into a readily intelligible whole." The book desperately needed careful "textual analysis that patiently weighs every sentence against every other, that wrings from each phrase its last elusive scrap of meaning." Only through such analysis might readers really understand what "its author was trying but could not quite manage to make it say." Then Kendall suggested that the book's "central doctrine," practical or not, was that "in accepting the permanence of the large state we resign ourselves to perpetual bondage."[38]

In 1953 and 1954 Kendall assisted Buckley and Bozell in writing *McCarthy and His Enemies*. He carefully edited the prepublication typescript. As noted by Bozell's biographer, Kendall's "ideas on social consensus and its enforcement, furnished the book's underlying interpretative framework." In an early draft of one chapter, for example, Buckley castigated the anti-McCarthyites for lacking evidence and merely citing "a line from the Areopagitica" or "a line from J.S. Mill." These were themes and authors which Kendall took up in his classes and on which he later published scholarly articles. Another key point in the book first elucidated by Kendall (in the Cohen case) was that loyalty investigations should not focus on determining the guilt or innocence of their subjects but adopt a standard of "reasonable doubt." Published by Regnery and condemned by critic Dwight Macdonald before it was written, the book examined McCarthy's record in matter-of-fact language. It criticized his sloppy use of evidence, recognized that he occasionally lied, and admitted his investigations sometimes smeared the innocent. More fundamentally, the book suggested that communist infiltration was a real and existential threat. Examining McCarthy's work case by case, it concluded that his efforts in rooting out Marxist moles had been mostly positive. If the Cold War was a war, the authors maintained (taking a "radical" Kendallian line) that individual liberty had to take second place to national security. Such liberals as Arthur M. Schlesinger, Jr., condemned *McCarthy and His Enemies* as "sick" while the conservative press mostly praised it. The book sold well. It came out in March 1954 when McCarthy's power was at its height. Shortly afterward came the Army-McCarthy hearings, which discredited the Wisconsin senator. Bill later wrote a funny account of Ken and Brent watching the televised hearings over drinks. Kendall tells Bozell that "his boy" McCarthy was hurting the anticommunist cause by bullying witnesses in front of a huge audience. Appalled and entranced by the spectacle of the hearings, the men agreed to meet the next day to watch another round.[39]

In 1954 Kendall was building a new house for himself and Anne. Cleanth Brooks and Willmoore had gone in together to become "co-owners" of a piece of rural real estate outside New Haven in the Spring of 1950. Kendall had taken this step "to remind people I had tenure and would be staying until *I* decided to go elsewhere." Marriage to Anne energized Ken to build a nice house for himself and his new spouse, on this property in Northford, Connecticut. He devoted lots of attention to the construction process, hired a Yale architect to design a modernist structure, personally hauled building materials to the site, and got himself into considerable financial difficulty. Construction began in 1953, as Kendall knew he would return to Yale the following year. Going into debt related to this Northford domicile, Kendall later confessed, had pushed him into taking on "more Washington consultantships and more non-scholarly but remunerative writing than I'd any business doing."[40]

As he prepared to return to Yale for the Fall Semester of 1954, Kendall was pleasantly surprised that he was not shunted aside into the obscure "periphery" of the department. He learned that he would still be teaching his beloved class in local government. He would also be teaching incoming graduate students the basic class in political theory.[41] Perhaps a new beginning was in the offing. Perhaps he could move his academic career in a more positive and harmonious direction. Instead of going along to get along on this new path, however, Kendall girded his loins to wage a campaign against what he saw as the corruption and wrongheadedness of the American political science profession. In Spring 1954, for example, Charles Hyneman invited Kendall to speak at Northwestern University. Willmoore stayed at the Orrington Hotel where, a quarter century before, he had worked as a busboy. He delivered a speech berating the profession for failing to solve "problems that the community wants solved." Rather than trust experts, it would be better, said Kendall, to trust the people. "For the community is wiser about its needs than men know, and one of the things it cannot do without in the long pull, is a political science that can speak to it with the authority of true learning about the predictable consequences of its political acts." He received enthusiastic feedback from the Evanston crowd, which included future acolyte George W. Carey. This response gave Kendall hope about "getting listened to a little."[42] Meanwhile, with a taste of popular success from behind-the-scenes work on *God and Man at Yale* and *McCarthy and His Enemies*, Kendall looked forward to helping Buckley launch a new magazine of conservative opinion.

NOTES

1. WB, "McCarthy: A Votary's Account," B5, Series Accession 1997-M-160, BP.

2. WK, Review of *Prophets and Peoples*, by Hans Kohn, *Journal of Politics* 8, no. 3 (August 1946): 425–27; WK to EV, June 17, 1949, "VK," 372.

118 Chapter 5

3. "Sooner Named," *Daily Oklahoman*, April 15, 1946, p. 21; CH, Guggenheim Reference Letter for WK, January 16, 1945, and WK to CH, December 1946, B7, CHP.

4. Yale University to WK, June 16, 1947 and WK to Sid Lovett, January 29, 1957, B1F39, Pierson College Fellows Records, Manuscript and Archives, Yale University Library; WK to CH, December 1947 and [February 1948], B7, CHP; WK to YM, [Fall 1949], B5F3, KP.

5. WK to P.E. Corbett, April 2, 1947, B30F14, KP; WK to J. Raymond Walsh, June 16, 1942, B1F2, CCR; FW, Willmoore Kendall Memories, 2, WKC.

6. Judis, *Buckley*, 59; WK to WKS, October 16, 1933 and July 28, 1934, in *OxY*, 284, 374; WK to CH, 1948 and Spring 1950, B7, CHP; Lynn Speer Lemisko, "The Historical Imagination: Collingwood in the Classroom," *Canadian Social Studies* 38, no. 2 (Winter 2004), www.quasar.ualberta.ca/css; *YDN Critique*, April 1950, 73, 77–79, Series Accession 1997-M-160, B5, BP; WB, Foreword to *WKM*, xi–xii.

7. *News Critique*, April 1950, 78, and WB, "The Colossal Flunk," B5, Series Accession 1997-M-160, BP; Judis, *Buckley*, 59–62.

8. WK to EV, April 2, 1948 and WK to EV, April 2, 1948, April/May 1948 and September 27, 1948, "VK," 367–68, 370–72; WK to CH, February 1948 (3 letters), and WK to CH, Spring 1948, B7, CHP.

9. WK and WB Statements, *YDN*, May 14, 1948, p. 4; Richard B. Fisher Letter, *YDN*, May 17, 1948, pp. 4–5; "Rather Be Right?," *YDN*, January 25, 1949, p. 12; Judis, *Buckley*, 64.

10. Sigmund Diamond, "God and the F.B.I, at Yale," *The Nation*, April 12, 1980, pp. 423–28; "Conservative, Liberal Factions," *YDN*, October 24, 1949, pp. 1, 8; "First Time," *YDN*, October 31, 1949, p. 6; Thomas H. Guinzburg, "Bureau Chiefs," *YDN*, October 25, 1949, pp. 1, 5; Robert S. Cohen Letter, *YDN*, October 26, 1949, p. 4; WK Letter, *YDN*, October 28, 1949, B7, Series Accession 1997-M-160, BP; "Robert S. Cohen (1923–2107)," http://www.bu.edu/cphs/about/robert-cohen/.

11. "On the Verdict," *YDN*, October 17, 1949, p. 4; "U.S. Communists" *YDN*, March 24, 1950, p. 1.

12. John Koch, "Faculty Clash," *YDN*, April 18, 1950, pp. 1, 3; Bourne Dempsey Letter, *YDN*, May 8, 1950, p. 4; F. Reid Buckley Letter, *YDN*, May 9, 1950, p. 4.

13. "Debating Teams," *YDN*, April 24, 1948, p. 1; "Brent Bozell," *YDN*, October 24, 1947, p. 1; "Bozell Will Speak," *YDN*, October 13, 1948, p. 1; "Bozell Wins," *YDN*, February 13, 1948, p. 1; "UWF, PCA Heads," *YDN*, January 16, 1948, pp. 1, 5; H.S. Weaver, "Bozell, Vecchione," *YDN*, January 22, 1948, pp. 1–2; L. Brent Bozell, Jr., "Bozell Statement," *YDN*, February 19, 1948, pp. 9–10; Tom Guinzburg, "Bozell, Vecchione," *YDN*, February 26, 1948, p. 1; "'Students for Wallace," *YDN*, April 17, 1948, pp. 1, 3; Daniel Kelly, *Living on Fire: The Life of L. Brent Bozell, Jr.* (Wilmington, DE: ISI Books, 2014), 11–13; WB, Speech to Yale Political Union, October 24, 1962, Series Accession 2009-M-035, B3, BP.

14. "PU to Broadcast Discussion Series," *YDN*, October 16, 1948, p. 1; "PU Holds Meeting," *YDN*, February 11, 1949, p. 1; "Political Union Award," *YDN*, January 12, 1950, pp. 1, 6; "Varsity Debaters," *YDN*, May 14, 1949, p. 1; "Caudle Wins Moot

Court Prize, *YDN*, May 10, 1951, p. 1; "Civil Rights," *YDN*, October 23, 1952, p. 1; "Weiss-Bozell," *YDN*, March 4, 1953, p. 1.

15. Wills, *Confessions*, 23–24; WK to CH, Spring 1951, B7, CHP; WK to V.O. Key, July 26, 1950, B22F9, KP; WK to CH, Spring 1950, B7, CHP; WK to YM, 1952, B5F3, KP.

16. WK to EV, August 21, 1949, in "VM," 376–77; WK to Lawrence Dennis, November 26, 1947 and [1950], B4F3, Lawrence Dennis Papers, Hoover Institution, Library and Archives; Nash, "Iconoclast I," 131.

17. WK, "Prolegomena to Any Future Work on Majority Rule," *The Journal of Politics* 12, no. 4 (November 1950): 694–713.

18. WK, "The Function of Intelligence," *World Politics* I, no. 4 (July 1949): 542–52; Davis, "Kent-Kendall," 95–97; Anthony Olcott, "Revisiting the Legacy: Sherman Kent, Willmoore Kendall, and George Pettee—Strategic Intelligence in the Digital Age," *Studies in Intelligence* 53, no. 2 (*Extracts*, June 2009): 21–32; Josh Kerbel and Anthony Olcott, "Synthesizing with Clients, Not Analyzing for Customers," *Studies in Intelligence* 54, no. 4 (Extracts, December 2010): 11–27; Shaun P. McCarthy, *The Function of Intelligence in Crisis Management: Towards an Understand of the Intelligence Producer-Consumer Dichotomy* (Farnham, UK: Ashgate Publishing), 45–51; William C. Spracher, "National Security Intelligence Professional Education: A Map of U.S. Civilian University Programs and Competencies" (PhD diss., George Washington University, 2009), 34–47; WK to James W. Fesler, November 13, 1951, B22F9, KP.

19. WK to CH, Spring 1951, B7, CHP; WK to YM, 1952, B5F3, KP.

20. WK, ed. *A Communist Party in Action: An Account of the Organization and Operation in France*, by A. Rossi (New Haven: Yale University Press, x–xxiv, 270; Olcott, "Revisiting," 32; WK to YM, [Fall 1949], B5F3, KP; WK, "Bipartisanship and Majority-Rule Democracy," *American Perspective* IV, no. 2 (Spring 1950), reprinted in NK, *Willmoore Kendall: Contra Mundum* (New Rochelle: Arlington House, 1971), 118–28.

21. WK to CH, December 1947 and George Pettee to CH, August 15, 1950, B7, CHP; George Pettee to CB, August 15, 1950, B6F147, CBP.

22. CB to George Pettee, August 29, 1950, B6F147, CBP; CH to George Pettee, August 25, 1950, B7, CHP; Olcott, "Revisiting," 28–30.

23. *Revised Summary of ORO Projects, Special Studies and Field Operations*, Volume I, DTIC AD0007783 (Chevy Chase, MD: Operations Research Office, 1952), 85–90; Kevin M. Woods, "Creating the Capacity for Innovation: U.S. Army 1945–1960" (PhD diss., University of Leeds, 2011), 74; YM to George H. Nash, April 20, 1972, B21F13, KP; WK to YM, October 27, 1950 and 1952, B5F3, KP; WK to CH, March 1951 and Spring 1951, B7, CHP; WK to CB, October 26, 1950, B6F147, CBP; Richard Schumacher, "Blue Chips," *YDN*, October 4, 1950, p. 5; WK to HR, February 11, 1951, B38F2, HRP; WK to Tinkum Brooks, [Late 1950], B6F148, CBP.

24. *ORO Projects*, 87–88, 150–52; Sora Kim and Eric Haley, "Propaganda Strategies of Korean-war era Leaflets," *International Journal of Advertising* 36 (2017): 1–21; *Report on the Possible Uses of the Polygraph and Supplemental Report*

of the Examination of Korean Nationals and Communist Chinese, ORO-S-85 (Chevy Chase, MD: Operations Research Office, 1951), 5–6, 9; WK to CH, [1951] (2 letters) and October 22, 1951, B7, CHP; WK to YM, Fall 1951, 1952 and [1954?], B5F3 and WK to YM, August 6, 1951, B6F1, KP; WK to HR, December 26, 1962, B38F2, HRP.

25. Andrade to Nash, January 8, 1974, B4F18, KKP; WK to YM, Fall 1951, B5F3, KP; *ORO Projects*, 90–91; WK to CH, Spring 1951, B7, CHP; WK to CB, October 2, 1950, B6F147 and WK to CB, March 7, 1951 and [1952], B6F148, CBP; WK to EV, September 27, 1948, in "Kendall-Voegelin Correspondence," September 27, 1948, 371; WK to CH, January 31, 1952, B16F9, KP.

26. WK to Edgar S. Furniss, March 29, 1951, B22F9 and WK to James W. Fesler, February 9, 1952 and February 13, 1952, B30F14, KP; WK to CB, [1952], B6F148, CBP.

27. WK to YM, 1952, 1953 and [1954?], B5F3, and WK to YM, 1954, B5F4, KP; WK to CH, Spring 1954, B7, CHP; WK to CH, January 31, 1952, B16F9, KP; George Pettee to Howard K. Brown, February 9, 1962, KP.

28. Hsia Chih-tsing, et al., *China: An Area Manual: Volume I—Geographical, Historical, and Military Background* (Chevy Chase, MD: Operations Research Office, 1953), 126–27, 131–32; Wilbur Schramm, *The Nature of Psychological Warfare* (Chevy Chase, MD: Operations Research Office 1954), 8–10; Olcott, "Revisiting," 27.

29. WK to YM, March 1948, [Early 1949], Spring 1950, October 27, 1950, December 12, 1950, and Spring 1951, B5F3, and WK to YM, [Fall 1960], B6F2, KP; WK to CH, February 15, 1950, March 1951, B7, CHP; WK to EV, April 2, 1948, "VK," 367; Brandwein, "Katherine," 108–09; WK to FGW, [1964], B3, KP.

30. Andrade to Nash, January 8, 1974, KKP; WK to YM, Early 1951, Fall 1951, Early 1952, 1952, 1954 and Anne B. Kendall to YM, 1954, B5F3 and WK to YM, 1954, B5F4, KP; Wedding Invitation for WK and Anne Brunsdale, June 7, 1952, B1F39, Pierson Records; "Anne Brunsdale Wed," *Minneapolis Star-Tribune*, June 8, 1952, p. 55; "Just Married," *Minneapolis Star-Tribune*, June 10, 1953, p. 9.

31. WK to YM, December 12, 1950, 1952, [1952?], and [1953?], B5F3, KP; WK to CB, January 3, 1951, B7F147, CBP; WK to CH, January 31, 1952, B16F9, KP.

32. WK to YM, [1953?], B5F4, KP; WK to CH, January 1953 [probably misdated by archivist, likely either late 1953 or early 1954], B7, CHP; Davis, "Kent-Kendall," 94.

33. WK to CH, January 31, 1952, B16F9, KP; James W. Fesler to WK, October 26, 1951; WK to James W. Fesler, November 13, 1951, B22F9, KP.

34. "Bill's Book," *YDN*, October 15, 1951, pp. 4–5; Theodore M. Greene, "The Christian Speaks," and John Perry Miller, "The Economist Speaks," *YDN*, October 15, pp. 4–5; Anthony M. Astrachan, "An Undergraduate's View," Francis Coker, "An Historical View" and William K. Wimsatt, Jr., "A Conservative View," *YDN*, October 16, 1951, pp. 4–5; Dan Fastenberg, "God and Man at Yale," *Time*, August 17, 2011, https://entertainment.time.com/ 2011/08/30/all-time-100-best-nonfiction-books/slide/god-man-at-yale-by-william-f-buckley-jr/.

35. William F. Buckley, Jr., *God and Man at Yale: The Superstitions of "Academic Freedom,"* 50th Anniversary Edition (Washington, DC: Regnery Publishing, 1986), lxvi; Judis, *Buckley*, 86–87.

36. WK to WB, April 1963, B26, BP; Judis, *Buckley*, 86–87.

37. WK to CH, Spring 1951, B7, CHP; WK to YM, 1952, B5F3, KP.

38. Austin Ranney and WK, "Democracy: Confusion and Agreement," *Western Political Quarterly* 4, no. 3 (September 1951): 430–39; HR to WK, November 3, 1950, B38F2, HRP; WK, "Introduction: How to Read Rousseau's *The Social Contract*," *The Social Contract*, ed. WK (Chicago: Regnery, 1954), vi–xiii.

39. Wills, *Confessions*, 22; Judis, Buckley, 106–07; Dwight Macdonald to HR, December 4, 1952 and HR to Dwight Macdonald, December 8, 1952, B5, Series Accession 1997-M-160, BP; WK to HR, March 4, 1953 and HR to WK, May 4, 1954, B38F2, HRP; WK to YM, Spring 1954, B5F6, KP; Kelly, *Fire*, 25–29; "McCarthy Debate," *YDN*, April 12, 1954, p. 1; "McCarthy and His Enemies," *YDN*, April 22, 1954, p. 2; WB, "Votary's Account," B5, Series Accession 1997-M-160, BP; JH, *The Making of the American Conservative Mind: National Review and Its Times* (Wilmington, DE: ISI Books, 2005), 85; WB, Foreword xviii–xxi.

40. WK to CH, Spring 1950, July 6, 1950, Spring 1954, B7, CHP; WK to YM, 1954, B5F4, KP; WK to YM, 1953 and Spring 1954, B5F6, KP; WK to HR, July 25, 1953, B38F2, HRP; WK to Sid Lovett, January 29, 1957, B1F39, Pierson Records; Mark Royden Winchell, *Cleanth Brooks and the Rise of Modern Criticism* (Charlottesville: University Press of Virginia, 1996), 286.

41. WK to CB, [1954], B6F148, CBP.

42. WK, "The Social Determinants of Political Science," Northwestern University, April 27, 1954, B6F148, CBP; WK to CH, Spring 1954, B7, CHP; GWC, "Doctrine," 17.

Chapter 6

1954–1959

"Why Are You So Damn Logical?"

On November 19, 1955, the premier issue of *National Review* hit U.S. newsstands. Unsurprisingly—with senior editor Willmoore Kendall's name on the front cover—the magazine immediately went on to the attack against liberals. Its editors asserted that "the nation's opinion-makers for the most part share the Liberal point of view, try indefatigably to inculcate it in their readers' minds, and to that end employ the techniques of propaganda." Therefore, "we may properly speak," they continued, of "a huge *propaganda machine*, engaged in a major, sustained assault upon the sanity, and upon the prudence and the morality of the American people." Liberals had set themselves in opposition to "the goals and values appropriate to the American tradition." Moreover, the sanity of liberals themselves was suspect, proclaimed the editors, "because the political reality of which they speak is a dream world that nowhere exists."[1]

Liberal intellectuals responded by heaping scorn on the infant magazine. A negative comeback from social critic Dwight Macdonald was predictable. But the nastiness of his attacks—labeling *National Review*'s staff "Scrambled Eggheads of the Right"—was startling. James Burnham was a traitor to Trotsky with clichéd ideas, Suzanne La Follette an angry incompetent, and Willi Schlamm a "lowbrow" mediocrity. Kendall, said Macdonald, was "a wild Yale don of extreme, eccentric, and very abstract views who can get a discussion into the shouting stage faster than anyone I have ever known." An unkinder cut for Kendall came from old classmate John Fischer, then editor of *Harper's*. Over lunch Kendall had solicited him to write a piece about the new magazine. In "Why is the Conservative Voice so Hoarse?," Fischer, in his column "From the Editor's Easy Chair," linked *National Review* with other "extremist little magazines." The new publication, he wrote, "aimed primarily at an audience of True Believers . . . who throw themselves frantically into a cause—often to make up for some kind of frustration in their private lives."[2]

Harder yet for Kendall and his fellow editors to swallow was disapproval from fellow conservatives bothered by the magazine's take-no-prisoners style. Kendall had a hard time attracting fellow academics to write for the magazine. His only real success in this regard was in getting Revilo Oliver, then an obscure classicist at the University of Illinois, to write the occasional article. Eric Voegelin thought Kendall was wasting his time "mangling" leftwingers. R. B. McCallum, Kendall's old tutor, saw *National Review* as intemperate. He gently suggested that instead of calling Franklin Roosevelt the "worst ever" president it might have focused a specific failure such as getting "duped" at Yalta. Though often wooed by Buckley and Kendall, Bertrand de Jouvenel, prominent French conservative and Willmoore's close friend, refused to write for the magazine because it supported McCarthy. The tone of *National Review*, he said, was inappropriate for how "Christians should fight their battles." Even Charles Hyneman criticized the new magazine for so severely "slamming the liberals."[3]

Despite such reactions, *National Review*, during the time Kendall worked actively there, rapidly expanded in circulation and influence. By 1958 William F. Buckley, its editor-in-chief, proclaimed that the magazine had become "an institutional fact of American life." No longer was it "a flash-fire from the Neanderthal right" but had become "the voice of American conservatism." These first years, then, were key to making the magazine a major player on the American political scene, a role it would hold (and expand) for decades afterward. In the fall of 1958 Kendall moved to California to take up a visiting professorship at Stanford. At that point, his contributions to the magazine decreased significantly. By then, however, *National Review* had boosted its circulation to almost thirty thousand (six times its initial run) and was turning a small profit.[4]

Given the subsequent mainstreaming of its message, its association with the conservative triumphalism of the Reagan era, and its later power to define "the American conservative mind," scholars sometimes forget how radical *National Review* once was. Its original editors were united in their "support for McCarthyism." Minimizing this militancy has worked to dim the significance of Kendall's contributions to *National Review*. Kendall died when conservatism was still seeking but had not reached mainstream status. In telling the magazine's history, then, Kendall has become an exotic figure used to illustrate its primitive past. In fact, as the only one of the original editors whom Buckley had known well, Kendall played a crucial role in the new enterprise. Especially in its first few years, *National Review* reflected his hard-hitting style. It set out to vilify the very term "liberal." To be sure, Kendall was long dead before this task was complete, when liberals had to rebrand themselves as progressives. Kendall (and the other editors) rejected the view that liberals were engaged in a general conspiracy with communists. Rather the "conviction" at *National Review* was that liberalism posed a serious independent danger to the nation and that the magazine should focus on fighting it. From 1955 to 1958, in his weekly column "The Liberal Line," Kendall analyzed, dissected, and lambasted the "liberal propaganda machine." In this role it was he who launched the campaign to make "liberal" a dirty word, serving as the tip of the conservative spear.[5]

As an experienced propagandist, Kendall recognized the "wheel-spinning operation" of the American left. He set out to craft counternarratives to it. "The Liberal Line" involved a long-running, partly tongue-in-cheek propaganda metaphor. Liberal "operatives" and "echelons" received "directives" from a vaguely defined "central headquarters." Kendall named, and tried to shame, "leading opinion-makers" he believed were misleading the public. Favorite targets included Joseph Alsop, Stewart Alsop, and Walter Lippmann in journalism and Chester Bowles, Arthur Schlesinger, Jr., and John Foster Dulles in academia and government. The column suggested that such men—however they designated themselves politically—were liberals who supported large-scale government spending (except for the military), minimized the threat of global communism, and sought to control both parties. In 1955, for example, Kendall claimed liberals wanted "Republicans to nominate, as usual, an anti-Republican Republican," that Bowles sought to defeat "the world Communist movement without firing a shot or mussing a shirt-cuff," and that writer Lewis Mumford advocated neo-communist economics to stave off actual communist economics. Sociologist Norman Birnbaum, Kendall claimed in 1959, "does *not* say that Western democracy is no more democratic than you know what, but he's thinking it mighty loud."[6]

Columnist Kendall loved pointing out the "smugness" and "humorless confidence" of liberal leaders sure of a supper, sure of an easy chair, and sure of the truth. Liberals, he said, viewed discussion as "a one-way transmission belt for their superior wisdom and values." They constituted a "mutual admiration society" which considered itself "infallible" and suppressed alternate views. Never questioning their own righteousness, they patted "one another's backs." Kendall said John Fischer had made "intentionally inaccurate" claims about "heavy clerical overtones" at *National Review*. He then added that liberals tolerated such lies because they "ought to be true." When Lippmann engaged in an "examination of conscience" about China, he did not look into "his own conscience, but rather that of Chiang Kai-shek." Cocksure left-wing journalists were quick to dismiss the "crass ignorance" of well-trained American military leaders. Instead they looked for guidance from the great strategic minds at work "writing columns for newspapers." Regarding the paramount issue of the day—the struggle against communism—liberals ignored advice contrary to their own pacifistic predilections and embraced a "fatalistic defeatism." In damning the book *Conscience*, Kendall ridiculed author Robert Burlingame's overactive sense of guilt. Equating "the American conscience with his own," the author combined superficial generalities, such as "war never solves problems," with naïve faith in a new morality.[7]

Kendall could produce solid work as a reporter for the magazine, especially when covering geographical regions he knew well. In September 1956, for example, he traveled to Bolivia to write a firsthand account of that country's left-wing regime. Once in the country he described power shortages, large-scale corruption, food lines, and galloping inflation. He ascribed these faults to the unwise nationalization policies of the Bolivian government. The ruling National Revolutionary Movement (MNR), he wrote, was motivated by anti-American animus which caused it to make "mad" decisions like nationalizing its tin mines. The MNR was the de facto "jailer of Bolivia's workers and peasants." Yet only massive American financial and technical aid kept its abominable regime afloat. The real failure of the country's former mine owners, Kendall said, had not been paying their workers poorly. Rather they had failed to subsidize churches and schools to combat pernicious communist ideas. Kendall then denounced "idiotic" American policies which decoupled financial grants from whether a recipient country observed decent "standards of public morality."[8]

The next year Kendall combined his expertise at book reviews with some firsthand reporting on Spain. This episode started out with an assessment of Herbert L. Matthews's book on the Spanish Civil War, *The Yoke and the Arrows*. Matthews had reported on the war for the *New York Times*, and Kendall had known him in Madrid. By minimizing communist influence among the Loyalists and excusing church burnings, Kendall said, Matthews revealed a deep liberal bias. The author was determined to portray the Nationalists as "children of darkness" and the Republicans as "children of light." Kendall concluded his review by proclaiming that he was not "disappointed" in the author because "he had never thought much of him anyhow." The Spanish government was paying attention. It contacted Kendall to undermine a controversial assertion in *The Yoke and the Arrows* that a celebrated incident in the 1936 siege of the Alcázar fortress in Toledo had never happened. When the Republicans threatened to kill his hostage son if he did not surrender, the usual story went, the Nationalist commander told his son to commend his soul to God, shout long live Spain, and die as a patriot. Upon the commander's refusal to surrender, the Loyalists shot their hostage. Complete fiction, wrote Matthews. With primary documents and eyewitness testimony provided by Spain, Kendall published a follow-up piece in *National Review* which affirmed the original story.[9]

As a journalist Kendall could be discerning about liberal trends. In 1956, for example, he discovered a "position that the machine has been at pains to stake out," namely that Eisenhower had allowed the Soviets to surge ahead of the United States in its nuclear capabilities. So important was this new initiative, headquarters farmed it out "to top-echelon machine operatives of unimpeachable respectability; namely, the Alsops." Kendall recognized this theme of supposed American military weakness as a way to get "Republicans out of power." He then suggested the machine only adopted "positions" when it had "a firm lead from our colleagues in the upper reaches of the government service." It was not really in favor of a tough anti-Soviet stance, but wanted to counter charges "that might undermine [liberal] prestige." Currently, "because of certain highly placed officers in the armed forces," the machine lacked the "free hand" on military questions that it enjoyed elsewhere. Years in advance, then, Kendall perceived the false "missile gap" narrative which Democrats, encouraged by Joseph Alsop, used in 1960 to put John F. Kennedy in the White House. In November 1957 Kendall saw even further into the future of liberalism when he suggested that the American left had come to treasure equality above all other values. Hence, he decided to expose its ultimate plan, which he called "Operation Blurring-of-Distinctions." Its purpose was

> to rear up a breed of human being that looks out on its world and sees not men and women, whites and Negroes, aristocrats and plebeians, saints and sinners, etc. but indistinguishable units bearing identical rights (to equality of opportunity, to a job, to a high standard of living, to security, to die peacefully in bed rather than get killed in a war)—all without interesting distinctions among them except, of course, that between rulers (that is, bureaucrats of various ranks) and ruled (that is, people who obey bureaucrats of various ranks).

Liberals would never give up this quest for equality until "the last molehill of privilege shall be steamrollered level with the plain." Few people in the 1950s could foresee the rise of gender fluidity as part of the liberal agenda, but Kendall did grasp this tendency.[10]

The editors of *National Review* valued good writing and wanted to maintain a high level of intellectual discourse. But issues of writing style eventually came to affect Kendall's position at the magazine. For *National Review* to achieve popularity, Buckley knew he had to rid its pages of overly scholarly elements, sometimes linked to Kendall and friends. In 1956, for example, Revilo Oliver criticized the magazine for lacking "intellectual finish and stylistic polish." He said it was "too journalistic" and focused too much on fleeting issues of the day. From the beginning, however, the magazine's editors—particularly James Burnham—wanted to reach a large audience in order to affect public affairs. Buckley had developed a friendship with Oliver in the mid-1950s but quickly decided that the Illinois professor was "dead wrong." To survive *National Review* had to attract readers. Therefore, it had to become "more journalistic" and needed to keep focusing on contemporary events even if it lost a few highbrows. When the magazine began, Kendall had been in charge of the book review section. In 1956 the editors removed him from this position because he appeared "inattentive and given to academicism."[11]

At *National Review* Kendall sometimes tried to write in the desired popular vein. He would mix his sarcasm together with folksy Oklahoma idioms. Able to write chatty, accessible copy since his *Tulsa Tribune* days, he had sharpened his ability to appeal to the public working as a propagandist. Nevertheless, much of his work for the magazine proved challenging for readers. When Kendall wanted to say something important—something beyond mere propaganda—he slipped into the style pioneered in his Locke book, that is, careful textual analysis. To find the treasures lurking in Willmoore Kendall's best prose, then, readers had to put their brains to work. In his *National Review* articles, Kendall sometimes took several weeks, with continuations over several issues, to reach a thoroughly logical conclusion about a subject. "Readers of considerable education," conservative rhetorician Richard Weaver told Kendall, often found his elaborate "schematism" to be "a thing of beauty," but even they might find it "too rigorous." Such "relentless logical progression," Weaver went on, made "the average man uneasy." To appeal to a popular audience, he said, Kendall needed to write in a more "relaxed and 'natural' way." Long before, Kendall's father had told him that a journalist should avoid "logical syllogisms" in favor of sprightly accounts of "personal doings." At that time, Willmoore defended his style as adopted from his "great and good friend R.G. Collingwood." Decades later, for better or worse, Kendall had not purged his prose of Collingwood's influence, and, in the end, he never would.[12]

Willmoore had thrown himself into work at *National Review* in part to revive his sagging spirits. Now in his forties, he had begun to feel the effects of his age and "high living," and his marriage to Anne was breaking up in an ugly way. In August 1955 she moved out amid accusations of his drunkenness and philandering, and even domestic violence. Anne accusing Ken of throwing a knife at her during an argument. Attempts to reconcile proved futile. Willmoore claimed Anne "had built a wall around herself emotionally." He became distraught when she refused to forgive his misdeeds and saw him as "a liar, a cheat, and a scoundrel." Financial worries compounded these anxieties, with Willmoore thinking he might lose all his assets and face prosecution for unpaid debts. Then, shortly after Christmas in 1955, Kendall had "a profound religious experience," which, he said, would "make a different man of me." Gerhart Niemeyer was present. He later described the moment "when Willmoore, hitherto atheist, had encountered God one morning on the road, and broke into tears that would not dry for days. I have always felt that that moment of deepest humility was also his moment of greatest glory that can never be expunged." Still hoping to salvage his marriage, he admitted causing most of its problems, saying he had gone "plain off his rocker" with financial worry. Unimpressed, Anne moved forward with the divorce. A new "miracle" occurred on New Year's Day 1956 which allowed Willmoore to sell some Virginia property for a good price. As he moved into his new house in Connecticut "to rattle around absurdly in its several square miles of floor space," he confessed that losing Anne caused him "a kind of pain I have never known." Receiving a bell as a gift from Yvona "clearly intended for the calling of the children we intended to have at Northford," he said, "was the most traumatic experience of Christmas day."[13]

The divorce became final in July 1956. Kendall's major remaining asset was the Northford property which he called "virtually useless to me without Anne." Though not much interested in other women since meeting Anne, he hoped for a new love interest at *National Review* whose office would surely "have some females in it." (Kendall did not find true love at the magazine but was discovered *in flagrante* with a secretary at its office.) After mentioning to his sister that he was "entering the Roman Catholic Church," Kendall told Yvona that he took solace that Bill Buckley, his most "intimate" friend for the last five years, held him in high esteem. Buckley's devout Catholicism and sunny disposition provided an attractive model for Kendall during this crisis. When Kendall was confirmed as a member of the Catholic Church, Buckley served as his sponsor. Kendall's Yale graduate student, the political theorist Father Stanley Parry, CSC, officiated at the ceremony. On his conversion Kendall received a hearty note of congratulations from Bertrand de Jouvenel. The French political theorist told Willmoore that "what has happened to you is the most important thing which can happen in a man's life."[14]

Kendall took his new faith seriously enough that—even as he contemplated his second divorce—he was thinking about obtaining annulments. He hoped eventually to remarry as a Catholic. Later, in assisting Kendall in the annulment process, Buckley testified to his mentor's lack of maturity about marriage. Shortly before marrying Anne Brunsdale, he said, Willmoore had declared marriage to be "a quasi-commercial relationship which should be ended the moment incompatibility results." Willmoore married Anne, he said, because she was the nearest "of operative stimulants" and, he, "as was his habit, yielded to them." Months before, Buckley continued, Kendall had wanted to "marry one of my sisters." Shortly thereafter he said he would move to France to find his "ideal woman." Ken certainly knew, said Bill, that "the conditions of a permanent marriage" were lacking in the relationship with Anne. Then he married her anyway.[15]

As Willmoore's second marriage collapsed, his professional situation at Yale worsened. Kendall tried to get along upon his return to campus but by now he had a well-developed, mostly negative reputation on campus. He passed students in graduate exams he wanted to fail, applying the "behaviorist" standards of other Yale professors. Nevertheless, his efforts to teach traditional political theory—that is, philosophical ideas grounded in the great thinkers of Western philosophy—were blocked at every turn. Even teaching classical theory as a window into "empirical" theory proved impossible. Regarding contemporary politics, Willmoore refused to pull his punches. In 1954, said the *Yale Daily News*, Kendall "was the only person" it interviewed in the political science department who thought Joseph McCarthy should not be censured. Kendall praised the senator's "conspicuous service in the struggle against domestic communism," criticizing senators "who still don't know the score on internal security." At a December 1954 campus event, Kendall debated two scientists, maintaining that "the government . . . should only employ scientists who can be proved to be loyal Americans."[16]

The next year Kendall became less visible on campus. In 1955, for example, the only mentions of Kendall in the *Yale Daily News* were in two articles about *National Review*. Within a couple of years he had become busy enough at the magazine that Yale noticed. Renting out the Northford property, he took an apartment in New York. In previous years Yale administrators had criticized Kendall for spending too much time "courting" students. Although he was on campus four days a week and present for his classes and office hours in 1955 and 1956, Provost E. S. Furniss admonished him for offering "part-time service to Yale." Furniss assured him that such criticism had nothing to do with the political slant of the new magazine. Yale, thought a frustrated Kendall, seemed sure to damn him if he did and then to damn him if he didn't.[17]

Stung by Furniss's criticism, Kendall increased his activity but not in a way to win over campus liberals. In a public lecture at Yale in April 1957, followed by "a vigorous question-answer series," Kendall said Americans "should preach what we practice." The people should refuse to tolerate communists, not as a clear and present danger but because their views were dangerous and false. "America," he continued, "is a country with a deep sense of orthodoxy. It is better to be overzealous than underzealous in guarding the orthodoxy of a community. America is now underzealous." Going on, Kendall said that he hoped he was "enormously brighter" than Joseph McCarthy but had "no quarrels with" the senator. If "a majority of the people" thought a person "wrong in his opinions," even if it were Kendall himself, that person might rightly "be barred from government service." In fact, he noted, his own support for Joseph McCarthy had made it difficult to find a post in Washington. When McCarthy died the next week, Kendall was "deeply shocked." He mourned the controversial anticommunist as "a courageous patriot." McCarthy's monument would be "the improvements he wrought in our internal security system."[18]

Kendall and Buckley, whatever their national impact, were losing the battle for Yale. In June 1957 the *Yale Daily News* praised students for towing a moderate line, ignoring the radical left and "rantings of . . . the Far Right" (represented by Kendall) and for shunning the "consistent madness" of Buckley. When Kendall, in the "super-right National Review," dared suggest Yale President A. Whitney Griswold was part of the dominant liberal establishment, the *News* expressed regret that tenure protected his job. Two letters criticized the *News* for its attitude. Philosophy professor David Braybrooke suggested that by arguing to quash Kendall the article confirmed his hypothesis of repressive liberal hegemony. Undergraduate Stephen Williams called Kendall a "well-known Fascist-beast." But he also accused the *News* of practicing McCarthyism by falsely claiming Kendall had attacked Griswold. In February 1959 the *News* scoffed at Kendall's pretensions about perceiving "The Truth." It labeled his support for a binding public orthodoxy "Orwellian" (perhaps not realizing that the origins of this teaching came from Aristotle).[19]

Throughout these troubles at New Haven, Kendall remained an influential teacher. In well-honed Socratic style, he continued to attract favorable attention from many students. Ilie Smultea, for example, had come to Yale from Romania as an anticommunist refugee. He soon came under Kendall's influence. Kendall, he said, was "a great and very generous man" and "the most brilliant intellectual" he had known in the United States. Kendall inspired Smultea to obtain a doctorate in political science. Meeting Kendall was life changing for Yale undergraduate Oscar Pemantle, a native of India. In 1955, having just flummoxed conservative poet E. Merrill Root with a probing question at a public presentation, a self-confident Pemantle felt a tap on his shoulder. He turned around to meet Kendall. Introducing himself, Willmoore proceeded to demolish the arguments which had stumped the poet. Pemantle was so impressed that he changed his major to political science. Kendall was the best teacher he ever knew, a "matador" in the classroom, who provoked students through dialogue to think for themselves. Despite Willmoore's well-known political beliefs, he avoided indoctrinating students. He worked them hard, said Pemantle, to support their own positions logically. Pemantle was a leftist and appalled by his teacher's McCarthyism, but Kendall became and remained his "loyal and steadfast friend." Pemantle in turn became a lifelong champion and promoter of Kendall's interactive teaching style.[20]

In his scholarship Kendall remained an advocate of a Rousseauian, "absolute-majoritarian" position. Under pressure of personal and professional difficulties, however, he began to modify this outlook in 1957. Throughout this period Kendall's scholarship continued to show contrarian brilliance. In September 1956, for example, Willmoore delivered an important series of lectures to a conference of conservative academics in Buck Hill Falls, Pennsylvania, a resort in the Poconos. It was if Daniel had volunteered to enter the lion's den. In the lectures, Kendall defended the right of the people to rule themselves and to resist the aggrandizement of experts. He also suggested that the people of Athens were right to put Socrates to death and voiced support for Rousseau's philosophy of the general will. Traditionalist Russell Kirk, center-right historian Clinton Rossiter, and libertarian Murray Rothbard were all in the audience. They were, respectively, amused, intrigued, and horrified. Both Kirk and Rothbard abhorred Rousseau but for diametrically opposed reasons (Kirk as an enemy of tradition and Rothbard as an enemy of liberty). Rothbard recognized Kendall's arguments as an attack on libertarianism. He labeled him "the philosopher *extraordinaire* of the lynch mob," whose majoritarian principles might be used to justify the crucifixion.[21]

In these lectures Kendall conjoined several themes which later appeared as scholarly publications. Kendall claimed that he hated and feared liberalism because it was antidemocratic. He argued that an unholy trinity of self-proclaimed experts—bureaucrats, academics, and journalists—dominated American society and politics. His ideas here mirrored those of Italian communist thinker Antonio Gramsci. Instead of emphasizing class conflict, Kendall focused on conflict between ruling elites and the people, tout court. Without reference to Gramscian hegemony (not yet de rigeur in American universities), Kendall discussed how an interconnected liberal elite exercised dominion over the people. By controlling elite universities, leading media, and the federal bureaucracy, these groups—all dominated by liberals—monopolized not just how important political questions were decided but even how they were framed and the factual narratives underlying them.[22]

Kendall then argued that the American people often acquiesced to such dominance because much of it was hidden and because they overprized elite claims to expertise. Pursuing this point, Kendall dissected John Stuart Mill's *Considerations on Representative Government*. He agreed with Mill that that any modern society required specialists for administrative expertise and guidance. Insofar as they possessed genuine know-how, such experts might provide accurate predictions about the consequences of certain courses of action. Yet such experts had no special capability to determine what the nation *ought* to do in a particular case. They had no special insight into what was *good* for the country. Rather the people of a democracy—once properly informed—should decide what course to pursue to promote their own welfare. Mill and followers paid lip service to representative government while arguing that experts—not the hoi polloi—should make the important decisions.[23]

Entranced with its own cleverness, this "Great Bureaucracy" then reified individual rights to undermine democracy. Like Mill many liberals argued for an absolute right to free expression, what Kendall called the "simon-pure" theory of free speech. In practice most American liberals, aping the Supreme Court, added an "escape clause" to Mill's doctrine. They would only ban expression which constituted a "clear-and-present danger" to the nation. The simon-pure notion, said Kendall, was "root and branch false." It provided individuals with a degree of freedom which no nation could actually tolerate. Adding the escape clause also demonstrated liberal hypocrisy. It often applied to rank-and-file American communists who were not a serious danger to the United States. Both groups of liberals were relativists. Skeptical toward all claims to truth, they applied this principle selectively. They believed, for example, that "all questions were open questions . . . except the question whether all questions are open questions . . . which [was] a *closed* question." Within their own bailiwicks of power, and especially within the three-headed "Great Bureaucracy," liberals ruthlessly suppressed views which contradicted their own ideas about protecting free expression.[24]

Kendall argued that individual rights, including free expression, were great social goods. He cited his own willingness to debate all comers to show the real value he put on the free exchange of ideas. Though valuable, free speech (and other individual rights) were not, and could not be, the only or the greatest goods for a functional society. The people ought to have serious reasons to limit these social goods (aka individual rights), but in a democracy they had to possess the power to do so at their discretion. Kendall illustrated this point with a long analysis of Plato's "Crito" and "Apology." The Athenian Assembly, he said, had been within its rights to execute Socrates because he refused to stop condemning the Athenian "way of life." The assembly, whose very reason for being was "to preserve this society and way of life," came to see Socrates as a public enemy who deserved death. The philosopher refused to moderate his charges that Athenians were so focused on fame and fortune that their way of life was "not worth living." He also recognized that as a citizen of Athens, the assembly possessed legitimate authority over him and refused to flee the city. Therefore, Socrates himself was no defender of the "simon-pure" doctrine of free expression. He accepted the principle, even at the cost of his life, that the Athenian people possessed legitimate authority to silence him.[25]

A couple of years later Kendall published a condensed version of these views on Socrates in *Modern Age*. The article reiterated that to survive every society must impose limits on freedom, including freedom of expression. Kendall again argued that not only was Athens correct to force Socrates to drink hemlock but that Socrates validated the principle of majority rule by accepting death at the hands of the people. Richard Weaver wrote to Kendall to praise his Socrates article. Clinton Rossiter let Kendall know that he had encountered the article in *Modern Age*. Reading it, he said, "brought back warm memories of a famous time together we had in the Poconos." Although Rossiter still could not "go along" with Kendall's thesis, he could, "by God, say this: you are the number one Socrates in the United States today." Rossiter then asked Willmoore: "What makes you so damned logical?"[26]

In 1956, at the very end of his absolute majoritarian phase, Kendall coauthored *Democracy and the American Party System* with Austin Ranney. A college-level textbook published by Harcourt-Brace, the book aimed to counteract "the unfriendliness of American political science literature" toward the U.S. political "system and its workings." The first four chapters, written by Kendall, set up a model of democracy which upheld his vision of majoritarianism. Ranney completed the next fifteen chapters, detailing the historical nuts and bolts of American parties. The two men apparently worked more closely together on the book's last three chapters. They concluded that American parties had contributed to the continuing health of democracy in the United States. Rossiter called Kendall's contribution to the book "the best thing that had ever been done on the American parties." Most reviews of the book were disappointing. Even so, the textbook sold relatively well. It remained in print for years, was adopted in many college classrooms, and earned lasting royalties for its authors.[27]

Although mostly neglected by scholars, *Democracy and the American Political System* provided the most complete statement of Kendall's absolute-majoritarian position (before he modified it in ensuing years). Kendall defined democracy as a "purely political conception" rather than as a feel-good, catchall synonym for the good life, as John Dewey used it. His definition, said Kendall, had the advantage of precision. By focusing on democracy as a form of government, he defined it as a political process. He looked at how its laws were crafted, not whether such laws were in themselves right or wrong. Kendall then went on to argue that only "unlimited majority rule" was fully democratic. Any system which prevented the majority from changing the governing system—say by putting the individual's right to free speech or to bear arms off limits—involved, ipso facto, rule by the minority which opposed such change. He dismissed fears of "majority tyranny" against a minority as applying even more strongly to minority tyranny against the majority.[28]

In the real world compromises of democratic purity were inevitable. Kendall therefore developed a model to judge *how* democratic any particular system of government was. To be democratic in more than name, he said a polity must, to a significant degree, operate in accord with four component principles. These principles included popular sovereignty, political equality, popular consultation, and majority rule. By popular sovereignty Kendall meant that sovereignty needed to rest with the people, not with an individual or with a small group. Political equality required "an equal chance for each member of the community to participate in the total decision-making process of the community." Popular consultation signified the necessity of regular, peaceful methods to learn the people's will. By majority rule, Kendall meant that a democratic government must "justify its actions on the grounds that they accord with the wishes of a majority of the enfranchised members of the community."[29]

A perfect democracy, for Kendall, meant the unanimous, harmonious, and direct consent of all community members. But such a system was impossible in large nations. For a good model of operational democracy, Kendall looked at New England town meetings. He showed how, on a small scale, they accorded well with the model he had developed. Then he attempted "blowing up" the town meeting to carry its attributes up to the level of the nation-state. One key difference soon became obvious. Large-scale government was necessarily representative, rather than direct. As citizens could not control administrative personnel face to face, they had to elect persons to "ride herd" on bureaucrats. Large-scale democracy required that citizens possess accurate information so that they could make informed decisions on issues about which they lacked direct knowledge. Another key issue in scaling up small-town democracy involved maintaining consensus over a wide and varied area. Keeping a large, democratic country together required frequent, conciliatory discussion among elected representatives. Such consultations, he argued, served to maintain harmony among multifarious factions. To Kendall, then, making democracy work in a large country required electing representatives to enact the will of the people. To maintain social consensus, democracy also required careful deliberation among these representatives.[30]

In the concluding chapters of *Democracy and the American Party System*, Kendall (writing with Ranney) showed that he still accepted the historical consensus of his day of the American founders as antidemocratic reactionaries. They had designed a system to protect property—from what they saw as excesses of democracy. Kendall did criticize former muse J. Allen Smith for exaggerating the antidemocratic aspects of American politics. He also suggested that nonideological political parties with overlapping platforms helped maintain American political consensus. With deep social and economic divisions and a long tradition of violence, the United States, Kendall and Ranney argued, had real "civil war potential." By avoiding purely ideological foci and by seeking to include many groups with diverse perspectives from every region, the parties had kept many different social groups within the political system. With each faction working within the party system to achieve its ends, national cohesion was maintained even over the wide expanses of a diverse and turbulent nation.[31]

Within a year, however, Kendall's political theory began to change significantly. In light of his conversion to Catholicism, reading Eric Voegelin and Leo Strauss, and being stung by Rothbard's criticism at Buck Hill Falls, Kendall abandoned his previous value-neutral approach. Aside from the value of democracy itself, his theory had been largely neutral about ethics and religion. Kendall had known Eric Voegelin for years. He was stunned, however, when he read the German scholar's book *Israel and Revelation*. He called it "the most breath-taking book I have ever seen." Following Voegelin, Kendall came to the "breathtaking" conclusion that civilization began with human realization of the existence of God, of a purpose bigger than itself, a purpose outside history. Human beings thereafter could help create and sustain society by using their reason and knowledge to serve divine and eternal purposes. No longer did they need to serve transient human desires within history. Voegelin, said Kendall, argued that whenever "men establish a government," they repeated, by analogy, God's creation of the universe. They willed into existence a new order. Human societies and political constitutions existed "under God." Therefore, to organize a society as if its purpose "were *within* History" was "self-defeating." Rejecting revelation, said Kendall per Voegelin, had led modern societies to treat religion as a "'value preference,' in the same category with a fondness for Bel Paese cheese." Accepting Voegelin meant that "all modern political theory is an attempt to square the circle." Awakened, Kendall began to assign Voegelin to his students at Yale. He also attempted to integrate Voegelin's ideas into his own political theory.[32]

The ideas of Leo Strauss also had a great effect on Kendall's teaching, inspiring him to focus more on formal political theory and less on activism. Although ambiguous about the value of religious belief, the Straussians rejected relativism. They thought eternal truths existed and were accessible to reason. Strauss and company rejected relativism, including historicism (truth varies by historical era) and conventionalism (humans establish truth through agreed-upon conventions). Thus, the job of political philosophy was to discover truth and the good and to promote a society based upon them. Strauss disliked, together with Kendall, "behaviorists" who focused upon "statistical analysis of the phenomena of political 'behavior.'" Unlike most American political scientists, Kendall said, the Straussians knew Plato and penned pleasing prose. Unusually deferential to the University of Chicago professor, Kendall began to funnel students to him for doctoral work. He praised the Straussians as a "new breed" of political scientists. In 1957, for example, Kendall commended Strauss disciple Walter Berns, then at Yale, for his book *Freedom, Virtue, and the First Amendment*. Kendall agreed with Berns that the federal courts by exalting free speech had undercut the ability of localities to act as "custodians of community" who could protect "social decency" from abuses of freedom.[33]

An unpublished article from 1957 showed Kendall transitioning away from his absolute majoritarianism. He rested this new stance on the Declaration of Independence. When inalienable rights and popular desires conflicted, Kendall argued that rights possessed a logically "superordinate" position. He claimed that the Constitution created a flawed system in which inviolable principles came up for debate at each election. This article revealed Kendall's first effort to integrate moral verities—beyond that of democracy itself—into his political theory. He argued for constructing public policy for "reason of God," even at the cost of overturning the American "constitutional order." Kendall's former students were puzzled. Buckley found "unconvincing" Kendall's notion that the Constitution amounted to "a previously undiscerned *volte face*" by the founders. He also criticized the article as too scholastic. Brent Bozell defended the article. He argued that Kendall was "the best man in the business at proving what something says." *National Review* ought to "turn him loose on the country's basic political documents" for the edification of readers. Ultimately, the magazine rejected Willmoore's article. Annoyed at the time, Kendall eventually realized that this failure to publish saved him embarrassing retractions in the future.[34]

In the Spring Semester of 1957 Kendall suffered a far harsher rejection, as Yale denied his application for promotion. Bertrand de Jouvenel was a guest at Kendall's house at Northford when this rebuff occurred. He recalled that night as one of "desperate unhappiness." Kendall moaned and shouted in his sleep. It became apparent to the reluctant listener that Willmoore's pain stemmed not just from "immediate disappointment" but from long-standing psychological hurts. In June, James Fesler told Kendall that he would never win promotion to full professor at Yale because he had not published enough. One might agree—with Jeffrey Hart—that Yale's evaluation was reasonable, that Kendall had not produced enough top-notch scholarly work for an Ivy League professorship. Yet, others in the department had become full professors with fewer publications. Strauss had informed Yale that Kendall was a serious, thoughtful, and insightful scholar. In its evaluation the department excluded the Ranney-Kendall textbook, publications for ORO, and work for *National Review*. Fesler said none of this work involved scholarship in political theory and so should be disregarded. Voegelin undercut Kendall, putting his "publicistic activities for the cause of ideological conservatism" on the "debit side" against him. Though Kendall saw such work as a "public service," Voegelin called it as a "waste of time and energy." Fesler also "let slip" that the university thought Kendall did "real harm in the classroom." Kendall's critics, that is, feared his allure as a teacher. They worried that his prowess in the classroom would entice talented students to conservatism. Other evidence showed that Kendall's exclusion had to do with lack of collegiality, that he "was an S.O.B." However one evaluates his scholarship, personal and political issues were unquestionably involved in Yale denying him promotion.³⁵

Despite disappointment, Kendall soldiered on, vigorously upholding his views on and off campus. On October 21, 1957, for example, he debated philosopher Paul Weiss, a strong leftist, before a packed audience at Yale's John Dewey Society. The topic was academic freedom. Weiss argued that universities should serve all mankind and tolerate virtually all shades of opinion. Kendall defended academic standards against a view of education as a scholastic free-for-all. A university, he added, "is a place where the talking of foolishness should be discouraged as a matter of course." Anticipating arguments philosopher Thomas Kuhn made a few years later, Kendall suggested that academic disciplines did not tolerate all opinions. Certain views were taboo in the academy to the point of making their advocates unemployable pariahs. A university was "the carrier of a congeries of orthodoxies." It should not be free "to defy the broader society" without expecting "retaliatory measures" from said society. To maintain itself, freedom, including academic freedom, implied limits. The debaters enjoyed their "lively and friendly" exchange even though, said the *Yale Daily News*, "each thought the other was a schnook." A few months later, Kendall delivered a campus speech assailing the Eisenhower administration. Eisenhower, he said, had delivered "himself into the hands of the liberally dominated bureaucracy." Ike's administration, he added, had disappointed conservatives. It "appeases the Soviet Union, neglects the nation's defenses, and dedicates itself to egalitarian social reform."³⁶

In his double role as professor and spokesman for the new conservatism, Kendall remained in the public eye. He gave frequent speeches, signing petitions, engaging in debates, and appearing on television and radio. In these endeavors, he reaffirmed his reputation as a contrarian ever ready to challenge conventional wisdom and deflate overblown egos. That fall, together with Medford Evans, he debated two ACLU lawyers. The question was the propriety of Harvard inviting J. Robert Oppenheimer, a former communist, to deliver its prestigious William James Lectures. Harvard tried to obstruct the event, but, said author M. Stanton Evans, the hall "was crowded with students and townspeople; it was a rousing debate, thoroughly enjoyed by all concerned." Then in April 1958 Willmoore appeared at the National Conference on Political Parties in Hayden Lake, Idaho. As the conference opened, he had a "fiery exchange" with Minnesota Congressman Eugene McCarthy. Kendall maintained that the Supreme Court was engaged "in a conspiracy against the Constitution." By promoting an "open society," the Court was preventing the "stringent regulation" of communism which most Americans favored. McCarthy admitted a need for "some restraints on liberty" but argued that the Court had not weakened "internal security" while protecting individual freedom. As the meeting concluded, Kendall launched a two-pronged attack on Paul Butler, national chairman of the Democratic Party, and on Bertha Adkins, assistant national Republican Party chair. In this exchange Kendall defended the proposition that the country ought "to have two parties which have no basic differences." He suggested that making parties more ideologically distinct and nationalizing most political issues—a development Butler and Adkins both advocated—would "divide the nation."[37]

In February 1957 Kendall commented publicly on Rev. Billy Graham's recent visit to Yale. He called Graham a "powerful" speaker. He praised how he stimulated campus discussions but believed this effect would be short-lived. He thought Graham "too slow afoot intellectually" to appeal to Yale students. He was a "remarkable pleader . . . who almost reduces Christianity to Madison Avenue." In 1958 Kendall moved on to condemn the "great and good" Albert Schweitzer for bad logic. The famous theologian and missionary, Kendall argued, had proposed that anything "intolerable" could not also be valid or true, that is, Schweitzer suggested that communism could not be that bad because to fight it robustly risked nuclear war which was "intolerable." In 1959 Kendall met Karl Barth, the famous liberal Swiss theologian. Barth complimented Kendall. He told him that their half hour conversation gave him "a new understanding of the Right-wing position." The response was vintage Willmoore. "All that proves," he replied, was that: "You have not been doing your homework, and don't understand the position you are attacking."[38]

Nor was Kendall getting warm and fuzzy in his scholarship. In June 1958 he published a devastating reply to Herbert McClosky in the *American Political Science Review*. McClosky, an old rival, had put together a "team" to write an article called "Conservatism and Personality" for the *APSR*. This team discovered that conservatives were ill-informed, "backward," "rigid," "obscurantist," authoritarian, and "alienated." Considering the article "asinine" and "manifestly idiotic," Leo Strauss did not deign to reply. Kendall, however, used his gift for textual analysis in a "shattering" rejoinder to McClosky. The article claimed that conservatism lacked real substance, except resistance to liberalism. Kendall pointed out that this same rubric applied in reverse to liberalism. Kendall showed the study's questionnaires were designed to make liberals look smarter than conservatives. Its population quartiles, for example, ranged from "extreme conservative" to "liberal," with no extreme liberals in sight. More damningly the behaviorist "team" made key reasoning errors. It treated personality characteristics as if as easy to measure as "weight and height." It then logically failed to connect its list of conservative characteristics to the forty-three point conservative creed it used to measure responses. To appear in print, this rejoinder had to overcome objections from a board member who said he would support publishing it if anyone but Willmoore Kendall had written it.[39]

To escape his situation in Yale, Kendall planned a research sabbatical in Spain, funded by the conservative Relm Foundation. Then he got a surprise offer from Stanford. He put his sabbatical on hold and went west to take up a yearlong post as visiting associate professor in political theory. This move, he said, freed him from the "crushing burden" of his "commitments to *National Review*." With Kendall gone, "The Liberal Line" disappeared permanently. The upcoming year in Palo Alto—despite some embarrassing moments—would prove productive, even redemptive for him, both professionally and personally. At Stanford Kendall replaced Mulford Sibley. Sibley's pacifism and socialism had prevented him, at the last minute, from obtaining a permanent post in political theory. The "fundamental ugliness of the events" in the Sibley matter led Kendall to believe he had little chance of getting a permanent position. Despite their political differences and his own disappointment, Sibley helped Kendall find a place to live.[40]

Kendall hardly got settled in before serious trouble arose. Early in the semester he showed up for work smelling of alcohol. He made the excuse that he had been suffering from the flu and had medicated himself with his traditional remedy of "hot-buttered rum." More serious was an incident which occurred shortly thereafter. Menlo Park police stopped Kendall and charged him with drunk driving. Kendall had been driving the wrong way on a one-way street. He pleaded guilty, but because he had been wearing a tuxedo after attending a formal dinner party and was a Stanford professor, the story made it into the papers. Both incidents occurred within a few weeks of arriving on campus. Provost F. E. Terman informed Willmoore that further incidents of the kind, "either on campus or off," meant immediate termination.[41] Hardly an auspicious start.

Although relocation had freed Kendall from the pressures he felt at New Haven, Northford, and New York, he found himself isolated. He seldom socialized with the political science faculty, most of whom remained aloof. As reported by one student, Kendall scandalized the faculty wives by appearing at a Christmas party, accompanied by a beautiful young graduate student in a "spectacular" red dress. Perhaps this companion was Nellie Cooper, a local librarian fifteen years Kendall's junior. During his first semester at Stanford, Willmoore put an entry into the local "Lonely Hearts Club." Answering his missive was Ms. Cooper, an attractive, Canadian-born, ex-Marine, who was looking for excitement in her life. When she met Willmoore Kendall, she perhaps got more excitement than she bargained for. The two lonely hearts hit it off and remained together for the next decade. Cooper, a Catholic, was less intellectually inclined than either of Kendall's first two wives. She did not come from a privileged background like Anne Brunsdale. On the other hand, Nellie had a strong determination to pursue her goals. Officially serving as Kendall's live-in secretary for a number of years before they became engaged, her mental toughness allowed her to brush off Willmoore's often outrageous behavior in a way many women could not have done. Her devotion to Kendall was genuine and continued unabated for decades after his death.[42]

Meanwhile, Kendall flourished both as a teacher and as a public speaker at Stanford. Overcoming his "neurosis" about lecturing (and making exaggerated claims *never* to have led a lecture-based class), he got up regularly at 5:00 a.m. and worked until 1:00 p.m. on class days, then went immediately to deliver the resulting lecture. The lectures often included explication of Strauss and Voegelin. "The first ten days were hell," he told Charles Hyneman, but then "overnight, I got the knack of it." Kendall kept himself busy that year by working up 120 lectures from scratch. Kendall had an "electrifying" effect on Stanford students. Attendance at his lectures was

Figure 6.1   Nellie Cooper Kendall. *Source:* Photo by Wilfred Cooper, Courtesy of Chuck and Pam Graham.

standing room only with classroom turnout "running 150% of enrollment." Through careful preparation of these lectures (keeping an eye toward future publication), Kendall said he felt himself "'coming to' intellectually." He was moving forward again after years of avoiding the reading he felt was necessary to move his scholarship forward. His numerous public lectures and debates—including the well-attended showdown with Sibley—had made a positive impression and lifted his mood. The year at Stanford, Kendall told Buckley, had made him "about as uninhibited as you about speaking," then added: "May God forgive me."[43]

While teaching at Stanford, Willmoore had an intellectual epiphany. This one was more lasting than that he had about the Declaration of Independence in 1957. Kendall became a Madisonian. "*Nobody*," he told Buckley in June 1959, "understands the sources of the American political tradition anymore: in scholarship, the whole business has got to be re-examined; and I look forward eagerly to doing the re-examining." It was in Palo Alto, then, that Kendall made his last major intellectual turn. He acquired an intellectual perspective which he would retain and work to elucidate for the rest of his life. "The key issue," he continued, was "that Madison was not trying to prevent majority-rule but majority tyranny," that is, "'unjust' actions by majorities." Contra his unpublished 1957 article, Kendall now defended "the Framers for not having included a Bill of Rights." Moreover, he now regarded "Madison, not Rousseau," as the foremost political thinker of the eighteenth century.[44] Kendall was ready to formulate a new and improved version of his political theory.

By the end of the academic year Kendall had come to view his time at Stanford as "a smash success." The incidents with alcohol early in his tenure and a national letter-writing campaign from liberal political scientists meant that he would get no permanent post. Four Stanford faculty had approached Kendall with a proposal to have him appointed as a tenured associate professor with control of teaching political theory at the university. This position was to involve a large increase over his Yale salary. Except for his "brush with the police," Willmoore claimed, the proposal would have envisioned a full professorship. Ultimately, "feuding" within the department prevented the extension of an official offer. There was also talk among students about raising money for an endowed Herbert Hoover Chair of Political Philosophy. This effort fizzled out quickly. At the end of the year, Provost Terman wrote Kendall a surprisingly warm letter. He praised Willmoore for "presenting your views vigorously yet temperately." By participating "in public events on the campus" Kendall had helped make it a "lively" year. He had helped students to think and sparked their "interest in political and social questions."[45] Happy to avoid Yale, Kendall headed to Madrid for a two-year research sabbatical.

By the late 1950s Kendall knew he had moved, as Hyneman put it, from being a "controversial figure" into a "subject of near-universal disapproval." Hyneman attributed this development to Kendall playing "too rough in oral communications" and Kendall's "vigorous anti-communism" including association with McCarthy and Buckley. However, Hyneman praised Kendall's "rigorous pursuit of logic" and regarded his political theory as original and of the highest order. Some might regard Kendall's positions "as outside the limits of legitimacy," but Hyneman disagreed. He compared Kendall to Paracelsus whose contrarian views were accepted by later generations as truth. By being unconventional, his path to success was more difficult than for a tamer scholar who might easily publish books while mingling with likeminded colleagues. Libertarian Murray Rothbard was tougher and recognized the irony in his antagonist's situation. Using Willmoore's *"own* premises," said Rothbard, "Sherman Adams [Eisenhower's Chief of Staff] should put Kendall to death this instant."[46]

NOTES

1. "The Editors of *National Review* Believe:" *NR*, November 19, 1955, p. 8.
2. Dwight Macdonald, "Eggheads"; John Fischer, "The Editor's Easy Chair: Why is the Conservative Voice So Hoarse," *Harper's*, March 1956, pp. 16–22.
3. RPO, *Jewish Strategy*, vii; EV to WK, March 20, 1957, B15F1, KP; R.B. McCallum to WK, July 23, 1956, B30, Folder 12, KP; WK to BDJ, November 15, 1955 and [1956], B16F2, KP; WB to BDJ, February 5, 1958 and March 24, 1958, B5, BP; WK to CH, January 6, 1956, B7, CHP.
4. WB Statement to *National Review* Board of Directors, April 28, 1958 and William to *National Review* Directors, November 26, 1958, B5, BP.
5. Judis, *Buckley*, 130–34; WB, *Miles Gone By: A Literary Autobiography* (Washington, DC: Regnery, 2004), 283–86; WK to CH, January 6, 1956, B7, CHP; Susan Currie Sivek, "Editing Conservatism: How *National Review* Magazine Framed and Mobilized a Political Movement," January 1, 2007, p. 5–11, Linfield University, http://digitalcommons.linfield.edu; Hart, *Mind, passim*; Wills, *Confessions*, 33–35; Sam Tanenhaus, "Choosing Sides: The Writers and Politicians Who Sculpted Today's Extreme Divisions," *New Republic*, November 2018, p. 58.
6. Nash, "Iconoclast II," 247; WK, "The Liberal Line," *NR*, November 19, 1955, p. 8, November 26, 1955, p. 22, December 7, 1955, p. 24, December 14, 1955, p. 8, December 21, 1955, p. 8, December 28, 1955, p. 8, March 7, 1956, March 14, 1956, p. 14, April 25, 1956, and October 26, 1957, p. 370; WK, "The Printed Word," *NR*, January 3, 1959, p. 431.
7. WK, "The Liberal Line," *NR*, January 4, 1956, p. 8, January 18, 1956, p. 8, March 14, 1956, p. 14, June 13, 1956, p. 16, and September 14, 1957, p. 229. WK, "*Whose* American Conscience?," *NR*, April 20, 1957, pp. 383–84.
8. WK, "Bolivian Follies," *NR*, October 6, 1956, pp. 11–13.

9. WK, "The Liberal Line," June 8, 1957, p. 540; WK, "Spain Talks Back to the '*Times*,'" July 20, 1957, pp. 87–88.

10. WK, "The Liberal Line," *NR*, March 28, 1956, p. 8, April 4, 1956, May 23, 1956, p. 8; November 9, 1957, p. 416, and January 4, 1958, p. 11.

11. WK, "The Liberal Line," *NR*, April 11, 1956, p. 10, November 1, 1956, p. 14, February 9, 1957, p. 136, March 30, 1957, p. 302, August 3, 1957, p. 131, September 28, 1957, p. 272, and August 30, 1958, p. 160; WK, "The Printed Word," *NR*, March 8, 1958, p. 228; James Burnham to WB, October 23, 1957 and November 24, 1957, B2, BP; RPO to WK, March 30, 1956, WB to RPO, April 18, 1956, and WB to WK, July 31, 1956, B3, BP; James Burnham to WB, July 15, 1958, B5, BP; Willi Schlamm to HR, May 21, 1954, Series Accession 1997-M-160, B4, BP; WK to EV, October 14, 1955, in "VK," 379; Hart, *Mind*, 30. Frank Meyer to WK, May 28, 1960, B21F8, KP; Judis, *Buckley*, 146, WB, *Miles*, 284.

12. WK, "The Liberal Line," *NR*, May 9, 1956, p. 9; WKS to WK, February 9, 1935, in *OxY*, 474; Richard Weaver to WK, March 27, 1956, B30F16, KP; WK to WKS, July 10, 1935, in *OxY*, 500; WK to Leo Strauss (hereafter LS), August 29, 1960, in *WKM*, 228; Pemantle, *Contrasting*, 192–93.

13. WK to YM, [1955?], Two Letters, November 1955, January 1956, and [1956?], B6F1, KP; Gerhart Niemeyer to NK, June 30, 1967, B22F22, KP.

14. WK to YM, [1956], 2 Letters, B6F1, KP; BDJ to WK, [1956], 2 letters, B16F2, KP; Hart, "Deliberate Sense," 77.

15. William J. Mullen to WB, April 27, 1959 and WB to Eugene A. Moriarity, May 19, 1959, B8, BP.

16. WK to FGW, December 10, 1960, B2, WP; "McCarthy Censure," *YDN*, November 19, 1954, p. 3; G. Morgan Browne, Jr., "Pollard, Phelps," *YDN*, December 15, 1954, p. 1; Byrum Carter Testimony, American Political Science Association Oral Histories, p. 41, B16F9, KP.

17. "Buckley to Head," *YDN*, October 19. 1955, p. 1; Edward A. Kent, "Required Readings," *YDN*, December 14, 1955, p. 2; "Kendall Review," *YDN*, March 13, 1958, p. 4; WK to CH, January 6, 1956, B7, CHP; WK to Edgar Furniss, December 13, 1956, B22F9 and Edgar Furniss to WK, January 15, 1957, KP; WK to Edgar Furniss, December 20, 1956, B3, BP; "Two to Watch," *YDN*, January 7, 1958, p. 2.

18. Paul Resnick, "Kendall Cites," *YDN*, April 24, 1957, p. 1; "McCarthy Succumbs," *YDN*, May 3, 1957, p. 1.

19. "Some Generalities," *YDN*, June 10, 1957, p. 2; "View With Alarm," *YDN*, October 12, 1957, p. 2; David Braybrooke and Stephen Williams Letters, *YDN*, October 17, 1957, p. 2; "Right Think," *YDN*, February 9, 1959, p. 2; Jeremy C. Herndon, "Voegelin's *History of Political Ideas* and the Problem of Christian Order: A Reappraisal" (PhD diss., LSU, 2004), 24.

20. Ilie Smultea to NK, April 12, 1968, B19F4, KP; Pemantle, "Trial by Drury," *passim*; Oscar Pemantle to NK, July 27, 1967, B20F6, KP; Pemantle Email, June 21, 2019; Pemantle, *Contrasting*, 56–57, 214.

21. Russell Kirk, Excerpt from *The Wanderer* [1986], B23F2, KP; Clinton Rossiter to WK, June 13, 1956 and March 26, 1959, B20F19, KP; Rothbard, *Strictly Confidential*, 35–50.

22. WK, "The Layman-Expert Dilemma," Lectures to the Foundation for American Studies, Escondido, California, [1957?], F40, Eric Voegelin Papers, Hoover Institution, Library and Archives; I follow Rothbard's dating for the talks. Kendall's vita lists them as 1955. Kendall delivered the lectures again in Escondido, California, probably in 1957. A manuscript of these talks has survived.

23. Ibid.

24. Ibid.

25. Ibid.

26. WK, "The People Versus Socrates Revisited: The Perplexities of the Athenian Jury System Are Our Own Problem," *Modern Age* III, no. 1 (Winter 1958–59): 98–111; John Bloxham, "Willmoore Kendall's 'McCarthyite' Socrates in Conservative Free Speech Debates of the 1950s and 1960s," *International Journal of the Classical Tradition* 25 (2018): 72–88; Richard Weaver to WK, January 31, 1959, B16F13, KP; Clinton Rossiter to WK, March 26, 1959, B20F19, KP.

27. WK to FGW, July 3, 1956 and July 13, 1956, B2, FGW; GWC, "Doctrine," 18, 22; CH to WK, August 4, 1957 and April 8, 1960,, B7, CHP; Frank Meyer to WK, March 14, 1960, B21F8, KP; Austin Ranney to NK, October 5, 1967, B20F11, KP; Arthur Strimling to NK, October 12, 1967, B17F6, KP.

28. Austin Ranney and WK, *Democracy and the American Party System* (New York: Harcourt, Brace, 1956), 12–15, 32–38.

29. Ranney and Kendall, *Democracy and the American*, 23–39.

30. Ibid., chs. 3–4.

31. Ranney and Kendall, *Democracy and the American*, 465–82, 519–32; GWC, "Doctrine," 22–24.

32. WK to EV, August 27, 1949 and October 15, 1956, in "VK," 378, 380; WK, "A Purpose Outside History," *NR*, March 2, 1957, pp. 210–11; WK, "Thoughts on EV," *NR*, February 14, 1959, pp. 530–31; WK to LSU Press Director, March 7, 1959, F40,Voegelin Papers; Richard Weaver to WK, March 11, 1959, B16F13, KP; EV to WK, March 20, 1957, B15F1, KP.

33. WK to LS, January 9, 1957, February 9, 1959, February 18, 1959, October 27, 1959, and August 10, 1960 in *WKM*, 198–99, 202, 204–205, 210, 223–24; LS to WK, February 13, 1959, in *WKM*, 203; WK, "The Liberal Line," November 16, 1957, p. 448 and November 23, 1957, p. 468; Alvis and Murley, Preface to *WKM*, xxvii–xxviii.

34. FGW, "Political Science," 41; WB to LB and WK, February 5, 1958, B6, BP; Alvis, "Evolution," 53–57; WB to Editors, November 19, 1957 and LB to WB, December 9, 1957, B2, BP; LB to WB and WK, July 20, 1961, B15, BP; WK to WB, June 15, 1959, B8, BP.

35. Hart, *Mind*, 40; James Fesler to WK, June 6, 1957, B22F9, KP; WK to Tinkum Brooks, August 13, 1960, B6F147, CBP; EV to James Fesler, March 20, 1957, in "VK," 383–84; BDJ to NK, December 30, 1967, B16F2, KP; WK to FGW, November 26, 1960, B2, WP; WK to CH, September 1, 1959, B7, CHP; WK to LS, August 29, 1960, in *WKM*, 227; Austin Ranney Testimony, American Political Science Association Oral Histories, p. 8, B16F9, KP; Nash, "Iconoclast I," 134; Statement on WK, [1962], B29F5, KP.

36. WK, "The Function of a University," B6F148, CBP; Robert B. Semple, Jr., "Kendall, Weiss," *YDN*, October 22, 1957, p. 1, 3; Mike Thomas, "Looking Down," *YDN*, October 24, 1957, p. 2; WK letter, *YDN*, October 24, 1957, p. 2; "Kendall to Challenge," *YDN*, February 17, 1958, p. 1.

37. "Katanga," *The Bee*, December 19, 1961, p. 8; "WITV Facts," *Fort Lauderdale News*, February 23, 1956, p. 54; M. Stanton Evans, *Revolt on the Campus* (Chicago: Regnery, 1961), 225–27; "It's Not Easy," *Tablet*, April 20, 1957, p. 4; "Dr. Manion Talk," *Tablet*, October 12, 1957, p. 4; "Will Discuss Freedom," *The Times Record* (Troy, NY), May 2, 1958, p. 54; Jack E. Fischer, "Yale Teacher," *Semi-Weekly Spokesman-Review* (Spokane), April 14, 1958, p. 5; "Highest U.S. Court," *Spokane Chronicle*, April 11, 1959, p. 59; "Similarity of Political Parties," *Arizona Daily Star*, April 14, 1958, p. 12.

38. "Graham Causes," *YDN*, February 19, 1957, p. 5; WK to WB, June 15, 1959, B8, BP; WK, "Intolerable?," *NR*, October 25, 1958, pp. 279–80.

39. LS to WK, April 1, 1959 and September 28, 1960 in *WKM*, 208, 229; WK, "Comment on McClosky's *Conservatism and Personality*," *American Political Science Review* 52, no. 2 (June 1958): 506–10; Pemantle, *Contrasting*, 188; WK, "Liberal Line," *NR*, July 5, 1958, pp. 63–64; WK to CH, Summer 1960, B7, CHP.

40. WK to EV, March/April 1957 and March 26, 1959, in "VK," 386, 389; WK to LS, February 9, 1959, in *WKM*, 201; Cady, "Sibley;" Mulford Q. Sibley to WK, July 11, 1958, B19F5, KP; WK to WB, Fall 1958, B6, BP.

41. WK to FGW, March 25, 1959, B2, WP; WK to LS, February 19, 1959, in *WKM*, 204–205; Hart, *Mind*, 39; F.E. Terman to WK, December 5, 1958, B19F13.

42. NK to LS, October 18, 1970, in *WK*, 258; Schrock Email, 2017; Interview with Pat and Connie Smith, Dallas, September 29, 2018; Interview of Mary Brian Bole, Dallas, September 28, 2018.

43. WK to CH, September 1, 1959, B7, CHP; CH to LSU Political Science Chair, March 17, 1962, B16F9, KP; Leo Paul de Alvarez, "Willmoore Kendall: Teacher, Obituary Clipping from *Phalanx*, 1967, B16F7, KP; WK to FGW, March 25, 1959, B2, WP; WK to EV, March 26, 1959, in "VK," 389–90; WK to WB, Fall 1958, B6, BP; WK to WB, June 15, 1959, B8, BP.

44. WK to WB, June 15, 1959, B8, BP.

45. WK to LS, February 18, 1959, in *WKM*, WK to WB, December 1958 and Fall 1958, B6, BP; WK to FGW, March 25, 1959, B2, WP; F.E. Terman to WK, June 26, 1959, B19F3, KP; WK to Tinkum Brooks, May 19, 1959, B6F147, CBP.

46. WK to LS, February 9, 1959, in *WKM*, 201; CH to Fulbright Committee, 1956 and CH to Richard Ware, March 11, 1958, B7, CHP; Rothbard, *Strictly Confidential*, 49; WK to LS, May 10, 1962, in *WKM*, 242.

Chapter 7

1959–1963

"In Open Air Again"

In the summer of 1960 Harvey Mansfield, Sr., professor of political science at Ohio State University and editor of the *American Political Science Review* found himself in a pickle. From Spain he had received an article from Willmoore Kendall. The article criticized the right to free speech, a right which ordinary Americans and political scientists held almost sacrosanct. Mansfield recognized the quality of Kendall's "incisive" analysis but knew that he had a problem. Finding a "neutral" reader for evaluating the article, given Kendall's status as a conservative "symbol and stereotype" proved impossible. Giving up on this task, Mansfield evaluated the article himself. He made several suggestions for revision. He wanted Willmoore to tone down his "rhetoric" and edit out "anything that will appeal only to Catholics and the natural law people." The author was annoyed by these comments but accepted several of Mansfield's suggestions as legitimate. Others he rejected, refusing to back off, for example, in his harsh attacks on John Stuart Mill. Kendall was therefore pleasantly surprised when Mansfield—despite the article's "unabashedly egghead McCarthyism"—published it in the *APSR*.[1]

Had he not used a similar title in his Socrates article, Kendall might have called this article: "The Case of the People vs. John Stuart Mill." In it he took on the role of prosecuting attorney, cross-examining Mill relentlessly, and seeking a harsh sentence. Karl Popper, who popularized the term "open society," merited less attention in his analysis. Refining his Buck Hill Falls lectures, Kendall set out to show the import of Mill's ideas through close reading and analysis of *On Liberty*. He demonstrated that Mill (with few exceptions) favored "absolute freedom of thought and speech," even when—perhaps especially when—such expression involved subversive subjects. Mill, said Kendall, insisted that freedom was society's first duty, demanded that all questions be treated as open questions, and denied "existence . . . of any truth whatever." Mill posited no "right" to free speech because that would demand recognizing an objective order of rights and duties. "In full rebellion against both religion and philosophy," Mill rejected previous treatments of his subject and regarded himself as "standing not upon the shoulders of giants but of pygmies." In summation, prosecutor Kendall called his nineteenth-century defendant "a teacher of evil."[2]

In the rest of the article, Kendall showed why an open society cannot work. Mill treated society as if it were a *"debating club* devoted above all to the pursuit of truth," whereas real societies cherish many goods. Most want to preserve ideas and practices which their members regard as true and by which their members try to live. Mill assumed free speech could do no social hurt. Most people disagreed with him on this point and feared social hurts resulting from what others said, or wrote, or thought. Therefore, Kendall argued, the only way to establish an open society was to coerce people into accepting a kind of society which they did not want. Society must silence those who oppose freedom of speech. Moreover, without belief in truth, "extremes of opinion will . . . grow further and further apart so that . . . their bearers can less and less tolerate even the thought of one another, still less one another's presence in society." Amid universal skepticism, noisy clashes of opinion would substitute "phosphorous" for "philosophy." Society would abandon the search for truth and tolerate injustice, ignorance, and oppression. Rather than modeling society on a debating club, Kendall suggested comparing it to an academic discipline. Among scholars discussion is valued, preparation for serious discourse required, and disciplinary "orthodoxy" assumed. Anyone who wanted to promote change had to work within the system's parameters and "persuade the community to accept his point of view." For the adamant change agent, if the academic discipline (or society) rejected his initiative, the alternatives were "isolation" or "banishment."[3]

Coming out in December 1960, the "Open Society and Its Fallacies" was one of the most insightful and provocative pieces of Kendall's oeuvre. Yet, only a month before, Kendall had published another article which was also among his most important. In it he articulated a carefully calibrated vision of Congressional supremacy. Entitled "The Two Majorities" and appearing in the *Midwest Journal of Politics*, this piece developed Kendall's conception of U.S. representative democracy. Presidential campaigns of both parties, he argued, tend to promote change and to seek *"popular mandates"* based on "lofty and enlightened principle." They proclaimed broad, vaguely defined plans to attract voters in a country with many different interest groups. Presidential elections thus tended toward a "plebiscitary political system." Congress, on the other hand, was linked to actual interests in "structured communities" in specific locales. Its representatives sought real gains for constituents through pork barrel projects and grounded the body politic in a healthy way.[4]

Clarifying the Madisonian vision he had first seen at Stanford, Kendall argued the Framers had designed Congress to make most important national decisions. Sometimes those decisions meant rejecting principled presidential initiatives. Leaders of the political science profession, especially Robert Dahl, had done a disservice to American politics. They had creating a false dichotomy that "either the majority rules through the presidential elections . . . , or it does not rule at all." Such political scientists thus denied "legitimacy . . . to Congress as a formulator of policy." Dahl and company portrayed Congress—with its staggered elections, seniority system, filibuster, and so forth—as a barrier to democracy, created because of the "anti-democratic, anti-majority-rule bias of the Framers." To question this consensus, admitted Kendall, "may seem an act of perversity." But academic perversity was Willmoore's stock-in-trade. He then argued persuasively that the Framers—contra Charles Beard, J. Allen Smith, et al.—possessed a deep *"commitment to the majority principle."* In creating the nation's framework, they had sought to facilitate popular control over the government, not to prevent it. They feared inflamed majorities "bent on injustice," but majority rule per se did not frighten them. As father of the Constitution, for example, Madison had no problem with "popular majorities having their way. He simply wanted . . . the majority to be articulated and counted in a certain way." Congress, then, was not a barrier to democracy but one of *"two* popular majorities."[5]

The Congressional majority involved selection by the people of uninstructed legislators with time and temperament to consider the national interest and the interests of their own communities. Localities vote not mainly on issues but for individuals. They select their "virtuous men," the natural aristocrats of their particular places. Such individuals, with deep roots at home and well connected with local business leaders and professionals, represent the "interests and values" of hierarchically structured local communities in ways no distant president ever could. Political discourse at the Congressional level dealt with concrete situations. Thus, candidates could "talk about something." In presidential elections, using "pleasant-sounding maxims," candidates mostly talked "about nothing." In this scholarly tour de force, one sees Kendall's long-standing interest in Rousseau and in local government bear fruit. By representing the will of many distinct communities, instead of upholding theories popular among liberal academics, Congress helped preserve democracy. It embodied the consensual will of the people which Rousseau believed must be lost in any large state. Frank Meyer, Willmoore's *National Review* colleague, recognized the article as "a brilliant piece of analysis." But Vernon Van Dyke, editor of the *Midwest Journal,* had to think long and hard before publishing it, given Kendall's notoriety.[6]

Though under contract with Yale until 1961, Kendall never returned there after 1958. In fact, his most productive years as a scholar came after leaving New Haven. After Stanford Kendall develop an increasingly nuanced and intricate political philosophy. From 1959 until his death in 1967, Kendall's publications increased in quantity and in quality. His many articles, and one book, from this period comprise his best scholarly work. They witness the maturation, extension, and articulation of ideas he had been pondering for the previous three decades. Later in 1960, for example, Kendall published yet another important article, "How to Read Milton's *Areopagitica*." This one appeared in the *Journal of Politics*. Arguing that the English Puritan was not a strong defender of free speech, he again faced considerable skepticism from the editor before having the article accepted for publication. The next year, together with Frederick Wilhelmsen, Kendall's piece on Cicero and the necessity for maintenance of a "public orthodoxy" appeared in French in *Table Ronde*.[7]

By 1960—having served his country in World War II and Korea, lived through scarring controversies at Yale, helped start *National Review*, and absorbed the ideas of Leo Strauss and Eric Voegelin—Kendall was at the height of his intellectual powers. His thought was reaching full maturity. For a time, he focused on publishing in prestigious journals hoping such articles would win him promotion at Yale. Under the sponsorship of the Relm Foundation, Kendall lived and worked in Europe from 1959 to 1961, mostly in Spain. Having more time to write facilitated this burst of scholarly productivity. Together with seventy other scholars, he lived for a time at the *Residencia* of the Spanish National Research Council, a government-sponsored think tank in Madrid. Here he found pleasant lodgings and was provided meals, domestic servants, and ample office space. Nellie Cooper came with him as his research assistant. Charles Hyneman believed this time in Spain helped Willmoore rediscover his muse. After "a long time in the woods," Hyneman took heart to see his old friend "out in clear ground and in open air again."[8]

Looking for like-minded company, Kendall began to associate with right-wing critics of the Franco regime. Among these were the Catholic traditionalists of *Opus Dei* associated with the University of Navarre in Pamplona. He befriended the Spanish historian and political activist Rafael Calvo Serer. He also admired philosopher Rafael Gambra Ciudad, whom he called "the only interesting person I found in Madrid." Many of these persons, including Calvo and Gambra, were monarchists disenchanted with the Franco regime. Some were Carlist legitimists. They supported the claims of the descendants of Don Carlos, Count of Medina to the Spanish throne and were often at odds with the Franco regime. The Carlists, Kendall admitted, were "a little crazy," but he admired their verve and self-assurance. He came to believe that even his "friends" in Spain remained constrained in their thinking and creativity. He did not blame the "dictatorship" for creating such intellectual stagnation. Rather he viewed the regime as "the result not the cause of the intellectual degradation of Spain." Frederick Wilhelmsen (deeply influenced by the Carlists) and his family were part of this circle. When Willmoore came to see the Wilhelmsens, he boomed out to their children that: "God has arrived." Alexandra Wilhelmsen, then a little girl, remembers that Kendall's Spanish was perfect but spoken slowly, similar to the southern-inflected drawl of his English. Although she called him Uncle Willmoore, he also frightened her a little.[9]

Kendall had difficulty completing a proposed book on Rousseau. In April 1960 he wrote Richard Ware of Relm to ask for renewal of his grant despite failure to complete the book. Part of this delay came because Kendall was reformulating his work in light of reading Leo Strauss and Eric Voegelin. He asked Ware to consider the quality of his work rather than its quantity. He noted that he could turn out "Polemical work" quickly but that "scholarly work" took time. Kendall told Ware that he had been more productive than ever in writing scholarly articles, but he had to write carefully, completing 700–800 words a day, all the while reading lots of scholarly material. Indeed, he was coming to understand that his forte lay in writing short expository pieces rather than lengthy monographs. When Willmoore pleaded greater productivity as a scholar, he spoke truly. He was formulating or completing much of his best scholarly work during this time. Recognizing the value of his efforts, Ware granted a second year of funding.[10]

Kendall did write a book in Spain, but it was unpublishable. Tentatively titled *The Long Farewell to Majority Rule*, it involved a close reading, textual analysis, and refutation of Robert Dahl's *Preface to Democratic Theory* (1956). By reading and rereading the book and reducing Dahl's arguments to logical form, a new vision of democracy "opened up" for Kendall, the implications of which, he said, Dahl did not see. By engaging with Dahl, Kendall realized his own previous ideas about "majority-rule democracy" had been wrong. Few Americans ever actually questioned "the majority-principle." Yet he was skeptical of Dahl's number crunching to measure democracy. He thought the author's anti-Madisonian views incompatible with the main arguments in *Preface*. Kendall then reached the "shocking" conclusion that "the whole anti-majoritarian interpretation of Madison and Hamilton is an historicist fallacy." As a book, this effort did not work. Rigorously argued point by subpoint, full of explanatory ellipses and references to Dahl's *Preface*, it made tough reading, even by Kendall's demanding standards. Public dissection of famous works by Locke or Socrates or Mill might pull in readers, but Dahl's name lacked similar cachet. Kendall did get interest from publishers, but eventually they shied away.[11]

Kendall wrote only sporadically for *National Review* while in Europe, with his contributions intertwined with his academic work. In May 1961 a crisis in Kendall's relationship with the magazine arose over his review of Arthur Whitaker's *Spain and the Defense of the West*. When Willmoore submitted a twelve-page typescript, Buckley pruned it. Believing his original version would help "our friends in Spain," Kendall found the edits to be unacceptable. He threatened resignation and expected that his stance would "probably result in the disappearance of my name from the masthead of *National Review*." A month later, he told Francis Wilson that the coming "liquidation" of his connection with the magazine would be "a relief." In reality, Buckley's refusal to rescind his cuts and his willingness to accept Willmoore's resignation shook Kendall so badly that he ended a long period of sobriety. Brent Bozell was able to reconcile the two men which allowed Kendall to continue for a time with *National Review*. In July Kendall apologized to Buckley and agreed to accept Buckley's editorial discretion as the final word about what got printed.[12]

Thus, not everything went swimmingly for Willmoore on his European sojourn. Despite a year of successful writing, Kendall was drinking to excess and determined to enter a hospital for treatment of this "long-standing malady." In October he checked in for a long hospital stay in Pamplona. He expressed hope that that this break from routine would help him start afresh in his scholarly pursuits. Responsible for his treatment was Dr. Juan José López-Ibor, the most famous psychiatrist in Spain. Hospital costs were cheap by American standards, and López-Ibor agreed to offer "his own services for free—as a friend." After months of treatment, the psychiatrist, using an early form of cognitive therapy, told Willmoore that what he most needed was "to apply to my own problems the kind of intelligence I apply to the problems I write about." López-Ibor also prescribed the drug disulfiram (Antabuse), "the famous little pills," said Willmoore, "which make you allergic to alcohol." By November, Kendall had given up all intoxicating beverages. He found the change to be quite "a shock," but López-Ibor stressed the need to "abstain totally." For a time Willmoore kept the nature of his malady quiet, and he always remained defensive about it. He told Hyneman he had been hospitalized for "fatigue" and "pneumonia." Only in early 1961 did he admit the alcohol dimension of his hospitalization to Bill Buckley. Even then he claimed López-Ibor was providing him "advice, not therapy" and that his hospital stay was "purely medicinal" in nature.[13]

For a time, Kendall thrived under this treatment. In December 1960 he welcomed Brent Bozell, Patricia (aka Trish or Tish) Buckley Bozell, and their eight children. They were coming to Spain so Brent could write. Willmoore devoted lots of time to finding a suitable dwelling, hiring a cook, two maids, a nanny, and buying a week's worth of groceries. Said Trish:

> Ken remains a jewel. When we arrived here he had the guards hand me the keys to the place and all the maids lined up in spanking uniforms (gotten by Ken) to greet me. Then a delicious four course meal with flowers around (another Kenism) and a sign in front of each bedroom designating which person went where. Yes, we were met at the airport by Ken, Reid, and two nurses. This allowed me to clutch Kiki, and after a plush reception at our home, I followed Kiki under the bed.

All in all, she thought, her family had come to live in "one of the more beautiful spots on earth," located near the magnificent royal monastic complex of El Escorial and surrounded "on all sides by snow-topped mountains."[14]

Mrs. Bozell, however, was also suffering from alcoholism. Drinking no alcohol on the plane trip over was the start of her attempt to dry out. At this point Kendall, months into his own treatment, spoke confidently about his "complete break with alcohol." It was a development he found a "quite 'liberating.'" He offered assistance to Trish, of whom he was quite fond. At social gatherings, their circle sometimes refrained from serving alcohol. When the alcohol did flow, Trish and Ken happily "drank mineral water." A few days after the Bozells arrived in Spain, Ken and Trish sat up to 5:00 a.m. talking "candidly for the first time about the problem." Willmoore was optimistic after this private conversation. He saw Trish "falling in love all over again with life," fondly recalling "how she loved it when I first knew her!" He expressed hope to Bill that he had "been of some use to her," then noted "how young and beautiful she is," despite her recent struggles with alcohol.[15]

By March things were going less well. Mrs. Bozell appeared to abstain only because of the insistence of her husband. Her abstinence had lasted six weeks. On March 5, 1961, the Bozells planned a birthday dinner for Ken, for which Trish prepared roast beef and cake. In the meantime, Brent discovered a "fifth of gin" his wife had snuck into the house and threw it away. A furious Patricia began slamming doors, then refused to talk to her husband. "Poor Ken," said Brent, "even he, I am sure, has had happier birthdays." Kendall then put the Bozells in touch with Dr. López-Ibor and was hopeful his treatment would help Trish. The initial results were unhappy. Brent soon found himself a "prison guard" to his wife, as his efforts to empty the house of liquor failed. "On Willmoore," Brent told Bill, "Good God." Kendall soon lapsed back into his own alcoholism. Upon receiving a letter from Buckley in the Spring of 1961 accepting his resignation from *National Review* (in the Whitaker dispute), Willmoore had gone "to the can and vomited," then telephoned Brent. Two hours later—when Willmoore showed up to lecture at the Madrid Ateneo—he "was stinko." As Bozell patched things up, he suggested that clarification of Buckley's editorial authority must come from him alone, that "no one else will do."[16]

Another untoward incident occurred in France in early 1961 when Kendall mailed some jewelry from Paris back to the United States. He sent it to Bill Buckley with instructions to forward it to Evan (Van) Galbraith. Galbraith was chairman of the board of *National Review* and Buckley's closest friend. Nancy Galbraith, Van's wife, had left two valuable gems in the poor box of a Paris church. Having convinced the priest to give them to him for safekeeping, Kendall chose not to return the jewels to Mrs. Galbraith herself. There "was some question as to Nancy's present competence." Over the next couple of years this situation got more complicated. Van Galbraith accused Kendall of having committed adultery with his wife, apparently during this visit to France. The Buckley circle mostly sided with Ken in the matter, regarding Nancy as "a mad woman" who was either lying or who herself had seduced Kendall. After Kendall's return to the United States, this matter got entangled in the Galbraith divorce. Named as corespondent in adultery, Willmoore had to testify in the case, amid accusations of homosexuality against Van and insanity regarding Nancy.[17]

Kendall, Buckley, and Bozell had developed a deep emotional bond in their shared battles at Yale. Despite bitter disputes in coming years, that bond never really disappeared. By 1960 the Buckley-Kendall relationship had experienced a role reversal. Buckley was acting as father figure to his former teacher. Some of Bill's letters to Willmoore in Spain sound eerily like those from Reverend Kendall to his son decades earlier, with Bill urging Ken to finish his book. Buckley also assisted Kendall with financial matters, including his taxes. Meanwhile, Bill and Brent were coming to know Nellie Cooper, and Brent was not impressed. Nellie, he said, "was nice, but terribly stupid . . . and mostly vegetable." He knew "how bad off Willmoore" was when he "presented her to us as his fiance." Bozell noted that Kendall had "taken refuge in her in the way one heads for the shade of a favorite old oak when the world seems too much to bear." By that summer, Bozell was also feuding with Kendall, but he hoped that Nellie would force Ken "to face reality and go after a cure." Willmoore seems to have planned to marry Nellie before this announcement. In 1960 he asked Yvona not to think it "silly" that he still hoped for "a son or daughter of my own." He went on to say that he had hired "the Roman equivalent of a Philadelphia lawyer" to help "his canonical case." He thought "the Church is going to free me to get married" and told his sister that the lower cost of living in Spain would make it easier to raise a family.[18]

As Kendall's time in Spain wound down, he had to face returning to Yale, a prospect neither he nor the university relished. When considering his position at Yale, however, Kendall took into account the "standpoint of the national Right." Conservatives prized having one of their own at the renowned university. Conservative activists regarded his employment at

Yale as a strategic beachhead. Buckley, said Kendall, had convinced him to return to Yale from a better-paying job at ORO to serve the purposes of the conservative movement. Relm had provided the research grant for Kendall to go to Spain in part to bolster his cause for receiving promotion at Yale. In 1959, when Stanford students wanted to raise money to establish an endowed chair for Kendall, Buckley discouraged their efforts. His old mentor, he said, could "do more for the cause of Conservatism teaching in the cosmopolitan fortress of the Liberal ideology than he can in the relatively robust colleges of the midwest and far west."[19]

Yet, Kendall often talked about quitting Yale. He came to believe that being at some other university where he could turn out PhD students, a privilege denied him at Yale, might help American conservatism more than remaining at the Ivy League school. In 1959, before he left for Spain, he thought he had arranged a buyout of his contract. Then, he said, President A. Whitney Griswold had "got cold feet at the last minute." Eventually Kendall decided that he could no longer be a martyr to the conservative cause by staying at Yale. He still wanted to boost the cause of conservatism and was willing to sacrifice for it. As regards Yale, however, he told Buckley that he had now to distinguish between loyalty and "quixotism."[20]

By early 1961 Kendall thought that Yale might accept another buyout proposal. His "self-respect" required him to leave, he said, given the impossibility of promotion and the pervasive hostility he faced in New Haven. In February 1961 he made a proposal to leave if the university would pay him ten years salary. The request did not result from a spur-of-the-moment drunken phone call to President Griswold, as sometimes portrayed. Kendall had long considered this move, then perhaps he made such a call. Dahl, on behalf of Yale, accepted Kendall's offer. Willmoore believed Buckley would "put great pressure" on him not to go through with his resignation. Kendall received Dahl's letter "with mixed emotions" but felt "pretty good about it." After negotiations, Kendall signed his letter of resignation on May 10, 1961, with Provost Norman Sydney Buck signing for Yale. The final terms of the settlement were two payments of $4,250 each year for the next five years. University officials denied they had forced out Kendall for political reasons. One political scientist did wryly suggest that their former colleague would find Spain's political climate more "congenial" than New Haven's.[21]

When Willmoore came back to Connecticut in late June 1961, he vowed never to set foot on the Yale campus. Without a job he began to look around for an outlet for his energies and for ways to boost his income. Always a poor money manager, and with heavy expenses related to legal matters and frequent travel, Willmoore struggled financially. His financial prospects began to improve at the end of 1961. The Yale settlement money helped, but he also began to sell gravel from his creek at Northford. This attempt to draw profit from his land attracted the attention of neighbors, the closest of whom were Cleanth and Tinkum Brooks. When Tinkum complained to Willmoore about trucks entering the property to remove the gravel, Kendall, who had been drinking, exchanged words with her. This confrontation ended a decades-long friendship with the Brookses.[22]

Kendall claimed at times that his drinking problem remained in abeyance upon returning to his home country. In November, for instance, he wrote to Hyneman that: "I took the vow in Spain and am sticking to it pretty good I *must* say." Doing "pretty good" was either intentionally untruthful or delusional. Those closer to Kendall knew better. In August Buckley and Bozell warned Willmoore that he was "dangerously ill" and should return to Spain for treatment. Kendall did not respond well to these admonitions. He temporarily cut off contact with Bozell for wielding "the weapon of alleged illness" like a "baby" brandishing "a razor." In September 1961 he went on "a bender" which caused grave concern to his mother, sister, and Buckley. In October Bill got Ken to agree to make continued employment at *National Review* contingent on remaining sober. He even agreed to pay him a $2,000 retainer if he refrained from drink. Buckley informed Pearl Kendall that her son "was looking for an incentive to take that little pill every morning."[23]

Meanwhile Kendall was searching out professional opportunities. Building on established contacts, for example, he explored working for the Dominican Republic. He had previously served that country as a public relations consultant. As part of this work Kendall had worked as ghostwriter and translator for Rafael Trujillo, the country's controversial dictator. In January 1957 the Dominican government had rejected his proposal to write a book about the "inner workings of the regime." Kendall viewed the country's public relations efforts as "inept," but he remained fascinated with the Trujillo experiment. He saw the regime as translating "into palpitating reality" the "'public-spirited' political philosophy" of Thomas Hobbes, with Rafael Trujillo as a Hobbesian Leviathan trying to bring order to his society. The Dominican boss, Kendall thought, was seeking to promote the good as Hobbes said strong rulers should do. Labeling the country's government a "dictatorship based on something called force," Kendall argued at the time, failed to catch its complexity.[24]

By the summer of 1961 the regime was in serious trouble. In May, shortly before Kendall returned to the United States from Spain, Rafael Trujillo—who in the previous two years had repelled a Cuban invasion and attempted to blow up the president of Venezuela—was assassinated in a CIA plot. Desperately holding onto power, the Trujillo family reached out to Kendall. Besides intellectual interest in the regime and experience working with it, Willmoore had a personal connection to the dead dictator's family. Flor de Oro Trujillo, Rafael's oft-married daughter, was an "old flame." Therefore, in July 1961, he took a trip to the Republic to explore working for the tottering government. It was, he said, a "sorely needed job." Kendall viewed his mission as showing the regime how "to make itself acceptable" to American conservatives, that is, what "self-surgery" would be necessary to make it agreeable to a Barry Goldwater. Afterward he flew to California to give a speech to Hollywood conservatives in which he praised the anticommunism of the rump government. If American liberals forced regime change on the country, they would, he argued, facilitate the spread of Castroism. Kendall doubted he would get the job because "the course I'd advise them to follow . . . would take more imagination than I suppose them to have." After about a month, he gave up the project as a waste of time. Shortly thereafter the remaining Trujillos fled to Europe. Kendall believed an opportunity to establish a firmly conservative Dominican government, "a la Chiang," had been missed.[25]

Longer-term prospects beckoned on the American speaking circuit. When he returned from Spain in 1961, Willmoore discovered that "an unprecedented demand for 'conservative' oratory" had developed in the United States. He believed he could earn a tidy income from such "performances." To maintain his market value, he told his sister, he would have to keep "my name on the masthead of *NR* at a time I would like to break with it." Kendall consulted with Buckley about possible engagements. He signed on with a speaker's bureau which advertised six different topics which he could deliver. These included: "'Academic Freedom and Its Fallacies, "Freedom of Speech" and Its Fallacies,' Conservatism and the Right-Wing Dictators, Conservatism and the Welfare State, The Fallacy of 'Christian' Pacifism, [and] Conservatism and the 'Individualist' Fallacy." Another flyer from following years included an illustrated portrait of a dapper Willmoore smoking a cigarette. It included testimonials from Brent Bozell and Stanley Parry.[26]

Over his lifetime Willmoore Kendall often showed himself to be a mesmerizing speaker and debater. When facing a challenging opponent such as Mulford Sibley, Paul Weiss, or James MacGregor Burns, he more than held his own. In the autumn months of 1961, however, he experienced a series of public embarrassments in this role, mostly related to his worsening alcoholism. Even when not obviously liquor related, one suspects covert drinking caused Kendall to misjudge his audiences. On August 19, 1961, for example, he delivered a speech at Hollywood High School in Los Angeles and praised Keynesian economics. In response Buckley received a cascade of letters criticizing his editorial "left hand man." A Phoenix-area physician complained that Willmoore sounded like "a Fabian socialist, perhaps a new frontiersman." Another listener said Kendall was rude and that he championed the "commie-line" of farm subsidies, the Marshall Plan, and the minimum wage. When Kendall proclaimed it "was the Russian communists we had to worry about" not "creeping socialism" at home, the crowd started "booing & protesting." Defending his mentor, Buckley admitted Kendall was fond of Keynes. Remembering the Yale years, however, Buckley told one correspondent that Willmoore had been "the only man on campus defending: 1) free enterprise 2) Senator Joseph McCarthy" and that "I saw him bleed rather profusely in defense of his beliefs." Therefore, Willmoore deserved "a certain amount of patience."[27]

Then things got worse. In Seattle on November 15, 1961, Kendall set out to debate liberal activist Carl Braden, recently freed from a year in jail for refusal to testify to the House Un-American Activities Committee. That night Kendall denounced the Bill of Rights, called Americans a "persecuting people," claimed Braden should be persecuted, and labeled himself a "Jacobin." According to a friendly witness, he "was obviously drunk and had been drinking all day." All in all, said one attendee, "it was a Field Day for Liberals." The next day—November 16, 1961—Kendall spoke at a California university and again appeared inebriated. Buckley wrote sternly to Kendall. Willmoore had denied being drunk, marshaled favorable testimonials, and defended his arguments in the speech. Buckley knew better and urged his former teacher to get "back to the antabuse." Bill then smoothed over the matter. He settled on (and asked others to share) the story that the controversial performances had resulted from "barbiturates taken in an accidentally heavy dose, and fatigue." He then sent an encouraging telegram to a thankful Ken. "EVIDENCE IS CLEAR. YOU WERE AMBUSHED BY BARBITURATES AND LET'S GET ON WITH PUTTING BRADEN BEHIND BARS."[28]

Continuing to drink heavily and not taking his Antabuse, Kendall was not yet ready to "get on with" anything. On December 1, he again embarrassed himself in front of a crowd, this time on a visit to Georgetown University, where he was set to teach the next semester. After a lackluster talk, he annoyed his audience by answering questions in a "boorish" manner. Then, at a dinner party at the home of Karl Cerny, former Yale student and (together with George W. Carey) a member of the Georgetown political science department, Kendall passed out. Carey attributed such behavior to Kendall's "heavy drinking," which was "well in excess of a fifth a day." Willmoore was often drunk before going out in public. In such state, said Carey, Kendall was a danger to himself, "falling asleep with lighted cigarette, falling out of chairs, etc." Ken reported this incident to Bill, apologizing for "getting very drunk." Buckley showed the letter to James Burnham, with the comment: "Read it & weep." Kendall remembered nothing about the night in question but promised to be "less grand" in promises about future sobriety. For a time, Kendall again dried out. He reported in mid-January to Buckley and Hyneman (who had heard of his troubles with "John Barleycorn") that he had not taken a drink in six weeks.[29] Buckley ignored his own pledge to fire Kendall from *National Review* if he did not stay sober.

In fact, when Kendall traveled to Dallas later in December to pursue yet another professional opportunity, he served as an emissary for Buckley, then sounding out a potential alliance with General Edwin A. Walker. Willmoore hoped to become a speechwriter for Walker, a right-wing critic of Eisenhower and Kennedy, who had just resigned his army commission to enter politics. In terms of political influence, the potential job would be "the most important operation I was ever involved in," Kendall told his sister. He added that he needed to stop Walker "from using his mouth to put his foot in." He told Francis Wilson that he would take the job only if Walker dropped "the whole topic of domestic communism, on which his thinking varies from silly to just plain mad." Kendall met Medford Evans, Walker's chief advisor, but the men could not agree about the nature of the Communist menace. Kendall toed the *National Review* line, arguing that American communists were no real danger and that the focus should be on the external Soviet threat. Evans maintained that American political leaders were deeply under the influence of communists and had to be denounced as such. Kendall replied that if the General did not change his mind he would "lose his respectable support." Asked to explain "respectable support," Kendall told Evans, "I mean *National Review*." Willmoore did not get the job. He informed Buckley that "real communication on the issues at stake" with Evans and Walker was "out of the question" because of "how they hate the 'respectable' Conservatives!" Kendall soon wrote a note to Evans which ended with the admonition, *"C'est la guerre."*[30]

Such outreach to Walker was connected to the magazine's increasingly testy relationship with the John Birch Society, to which both Walker and Evans were closely connected. After discovering in 1958 that Robert Welch, Society founder, thought President Eisenhower, and numerous other American government leaders, were communist agents, Buckley determined to break with the society. As Willmoore explained to Yvona, any such ideological divorce was a perilous step for the magazine "as many of our most powerful and wealthy supporters are also supporters of the Birch Society." Kendall was never a Bircher and said he could not understand why anyone would support the group. He believed Buckley had handled the question of *National Review* distancing itself from the Society "just brilliantly."[31] A key question in this dispute, then, was how to distinguish between the dangers of liberalism and communism. Those associated with Walker, Evans, and the Birch Society wanted to merge these threats. On the other hand, Buckley, Kendall, and the other editors of *National Review* had long sought to portray liberalism and communism as distinct dangers. The former was domestic and the latter external.

By backing Buckley, Kendall lost the friendship of Revilo Oliver. Oliver was a founder and board member of the Birch Society, and he wrote regularly for its magazine *American Opinion*. His final break with *National Review* came in 1960 when anti-Semitic statements delivered in his speeches appeared in *Common Sense* and *American Mercury*. Magazine editors already knew Oliver was a Nietzschean who viewed liberalism as exemplifying *Sklavenmoral*, but they found his increasingly open and outright anti-Semitism unacceptable. Buckley asked Oliver to repudiate his published remarks as "unauthorized." When Oliver refused, his name disappeared from *National Review*. Kendall applauded Buckley's approach to the matter. Heading east from Dallas in December 1961, Kendall stopped by Urbana to mend fences with his old friend. Oliver, he said, had "become very bitter about the world in general" and "seems to be asking for trouble as eloquently as anyone can." Willmoore had urged Revilo to avoid politics after being forced out at *National Review* but to no avail. He told Oliver that his anti-Semitism and conflation of liberals and communists was unacceptable to him personally and to the magazine. Revilo, however, had "gone John Birch Society crazy." To Wilson, Kendall added: "All of this is very sad to me, as Revilo has been my closest friend for 30 years now." On his visit Kendall tried to convince his friend that he was making unsubstantiated claims in his political writings that he would never tolerate in his scholarship. This outreach failed, and the men had little contact afterward. Oliver understood that in commencing "to write on political subjects," he had made a "grave mistake" career-wise, but, said Kendall, Revilo's "hatred for NR dominated all else in his emotions." Eventually, Oliver's anti-Semitism became too much for the Birch Society, which pushed him out in 1966.[32]

As it began to separate from the Birch Society and associated groups, however, the Buckley circle was distancing itself from an approach much like it had once championed. The magazine had always distinguished between liberal and communist threats. But it had also warned that liberal "fellow-travelers" facilitated communist subversion. As Buckley was getting *National Review* off the ground, critics had called such attacks disreputable. Now it was Buckley who was calling out his opponents on the right as scrambled in the brains. In part this change came because Buckley, Kendall, Burnham, and associates believed their battles in the 1950s—waged in their words and through the actions of McCarthy and the House Un-American Activities Committee—had worked. That is, under conservative pressure, the United States had tightened up its internal security procedures enough to minimize communist infiltration of American institutions. This fissure also occurred because Bircher claims were more extravagant, and less evidence based than the charges of their predecessors. As always, *National Review* continued to lambaste liberals. Insofar as this fight derived from the anti-Semitism of those to the magazine's right, there was little change. Buckley, Kendall and company had long denounced this tendency among conservatives.[33]

Willmoore had a relatively uneventful and productive semester at Georgetown in the Spring of 1962. For the first time in his life, he held the rank of full professor, albeit on a visiting basis. He continued to integrate the various strands of his career as a public intellectual together, working up speeches and lectures and then revising them for publication. An April 1962 speech he delivered in Madison, Wisconsin, for example, provided the basis for an article in *National Review* and for a key essay on McCarthy in his upcoming book. He suggested in this speech, that each side could claim victory in the McCarthy struggle. "McCarthyites . . . got the persecution of the Communists which their understanding of American consensus demanded." But "the anti-McCarthyites" saw that such efforts "went forward" using "the clear and present danger doctrine." Despite his inauspicious debut, Kendall performed creditably at Georgetown. He roomed with George W. Carey, developing an intellectual partnership that blossomed in the upcoming years. As usual, he won "devoted fans" among conservative students. When offered a teaching post in California, Kendall delayed accepting the position. The Jesuit university wanted to see if it could match the offer.[34]

After returning to the United States in 1961, Kendall continued to write occasionally for *National Review*. But he never wielded the influence or experienced the camaraderie he had enjoyed there until 1958. Privately, he expressed reservations about the magazine. He told Wilson that *National Review* "was a menace to US conservatism in its present form" and complained about being shunted aside as a "dreamy college professor." Kendall expressed dismay "at seeing myself passed up in the race for fame and fortune by persons who once in one way or another had been very close to me and distinctly below me in pecking order." Among these persons were John Fischer, Carl Albert, Robert Dahl, and Henry Kissinger. Much of this dissatisfaction centered on Buckley himself. As Ken told Bill in 1962, "You're *already* famous, and don't have to work on it so hard from now on. Some of the rest of us want to be famous, too." He fumed that the magazine had become *"Burnham's Fortnightly."* Predictably, Kendall came to resent Buckley's advice about his drinking, and in April 1962 he told his former student he had stopped taking Antabuse.[35]

That summer the Bozells paid for Ken and Nellie to return to Spain. Brent hoped Willmoore could help him finish his book. He also needed Kendall's translation services to help with Trish's treatment whose various nuances were beyond Bozell's Spanish. Trish continued to receive residential treatment for alcoholism from López-Ibor, and Bozell feared she would need institutional care upon return to the United States. Willmoore certainly did not lead by example. After a summer of sobriety, said Trish, Kendall partied "all night" with his friends for a "lost weekend" in Spain, leaving him *"muy soplado."* Then, "when he was on his 22nd hour of drinking, slobbering and fuming all over me, he garbled: 'Tish, you don't know how well you look. You see, some of us can take drink, some like you can't.' Isn't that cute?" Willmoore, she went on, "looks awful & is sick and not just from booze . . . Poor everybody." Trish reassured a worried Bill about Ken's health but mentioned his "shortness of breath." In fact, Kendall had his first signs of angina pectoris during the Spring Semester of 1962 at Georgetown. That fall he was diagnosed with serious heart trouble in Los Angeles.[36]

Kendall arrived back in the United States in late August 1962 and prepared to move west to take a new post at Los Angeles State College. He knew he was taking a step down from Yale or Georgetown but needed the money. Offered a tenured post, Willmoore took a visiting professorship instead. The job market for political scientists was quite good, and he did not want to tie himself down. He was interested in raising funds to push the annulment process forward so he could marry Nellie. "This business in Rome," he told Yvona, "is gonta be expensive." Kendall was also ready to relocate. The East, he said, was for him too tied up with his "mistakes" of going to work for the ORO, committing too much time to *National Review*, going into debt at Northford, and marrying Anne. He was happy to move to California whose "fluidity" offered a chance to start offer. Kendall enjoyed teaching his classes at his new post but discovered students less prepared than those he was used to. He considered coming back for a second year, but his contract was not renewed. He experienced "pangs of guilt" about not contributing more to *National Review* but preferred focusing on his academic work.[37]

Kendall's biggest achievement that year was to complete his long-awaited book. He finished the manuscript in February 1963 for submission to Regnery. The book's original title was *What Is Conservatism?*, patterned after Leo Strauss's *What Is Political Philosophy?* At the suggestion of the publisher, Kendall agreed to call the book *The Conservative Affirmation*. Kendall had high hopes for the book. He cultivated reviews in mass circulation magazines, including *National Review* and told Francis Wilson that Regnery was thinking "he's got another *God and Man at Yale*." William Rusher, publisher of *National Review*, wrote to Kendall saying he was eager to read *The Conservative Affirmation*. Rusher found Kendall's writing style "overwhelmingly attractive, and I am forever running around larding my sentences with 'over against' and 'off at the end.'" Into the early summer of 1963 Kendall continued to hope that sales of *The Conservative Affirmation* would take off. By July, however, it had become apparent to Kendall that his book, in terms of sales, "was going to be another Right-wing flop."[38]

One can understand why the book disappointed some of Kendall's fellow conservatives. It was a collection of seven essays, several already in print, together with thirty-one previously published book reviews. For one who already knew his work, Willmoore appeared not to be breaking much new ground and had not produced the "*book book*" which they expected. Moreover, *The Conservative Affirmation* seemed to lack focus. Bertrand de Jouvenel criticized it for not affirming conservatism but attacking liberals and Lockeans. In fact, the book was more carefully structured than it appeared. Kendall, for example, placed the essay "The Social Contract: The Ultimate Issue between Liberalism and Conservatism" at "what Strauss would call the center of the book, where the reader is led to the deepest philosophical level attempted in the book, and where at last the purpose is to instruct him philosophically, not to propagandize him." Kendall wanted that piece "to stand out like a sore thumb, i.e. as quite different in character from the rest of the book." Henry Regnery knew the book was not just slapped together. But he believed its centerpiece was "McCarthyism: The Pons Asinorum of Contemporary Conservatism," which argued for the necessity of social orthodoxy and showed that liberalism, in trying to undermine that orthodoxy, was a revolutionary enterprise.[39]

Despite these disparate interpretations, *The Conservative Affirmation*—every part of it—was, and still is, worth reading. Republishing book reviews might seem like cheating, but Willmoore Kendall was a master of that form. Indeed, he was a connoisseur of reading. Like a wine critic, he savored the essence of each book he was appraising, then rendered his carefully considered judgment upon it. He could be vicious. The new edition of Clinton Rossiter's *Conservatism in America: The Thankless Persuasion* was "even more ignorant or perverse" than its original version. He said Rossiter ignored actual conservatives and judged political movements by liberal principles. "One is tempted," concluded Kendall, "to explain the book in terms of perversity, not ignorance. But that might be ungenerous since the book is shot through and through with methodological confusions." His evaluations could also be generous. In analyzing *Our Public Life*, by Paul Weiss—his old Yale debate antagonist—Kendall admitted that conservatives would deplore its "liberal programmatic aspect." Then he praised Weiss's defense of natural law, "piety" toward the "American political tradition," and openness toward religion. Weiss, he concluded, "is that Liberal we've all been looking for who truly values the discussion process." Or, Kendall might combine deep analysis, severe criticism, and praise in his reviews. He criticized Richard Weaver's *Ideas Have Consequences* for having an "ill-tempered, name-calling emphasis." He suggested Weaver did not have enough familiarity with England or Scandinavia to analyze them. Then he compared Weaver favorably to Ortega y Gasset. Weaver just needed to realize that his real enemies were liberals, not Americans as a whole. If he did so, he would get Kendall's "vote for the captaincy of the anti-Liberal team."[40] In these reviews, one sees that Kendall had intellectually absorbed these books and would never forget them. His erudition, admitted even by enemies, was not faked, it was earned.

The book's essays also demonstrated Willmoore's characteristic style in all its intricacy. To readers unfamiliar with his work, his analyses of the open society, Christian pacifism, and the two majorities in American politics would appear as novel and meticulously reasoned. Two new essays also showed Kendall at the top of his game. "What is Conservatism?" began by limiting itself to the American situation. It dismissed "vulgar" conceptions of who the real conservatives are, that is, religious believers, anticommunists, and so forth. Kendall then posited an elaborate "battle-line" metaphor. He suggested that conservatives were those people who resisted—right down the line and on a whole host of issues—the "Liberal Revolution." The liberals were the enemy across this line of battle who, in an increasingly self-conscious way, sought "to overthrow an established and traditional social and political order." The enemy called its goal equality. Kendall labeled it egalitarianism. Liberals, that is, did not champion "an equal right to compete with others." Rather they wanted government to level all significant differences within the populace. Moreover, this liberal "revolution must go on and on forever, since if you are in the business of making people equal, there is and can be no stopping place." Kendall called on the resisters to coalesce in a self-conscious movement. Thereby, they could, on the line of political battle, work together to defend their tradition—a tradition grounded in the "high principles" of the "great documents" of the American founding. Thus might they thwart leveling liberal designs.[41]

In the book's keystone essay, "The Ultimate Issue," Kendall admitted he would work readers "somewhat harder" than "in earlier chapters." Then Kendall explained how American conservatives could not be Lockeans. This essay briefly summarized Western political philosophy. Starting with the Greeks, Kendall showed that the Sophists had argued for society originating in agreements between individuals designed to promote their own self-interest. He then demonstrated how Socrates, Plato, and Aristotle had defeated these propositions. They had argued that society was natural not conventional. The principles undergirding it were to be discovered, not invented. Moreover, the good society allowed the best aspects of human nature to flourish. Individuals thus had a duty to promote human good by preserving society. For two thousand years, this "Great Tradition" reigned in the West until challenged by Hobbes, Locke, and Rousseau. More modern philosophers had further reduced the insights of the three contractarians to a ruined remnant. Only two principles remained: (1) society must be based *exclusively* on the consent of the governed as to what is right and what is wrong and (2) the purpose of society "is to minister to the self-interest" of its members. Conservatives were those who affirmed the Great Tradition. Their ideas stretched back to Aristotle. They believed in a higher law discernable through reason which individuals were duty-bound to obey. Liberals were those who embraced the "relativism" of human convention and held individuals bound only by self-interest. "The Lockeans in America," said Kendall, "are the Liberals," and "Conservatives . . . must learn to understand themselves as the anti-Lockeans."[42]

Late that spring, a university which appreciated Kendall's ideas approached him with a job offer. The University of Dallas—seeking to build its brand as a superior, conservative, and Catholic institution of higher education— wanted Kendall to head its department of politics. Winding down his year in Los Angeles, this offer was a godsend for Willmoore, but it did not come out of the blue. He had received hints of the university's interest as early as 1960. As he pursued other opportunities, he remained in contact with Dallas about possible employment. When the offer came, he was excited. A light work schedule would leave him time "for writing, lecture engagements, etc." The money was almost as good as he was used to, and he could "call the difference . . . a gift to the Church." Kendall would lead a department of politics, not of political science. It would focus on "political philosophy and comparative government," as Aristotle did, with no behaviorist "nonsense." At Dallas, Kendall could combine his love of belles lettres and politics, a puzzling blend to many political scientists, but one to which Kendall had clung since Oxford. Happily, he told Wilson, "I shan't even *see* a Liberal in the course of a week's work." In his new post, he rhapsodized: "I can be Moses back from the 40 years of his preparation, among his people—I found myself sinking into the local accent, which was mine forty years ago, as a weary man sinks into a warm bath." In brief, he went on, "God has been very good to me."[43]

In April 1963 Kendall, seemingly chastened by his recent experiences and heartened that his book had come out, wrote to William F. Buckley. He thanked him for having borne patiently with him over the previous few years. He suggested a quieter future ahead, that most of his personal challenges from previous years were now in the past. He would also have the "*enforced* calm of being a heart patient."[44] As so often in the life of Willmoore Kendall, this period of contentment, especially in regard to his personal relationships, would be the calm which preceded a storm.

NOTES

1. WK to FGW, March 4, 1960, August 4 1960, and October 11, 1960, B2, WP; WK to LS, August 10, 1960, August 29, 1960, and October 12, 1960 in WKM, 222–23, 226–27, 230; Austin Ranney to WK, April 10, 1960, B20F10, KP.

2. WK, "The Open Society and Its Fallacies," *American Political Science Review* 54, no. 4 (December 1960): 972–76.

3. Ibid., 977–79; Sulma M. Portillo, "Unequal Benefactors and Beneficiaries: The Utilitarian Inadequacy of Mill's Arguments for Freedom" (PhD, diss., University of Windsor, 2007), 108.

4. WK, "The Two Majorities," *Midwest Journal of Politics* 4, no. 4 (November 1960): 319–24, 340.

5. Ibid., 321–25, 330–36.

6. WK, "Two Majorities," 336–45; Robert M. Reinsch II, "A Tale of Two Majorities," *Law & Liberty*, August 31, 2016, https://www.lawliberty.org/2016/08/31/a-tale-of-two-majorities/; Frank Meyer to WK, May 28, 1960, B21F8, KP; Vernon Van Dyke to FGW, February 2, 1960, Van Dyke to WK, March 7, 1960, and Van Dyke to WK, April 4, 1960, B2, WP; WK to FGW, March 8, 1960, B2, WP.

7. WK to FGW, January 24, 1960, B2, WP; WK to HR, [1960], B38F2, HRP; WK to FGW, March 4, 1960, September 22, 1960 and January 1961, B2, WP; WK to WB, January 26, 1961 and W. Morris Clarke to WK, January 21, 1961, B15, BP.

8. WK to FGW, 1960, B2, WP; CH to WK, April 16, 1960, B7, CHP.

9. WK to FGW, November 9, 1957, March 4, 1960, May 18, 1960, and June 1960 (2 letters), B2, WP; FW, Memories, WKC; Alexandra Wilhelmsen, Interview with the Author, Dallas, Texas, September 28, 2018.

10. WK to Richard Ware, April 4, 1960, B19F3, KP; WK to WB, November 15, 1959 and December 4, 1959, B8, BP; Austin Ranney to WK, March 29, 1961, B20F10, KP; WK to LS, August 10, 1960, in *WKM*, 223; WK to CH, September 1, 1959, April 8, 1960, B7, CHP.

11. WK, "The Long Farewell to Majority Rule," B31, BP; WK to CH, Summer 1960, B7, CHP; LS to WK, June 20, 1960, June 23, 1960, and December 3, 1963, in *WKM*, 220–21, 248; WK to FGW, June 1960 and June 29, 1960, B2, WP; WK to CH, April 8, 1960, Spring 1960, May 4, 1960, and May 22, 1960, B7, CHP; WK to FGW, 1963, B3, WP; WK to WB, January 23, 1962, and March 1, 1962, B26, WB; CH to WK, May 31, 1960, B7, CHP; GWC, "Doctrine," 27–32.

12. WK, "Do We Want an Open Society?," *NR*, January 31, 1959, pp. 491–93; WK, Draft Review of *Spain and the Defense of the West*, 1961, B15, BP; WK to Priscilla Buckley, May 7, 1961 and WK to WB, May 9, 1961 and July 20, 1961, B15, BP; LB to WB, May 1, 1961, Series Accession 2008-M-067, B7, BP; WK to FGW, May 2, 1961, June 5, 1961, B2, WP; LB to WB, May 28, 1961, B15, BP; WB to WK, May 25, 1961 and July 1961, and July 20, 1961, B15, BP.

13. WK to Tinkum Brooks, August 13, 1960, B6F147, CBP; BDJ to WK, August 16, 1960, B16F2, KP; WK to YM, August 5, 1960, November 22, 1960, and Fall 1960, B6F2, KP; WK to FGW, November 26, 1960 and December 10, 1960, B2, WP; WK to CH, November 20, 1960, B7, CHP; WK to WB, January 12, 1961, B15, BP.

14. WK to FGW, December 11, 1960, B2, WP; WK to YM, December 18, B6F2, KP; Patricia Bozell to WB, January 27, 1961, Series Accession 2008-M-067, B7, BP.

15. WK to FGW, January 1961, B2, WP; WK to WB, January 25, 1961 and January 26, 1961, B15, BP; LB to WB, March 9, 1961 and March 21, 1961, Series Accession 2008-M-067, B7, BP.

16. WK to WB, March 20, 1961 and April 17, 1961, B15, BP; LB to WB, Spring 1961, April 21, 1961, May 1, 1961, and June 1961, Series Accession 2008-M-067, B7, BP.

17. WK to WB, February 3, 1961, B15, BP; Patricia Buckley Bozell to WB, September 8, 1962, B18, KP; WB to WK, October 15, 1962, October 30, 1962, November 27, 1962, B20, KP; WK to WB, January 13, 1962 and WB to WK, February 15, 1963, B26, BP.

18. WK to WB, November 1, 1959, B8, BP; WB to Mrs. Oscar Samuelson, October 27, 1961 and YM to WB, October 1961, B15, BP; WB to WK, April 6, 1959, December 15, 1959, and WK to WB, May 15, 1959 and June 15, 1959, B8, BP; LB to WB, Summer 1961, Series Accession 2008-M-067, B7, BP; WK to YM, October 13, 1960, B6F2, KP; WK to FGW, May 18, 1960, October 10, 1960, and May 2, 1961, B2, WP; WK to YM, April 1961, B6F3, KP; WK to CH, March 3, 1961, B7, CHP; WK to LS, May 10, 1961, in *WKM*, 236.

19. WK to LS, May 10, 1961, in *WKM*, 235; WK to WB, January 12, 1961, B15, BP; WK to Richard Ware, April 4, 1960, B19F3, KP; WB to Richard Noble, June 3, 1959, B21F6, KP.

20. WK to WB, May 15, 1959 and 1959, B8, BP; WK to CH, September 1, 1959, B7, CHP; WK to WB, January 12, 1961, B15, BP.

21. Hart, "Deliberate Sense," 76; WK to FGW, December 10, 1960, February 25, 1961, and February 28, 1961, B2, KP; WK-Yale Settlement Letter, May 10, 1961, B29, KP; Ross D. Mackenzie, "Kendall Leaves," *YDN*, October 18, 1961, p. 1.

22. WK to FGW, June 26, 1961, B2, WP; WK to WB, November 11, 1959, B8, BP; WK to FGW, January 1961, Fall 1961, and October 24, 1961, B2, WP; WK to Tinkum Brooks, May 19, 1959, B6F147, CBP; WK to WB, Fall 1959, B8, BP; Winchell, *Brooks*, 304–05.

23. WK to CH, November 19, 1961, B7, CH; WB to Stanley Parry, August 23, 1961, B16, BP; WB to PGK, October 3, 1961, B15; WK to WB, April 30, 1962, B20, BP.

24. WB to WK, July 31, 1956 and August 6, 1956, B3, BP; WK to WB, August 7, 1956, B3, BP; José Maria Troncoso to WK, October 2, 1958, B6, BP; Murray Kempton, "Until Sundown," June 18, 1958, Newspaper Clipping, B6, BP; WK to WB, Fall 1959, B8, BP; WK to Leo Strauss, January 9, 1957, in *WKM*, 199.

25. WK to YM, April 1961, B6F3, KP; WK, "American Conservatism and Right-Wing Dictatorships," in *Contra Mundum*, 54–70; WK to FGW, 1961 and September 22, 1961, B2, WP; WK to WB, July 20, 1961 and September 5, 1961, B15, BP; WK to CH, November 19, 1961, B7, CHP.

26. WK to YM, April 1961, B6F3, KP; WK to FGW, July 26, 1961, B2, WP; WK to WB, 1961, B15, BP; WK to FGW, July 16, 1961, October 24, 1961, and December 1961, B2, WP; *Willmoore Kendall*, M. Catherine Babcock, Inc., Spring '62 Bulletin, B6F4, KP; *M. Catherine Babcock, Inc. Proudly Presents Willmoore Kendall* [1963?], B6F5, KP.

27. FGW, "Political Science," 40; Homer Greene to WB, August 21, 1961, Harold Kaemerle to WB, September 22, 1961, Mrs. F.L. Girard to WB, August 22, 1961, and Artemis Albertson to WB, August 28, 1961, B15, BP; WB to Mrs. Oscar Samuelson, October 27, 1961, B15, BP.

28. Elliott Walters to WB, November 23, 1962, Newspaper clippings of Letters from Giovanni Costigan and Milton Rowe, Fall 1962; Lynn Bouchey to WB, November 28, 1962, and Margaret F. Wendt to WB, November 27, 1962, B20, BP; Oscar Pemantle to WK, April 9, 1962 and Oscar Pemantle to David Lombard, September 4, 1962, B20F5, KP; WB to Elliot Walters, November 27, 1962, WB to WK, December 3, 1962, WB to Lynn Bouchey, December 7, 1962, WB to Victor Milione, December 7, 1962, WB Telegram to WK, December 7, 1962, B20, BP; WK to WB, November 1962 and December 1962, 1962, B20, BP.

29. GWC to CH, December 5, 1961, B7, CHP; WK to WB, December 4, 1961 and January 17, 1962, B15, BP; GWC to WK, January 3, 1962, B17F4, KP; CH to WK, December 20, 1961, B7, CHP; WB to WK, February 4, 1962, B20, BP; WK to CH, January 2, 1962, B7, CHP; WK to CH, January 26, 1962, B16F9, KP.

30. D.J. Mulloy, *The World of the John Birch Society: Conspiracy, Conservatism, and the Cold War* (Nashville: Vanderbilt University Press, 2014), 52; WK to YM, [1961], B6F3, KP; WK to FGW, December 1961, B2, WP; WK to WB, December 4, 1961, B15, BP; GWC to WK, January 3, 1962, B17F4, KP; WK to WB, December 26, 1961, B20, BP; John F. McManus, *William F. Buckley: Pied Piper for the Establishment* (Appleton, WI: John Birch Society, 2002), 137–38.

31. WK to YM, April 1961, B6F3, KP; WK to FGW, April 20, 1961, B2, WP.

32. RPO, *Jewish Strategy*, vii–viii; RPO to WB, March 23, 1955, BP; RPO to WB, February 15, 1960, February 22, 1960, March 12, 1960, and December 24, 1960, B11, BP; WB to RPO, February 10, 1960 (2 letters), May 16, 1960, B11, BP; RPO to WB, April 8, 1961 and WB to RPO, April 15, 1961, B15, BP; WK to WB, April 17, 1961, B15, BP; WK to WB, September 16, 1960, B10, BP; WK to FGW, April [1961], April 20, 1961, October 24, 1961, and November 1961, B2, WP; WK to CH, November 19, 1961, B7, CHP; WK to FGW, November 26, 1960, B2, WP; WK to WB, December 26, 1961, B15, BP; Mulloy, *Birch Society*, 185.

33. Judis, *Buckley*, 130; LB, Statement of Independent Committee Against Communism in Government, October 30, 1952 and WB, National Weekly Prospectus, March 9, 1955, Series Accession 1997-M-160, B4, BP; WB to George S. Montgomery, Jr., February 16, 1952, Series Accession 1997-M-160, B4, BP; WK to LS, December 2, 1956, in *WKM*, 156–57.

34. WK to FGW, October 30, 1961, B2, WP; WK, Madison Speech on McCarthy, April 8, 1962, pp. 26–28, B20, BP; WK to WB, March 1962 and March 25, 1962, B20, BP; GWC to WK, Spring 1963 and 1964, B17F4, KP; WK to Addison Potter, 1962, B20F15, KP.

35. WK to FGW, July 6, 1961, B2, WP; WK to WB, September 21, 1961, B15, BP; WK to WB, January 17, 1962, WK to WB, February 14, 1962, March 22, 1962, April 19, 1962, April 30, 1962, and May 1, 1962, B20, BP.

36. Frank Meyer to WK, July 27, 1962, B21F8, KP; Patricia Buckley Bozell to WB, September 8, 1962, B18, BP; WK to YM, Summer 1962, Fall 1962 and Late 1962, B6F4, KP.

37. WK to YM, Summer 1962, B6F4, KP; WK to Addison Potter, 1962, 2 Letters, B20F15, KP; WK to YM, Late 1962, Two Letters, B6F4, KP; WK to YM, Late 1962, B6F4, KP.

38. WK to FGW, Summer 1963, B3, WP; BDJ to WK, August 5, 1963, B16F3, KP; William Rusher to WK, May 21, 1963, B19F8, KP; WK to YM, Spring 1963 and Spring/Summer 1963, B6F5, KP; WK to WB, July 1963, B27, BP; HR, *Memoirs of a Dissident Publisher* (Chicago: Regnery, 1985), 188.

39. BDJ to WK, August 5, 1963, B16F2, KP; WK to HR, July 16, 1962 and [1964?], B38F2, HRP; Russell Kirk, Excerpt of review of second edition of *The Conservative Affirmation* from *The Wanderer*, 1986, B23F2, KP; HR, *Memoirs*, 188.

40. WK, *The Conservative Affirmation* (Chicago: Regnery Gateway, 1985), 167–71, 177–80, 184–87.

41. WK, "What is Conservatism," in *TCA*, 1–20.

42. WK, "The Social Contract: The Ultimate Issue Between Liberalism and Conservatism," *Conservative Affirmation*, 83–99; Alvis, "Evolution," 77–79.

43. WK to YM, Spring 1963 and Spring/Summer 1963, B6F5, KP; WK to YM, December 18, 1960, B6F2, KP; WK to FGW, December 18, 1960 and January 1961, B2, WP; Donald Cowan to WK, January 19, 1962, B17F3, KP; CH Testimony, American Political Science Association Oral Histories, p. 36, B16F9, KP; WK to FGW, 1963 and Summer 1963, B3, WP.

44. WK to WB, April 1963, B27, BP.

Chapter 8

1963–1967
"Kendall for King"

At the University of Dallas, Kendall found a small, ambitious institution whose developing ethos meshed with his own. Founded in 1956, the university was intensely Catholic and strongly anticommunist. In its first years, Cistercian monks who had fled violent Soviet oppression in Hungary dominated its faculty. Other orders also played prominent roles on campus. The university president in 1963 was physicist Donald A. Cowan. In early 1962 Cowan wrote Willmoore. He told him that Dallas was in the "formative stage" of building a high-quality conservative university. It could use, he added, "someone of your learning and stature to open up for our students the full scope of the life of the intellect." Cowan was part of an academic power couple. His wife—Louise Cowan, professor of English—was a defining intellectual force at the university when Kendall arrived. As Vanderbilt PhD's, the Cowans, like Kendall, had lots of contacts with the Southern Agrarians. Sharing many of Kendall's pedagogical and political concerns, like him they loved long talks about philosophy, literature, and politics over "good booze." To his surprise, Kendall quickly became "associated with the highest policy decisions at U. of D." This role was new for him. At his previous academic posts, not only had he never held an administrative position, he had not even served on faculty committees. His position as head of the department of politics and economics, however, entailed significant administrative duties. Moreover, as Kendall said in a letter to Francis Wilson, he became "the conscience and bull whip" of President Cowan, pushing him to make various "difficult decisions" needed to transform the university in the direction that both he and the Cowans wanted it to go.[1]

At his new university, Kendall was happy to report that liberals "dwell in the fox-holes" while "Right-wingers . . . fly the MIG's." In late 1963 Kendall wrote to Addison Potter, department chair at Los Angeles State, to say he was enjoying an academic camaraderie he had been missing "since LSU days." The students at Dallas were good, he added, though "hardly Yale caliber." Kendall set out to build the academic program as he had long envisioned. The new department, he said, would break the empiricist mold. In politics the program would "develop in its students the skills, habits, and manners important among scholars to the discussion of 'important things.'" As "the only alternative to settling political issues by sheer force," such skill was vital to nourish. In economics the department would integrate the discipline's "specialized subject-matter" with "the higher purpose of man." It would transcend "the material and mechanistic." The program was not meant to attract "ordinary" students but those aiming for graduate school or law school.[2]

To staff this department, Kendall eagerly sought, but without much success, to attract well-known conservative scholars to teach at Dallas. He tried, for example, to get Harry Jaffa—Strauss student and posthumous Kendall nemesis—to accept a position with the university. Kendall was reluctant to hire professors who did not share the university's conservative vision. He badly wanted Frederick Wilhelmsen (whom he trusted) and worked hard to add him to the faculty. When Wilhelmsen did come in 1965, Kendall recognized that he had been "a sensational success." During this quest for staffing, Kendall also made new acquaintances in the profession. One was James McClellan, a young man on his way to becoming a prominent conservative scholar and political activist. Academic conservatives like themselves, confided McClellan to Kendall, often suffered from lack of conversation with like-minded persons. Too often they had to stand "against the 'wave of the future'" without ever hearing "a sympathetic voice."[3]

Dallas and Kendall needed one another. The university went out of its way to meet his demands. The administration supported him against in-house critics, publicized his teaching talents, and tolerated his grumpiness. Kendall sometimes faced criticism from clerical instructors who believed the new department, by questioning the "natural rights" teachings of Catholicism, was defying "papal & Church authority." In defending his political theory, Kendall found support from the Cowans and from Dean Damian Fandal. A Dominican priest, Fandal backed Willmoore on the curriculum while urging him to deal with detractors in "Christian Love." Such institutional support—and his agreement with the university's mission—made Kendall reluctant to leave. He turned down other employment opportunities, he said, "because I *approve* of what U.D. is doing." A routine statement for many people, but for an employer to win Kendall's approval in this way was unprecedented. He admitted to "being happy" in Texas but feared Donald Cowan was "playing a losing game" and that if he were ousted "the first head to roll will be mine." Kendall knew that he was "the symbol of the Cowan regime, and it doesn't help that the kids are wearing 'Kendall for King' sweat shirts."[4]

To showcase its well-known teacher, the university built a special classroom. It had student desks in a semicircle raised above a generously sized floor reserved for the instructor. Kendall continued to use the style he had adopted at Stanford, combining lecture and discussion. Pacing relentlessly, he mostly lectured without notes. He had perfected "his own peculiar and brilliant style of speaking, a style unornamented and sinuous whose sole purpose was to lay bare the path of argument." Said star student Leo Paul de Alvarez:

> There was always a tension in the classroom for the student knew that he would have to examine the assumptions of his life. Kendall allowed no compromises; he refused to leave the student alone until he could see first he had made a choice and secondly, that he had to *make* a choice. No student remained unchanged in Kendall's classes. A student either came to accept his conclusions or to oppose them fiercely. But both students were left with the same legacy and that was his method of argument.

Also attractive, said de Alvarez, "was the man himself. He thundered out [while] pacing restlessly up and down his classroom." Often he picked out a student, often a pretty girl or a nun. Then: "He would bend over his chosen victim and embark upon a prolonged and unmerciful cross-examination, clarifying point after point of his lecture by alternately teasing, prodding, coaxing, and bullying his somewhat terrified and embarrassed victim." Everyone "hugely enjoyed" this "comic drama . . . except perhaps the victim." These classes were full of "naughty" humor as when Willmoore conjugated the word "*fuckare*" in Latin for his students. Kendall's "rhetoric was his own mixture of Burkean prose, Oklahoman idiom, political science and sociological jargon (which he used merely for effect, for he hated pseudo-scientific jargon), and plain American slang, all undergirded by the rhythm of the King James Bible." Kendall would "go wherever the argument would lead him," which sometimes "surprised himself . . . but he would never tailor it to any ideological precepts."[5]

In the classroom, then, Willmoore turned himself into a flamboyant character for the entertainment of his students but—more importantly—for their edification. Fond of his collection of colorful sports coats, Kendall often joked about them in class. He even opened up new ones from boxes he just received in the mail in front of his classes. As he delivered his lectures and dialogued with his students, Willmoore smoked. Ashes from his cigarette sometimes threatened to drop on undergraduates he was questioning. Because they "never knew what Kendall was going to do or say," students "could always look forward to the unexpected in his classes." He sometimes had to pop

Figure 8.1 Teaching, University of Dallas. *Source:* University of Dallas, Archives and Special Collections.

Figure 8.2 Domestic Harmony, At Last. *Source:* Photo by Wilfred Cooper, Courtesy of Chuck and Pam Graham.

nitroglycerin pills for his heart condition. On one occasion, the class looked on horrified as Kendall's face turned blue. He swallowed a pill, remained silent for an entire minute, then continued on with his lecture. Decades later, one "victim" of his trademark classroom questioning remembered Kendall with "awe" and affection, as her "intellectual father."[6]

There were some hiccups in these Dallas years. That first semester, Willmoore told Charles Hyneman, he had only been downtown twice, "once to attend the luncheon at which Jack Kennedy was to have spoken." After the assassination Don Cowan went into crisis mode. He declared the university's "grief is unbounded," encouraged special masses, and closed classes the following Monday. Kendall was more sanguine. Heading to the meeting he told Louise Cowan that he had never met an American president in person, then joked after the luncheon cancellation that his streak was intact. Kendall believed JFK's presidency a disaster. He thought the president's decision to let the Bay of Pigs invasion go forward "without the intention of backing it up" amounted to "high treason." Upon the president's death Kendall commented that whoever lives by the sword dies by the sword. He referenced Diem's assassination and certainly remembered Trujillo's as well. Kendall thought the JFK assassination "a Russian intelligence operation" but thought the Warren Commission would never dare to say so. He did not go so far as Revilo Oliver who became "a national figure over night" by claiming the Soviets had killed JFK as a rogue "CP member." According to one account, Kendall stunned his grieving students by commenting in class that Kennedy's assassination was the best thing that could have happened "for the Republic."[7]

Closer to home were deteriorating relations with family and friends. In late 1963 Kendall went through a wrenching family crisis, breaking completely with his brother and mother. In the 1950s Walter Kendall had served as Willmoore's accountant. For years he failed to file his brother's taxes and left Willmoore with a large debt to the Internal Revenue Service. Eventually, this dispute involved Pearl Kendall. That Willmoore owned and made payments on his mother's house, and that Pearl had a bad relationship with Walter's common-law wife and son, complicated matters. Venting, Kendall told his sister that their mother needed to understand that he was "the head of this goddamn family." When Willmoore and Yvona decided to cut off relations with Walter, they warned Pearl to avoid further contact with him. A painful confrontation happened over Christmas 1963 when Mrs. Kendall visited Walter anyway. Willmoore and his mother never spoke again. Instead of helping his mother financially, he began to send money to Walter's poverty-stricken dependents. He then deeded his mother's house to Walter.[8]

About this same time Ken's relationship with Bill Buckley fell apart. In September 1963 Buckley suggested to Kendall that he be listed as contributor rather than as senior editor for *National Review*. Ignoring pleas to stay calm, Kendall demanded to be removed from the masthead altogether, then cut off contact. In December publisher William Rusher, pleading for donations, put out a newsletter for magazine insiders. Kendall responded bitterly. "Like most whores," he wrote Rusher, the magazine "richly deserved" its "mendicancy." Criticizing *National Review* for "continuing to kiss [Barry Goldwater's] behind," Kendall wondered how Rusher might "get him to respond to your advances." Angry that *National Review* had refused to run a pro bono advertisement for Dallas, Kendall wrote to Buckley. He called the magazine "the Right-wing organ of the establishment." Having recently come "to place a high value on my dignity," he went on, he could not continue to correspond with Buckley. Rusher replied in a conciliatory way to his first note. Kendall answered that the founders of the magazine had not "intended the bright undergraduate mag you publish from fortnight to fortnight." Drawing on his gift for invective, he said he felt "about NR, much as I would about an ex-wife of mine who'd become a call-girl."[9]

At this point Buckley blew up and responded with equal bitterness. Knowing Ken intimately, Bill understood his weak spots and struck them mercilessly. Buckley defended his friends who were not "conversant with your problem" and claimed Kendall's ongoing "deterioration" made him almost impossible to help. He suggested that Willmoore had contributed virtually nothing to the "practical and intellectual affairs" of *National Review*'s founding. He noted that the magazine had removed him from the masthead, rather than him voluntarily stepping down. Bill suggested that Ken had loved—and profited from—association with this mere "bright undergraduate mag." Sticking the knife in deeper, Buckley maintained that the financial hardships of the magazine came not from pursuing Goldwater but from "emoluments paid out over the years to non-performing editors." As for "wives and call-girls," he went on, "I can only welcome the news that you have finally learned to distinguish between the two."[10]

As this feud boiled over, Brent Bozell was launching a campaign for Congress, running in the Republican primary for the sixth district of Maryland. Kendall served as his advisor on domestic issues. Despite Buckley's depiction of the campaign as a quixotic quest to bring Carlism to America, it was a rather straightforward effort by a conservative insurgent to unseat Charles Matthias, the liberal incumbent. Kendall proved a competent strategist, offering practical advice. On Civil Rights the campaign urged that segregation be dismantled "voluntarily" through winning over the "hearts and minds" of both races. The campaign decried "the growth of big government" and "demagogic wars on poverty" and promised to "put prayer back in our schools." Bozell, echoing a Kendallian theme of public orthodoxy, proclaimed himself a "defender of the American way of life." Meanwhile, the campaign urged voters to elect "A REPUBLICAN WHO WILL *VOTE* REPUBLICAN." Bozell, a natural campaigner, ran a strong race. But he faced hardball tactics from his opponent and received only a third of the vote.[11]

During the campaign the Bozell-Kendall relationship got rockier. Trying to stay neutral in the dispute between mentor and brother-in-law, Bozell grew estranged from both. As Brent prepared to announce his candidacy in February 1964, Trish wrote Bill that things were "complicated by the presence of Willmoore whose performance was drinking, smooching (me), drinking, hating you, drinking, loving you—and somehow looking quite well and managing to be charming throughout. It must be his sense of humor." Another difficulty arose about *A World Without Communists*, a book Kendall wrote with Frank Meyer and Gerhart Niemeyer. Intended for a popular audience, the book needed a prominent titular author. Meyer and Niemeyer were content to be ghostwriters but insisted that neither they nor Kendall appear as author. Bozell promised to append his name to the book but then changed his mind. This decision meant the book was never published. An enraged Kendall broke completely with Meyer. Then in 1965 he wrote to Bozell calling him "the very symbol of disappointment, disloyalty, and . . . treason. All that might be possible to take from someone whom I loved less; from you, whom I do love, it is an intolerable ordeal." Contact continued until 1966. Kendall's name appeared on the cover of Bozell's new Catholic traditionalist magazine *Triumph*. But Kendall was still fuming over the book dispute. Thinking "God hard to manage," he disapproved of Bozell's increasingly religious approach to politics. He soon wrote Brent to: "Get my name the hell off the masthead of that damn rag." Kendall was also angry at what he saw as inadequate appreciation for the help he gave Bozell with his book on the Supreme Court, *The Warren Revolution*. Such paltry acknowledgments were, he said, typical for the Buckley circle. "The Buckleys," he told Brent, "consume people as a furnace consumes coal."[12]

Amid turmoil in his personal life, Kendall remained active as a public speaker. He demonstrated continued virtuosity on stage (without the embarrassments of 1961 and 1962). His most important public debate in these years occurred on February 23, 1964. He faced off with prominent political scientist James MacGregor Burns in Pasadena, California. The topic was: "The Deadlock in Washington is to be Deplored." Burns had just published a well-received book called *The Deadlock of Democracy*. Burns was the foremost scholarly proponent of strong presidential leadership. Kendall knew he could not convince Burns of his errors and so set out to clarify their differences. He agreed with Burns that Congress often blocked change. He disagreed that such fact was a problem. Just as homeowners used locks to frustrate thieves and preserve their property, Kendall said, Congress protected a prosperous polity from harmful change. Liberals sought to alter the rules to hasten change. Burns himself supported a host of reforms: abolishing midterm elections, ditching the filibuster, dismantling seniority in Congress, and promoting ideological distinct parties. By empowering the "sheer, naked will" of the majority, said Kendall, such reforms would destroy the design of the Framers. Yet this political scaffold had long promoted "a more perfect union" while preserving justice and liberty. Congress, Kendall continued, was the sovereign center of American government. "As I understand it—as Madison and Hamilton understood it—the sky has always been the limit about the content of [Congressional] decisions." But the Framers had built the system so that reforms—when made—would reflect "the deliberate sense of the community." The word deliberate as Kendall used it had several nuances. Deliberate change, that is, would be intentional, slow, and follow careful legislative discussion. Burns wanted to "cut the Gordian Knot" of the American politics. If he succeeded, American politics would unravel. As the majority imposed its principles by force majeure on large and resistant minorities, unrest would surely follow.[13]

The next month Willmoore debated liberal professor Åke Sandler in Los Angeles. In this talk Kendall suggested that an intellectual climate "dominated by liberals" blocked serious dialogue with conservatives, whose views they considered "indefensible, both morally and intellectually." Liberals, for instance, saw equality as axiomatic though "in reality, [it] does not exist and cannot exist." Even their generic calls for "equality of opportunity" were "utopian, idealistic, and dangerous" and would require abolition of "the family and of property." Conservatives, he said, possessed proper "piety toward the past" while liberals want us "to bow" in shame for our ancestors. To finish up, Kendall defended "the right of the people to adopt an orthodoxy and seek to hand it on to their descendants." Increasingly confident as a speaker, Kendall remained active on the lecture circuit right up until his death. On one tour in 1966, for example, he spoke in six states on thirteen different college campuses. And in April 1967 he debated Mulford Sibley in Northfield, Minnesota. Looking at one another "across the nave of the St. Olaf College chapel," the old rivals debated free speech.[14]

Thriving as a teacher and on the lecture circuit, Kendall was also working productively as a scholar. In the summer of 1964 Kendall published "American Conservatism and the 'Prayer' Decisions" in *Modern Age*. Here he brought his evolving theoretical views about democracy to bear upon a contemporary issue. He started by discussing a situation in North Brookfield, Massachusetts. There the local school board had voted to defy the Supreme Court decisions—*Engel v. Vitale* (1962) and *Abington School District v. Schempp* (1963)—which had prohibited officially sponsored prayer in public schools. After commending the school board for defying the court by voting to uphold the views of local people, Kendall attacked the court as antidemocratic. He acknowledged how hard it would be to dislodge the court's power. Long traditions of judicial review and strong arguments from Madison and Marshall favoring such review made the court hard to fight. Resistance appeared unseemly to New Englanders who feared looking like "Governor Wallace." Unseemly or not, however, Kendall argued that American citizens had to rein in the court. Citizens ought not "argue-bargue" about the extent of the court's legal authority. Rather they should reassert their own power, as citizens in a democracy, to make key prudential decisions, especially local decisions, concerning the good of society.[15]

Citizens, he argued, needed to prepare themselves to meet the onslaught of "liberal" elites determined to promote change and backed by federal authorities (and the court's prestige). If not reined in, the court, he claimed presciently, would ban "Christmas plays and public *crèches* and religious songs . . . invocations and benedictions at school graduation exercises." The Supreme Court would impose such changes, even though the people opposed them, showing that the judiciary was a danger to democracy. For Kendall, drawing on Aristotle, nothing was more vital for civilization than deliberation among citizens. On the national level, that meant that Congress, after due deliberation, ought to make most important decisions. To protect the people's right to deliberate and decide at local and state levels, Kendall believed Americans must "curb" judicial power. Real democracy depended on maintaining or rediscovering the "deliberate sense" of citizens through the give and take of elected assemblies. "Let the people of the local community work the matter out," says Kendall, "as part of their general problems of living together on their little portion of American real estate."[16]

In November 1964 Kendall hit some of these same themes at the annual meeting of the Southern Political Science Association in Durham, North Carolina. This time his talk focused explicitly on the ongoing civil rights struggle. After disavowing states' rights, Kendall admitted that the civil rights movement was powerful and effective. By avowing revolutionary intent and with an unwillingness to take no for an answer, however, the movement threatened a major political crisis. Traditionally, he said, the American political system required change agents to wait patiently until consensus had developed to support their goals. If a group short-circuited this system—even if a majority—and imposed its will on a sizable and recalcitrant minority, dire consequences could be expected. Perhaps one would see widespread defiance of the law (as with prohibitionism) or maybe civil war (as with abolitionism). Even if the civil rights struggle were just and moral (which Kendall seemed tacitly to admit), other political actors might violently disagree. Coercing them could disrupt the democratic process, substituting real conflict for continued discussion. Even righteous goals, he continued, must be balanced against other real social goods. In seeking rapid justice, the movement could endanger domestic tranquility and more perfect union. Kendall then voiced support for the Civil Rights Act of 1964. It was "the product of a consensus," reached by the people's representatives in Congress rather than by presidential edict or judicial fiat. The act's incrementalism, he suggested, would lessen the public's appetite for revolutionary change. Going forward, the law would thereby diminish the appeal of the civil rights movement.[17]

Willmoore knew the civil rights question was more explosive than the issue of school prayer. Wary about how academics would receive his talk, he felt sorely tempted to cancel. But he felt duty-bound to appear at the conference on behalf of the University of Dallas. The experience was worse than anticipated. When Florida State political scientist Marian Irish attacked Kendall's paper, she received an "80-second ovation." Moreover, Willmoore told Wilson, "all the discussants assumed, despite my disclaimers, that I'm against the poor Negroes." Writing to Willmoore, James McClellan said he found the Durham meeting "sickening," crowded with run-of-the mill "mental goose-steppers." Then he continued: "I must say I was most proud of you when you stood up to defend your paper. You could hear a pin drop . . . . When you stood up there, I thought of Cicero . . . admonishing his countrymen to take heed in their politics." Despite the negative reception in Durham, Kendall published the speech nearly verbatim a couple of months later in *Intercollegiate Review*.[18]

Kendall was untypically reticent in expressing his views on issues of race. In 1960, for example, he knew he had taken on a "hot potato" in reviewing a book by Nathaniel Weyl which argued racial differences had a scientific basis. Kendall cautiously praised Weyl's book without endorsing its views on black inferiority. Privately, he agreed with Weyl that "that there are races, and they do differ." More importantly, the growing militancy of the civil rights struggle alarmed Kendall and—because he quietly identified as a white southerner—sometimes angered him. In 1960, for example, he said that Nixon and Kennedy were "ideologues" who would "Littlerock everything in sight. And enjoy it." Two years later he wrote to Buckley, professing to be "a little shocked" at Bill's statement that he would "enforce Federal law in the South 'at bayonet point.'" In a July 1963 letter to Buckley, Kendall (for the only time the present author has found) specifically, if hesitantly, voiced support for segregation. Responding to an admonition not publicly to favor segregation, he confessed: "I guess I am, at this point, for the segregation for the bulk of the American Negroes" despite feeling "no particular prejudice against Negroes." Rather, he opposed desegregation because of the "methods" and "grounds" on which the struggle had been waged. His attitude had been shaped by his evolving views on the Bill of Rights and by African Americans making "demands" upon—rather than working within—"the political community." He also expressed belief that black radicalism "would trigger the latent anti-Negro, really anti-Negro, sentiment in the white proletariat itself, and then there really is going to be hell to pay."[19]

Like the academics at Durham, one might be inclined to dismiss such statements as rationales to disguise racial animus. For Kendall, however, these statements appear to be more than simple excuses. His views on the Bill of Rights and on how the community ought to treat dissidents had developed in the 1940s and early 1950s. They focused far more on communist subversion than on race. As early as 1954, Kendall had warned against the "genuine civil war potential" of pushing forward with the civil rights demands. And when Kendall talked about "hell to pay" if white racism were aroused, he was not speaking abstractly. Rather he spoke from personal experience (the fiery cross in Mangum and the ruined remnants of North Tulsa after the Race Massacre). In the Ranney-Kendall textbook, in the Bozell campaign, and in the Durham speech, Kendall suggested that the real answer was to change the "hearts and minds" of southern whites to realize that repression of African Americans was unjust. However, he feared such change would come too slowly to avoid bitter, massive, and destabilizing racial conflict. In a 1964 letter to Kendall, Garry Wills praised Willmoore's efforts to "prescind from the moral claim and talk about the demands of political order."[20] On this issue, however, Kendall was discovering that it was increasingly difficult to prescind.

Kendall expanded on such points in the classroom. He reiterated to his students—as he had said in Durham—that his political theory did not rest on states' rights. Whenever Congress, the President, and the Supreme Court agreed about something, there was a de facto "constitutional consensus." No one was left "to say No to We the people." The enumeration of rights in the Bill of Rights—which would otherwise have been left to the states to decide—had been "a clear invitation from the very first" to the federal government "to play games with the whole business of delegated powers." For example, he told students that the first Congress had set up a "Dept. of Agriculture," which, of course, was nowhere mentioned in the Constitution. About the Tenth Amendment, Governor Wallace might complain, but, he asked, "Who the hell cares, really?" The federal government had been expanding its powers for many decades. It would continue to do so as long consensus existed at the federal level. Kendall did not deny "the right" of a federal majority to govern. He did question whether it was "smart or prudent" for a "bare majority" to impose its choices on society.[21]

In a 1965 classroom lecture he denied responsibility for social injustice. A key divide in America, he told his students, was between "the guilty feelers and the non-guilty feelers." Many "liberal intellectuals" not only felt guilty about poverty and injustice but tried to shame others who did not feel such guilt. Kendall professed himself a nonguilty feeler. He rejected responsibility for problems he did not create, including "the fact Negroes don't vote in Selma" and "that a vast number of people continue to be born poor in America." He suggested liberal guilt was problematic from a Catholic perspective. He thought it wrong to accept guilt "for the sins of my father and grandfather" rather than for something he himself did. More fundamental was danger from the guilty feelers trying to end injustice. Kendall, as we have seen, reminded his students that pursuing justice at all costs could collapse a thriving political system, could cause "heaven" to fall and leave wreckage in its place. A student suggested that his teacher felt too little "brotherhood for your fellow man." Kendall responded that: "I have such a deep sense of brotherhood that I am willing to let people live their own lives."[22]

In class he also reiterated that impositions by the courts undermined democracy and threatened to unravel the consensus which allowed the United States to function. The Fourteenth Amendment, said Kendall to his Dallas students, set aside the Tenth Amendment. It made the Supreme Court into a "permanent constitutional convention so that until the sun goes down on Monday, you never know anymore what the Constitution of the United States is because the Supreme Court decisions are made on Monday, so always at 5:30 you will see me sitting there by the television to find out what the Constitution means this week." Change agents, making claims to "natural rights," had used the court to make "a whole series of demands . . . to step in and impose on certain groups in the community changes even down in their local way of life, of an extremely drastic, and to them unpleasant, character." Among these efforts were banning school prayer, mandating desegregation, and nationalizing educational standards. These efforts were an attempt of one part of the community to impose its will on another part of the community using the powers of government. The Supreme Court, for example, had crushed the efforts of "local censors" to restrict "pornographic literature." The problem would arise when the imposed upon group decided not to obey. If the citizens of North Brookfield decided to continue with school prayer, he asked his students, would the federal government send troops, as it did to achieve desegregation in Little Rock? On the other hand: "Give the Southerners their way on the whole civil rights movement or give the prayers-in-school people their way and you don't get anywhere because you simply make angry the people who have been supporting the Supreme Court decision; it is they who have to take it on the jaw now."[23] Whether the issue was prayer, civil rights, or pornography, Kendall thought real democracy demanded genuine give and take among *elected* representatives.

Applying these principles to the politics of his own day led Kendall in surprising directions. In 1964, for example, Willmoore recognized the nomination of Barry Goldwater as Republican candidate for president as a watershed. "Conservatism," he suggested in *New Guard*, published by the Young Americans for Freedom, had become "one of two realistic alternatives as regards the future of America." Conservatives would finally "have their voices heard" in a presidential election. The Goldwater candidacy constituted a challenge to "the whole governing class." *New Guard* readers must have been puzzled when Kendall mentioned "the grim significance of the Goldwater acceptance speech." The speech, he said, showed that Americans were "no longer a people in agreement on fundamentals." Having just written the speech, Harry Jaffa wrote excitedly to Kendall. Jaffa boasted that it was "the closest thing to a lecture in political philosophy" that the American people had heard "in this century at least." Hearing the famous line: "extremism in defense of liberty is no vice" and that "moderation in pursuit of justice is no virtue," Kendall hated it. "There's nothing wrong with that statement," he said, "that couldn't be put right by a hundred thousand well-chosen words." Treatments of Kendall's life have sometimes concluded with a surprise ending. Willmoore was a registered Democrat who voted for Lyndon Johnson in 1964. Kendall himself remained mostly quiet on this point. He apparently also voted for Truman in 1948 and Kennedy in 1960. But he recognized that not being Republican might make him look "ridiculous" among conservatives.[24]

Yet uneasiness about Goldwater and admiration for Johnson derived logically from Kendall's principles. Willmoore saw Goldwater as a (frequently) irresponsible radical and Johnson as a (mostly) responsible conservative.

Kendall's view here was a mirror image of the ideas of James McGregor Burns about presidential leadership. Contra Burns, Kendall believed presidents ought to serve (using Burns's later terminology) as "transactional" leaders who deferred to Congress. They should work deals within the existing system to advance a limited political agenda. He thought "transformational" (again using Burns's later terminology) leaders were dangerous. They moved rapidly and tended to bypass careful consideration in Congress. Yet it was Congress which assured that political changes reflected the "deliberate sense" of the American people. Thus, when Goldwater supported "extremism" and condemned "moderation," he embraced a vision of conservatism diametrically opposed to Kendall's own. Kendall was coming to see danger in the tendency of some Strauss students to support political visions of uncompromising moral rectitude. Those who sought an "enlightened statesmen" or "philosopher king," he feared, endangered democracy. The Straussians in turn were coming to see moral failings, especially in regard to civil rights, on the part of Kendall and his coterie.[25]

Kendall saw Johnson as a dealmaker not a crusading radical. Johnson understood and worked closely with Congress. In January 1967, writing Carl Albert (then House Majority Leader), Kendall claimed to remain "uncompromisingly Conservative." He then added that, "for the first time since I became deeply interested in politics," he had "confidence in the man in the White House." Viewing Johnson and Albert as conservatives at heart, he expressed willingness to serve in the administration if called. Expanding on LBJ, Kendall called him "the toughest anti-communist president of my lifetime." In this regard, he would have had in mind Johnson's stance in Vietnam and his 1965 intervention in the Dominican Republic to squelch a left-wing coup. Kendall also relished the fact that Johnson had "sent most of those liberal professors from Yale and Harvard back to the classroom." Speaking in Knoxville, Willmoore praised the president for building highways through Appalachia for "middle-class" people to use.[26]

In 1965 Donald Cowan wrote Kendall expressing "deep gratitude" for his services to the University of Dallas. He offered Willmoore a contract for $14,000 per year. The next year Kendall received another nice raise. Cowan told Willmoore it was "no light matter" for him to share the university's mission as "a keystone in this age's arch of history." In serving these grandly expressed purposes, Kendall brought his own earthiness onto the job. His lectures mostly focused on academics, rather than on current events. But after class he met students in the cafeteria to talk informally for hours. He attracted students with a persona of hearty, hospitable manliness. His house became a "gathering place" for student bonhomie complete with food, drinks, smokes, and political discussion. Kendall's conviviality convinced undergraduate student Don Erler to switch his major to politics. He advised Erler that he needed to get all A's to proceed to graduate school. He then added that Erler should "get married to eliminate a repeat of 'your ten or so years' of running around after a piece of ass." Erler, later a UD PhD, wrote to Kendall to affirm that he was getting all A's. He was also planning to get married in the near future but "certainly not because you suggested it." Erler said he felt free to ignore the advice of "good doctor" Kendall who had been "half-loaded and very facetious at the time."[27]

In the fall of 1965 Kendall, who had received another research grant from Relm, returned to Europe with Nellie, mostly living in Paris. Willmoore's increasing health problems cut their sojourn short after a semester. In October 1965 he suffered a recurrence of the boils that had plagued him since the 1930s. This time was serious enough to require surgery and hospitalization in Paris. Bored, he told Yvona, he started "drinking rather more wine than I should have." Then "getting annoyed with" himself he went back on Antabuse. Afterward he felt "typical wk pangs of guilt" about not getting more work done. To his sister Willmoore joked about Nellie, "living with a great man" but daring to disagree with him. "But I tell you this," he continued, "I love every square millimeter of her, even when she disagrees with me. She is the world's loveliest and most lovable woman, not even excluding— the phrase I have just embodied in my will—my 'dear sister' (Nellie appears in the will as my 'beloved Wife,' almost as if she had dictated it herself." Nellie and Willmoore spent that Christmas in their Paris apartment, drinking Bloody Mary's and dancing to music on the television.[28]

On this trip Kendall had two revealing meetings with other intellectuals. One involved a tense meeting with economist Wilhelm Röpke who was shocked when Willmoore lauded Rousseau. "I begin to think," Kendall wrote Regnery, that "Right-wing intellectuals (e.g. Kirk, e.g. Röpke) need a personal devil to blame for everything, an Arch-Enemy with a Great Name, and having adopted poor, humble Jean-Jacques, are going to be reluctant to give him up." Holding Locke accountable for liberalism's failures "is too distasteful" for them "to contemplate." Kendall also came to know Dartmouth English professor Jeffrey Hart that fall. The two men enjoyed one another's company when Hart invited him over to England where Hart was doing research. Hart reported back to Buckley that Kendall "was a lot of fun" and "as smart as it is possible to be." In reply, said Buckley: "You have the same impression of Willmoore everyone has. He is indeed a very charming man." Hart was amazed by Willmoore's capacity for alcohol. Kendall's belief that "his analysis of the constitutional question provides the *only* relevant structure for the discussion of contemporary political issues," disturbed the Dartmouth professor. Buckley replied with his own thoughtful analysis of his former teacher. "There is a strange sense in which Willmoore is all intellectual, another in which he is all ideologue. All intellectual in the sense he is remote from things; ideological, in that once he is parti pris to a position, absolutely nothing seems to budge him."[29]

The high point for Kendall of this stay in Europe came in November 1965 when he returned to Oxford. Willmoore's old tutor, R. B. McCallum, who was now Master at Pembroke College, invited him back to his alma mater. A delighted Willmoore wrote home to Yvona: "Had dinner at High Table at Pembroke on Sunday—as, if you please—Guest of Honor. An unforgettably pleasant experience, believe you me." McCallum later fondly recalled this visit during which Willmoore possessed "all his usual vigour and force." It had been a "splendid evening." McCallum, who regarded Kendall as one of the smartest students he had ever taught, gathered his colleagues to hear Willmoore speak. The crowd enjoyed the "knowledge, subtlety and penetration" with which their guest addressed "the civil rights issues in America." It was enlightening, McCallum said, to hear someone speak who was not the "stereotyped brand of American Liberal" with "predictable" and "uninteresting" views.[30]

While in Europe Kendall also continued to pursue his annulments. At the end of 1965 the ecclesiastical authorities granted his annulment to Katherine, meaning, he joked, that he was now again married to Anne. At this point his canon lawyer believed he would win the case for the second annulment but decided to appeal directly to the Pope Paul VI. Had his final annulment not been granted, Kendall was prepared to marry Nellie in the Orthodox Church. That step, he knew, would require him to leave the University of Dallas. In fact his 1965 sabbatical in Paris was partly to escape the embarrassment of his "uncertain" marital situation. University authorities wrote to the pope successfully urging him not to block the final annulment. Finally, at noon on August 5, 1966, with both annulments complete, Willmoore and Nellie, with Father Fandal presiding, got married as Catholics. That morning Ken sent a telegram to Bill. Speaking from "Godson to Godfather," he told his former student of the wedding. He said "it would mean much to us, if you would be in church at that time and offer a prayer for us." Buckley responded: "Will do. Wish you both a lifetime of happiness."[31]

After returning to the United States in 1966, health concerns kept Kendall from traveling to Europe again. Back in Dallas he threw himself into his work for the university, focusing on building a new graduate program. He soon came up with the idea of a PhD program in politics. Willmoore knew demand existed for such a program. Visiting Berkeley he had talked to eight conservative graduate students ready to transfer immediately into the program he envisioned. In 1966 Kendall wrote Voegelin, telling him he was building the new PhD program in politics and literature "in the image of you and Strauss." He had written a similar letter to Strauss the previous year. At Dallas, Kendall regarded himself as the bridge between Strauss and Voegelin. He and his program would hold "Athens" and "Jerusalem" in balanced tension with one another. The program's structure would eschew behaviorism, have serious language requirements, and admit only "a few select students each year." Kendall did not want the program to be chiefly Catholic in nature. He feared its graduates would have difficulty finding jobs in a market of mostly "non-Catholic institutions." He also knew most deep-pocketed donors in Texas were Protestants who would be suspicious of a program too overtly Catholic in character.[32]

Kendall himself had envisioned this program, but budget concerns gave him misgivings about opening it. In this case, university authorities pushed him forward. "WILLMOORE! WE MUST BEGIN!," wrote Dean Fandal. The university worked hard to keep Kendall happy. "For our part," continued Fandal, "it seems we must have whatever assurance is possible that WK remains on the scene as long as God grants him the grace to be among men." Dallas, he said, has "counted heavily on you to lend your name and your philosophy, and, indeed your pedagogy to the institution." He urged Kendall to put the university's "providential mission" before his own desires. In the end the launch went well. "As my graduate program enters its stretch for its first year," Kendall told Hyneman in 1967, "I view it with more satisfaction than anything I've ever done." In a report to the Texas Educational Association, he admitted difficulties. By the end of the year, for instance, four students had left. Some students had difficulty adjusting to the combination of literature and politics. Most had adjusted, and he spoke proudly of "high morale among the ten survivors." Kendall had attracted some grant money for the program but admitted that it needed more funding to thrive.[33]

As he built up the graduate program, Kendall's scholarship reflected increased intellectual self-knowledge. In a revealing letter to Henry Regnery, for example, Willmoore proclaimed that he had "arrived" at his philosophical position with publication of *The Conservative Affirmation* in 1963. The introduction to this book, he went on, had been an "open declaration of war on all right wing Intellectuals except Richard Weaver." Kendall had come to understand that he worked best by thinking out things sequentially. He now knew that his most effective work came in articles linked to his classroom lectures and extra-academic activities. His thinking, he told Regnery, had not remained stagnant. He had refined it over time:

> Twenty years ago there was *no* anti-Liberal literature, because up to a recent moment before that the Liberals hadn't seemed to warrant being taken all that seriously.... Since then, I was groping forward to something I felt sure was important, that I felt sure everybody was missing, that I felt that I had to find, but knew I'd be a long time a-findin' because that is how the mind squares off to an unknown problem.

Kendall's "teaching"—a word he liked to apply to his own work—thus included his scholarship, his work in the classroom, his public speeches, and his writing for popular magazines. As part of this intellectual epiphany, Kendall sometimes criticized scholars, including Voegelin, who purposely disengaged from contemporary concerns.[34]

After breaking with *National Review*, Kendall was able to focus more on the academic side of his work. He published several scholarly articles in the years before his death. Most important was "John Locke Revisited" which appeared in 1966. According to Fritz Wilhelmsen, Kendall wrote the article in a little bar in Madrid, getting up each morning writing for several hours on a legal pad in his famous green ink while "ordering one rum and coke after another." By now Kendall viewed Locke as "the most destructive . . . of all the Machiavellians." This article, Gerhart Niemeyer told Kendall, amounted to "a learned dialogue between you and Strauss." It showed a "fundamental agreement" about how to interpret Locke. Reviewing his own work from a quarter century before, Kendall saw it as insightful but naïve. He had noticed the contradiction between Locke's support for majority rule and his defense of natural rights. By reading Strauss, however, Kendall now understood that Locke had no "latent premise" for majority rule. Rather Locke had concealed his real views to make them palatable to contemporaries. Kendall now believed Locke had prioritized the individual right to property above all else, that his praise for Christian morals and majority rule simply disguised support for untrammeled individualism. Unfortunately, said Kendall, modern society had adopted Locke's ideology—individual rights without social duties—by assuming, as Kendall had once done, that Locke supported both individual rights and majority rule. Kendall finished by analyzing Peter Laslett's work on Locke. He criticized the English historian for claiming, without evidence, that Locke favored majority rule. That academics accepted Laslett's views and ignored Strauss's showed that "the political theory profession is suffering from a mortal sickness." A flattered Strauss expressed admiration for Kendall's "forceful and noble" work. He called Willmoore "the only man who vindicates the honor of our profession." Kendall was "the only man who, without being my student, understood marvelously what I thought and intended."[35]

Some of Kendall's best-known scholarly work appeared only posthumously. In March 1968, for example, two of his articles appeared in professional journals. In "The 'Intensity' Problem and Democratic Theory," coauthored with George Carey, Kendall addressed how democracies could deal with differing levels of political intensity in the populace. Demanding that the majority get its way (Kendall's previous "majority principle" and Dahl's "populistic democracy") could leave many people deeply dissatisfied and cause instability. Dahl and followers suggested that "weighing" votes, not just counting them, might be necessary. Kendall (and Carey) disagreed, thinking any such system unworkable. What were the weighing criteria and who did the weighing? They suggested the *"Federalist* model" as better for dealing with the problem. Rather than majority or minority *"dictation,"* this model focused on "consensus." Deliberation (in Congress) allowed different social groups to know one another, anticipate one another's reactions, and avoid destabilizing actions. Also appearing in March 1968, and coauthored with Carey, was "The 'Roster Device': J.S Mill and Contemporary Elitism." Here the authors dismissed notions that moral and intellectual capacities were identical, or that moral capacity was irrelevant for decision-making. Then they denied that those allegedly possessing "intellectual superiority" (aka more education) should necessarily make the most important political decisions.[36]

The best known of Kendall's posthumous publications was *The Basic Symbols of the American Political Tradition*. Appearing in 1970, and again coauthored by Carey, it remains in print fifty years later. As written the book was half Kendall (the first four chapters) and half Carey editing Kendall (the last four chapters). It applied Eric Voegelin's theory of "representative symbols" to the American political experience. Kendall had been using Voegelin for some years in the classroom and in public speeches. Kendall believed, for example, that LSU political theorist Ellis Sandoz failed in his attempts to apply Voegelin's ideas to the United States. Sandoz was wrong, said Kendall: (1) in choosing obscure events as important symbols, (2) in failing to distinguish between "Lockean" and "classical" symbolization, and (3) in suggesting that Americans were a "chosen people" whom God would ipso facto protect. Instead, Kendall suggested that representative assemblies were the most important symbols. While acknowledging Christian precepts and imploring divine assistance, these assemblies themselves decided, after careful discussion, how to proceed into the future.[37] To paraphrase Kendall's view here, God helped those communities which talked things through, then helped themselves.

Before his death Kendall had secured a promise from LSU to publish *Basic Symbols*. In it he laid out Voegelin's theory of symbolization. He then examined four key historical documents to suggest the roots of the American political tradition. Because many Americans had begun questioning "the national habit of identifying the traditional with the good," Kendall thought it is important to understand that tradition. He suggested the tradition had been falsely interpreted to valorize individual rights over the community's right to govern itself. Voegelin, he went on, had fruitfully used his theories of symbol and myth to analyze the Judeo-Christian and Greco-Roman foundations of Western civilization but had dealt little with America. In Kendall's retelling, then, symbols and myths were full of meaning, showed "each people's attempt at *self-interpretation*," entailed how a people saw itself in relation to "transcendent truth," and did not depend too much on actual "historicity."[38]

The next three chapters involved textual analysis of the Mayflower Compact (1620), the Fundamental Orders of Connecticut (1638), the Massachusetts Body of Liberties (1641), and the Virginia Declaration of Rights (1776). Because he wanted to highlight the uniqueness of the American tradition and break from a focus on natural rights, Kendall focused on documents produced in America, the first three of which predated Locke. Using Voegelin's terminology of compact symbolization and differentiation, Kendall noted that it was important to understand correctly when a people began to constitute itself and to note whether the people's subsequent actions corresponded "with the symbols we have in hand." At its beginning in 1620 the American people was religious, justice focused, but not focused on individual rights or equality. The Mayflower Compact was nevertheless "an exercise of freedom" by its signers creating a community. In the next two documents, Kendall discerned differentiation into a more complex mythos including *"higher law, supreme representative assembly, deliberation,* the *virtuous people."* Individual rights were still not part of the picture. By 1776 a vocabulary of individual rights had crept into American discourse. But the signers of the Virginia Declaration did not see rights in Lockean terms, that is, as universal and inalienable. Rather such rights remained subject to the legislature, acting with regard to principles of justice. By this time, however, government and religion had differentiated into distinct spheres.[39]

As with much of Kendall's writing, *Basic Symbols* "works" its readers, in this case doubly, because of the combination of Kendall's intensive textual analysis and Voegelin's complex symbology. The book has had many admirers, as well as lots of critics, because it has provided perhaps the clearest alternative interpretation, at least among conservatives, to the idea that individual liberty and equality were the keys to understanding the American political tradition. Furthermore, the book stated in positive form Kendall's views on the need to prioritize deliberation and popular self-governance. Friendly conservatives therefore urged him to prioritize the project. Perhaps, as some scholars have argued, by making the "myths" of Voegelin rather than the "principles" of Strauss central to the book, Kendall "betrayed" the nonrational basis of his own thought. Yet, he also recognized that myths helped ordinary people reverence their homeland without possessing knowledge of deep philosophical principles. Such love of country, with a political orthodoxy accessible to the masses, he proclaimed necessary for any nation to survive.[40]

Perhaps Carey overstated Kendall's negativity toward the Declaration of Independence and toward Abraham Lincoln in the last four chapters of *Basic Symbols*. But Kendall had worked out most of the ideas of the latter chapters before Carey edited them. He did think "natural rights" were undemocratic because they thwarted the people's will. He believed equality was both unrealizable and undesirable. By focusing on equality and aggrandizing presidential power, Lincoln changed the original emphasis of the Constitution on democratic self-governance through Congressional deliberation. Appalled by the book, Harry Jaffa waged a decades-long war against *Basic Symbols*. Jaffa viewed Kendall as his "real adversary" and saw Calhoun as Kendall's "supreme sage." Jaffa's "Kendall thesis" has been adequately refuted in several places and on several counts: (1) Jaffa's critique of *Basic Symbols* focuses on the fifth chapter of the book completed by Carey, not Kendall; (2) the book contains only a fleeting reference to Calhoun and nowhere praises him or defends slavery or the extension of slavery; (3) all issues, for Kendall, were up to Congress—not the states—to decide, with slavery, or its expansion, no exception; (4) there is nothing whatever in the book (or elsewhere in Kendall's work) about nullification, the concurrent majority, interposition, or whatnot. Following Kendall's political logic—which focused on the plenary power of Congress and emphasized negotiation and compromise—leads not to Calhoun (nor to the anti-Federalists, as de Alvarez maintained) but to Henry Clay. Kendall/Carey does however reveal its authors' strong sense of antiutopianism, an intense skepticism toward those who would remake the world with the wave of a wand or at the point of a bayonet. Kendall (and Carey) understood that delusions of political grandeur could end in bloody disaster. Any civil war, whatever positive results it might achieve, marked a political failure. According to this political theory, then, the way forward was to talk things through (allowing "honest controversy" even on basic principles), not fight them out; to negotiate, not impose; to work patiently for change, not demand its immediate realization. Thus, Kendall (and Carey) shunned notions of the United States as an exceptional nation divinely chosen to remake the world. (Even in his intelligence career Kendall had opposed requiring allies to fulfill American political ideals.) This stance—profoundly skeptical of rapid and radical change—had long aggravated liberals. It soon exasperated the emerging neoconservative movement, including Jaffa.[41]

While alive Kendall got more pushback from another proposed book entitled *The Sages of Conservatism* in which he critiqued conservative contemporaries. Henry Regnery, for example, bridled at Kendall's criticism of Russell Kirk but gave him a contract for the proposed book nonetheless. Kendall completed only fragments of it. Proposed targets included William F. Buckley (the Young Sage of Stamford) and James Burnham (the Muscle-Minded Sage of Kent). Trying to show how his own views were superior to those of conservative contemporaries, Kendall here did what he did best, close reading and critical analysis of the work of other intellectuals. He only finished (more or less) three chapters—those on Kirk (the Benevolent Sage of Mecosta), Clinton Rossiter (the Pseudo-Sage of Ithaca), and John Courtney Murray (the True Sage of Woodstock). Kendall's take on Murray was largely positive, agreeing with him that real truths existed and on the need for social consensus. Kendall remained on relatively friendly terms with both Kirk and Rossiter, but he viewed the former as an impractical antiquarian and the latter as a liberal "Trojan Horse." Perhaps only Willmoore Kendall could have used "benevolent" as a sneer.[42]

Most importantly, Kendall carefully critiqued lists of conservative characteristics compiled by Kirk and Rossiter. He accepted some of their ideas, rejected others, and modified some of their points to make them applicable to the United States. Hidden within these critiques, then, lay Kendall's own apophatic fifteen-point definition of American conservatism. As extracted by the present author and reformulated as assertions rather than refutations, these principles were as follows:

1) The nature of man is sufficiently constant to warrant certain firm propositions about him, namely that he is sufficiently capable of good and reasonableness and civility to deserve the means to his self-protection, sufficiently capable of bad and unreasonableness and barbarism to warrant the separation and limitation of power that characterize the Constitution of the United States.
2) Despite great and indisputable natural inequalities among them, all men *are* created equal, and are entitled in some respects, but not in others, to equal treatment.
3) It is the business of government in the United States to promote a just, not an equal distribution of rewards and privileges.
4) The people, in choosing the representatives who are to exercise the powers granted to officeholders under the Constitution, should seek the "best" men.
5) Political power, no matter by whom exercised, is potentially tyrannical, capable of injustice and of invading natural rights, and should therefore be restrained.
6) Because men are capable of injustice—of invading each other's natural rights—the most desirable state of affairs—politically, socially, economically—is one in which power is diffused.
7) Men are endowed with natural rights but forfeit their rights by not performing their duties.
8) Abrogation of the right to property, save as clearly necessary for the purposes set forth in the Preamble to the Constitution, is *theft*, and thus a violation of natural law.
9) A *good* institution is rendered the *more* sacred by having been handed down by the forefathers.

10) Organized religion plays a valuable role in the life of American society and should be regarded with favor even by American conservatives who are not themselves believers.
11) The proper function of American educational institutions, both public and private, is to inculcate upon their charges a belief in the *conservative* creed.
12) There are principles of universal justice, which man discovers through *reason*, that is, through the principles of *natural law speculation*.
13) Conservatism rejects both individualism and collectivism on grounds of reason.
14) The goals of *our* society should be "to form [an ever] more perfect Union, establish Justice, insure domestic tranquility, provide for the general Welfare, and secure the blessings of Liberty to ourselves and our posterity."
15) The best form of government for the *American* people is that stipulated in the Constitution of the United States, as explicated and justified in the *Federalist*.

This list specifies Kendall's ultimate stances on many issues—human nature, equality, democracy, individual rights, tradition, religion, reason—which he dealt with at more length but more obliquely elsewhere. Here one sees the influence of Strauss (on natural-law reasoning), Aristotle (on aristocracy and justice), Burke (on national particularity and tradition), Voegelin (on religion), Publius (on the Constitution), and Rousseau (on the people). Kendall's political teaching rested upon no one of these points but demanded maintaining a balance among them. His teaching cannot be subsumed under the umbrella of any other thinker, for Kendall quite consciously derived his political philosophy from many sources. He was a man who "never stopped thinking." His ideas were therefore always subject to revision. But the fifteen principles above define what, at the end of his life, Willmoore Kendall meant when calling himself a conservative.[43]

On June 30, 1967, shortly after meeting with a student, Willmoore Kendall had a heart attack. He lay down for a nap in Dallas and never woke up. The following Sunday students said a rosary and kept an all-night vigil with his body at Lynch Hall in the special classroom where Kendall had taught. Father Fandal said the requiem mass. According to Leo Paul de Alvarez, Kendall had discerned his real vocation as a teacher at Dallas. Typically, said de Alvarez, Willmoore had gained this insight by pondering the writings of another intellectual. Richard Weaver, Kendall believed, provided a key piece to the democratic puzzle "missing" from *The Federalist*. Weaver had deliberated upon how the people of a democracy might remain "decent" and "virtuous," that is, dedicated to justice and liberty and opposed to tyranny. The Framers had simply assumed such qualities to subsist in the people. Weaver, however, had suggested the need for a "select minority" to preserve the "historical memory" of the people lest "they forget what and who they are." Kendall's "final days," said de Alvarez, "were taken up with creating this band of teachers. He had pointed out the ultimate task of the teacher in America today, a task he himself had most nobly borne." As this sort of a teacher, then, Kendall was exercising his long-term vocation as a tribune. By helping the American people maintain its virtue and know its strength, this band of teachers could help the people protect itself from power-hungry foes, foreign and domestic. Had Kendall lived longer, the band would have been bigger. Even so one of its members (graduate student John Murley) moved immediately to defend his teacher's singular legacy from cooptation by Catholic traditionalists associated with Brent Bozell and Frederick Wilhelmsen. That fall Louise Cowan kicked off the new semester at Dallas by announcing that the Willmoore Kendall Graduate Program in Politics and Literature would be expanding.[44]

Remembering his longtime friend to colleagues, Charles Hyneman spoke of the real value of Kendall's scholarship. He emphasized his genuine prowess as a teacher while also frankly acknowledging his faults. Willmoore's "raging compulsion to expose error and force recognition of sound principles" had badly damaged his own career. Former Kendall students wrote Hyneman to thank him for the truth of this portrait. Dankwart Rustow, an important political theorist, and Charles M. Lichenstein, prominent Republican diplomat, had both fallen out with Kendall before his death. Rustow acknowledged that meeting Kendall had been "an intellectual turning point" for him. Lichenstein said of Kendall: "here is one sometime disciple of his who—however he messed up our border treaties—never will forget, never will reject, and never will apologize for his influence." Private praise poured into Nellie Kendall, including a note from Vice-President Hubert Humphrey. Mulford Sibley called Willmoore "one of my best friends" who possessed "one of the most brilliant minds it has ever been my privilege to encounter" and assured Nellie that Willmoore had loved her deeply.[45]

Many who knew Kendall, especially those closest to him, retained vivid memories of the colorful cold warrior. He appeared as a fictional character in several published tales, most famously in Saul Bellow's *Mosby's Memoirs* and William F. Buckley's *The Redhunter*. Pearl Kendall remained sad and bewildered about why her oldest son had shunned her in his last years. Father Fandal, later a key leader of the Dominican Order, found himself haunted by his "cussed" and "unforgettable" colleague. The atheist Revilo Oliver wrote of "the dolorous memories of my dead friend" now "dissolved into the universal void of irrevocable time." A month after Ken's death, Nellie wrote Bill. Having only met Buckley twice, she did not know him well but understood how important he had been to her deceased husband. She told him that

Figure 8.3 Home Again. *Source:* Photo by the Author.

her "Reason for hopping so madly over half the earth for almost ten years" was gone. She mentioned wanting to settle down in Dallas to work as a librarian and that she would continue as a "Little Mother" to Ken's students. The new widow told Bill that he had been "the source ... of some of Willmoore's greatest pleasure and pain." Then she added: "I know he never stopped loving you tremendously, no matter what you heard, or read, or saw—from whatever source, even WK himself."[46] In the end, Willmoore Kendall came all the way home. Today he lies buried near his father in six good feet of red heartland earth at Rose Hill Cemetery in the ancestral town of Ardmore, Oklahoma. His epitaph reads simply: "Teacher."

NOTES

1. WK to FGW, April 14, 1964, and March 23, 1965, B3, Kendall Student Interview, Name Withheld, September 28–29, 2018; WP; Donald A. Cowan to WK, January 19, 1962, B17F3, KP; Donald A. Cowan, "The Indelible Mark" (1964). *Speeches.* Paper 11. http://digitalcommons.udallas.edu/cowan_speeches/11; Donald A. Cowan, Draft Biography of WK, 1967, WKC; FW, Memories, 5, WKC; "Obituary of Louise Cowan," *New York Times,* November 19, 2015, p. B14.

2. WK to HR, August 10, 1965, B38F2, HRP; WK to RPO, [1963], Revilo P. Oliver, Online Papers; WK to Addison Potter, Fall 1963, B20F15, KP; University of Dallas, Department of Politics and Economics Flyer, [1964], B15F3, KP; WK to Robert Pass, February 19, 1964, B15F3, KP.

3. WK to EV, July 24, 1966, in "VK," 402–03; LS to WK, December 3, 1963, January 16, 1964, February 3, 1964, April 27, 1965, November 4, 1966, and November 18, 1966, and WK to LS, April 23, 1965, in *WK*, 248–50, 253–56; BDJ to WK, February 27, 1966, B16F3, KP; JH to WK, February 2, 1965, B17F5, KP; Harry Jaffa to WK, March 22, 1964, B17F13, KP; James B. McClellan to WK, April 15, 1964 and June 26, 1964, B21F5, KP; WK to FGW, June 18, 1964 and November 5, 1965, B3, KP.

4. Damian Fandal to WK, December 2, 1965 (misdated 1966), B18F11, KP; WK to FGW, [1964], March 20, 1964, and December 28, 1964, B3, WP; WK to YM, [1964], B6F6, KP; WK to CH, Spring 1964, Two letters, B16F9, KP; WK to YM, [1964], B6F6, KP.

5. "Politics and Economics at the University of Dallas," Flyer, 1966, B15F8, KP; Kendall Student Interview, Name Withheld, November 16, 2016; Interview with Leo Paul de Alvarez, September 29, 2018, Dallas, Texas; Leo Paul de Alvarez, "Willmoore Kendall: Teacher," Obituary Clipping from *Phalanx*, 1967, B16F7, KP.

6. Leo Paul de Alvarez, "Willmoore Kendall: Teacher," Obituary Clipping from *Phalanx*, 1967, B16F7, KP; Interview with Pat Smith, September 28, 2019; FW, Memories, 8–10, WKC; Student Interviews, Name Withheld, August 28, 2018, and September 28–29, 2018.

7. WK to YM, April 1961, B6F3, KP; WK to CH, December 1963, B16F9, KP; WK to FGW, [1963] and March 28, 1964, B3, WP; JH to WB, February 16, 1966, B39, BP; Donald Cowan Statement on JFK Assassination, November 1963, B1F5, Cowan Collection, MS 152, Archives and Special Collections, University of Dallas; Pat and Connie Smith Interview, 2018.

8. WB to WK, March 25, 1959 and WK to WB, March 26, 1959, B8, BP; WK to WB, October 13, 1961, B15, BP; WK to YM, [1960] and [Fall 1960], B6F2, KP; WK to FGW, July 6, 1961, B2, WP; WK to Tinkum Brooks, May 19, 1959, B6F147, CBP; WK to YM, [Summer 1962], B6F4, KP; WK to YM, [1964], 3 letters, B6F6, KP; WK to Tinkum Brooks, August 13, 1960, CBP; PGK to KK, August 8, 1965, October 1, 1966, December 30, 1966, February 8, 1967, February 28, 1967, and March 20, 1967, B5F7, KKP.

9. WB to WK, September 18, 1963 and September 26, 1963, B26, BP; WK to *National Review* Board, September 22, 1963, B26, BP; WK to William Rusher, January 1964 and February 1964, B31, BP; William Rusher to WK, January 29, 1964, BP; WK to WB, January 16, 1964 and January 19, 1964, B31, BP.

10. William Rusher to WK, February 4, 1964, B31, BP; WB to WK, February 13, 1964, B31, BP; Judis, *Buckley*, 211–12.

11. Judis, *Buckley*, 318–19; "Bozell for Congress," 1964 and "Bozell for Congress: The Matthias Record," 1964, B29, BP; Kelly, *Living on Fire*, 82–86.

12. Patricia B. Bozell to WB, February 6, 1964, B29, BP; WK to YM, [1964], B6F6, KP; Frank Meyer to WK, July 27, 1962, February 16, 1963, March 18, 1963,

and October 5, 1963, B21F8, KP; Elsie Meyer to WK, February 15, 1964, Contract Between Meyer and Kendall, October 8, 1964, and April 7, 1965, B21F9, KP; Gerhart Niemeyer to WK, March 13, 1965, B21F11, KP; WB to JH, March 1, 1966, B39, BP; WK to HR, [1966], August 3, 1966, and August 10, 1966, B38F2, HRP; John Tower to WK, August 2, 1966, B15F4, KP; Student Interview, September 28, 2018; LB, Handwritten Dedication, 1966, WK Copy of *The Warren Revolution*, Willmoore Kendall Memorial Library, University of Dallas; Bozell WK to LB, 1965, B35, BP; WK to LB, 1966, B39, BP.

13. "Kennedy Biographer to Debate," *Star-News* (Pasadena, CA), February 20, 1964, p. 1; WK, "Resolved the Deadlock in Washington is to be Deplored" and Review of *Deadlock*, in *Contra Mundum*, 266–89.

14. WK to YM, [1964], B6F6, KP; Walter M. Cunningham, Notes of Kendall Debate with Åke Sandler, March 2, 1964, Los Angeles, B19F7, KP; "Conservative to Debate Liberal," *Stanford Daily*, May 10, 1966, p. 1; "Speaking Itinerary for Prof. Kendall," May 5, 1966, WKC; Mulford Q. Sibley to WK, April 5, 1966, B19F5, KP; Kristin Serum, "Freedom of Speech Debated," *Minneapolis Star*, April 7, 1967, p. 6.

15. WK, "American Conservatism and the 'Prayer' Decisions," *Modern Age* VIII, no. 3 (Summer 1964): 245–59.

16. WK, "Prayer Decisions," 250–58; Alvis, "Evolution," 70–75.

17. WK, "The Civil Rights Movement and the Coming Constitutional Crisis," in *Contra Mundum, passim*.

18. WK to HR, October 29, 1964, B38F2, HRP; GWC to WK, Fall 1964, B17F4, KP; WK to Oscar Pemantle, Fall 1964, B20F5, KP; WK to FGW, November 19, 1964, B3, WP; James McClellan to WK, December 11, 1964, B21F5, KP.

19. Frank Meyer to WK, May 28, 1960, B21F8, KP; WK to Nathaniel Weyl, 1960 (Two Letters) and November 20, 1960, Nathaniel Weyl to WK, December 23, 1960 and February 10, 1961, B7F7, Weyl Papers; WK to WB, October 17, 1962, B20, BP; WK to WB, June 21, 1963, B26, BP.

20. WK, "Social Determinants," B6F148, CBP; de Alvarez, "Kendall and Constitution," 9–11, WKC; Garry Wills to WK, [1964?], 2 letters, B16F11, KP.

21. WK, Classroom Lecture, University of Dallas, Government 201, [1964?], B26F3; WK Classroom Lecture, University of Dallas, May 22, 1964, B26F2, KP; WK, Classroom Lecture, University of Dallas, May 15, 1964, B29, KP; WK to HR, January 18, 1964, B38F2, HRP.

22. WK, "The Divided Constituencies," clipping from *Tower*, (Fall-Winter 1994), excerpted from May 14, 1965 lecture, B24F7, KP; WK, Classroom Lecture, University of Dallas, Government 201, [1964?], B26F3.

23. WK, Classroom Lecture, University of Dallas, May 22, 1964, B26F2, KP; WK, Classroom Lecture, University of Dallas, May 15, 1964, B29, KP.

24. WK, "What Goldwaterism is All About," *New Guard*, October 1964, pp. 8–9, 12; Harry Jaffa to WK, March 22, 1964, May 7, 1964 and August 7, 1964, B17F13, KP; John O'Sullivan, "When Liberalisms Collide," *NR*, October 20, 2014, nationalreview.com; WK to Addison Potter, March 26,[1962?], B20F15, KP; Nash, "Place," 8–9; Wills, *Confessions*, 25; Nash, "Iconoclast II," 246; Judis, *Buckley*, 61; Archibald Cox to WK, October 17, 1960, B20F3, KP.

25. Havers, "Our Times," 23–24; WK to HR, October 13, 1965, B38F2, HRP; JH to WK, April 15, 1966, B17F4, KP; James MacGregor Burns, *Leadership* (New York: Harper & Row, 1978), *passim*; Joseph Postell, "Philosopher-Kings or the Sense of the Community? Jaffa, Kendall, and the Problem of Majority Rule," *Anamnesis* 7 (2018): 50–69; Walter Berns to WK, December 17, 1956 and December 31, 1956, B18F7, KP; Harry Jaffa to NK, August 13, 1974, B17F13, KP.

26. WK to Carl Albert, January 30, 1967, Box 43, Folder 9, General, CAC; "LBJ a Conservative?," Tennessee Newspaper Clipping, [1966], B6F8, KP.

27. WK to YM, February 25, 1965, B15F3, KP; Donald Cowan to WK, February 28, 1966, B17F3, KP; NK to WB, August 27, 1967, B44, BP; Student Interview, September 29, 2018; de Alvarez, "Missing Passage," 148; FW, Memories, 4–5, WKC: Don Erler to WK, December 8, 1965, B18F13, KP.

28. WK to YM, October 12, 1965, B6F8, KP; WK to YM, October 26, 1965, B6F8, KP; WK to YM, October 12, 1965, B6F8, KP; WK and NK to YMK, Late 1965, B6F7, KP.

29. WK to HR, November 14, 1965, B38F2, HRP; WK to FGW, November 16, 1965, B3, KP; JH to WB, September 7, 1965 and WB to JH, September 13, 1965, B35, BP; JH to WB, February 16, 1966, B39, BP; Hart, "Deliberate Sense," 77–78; WB to JH, March 1, 1966, B39, BP.

30. WK to YM, November 1965 and December 1965, B6F8, KP; JH to WK, October 21, 1965, B17F5, KP; Hart, "Deliberate Sense," 78; R.B. McCallum to NK, September 18, 1967, KP.

31. WK to HR, [1965?], B38F2, HRP; WK to FGW, March 23, 1965, B3, WP; WK to YM, December 31, 1965, B6F7, KP; Damian Fandal to WK, January 6, 1966, B18F11, KP; WK to YM, November 1965, B6F8, KP; Damian Fandal to WB, May 6, 1981, B22F22, KP; Damian Fandal to Pope Paul VI, [1965], WKC; WK to WB, August 5, 1966, and WB to WK, August 5, 1966, B39, KP.

32. Jeffrey Hart to WK, April 15, 1966, B17F3; WK to FGW, March 23, 1965, B3, KP; WK to EV, July 24, 1966, in "VK," 401–03; WK to LS, April 23, 1965, in *WK*, 253–54; FW, Memories, 10–12, WKC; Alexandra Wilhelmsen Interview, 2018; Student Interview, September 28, 2018; Kendall Student Interview, Name Withheld, September 28, 2018; KP; "Politics and Economics at the University of Dallas," Flyer, 1966, B17F8, KP; "Report to the Texas Educational Association," Spring 1967, B17F8, KP; WK to CH, December 1963, B16F9, KP.

33. WK to HR, [1966?], B38F2, HRP; Damian Fandal to WK, January 6, 1966, and February 24, 1967, B18F11, KP; Alex Hillman to WK, April 7, 1967, B17F17, KP; WK to Richard Ware , July 6, 1966 and May 26, 1967, B19F2, KP; "Report to the Texas Educational Association," Spring 1967, B17F8, KP.

34. WK to HR, [1964?] and WK to HR, January 18, 1964, B38F2, HRP.

35. WK to FGW, 1963, B3, WP; FW, Memories, 6, WKC; Gerhart Niemeyer to WK, May 28, 1965, B21F11, KP; WK, "John Locke Revisited," *Intercollegiate Review* 2, no. 4 (January-February 1966): 217–34; Alvis, "Evolution," 60–67; LS to WK, April 27, 1965 and June 2, 1967, and LS to NK, October 28, 1970, in *WK*, 255–58.

36. WK/GWC, "The 'Intensity' Problem and Democratic Theory," *American Political Science Review* LXII, no. 1 (March 1968): 5–24; WK and GWC, "The

'Roster Device': J.S Mill and Contemporary Elitism," *Western Political Science Quarterly* 21 (March 1968): 20–39.

37. WK to HR, January 28, 1964, B38F2, HRP; WK, "The Achievement of Eric Voegelin," March 14, 1964 and Louis H.T. Dehmlow to WK, March 20, 1964, B24F8, KP.

38. Richard Wentworth to WK, August 9, 1966, B22F11, KP; JH to NK, October 10, 1967, B17F5, KP; WK and GWC, *The Basic Symbols of the American Political Tradition* (Baton Rouge: LSU Press, 1970), ch. 1.

39. WK/GWC, *Basic Symbols*, chs. 2–4.

40. JH to WK, December 17, 1965, B17F5, KP; William Gangi, "A Scholar's Journey on the Dark Side," *Chapman Law Review* 11, no. 1 (2007): 40–41; de Alvarez, "Missing Passage," 152–53: East, "Political Thought," 232–33.

41. Harry V. Jaffa, Review of *Basic Symbols of the* American *Political Tradition*, by WK/GWC, *Loyola of Los Angeles Law Review* 8 (1975): 471–505; Student Interview, August 2018; Harry V. Jaffa, "Inventing the Past," *St. John's Review* XXXIII, no. 1 (Autumn 1981): 4; "Jaffa vs. Bork: An Exchange," *NR*, March 21, 1994, pp. 56–59; Postell, "Philosopher-Kings," 52; WK and GWC, *Basic Symbols*, 101 and *passim*; de Alvarez, "Missing Passage," 141–44; John A. Murley, "On the 'Calhounism' of Willmoore Kendall," in *WKM*, 101–07; McCarthy, "Constitution," *passim*; Joshua A. Tait, "The Right, With Lincoln: Conservative Intellectuals Interpret Lincoln, 1945–89" (M.A. thesis, University of Canterbury, 2013), 81–99; de Alvarez Interview, 2018; Leo Paul de Alvarez, Review of *Basic Symbols of the American Political Tradition*," by WK and GWC, *Modern Age* (Summer 1971): 323–35; Justin Blake Litke, "American Exceptionalism: From Exemplar to Empire" (PhD, diss., Georgetown University, 2010), *passim*.

42. WK to FGW, March 4, 1960, September 22, 1960, December 10, 1960, January 1961, B2, WP; HR to WK, March 22, 1963 and May 13, 1963, B38F2, HRP; WK to HR, [1960], February 2, 1962, March 25, 1963, and [1965], B38F2, HRP; WK to WB, January 26, 1961 and Morris Clarke to WK, January 21, 1961, B15, BP; WK to FGW, 1963 and [1966], B3, WP; WK, "The Liberal Line," *NR*, June 13, 1956, p. 16; WK, "Moon-Struck Madness," *NR*, June 13, 1956, pp. 20–21; WK, "The Liberal Line," July 18, 1956, p. 11; WK, "Three on the Line," *NR*, August 31, 1957, p. 179; WK to Francis Croker, October 18, 1957, B22F9, KP; Clinton Rossiter to WK, February 8, 1967, B20F19, KP; Nash, "Iconoclast II," 246; Herndon, "Voegelin's History," 25.

43. WK, "The Sages of Conservatism," in *Contra Mundum*, 29–89; FW, Memories, 10–12, WKC; Nash, "Place," 5.

44. Student Interview, November 17, 2016; FW, Memories, 12, WKC; Student Interview, September 28, 2018; State of Texas Death Certificate, Willmoore Kendall, Jr., Texas, Death Certificates, 1903–1982, Provo: Ancestry.Com, 2013; Damian Fandal to WB, May 6, 1981, B22F22, KP; Donald Cowan, "Willmoore Kendall," Newspaper Clipping, 1967, B16F7, KP; Leo Paul de Alvarez, "Willmoore Kendall: Teacher," *Law & Liberty*, March 5, 2018, https://www.lawliberty.org/ 2018/03/05/patriotism-is-not-enough-steven-hayward-conservatism-24683/; Obituary Clipping from Phalanx, 1967, B16F7, KP; Richard M. Reinsch II, "A Question of Patriotism,"

"Havers, "Strauss-Kendall," 25; John Murley letter to *Triumph*, July 21, 1967, B22F22, KP; Louise Cowan Speech, Fall 1967, B16F9, KP.

45. CH, "In Memoriam: Willmoore Kendall," *P.S.* (Winter 1968): 55–56, B4F18, KKP, Charles M. Lichenstein to CH, March 29, 1968, B16F9, KP; Dankwart A. Rustow to CH, March 8, 1968, B16F9, KP; Hubert Humphrey to NK, July 5, 1967, B22F22, KP; Ilie Smultea to NK, April 12, 1968, B19F4, KP; Mulford Q. Sibley to NK, December 20, 1969, B19F5, KP.

46. Chet Wolford to WB, June 2, 1997, B3, Series Accession 2009-M-035, BP; PGK to WK, August 28, 1967, B44, BP; Damian Fandal to NK, August 4, 1967 and May 9, 1968, B18F11, KP; RPO to NK, February 3, 1968, Oliver Papers; Damian Fandal to WB, May 6, 1981, B22F22, KP; NK to WB, August 27, 1967, B44, BP.

Conclusion
1977: "The Best Man of Bugtussle"

On the Fourth Floor Rotunda of the Oklahoma State Capitol hangs a curious portrait. Entitled "Carl Albert," painted in oil by distinguished Sooner State artist Charles Banks Wilson, it depicts the forty-sixth Speaker of the United States House of Representatives. Only 5'4" in real life, Carl Albert stands like a colossus in the foreground of the painting. Turned slightly to his right, left hand in his pants pocket, he is wearing a brown business suit, a pastel tie in a double Windsor knot, and has horn-rimmed reading glasses tucked neatly into a front coat pocket. With his graying temples, watchful eyes, and bemused smile, one senses this man possesses power and means business. Even without the clue of the U.S. Capitol in the background, one might suspect that his business is politics.

On both sides behind and below Albert, painted in muted tones, stand the schoolchildren of Bugtussle Elementary from 1914. Wilson adapted this part of his painting from a black and white school photograph which showed the real Carl as one of the shortest boys in the front row.[1] Yet the artist paints the kids in miniature. In brilliant color, larger than life, and in the full flush of power, the adult Speaker emerges out of the crowd of tiny, anonymous schoolchildren who are clad in drab overalls, wool coats, and homemade dresses. To the right, behind and above the children, stands the two-room Bugtussle School, a wooden structure with a few gothic flourishes. Above it stands the U.S. Capitol building. The artist depicts the buildings (and a few leafed-out hardwoods on the left side of the canvas) a bit hazily. The little people are more distinct, but Albert's image dominates everything—both by its size and by its vibrancy.

Wilson's painting invites interpretation. Obviously, it illustrates the greatness of Albert who, as Speaker of the House, reached higher political office than any other Oklahoman. Albert labored in the House for thirty years

Figure 9.1 Charles Banks Wilson, "Carl Albert." *Source:* From the Oklahoma State Capitol Art Collection. Image Courtesy of the Oklahoma Arts Council.

starting in 1947, serving as Democratic Whip from 1955 to 1961, House Majority Leader from 1961 to 1971, then Speaker of the House from 1971 until retiring in 1977. He represented the Third District of Oklahoma, in the southeastern quadrant of the state. Culturally akin to the Deep South, this region's nickname was "Little Dixie." The painting draws attention to Albert's humble beginnings, for he was born in a log cabin as the son of a tenant farmer. And the Bugtussle School really was a two-room affair (which went up to eighth grade). The rural poverty depicted in the painting was also real, for Little Dixie was the poorest part of a poor state. By portraying him as a giant, the portrait slyly addresses the question of Albert's physical stature. Viewing the painting, the nickname "Little Giant" (a title Albert embraced) leaps out from the canvas for anyone with knowledge of the Speaker's career.

Also clear is that Big Albert symbolizes the American dream in which hard work and talent overcome economic deprivation and inherited physical limitations. The school house and the U.S. Capitol appear to represent the power of education and government to lift the poor out of poverty. Indeed, Albert himself had methodically and quite intentionally used education as his ticket out of the cotton fields. He also had become an avid New Deal/Fair Deal/Great Society Democrat who believed federal intervention in the economy helped lighten the hardships of his constituents.[2] The historian will note a few brown faces but no black ones among the school children but understand that this absence depicts the realities of school life in segregated Oklahoma.

Beyond these observations, interpretation of the painting becomes more speculative. But one may still glean useful insights from pondering it. The absence of Charles Ross, the school's male teacher, is puzzling, for he appears in the original school photograph.[3] With Ross invisible, Albert emerges from the canvas as Bugtussle's all-powerful father figure. No man remains to contest his paternalistic authority. A libertarian art critic might read the painting as a metaphor for overmighty government. With Big Albert taking care of everything, no other adults are needed to care for the childlike citizens of Bugtussle. The small images of the school children, compared to the supersized Speaker, accentuate their dependency on him and, symbolically, upon government largesse.

Willmoore Kendall's political theory also provides a fruitful way to analyze the painting. Using this template, Albert emerges from the crowd of kids as the "best man" or democratized aristocrat of Bugtussle. Recognizing his talent, his constituents send him to Congress. Little Carl in the photo becomes Big Albert in the painting, but he remains part of the community. His old schoolmates do not linger in childhood. Rather, representing the people of Little Dixie, they recognize Albert as their larger-than-life leader whom they honor by reelecting repeatedly to represent their interests in the distant national capital. His dealings there are beyond their ken, but they know him, know that he remains one of themselves, and trust his good judgment for use in their service. He leads their locale. Albert's brown attire perhaps symbolizes his continued attachment to the soil of the district while the trees and school house bespeak his local roots. By depicting the U.S. Capitol, the painting portrays the proper place for Big Albert to exercise his outsized gifts. He is not to wield arbitrary power but to promote the well-being of home folks through mastering the processes of democracy.

In his three decades as United States representative for Oklahoma's Third District, Carl Albert embodied the ideal of democratic leadership as understood by his friend Willmoore Kendall and, more distantly, as elucidated by Aristotle. Perhaps it is not surprising that Kendall's teaching can help explicate the meaning of painted Big Albert. Willmoore and Carl, as we have seen, were old friends with shared connections and similar experiences. In his memoirs, Albert even claimed Kendall as a boyhood resident of his own Pittsburg County. Both Oklahomans were intelligent, ambitious, and politically engaged. Both suffered from heart trouble and drank to excess. But their differences were many and manifest. Albert was short and dark haired, Kendall tall and fair. Kendall was flamboyant, passionate, and contentious. Albert was outwardly modest, methodical, and calm. Kendall waged noisy intellectual war against all comers. Albert quietly cultivated powerful friends. He worked harmoniously with his colleagues and advanced relentlessly up the House hierarchy. After college the men remained in touch only sporadically, but in many respects they thought alike.

To an uncanny degree, Carl Albert put into practice the political theory Willmoore Kendall preached. He almost perfectly fit the mold of Kendall's democratic "best man," beloved by constituents and representing his district's particular interests in Washington. Like Kendall, Albert believed that a variety of viewpoints and interests within and between parties was an asset to democracy. He distrusted ideological divisions and believed Congress, particularly the House, properly reflected the diversity of the United States. Albert was a skilled practitioner of the art of Congressional deliberation which Kendall saw as the heart of American democracy. He prized the prerogatives of Congress and worked to uphold them against executive encroachment. Kendall believed that the American system of elected representation combined the best feature of democracy (rule by the people) with the greatest advantage of aristocracy (rule by the best) as defined by Aristotle. Should a representative's views diverge too dramatically from those of his constituents, the constituents could oust him at the next election. In normal times, however, voters would defer to representatives whom they knew face to face and admired. Kendall held that a majority elected to Congress in this manner was more representative of the desires of the American people—and more stable—than were fleeting presidential majorities.

Without explicitly consulting this teaching, Albert adopted it as his own. Looking back after retirement, Albert noted how service to his district had won him enough trust among local voters so that he could vote his "convictions" on important issues. From the beginning of his career, he understood that taking care of his "district's special needs" was vital to his political future. In his fascinating autobiography, *Little Giant: The Life and Times of Speaker Carl Albert*, Albert recounted many instances of mundane achievements, including preserving Oklahoma's share of the national peanut production quota, intervening with the Marines so the sole surviving son of a constituent avoided combat, and promoting initiatives for rural electrification and flood control. According to one scholar, Albert believed like Tip O'Neill, his successor as Speaker of the House, that "all politics were local." As Albert put it: "Because the Third District's voters knew and trusted me, they let me build a career of service. They knew that that career was more important than any vote I ever cast because they knew that my service embraced the best of their beliefs and the greatest of their needs."[4]

Reading only his biography, one might imagine Albert as a consistent liberal voice in Washington, dedicated to civil rights and solidly pro-labor. This impression would be misleading. In his autobiography, for example, Albert calls the Taft-Hartley Act of 1947 "viciously antilabor." He fails to mention that he voted to override Truman's veto of the act. In the same year, he voted no when the House voted to ban the poll tax. Albert also voted against the Civil Rights Act of 1957 (though he obscured this fact in his autobiography). Perhaps, deep down, Albert always cherished "the civil rights of all people," as claimed in *Little Giant*.[5] If so, he compromised these principles early in his congressional tenure, voting against his own beliefs to avoid antagonizing his constituents. Later, Albert became more visibly liberal. He provided great assistance to President Lyndon B. Johnson, for example, in securing passage of the Civil Rights Act of 1964. Having earned the trust of Third District voters, he apparently felt secure enough to lead them in what he had always known (or claims to have known) was the ethically right direction.

Throughout his career, Albert believed that an "active state, promoting equal opportunity, . . . could enhance the status of all Americans." Far from hostile to business, however, Albert believed New Deal-style liberalism had "saved capitalism." And like most Congressmen he was well connected to local business interests and professionals. Oklahoma coal mining, petroleum, and mercantile interests helped fund his political career. Nevertheless, qua Kendall, Albert's ideal was that of the aristocrat (the best man) and not that of the oligarch (the rich man). When he retired from the Speakership, Albert pointedly declined lucrative offers from vested interests seeking his influence with "old friends in Congress." For, he said, "Ernie Albert's boy was not for sale." Like Odysseus returning to Ithaca, Albert "went back to a little community called Bugtussle, near the town of McAlester in Pittsburg County, Oklahoma." For three decades Albert had been that community's best man in Washington. Then he came home. Sitting on his back porch after a long and successful career, he looked out nostalgically over old fields where he once picked cotton. But those fields were now underwater. A gigantic, manmade Lake Eufaula, funding for which Albert had shepherded through Congress, covered them.[6]

For much of the twentieth century, leaders of the political science profession had criticized the political processes of Congress, which Albert practiced so well. They had called for programmatic competition between ideologically distinct parties. Elected officials would possess clear mandates to enact the voters' wishes. Willmoore Kendall had strongly disagreed, arguing that the inchoate nature of American parties preserved stability and facilitated compromise. Albert realized in practice, even within his own party, he had to balance many interests, from "unreconstructed Dixiecrats" to "far out liberals." Each member of the House, he knew, represented a unique district. Some were urban and liberal, and others rural and conservative. Some were in safe seats, others more vulnerable. Like Kendall he understood Congressional elections not as one big national event but as 435 separate contests. Kendall had argued that these districts composed distinct communities. Each had a different set of voters, economic interests, and leaders. Albert learned the same lesson while in political harness. He understood the real distinctions between northern urban machines buttressed by "ethnic and working class voters" and southern Democrats who "represented a powerful establishment, an interlocking network of landowners, financiers, industrialists, and professionals, all men of power, all men of white flesh."[7]

Albert "never once forgot that" the political diversity of his own party—and of America—was reflected in Congress. Early on Albert cozied up to Speaker of the House Sam Rayburn and House Majority Leader John McCormack. Rayburn, "a Baptist from Fannin County, Texas," represented a rural district just across the Red River from Albert's own. McCormack, "a Catholic from South Boston," spoke for a very different set of constituents. These elder statesmen became mentors and patrons of Albert, a "Methodist from Oklahoma," because they recognized his intelligence and saw how diligently he worked. With their encouragement, Albert dedicated himself to a career in the House of Representatives. Left-wing Democrats distrusted Albert, seeing him as too conservative and too southern. These progressives in turn annoyed Albert with "the arrogance of the claim that the men who gave us most of the Democratic membership of Congress were not Democrats."[8]

Nor might one wish these distinctions between regions and districts away. Many Democrats chafed at the dominance of the southern caucus. To change Congress to what it should be, Albert understood, however, required working "with what Congress in fact was." Albert sought "to do as much as possible to win as much support as possible." This goal necessitated knowing "what was possible." Again, Albert did in real life what Kendall commended in theory. He sought to achieve incremental change through deliberation aimed at consensus. Kendall argued that railroading through major political changes, even beneficial changes, could lead to long-lasting political backlash. Albert also feared that disciplining "our largest single element [southern representatives]" might cause their "permanent estrangement."[9] Thus, Albert understood, with Kendall, that Congressional give and take among diverse interests, and across party lines, was vital for the continued health of the American system.

In breaking the southern stranglehold over legislation, for example, Albert showed that he could achieve the art of the possible through negotiation. In early 1961 Speaker Rayburn, with Albert (then Majority Whip) at his side, rejected intervention by newly elected president John F. Kennedy to break southern power on the House Rules Committee. With such internal

Congressional processes, said Rayburn, the "White House has no business at all." Instead, Albert and Rayburn hammered out a compromise among House members by adding new members to the committee. Behind-the-scenes negotiations in Congress—facilitated by Rayburn, McCormack, and Albert—achieved the desired result. Administration efforts to sway votes, said Albert, had achieved nothing. Thereby, he continued, this change lessened the power of the committee to block needed legislation. Yet it resulted in "no permanent division into embittered southern and anti-southern elements."[10]

Throughout his career, Carl Albert was devoted to maintaining the power and dignity of Congress. As a young Bugtussle lad, he had decided in first grade—after hearing a talk from Third District congressman Charles D. Carter—that he would pursue a career in the House of Representatives. Inspired by a teacher who admired Speaker of the House Champ Clark, little Carl had begun to consider the "great goal" of becoming Speaker. Albert always "loved the House of Representatives." He reveled in its history, such as the revolt Clark had led "to smash" the power of Speaker Joseph Cannon in 1910.[11] As a young Congressman, inspired by Sam Rayburn (and in good Aristotelian fashion), Albert would put on the virtuous "House Habit" of hard work, legislative deliberation, and consensus building. Never would he seek office outside its confines. In 1965 Albert took pride that key reforms to the Ways and Means Committee—which facilitated passage of various Great Society programs—had been "entirely conceived and executed by the House leadership." Pushing through the Budget and Impoundment Act of 1973, Albert faced down President Richard Nixon. Federal budgeting "would rest firmly where the Founding Fathers had placed it," that is, with Congress. In 1973 he also moved forward the most powerful House constitutional weapon by authorizing an impeachment inquiry against Nixon. After retirement, Albert proudly established the Carl Albert Congressional Research Center as the "only academic facility in America devoted to the study of its legislative branch."[12]

Although committed to the Democratic Party, Albert valued working across the aisle with the opposing party. He cherished friendships with Republican Speaker of the House Joseph Martin and future president Gerald Ford. During the Eisenhower administration, Albert (with the rest of the Democratic House leadership) frequently helped the president pass legislation which congressional Republicans opposed. On the other hand, when faced with recalcitrance in his own party, Albert could turn nimbly to House Republicans for help. In 1964, for example, he worked out a deal with House Minority Leader Charles Halleck (whom he disliked) to push through the landmark Civil Rights Act. Most famously, for several months in 1973, after the removal of Vice President Spiro Agnew, Albert stood next in line to the presidency. Even with Nixon facing impeachment, the Speaker played no games with the process. He urged the president to nominate fellow House member Gerald Ford to replace Agnew and then worked to assure Ford's confirmation.[13]

Willmoore Kendall died a few years before Carl Albert became Speaker of the House, but he had come to admire the achievements of his former housemate and badly wanted to see him "in that Speaker's chair."[14] The men's views on politics diverged significantly in some areas. Albert remained far more deferential to the federal courts than Kendall thought wise. Kendall saw great value in the arcane House procedures which Albert worked to dismantle. On the other hand—as regards the importance of public service in a democracy, disapproval of ideological parties, the centrality of legislative deliberation for good governance, and holding high the powers of Congress—Carl and Willmoore were on the same page. Kendall knew his old friend had become the best man of Bugtussle and that his career exemplified the healthiest aspects of American democracy. Surely, then, Willmoore would have appreciated the symbolism of Wilson's Big Albert which was unveiled in 1977, a decade after his own death, to commemorate the Speaker's retirement.

NOTES

1. Carl Albert and Danney Goble, *Little Giant: The Life and Times of Speaker Carl Albert* (Norman: University of Oklahoma Press, 1990), 42, 377; Christopher H. Owen, "The Man From Bug Tussle," *Chronicles*, February 2021, pp. 40–43.
2. Ibid., 156.
3. Ibid., 36–42.
4. Albert and Goble, *Little Giant: The Life and Times of Speaker Carl Albert* 175–81, 191–95; Dean J. Kotlowski, "Limited Vision: Carl Albert, The Choctaws, and Native Self-Determination," *American Indian Culture and Research Journal* 26, no. 2 (Spring 2002): 33.
5. House Vote #74 in 1947 (80th Congress), https://www.govtrack.us/congressvotes/80-1947/h74; House Vote #42 in 1957 (85th Congress), https://www.govtrack.us/congress/votes/85-1957/h42; Albert, 170, 274–75; Albert to Earl Q. Gray, April 15, 1948, Box 2, Folder 78, Legislative, CAC; Albert, 156, 379; "'Little Giant Dies at Age 91," *Daily Oklahoman*, February 6, 2000, p. 13A.
6. Kotlowski, 33; House Vote #49 in 1947 (80th Congress), https://www.govtrack.us/congress/votes/80-1947/h49; Albert, 146–49, 372, 375.
7. Albert to WK, February 2, 1967, Box 3, Folder 49, General, CAC; Albert and Goble, 214–17.
8. Ibid. Albert and Goble, 200, 230–31.
9. Ibid., 230–38.
10. Ibid., 239–42.
11. Ibid., 41–42.
12. Ibid., 200–02, 291, 351–53, 365–66, 376.
13. Ibid., 160, 208–12, 285–86, 359–65.
14. WK to Albert, January 30, 1967, Box 43, Folder 49, General, CAC.

Bibliography

Albert, Carl. "Carl Albert Center Congressional and Political Collections," University of Oklahoma.

Albert, Carl and Danney Goble. *Little Giant: The Life and Times of Speaker Carl Albert*. Norman: University of Oklahoma Press, 1990.

Allitt, Patrick. *The Conservatives: Ideas and Personalities Throughout American History*. New Haven: Yale University Press, 2010.

Alvis, John E. "The Evolution of Willmoore Kendall's Thought," in *WKM*, 86–94.

"Among Soldiers." *Stillwater Gazette,* August 23, 1918, 5.

Anderson, Claudia. "From the Archives of the *Weekly Standard*: Anne Brunsdale, 1923–2006." *Washington Examiner*, February 13, 2006, https://www.washingtonexaminer.com/weekly-standard/anne-brunsdale-1923-2006.

"Anne Brunsdale Wed." *Minneapolis Star-Tribune*, June 8, 1952, 55.

"Appointments." *Daily Ardmoreite,* November 10, 1909, 4.

Astrachan, Anthony. "An Undergraduate's View." *YDN*, October 16, 1951, 4.

"Average Child Can Be." *Tulsa Tribune*, November 16, 1923, 13.

"Baby Member." *Ogden Standard-Examiner*, December 27, 1936, 6.

"Baccalaureate Sermon." *Miami Daily News-Record*, August 22, 1930, 3.

"Beaumont Society," *Pembroke College Record: 1933–34.*

Bell, Daniel. *The End of Ideology: On the Exhaustion of Political Ideas in the Fifties.* New York: Collier, 1961.

Bellow, Saul. *Mosby's Memoirs and Other Stories*. New York: Viking Press, 1968.

"Bill's Book." *YDN*, October 15, 1951, 4–5.

"Blind But Qualified." *Hartshorne Sun*, July 16, 1914, 1.

"Blind Evangelist." *Chickasha Daily Express*, October 9, 1916, 4.

"Blind from Infancy." *Daily Ardmoreite*, October 24, 1920, 2.

"Blind Pastor." *Tulsa Tribune,* May 1, 1923, 5.

"Blind Pastor Paints Picture." *Tulsa Tribune*, November 19, 1923, 5.

"Blind Pastors." *Daily Oklahoman*, October 27, 1939, 1.

Bloxham, John. "Willmoore Kendall's 'McCarthyite' Socrates in Conservative Free Speech Debates of the 1950s and 1960s." *International Journal of the Classical Tradition* 25, no. 1 (2018): 72–88.

Bosemberg, Luis Eduardo. "The U.S., Nazi Germany, and the CIAA in Latin America during WW II," https://core.ac.uk/download/pdf/86445397.pdf.

Boudin, Louis B. *Government by Judiciary*. 2 vols. New York: William Godwin, 1932.

Bowers, Claude G. *My Life: The Memoirs of Claude Bowers*. New York: Simon and Schuster, 1962.

———. *The Tragic Era: The Revolution after Lincoln*. Cambridge, MA: Houghton-Mifflin, 1929.

"Boy Scouts." *New York Times*, October 8, 1922, 90.

Bozell, L. Brent, Jr. Handwritten Dedication to *The Warren Revolution*, 1966, Willmoore Kendall Memorial Library, University of Dallas.

———. Statement. *YDN*, February 19, 1948, 9–10.

"Bozell Will Speak." *YDN*, October 13, 1948, 1.

"Bozell Wins." *YDN*, February 13, 1948, 1.

"Brent Bozell." *YDN*, October 24, 1947, 1.

Braybrooke, David. Letter, *YDN*, October 17, 1957, 2.

Brewer, Landry. "Maurice Halperin: From Sooner Subversive to Soviet Spy." *Chronicles of Oklahoma* 96, no. 2 (Summer 2018): 156–68.

Brinkley, Alan. "The Problem of American Conservatism." *American Historical Review* 9, no. 2 (April 1994): 409–29.

Brooks, Cleanth. "Cleanth Brooks Papers." Yale Collection of American Literature, Beinecke Rare Book and Manuscript Library, Yale University.

———. *The Well-Wrought Urn: Studies in the Structure of Poetry*. New York: Harvest Books, 1947.

Browne, G. Morgan. "Pollard, Phelps," *YDN*, December 15, 1954, 1.

Brunello, Anthony R. "The Madisonian Republic and Modern Nationalist Populism: Democracy and the Rule of Law." *World Affairs* 181, no. 2 (Summer 2018): 106–32.

Buckley, F. Reid. Letter, *YDN*, May 9, 1950, 4.

"Buckley to Head," *YDN*, October 19. 1955, 1.

Buckley, William F., Jr. Foreword to *WKM*, ix–xxii.

———. *God and Man at Yale: The Superstitions of "Academic Freedom."* 50th Anniversary Edition. Washington, DC: Gateway, 2002.

———. *Miles Gone By: A Literary Autobiography*. Washington, DC: Regnery, 2004.

———. *The Redhunter: A Novel Based on the Life Senator Joe McCarthy*. Boston: Little, Brown, 1999.

———. Statement. *YDN*, May 14, 1948, 4.

———. "William F. Buckley, Jr. Papers." Manuscripts and Archives, Yale University Library.

Buckley, William F., Jr. and L. Brent Bozell. *McCarthy and His Enemies: The Record and Its Meaning*. Chicago: Regnery, 1954.

Burns, James MacGregor. *Leadership*. New York: Harper & Row, 1978.
Cady, Duane L. "What's On My Mind: Remembering Mulford Q. Sibley," May 20, 2019, https://duanelcady.com/remembering-mulford-q-sibley/.
"Campus Column." *Northwestern Alumni News*, December 1925, 11–12.
"Capacity Crowd Attends." *Stanford Daily*, May 4, 1959, 1.
Carey, George W. "How to Read Willmoore Kendall." *Intercollegiate Review* 8, no. 2 (Winter/Spring 1972): 63–65.
———. "Willmoore Kendall and the Doctrine of Majority Rule," in *WKM*, 17–46.
"Caudle Wins Moot Court Prize." *YDN*, May 10, 1951, 1.
"Chiefly About People." *Western Christian Advocate*, February 15, 1911.
"Church Services." *Advance Democrat*, December 13, 1917, 1.
"City Youth." *Daily Oklahoman*, December 13, 1931, 9.
"Civil Rights." *YDN*, October 23, 1952, 1.
Cohen, Robert S. Cohen. Letter, *YDN*, October 26, 1949, 4.
Coker, Francis. "An Historical View." *YDN*, October 16, 1951, 5.
Collier, Peter. *Political Woman: The Little Big Life of Jeane Kirkpatrick*. New York: Encounter, 2012.
"Commencement Exercises: Stillwater Public Schools," *Advance Democrat*, May 16, 1918, 5.
"Conservative, Liberal Factions." *YDN*, October 24, 1949, 1, 8.
Collingwood, R.G. *The Idea of History*. Oxford: Clarendon Press, 1946.
Continetti, Matthew. "'Genuine Civil War Potential:' Willmoore Kendall, Donald Trump, an American Conservatism," *Washington Free Beacon*, July 27 2018, https://freebeacon. com/columns/genuine-civil-war-potential/.
"County Vote," *Mangum Star*, November 9, 1922, 1.
Cowan Collection. MS 152. Archives and Special Collections, University of Dallas.
Cowan, Donald A. "The Indelible Mark" (1964). *Speeches*. Paper 11. http://digitalcommons.udallas.edu/cowan_speeches/11.
Damai, Paul K. "Radio Short Circuits," *Hammond Times*, August 13, 1944, 8.
Darroch, Doug. "Cain's Spirit," *Tulsa Tribune*, December 10, 1975, 10B.
Davis, Jack. "The Kent-Kendall Debate of 1949." *Studies in Intelligence* 35 no. 4 (June 1992): 91–103.
de Alvarez, Leo Paul. Interview with the Author. Irving, Texas, September 28, 2018.
———. "The Missing Passage of 'The Vanderbilt Lectures,'" in *WKM*, 141–55.
———. "Review of *Basic Symbols of the American Political Tradition*," by WK and GWC, *Modern Age* (Summer 1971): 323–35.
"Death Claims Rev. W. Kendall." *Miami Daily News-Record*, June 7, 1942, 1.
"Death Claims State Worker." *Daily Oklahoman*, October 28, 1932, 12.
"Debating Teams." *YDN*, April 24, 1948, 1.
Debo, Angie. *Tulsa: From Creek Town to Oil Capital*. Norman: University of Oklahoma Press, 1943.
Dempsey, Bourne. Letter, *YDN*, May 8, 1950, 4.
Dennis, Lawrence. "Lawrence Dennis Papers." Hoover Institution. Library and Archives.

Diamond, Sigmund. "God and the F.B.I, at Yale," *The Nation*, April 12, 1980, 423–28.
"Does Mangum Need." *Mangum Star*, January 5, 1922, 4.
"Dr. Eddy Hints." *Democrat and Chronicle*, February 26, 1941, 7.
"Dr. Jekel [sic] and Mr. Hyde." *Konawa Chief-Leader*, March 12, 1909, 1.
"Dr. Manion Talk." *Tablet*, October 12, 1957, 4.
"E.A. Grant." *Pembroke College Record*, 1988.
Ealy, Steven D. and Lloyd, Gordon. "The Eric Voegelin-Willmoore Correspondence," *Political Science Reviewer* 33 (2004): 357–412.
East, John P. "The Political Thought of Willmoore Kendall," *Political Science Reviewer* 3 (Fall 1973): 201–39.
"Editors of *National Review* Believe." *NR*, November 19, 1955, 8.
"Endorse Kendall." *Daily Oklahoman*, December 12, 1940, 6.
"Epworth Leaguers." *Glencoe Mirror*, March 14, 1941, 1.
"Eufaula Pastor." *Indian Journal*, June 11, 1942, 1.
Evans, M. Stanton. *Revolt on the Campus*. Chicago: Regnery, 1961.
"Farewell Sermon." *Miami Daily News-Record*, October 19, 1941, 7.
Fastenberg, Dan. "God and Man at Yale." *Time*, August 17, 2011, entertainment.time.com.
"Fiery Cadet." *Tulsa Tribune*, March 10, 1929, 1.
Finnegan, John Patrick. *Military Intelligence*. Washington, DC: Center of Military History United States Army, 1998.
"First Time," *YDN*, October 31, 1949, 6.
Fischer, Jack E. "Yale Teacher," *Semi-Weekly Spokesman-Review*, April 14, 1958, 5.
Fischer, John. "The Editor's Easy Chair: Why is the Conservative Voice So Harsh?" *Harper's Magazine*, March 1956, 16–22.
Fisher, Richard B. Letter to the Editor. *YDN*, May 17, 1948, 4–5.
"Former Miamians," *Miami Daily News-Record*, November 26, 1939, 25.
Frank, Bob. "Profs Differ," *Stanford Daily*, April 10, 1959, 1.
Frederick Daniel Wilhelmsen. UD Profile Series, I. Dallas: University of Dallas, 1998.
Frysinger, Galen S. "Philbrook Museum," "Philtower," "Boston Avenue Church," and "Westhope," http://www.galenfrysinger.com/oklahoma.
Gangi, William. "A Scholar's Journey on the Dark Side." *Chapman Law Review* 11, no. 1 (February 2008): 1–83.
"Garlick-Kendall." *Daily Ardmoreite*, December 22, 1907, 9.
"Garrett Biblical." *Chicago Tribune*, April 25, 1912, 8.
Gerkin, Steve. "Beno Hall: Tulsa's Den of Terror," *This Land*, September 3, 2011, thislandpress.com.
Gibson, Arrell Morgan. *Oklahoma: A History of Five Centuries*, 2nd ed. Norman: University of Oklahoma Press, 1981.
Goble, Danney. *Tulsa!: Biography of the American City*. Tulsa: Council Oak Books, 1997.
"Goble to Speak." *Evening Courier* (Urbana, IL), February 18, 1945, 7.
Godfrey, James L. Review of *John Locke and the Doctrine of Majority Rule*, by Willmoore Kendall. *Social Forces* 20, no. 3 (March 1942): 417.

Godfried, Nathan. "Fellow Traveler, Organic Intellectual: J. Raymond Walsh and Radio News Commentary in the 1940s." *Democratic Communiqué* 22, no. 2 (Fall 2008): 19–45.

Goldman, Jan, ed. *The Central Intelligence Agency: An Encyclopedia of Covert Ops, Intelligence Gathering, and Spies.* Santa Barbara: ABC-CLIO, 2016.

"Graham Causes," *YDN*, February 19, 1957, 5.

Greene, Theodore M. "The Christian Speaks." *Yale Daily* News, October 15, 1951, 4.

Guinzburg, Thomas H. "Bureau Chiefs," *YDN*, October 25, 1949, 1, 5.

———. "Bozell, Vecchione," *YDN*, February 26, 1948, 1.

Hadley, David P. *The Rising Clamor: The American Press, the Central Intelligence Agency, and the Cold War.* Lexington: University Press of Kentucky, 2019.

"Hagler Memorial," *Tulsa Tribune*, February 23, 1924, 3.

Hart, Jeffrey. "The 'Deliberate Sense' of Willmoore Kendall." *New Criterion*, March 2002, 76–80.

———. *The Making of the American Conservative Mind: National Review and Its Times* Wilmington, DE: ISI Books, 2005.

———. "Willmoore Kendall: Philosopher of Consensus," *National Review*, September 1, 1978, 1083–84.

———. "Willmoore Kendall: The Unassimilable Man," *National Review*, December 31, 1985, 84–89.

Havers, Grant. "The Politics of Paradox: Leo Strauss's Biblical Debt to Spinoza (and Kierkegaard)." *Sophia* (December 2015): 525–43.

———. "Leo Strauss, Willmoore Kendall, and the Meaning of Conservatism," *Humanitas* 18, nos. 1 and 2 (2005): 5–25.

———. "Who is to Say Nay to the People? Publius, Majority Rule, and Willmoore Kendall," *Law and Liberty*, May 28, 2012, https://www.lawliberty.org/2012/05/28/who-is-to-say-nay-to-the-people-publius-majority-rule-and-willmoore-kendall/.

———. "Willmoore Kendall for Our Times." *Modern Age* (Winter/Spring 2011): 121–24.

Hawley, George. *Right-Wing Critics of American Conservatism.* Lawrence: University Press of Kansas, 2016.

Haynes, John Earl and Alexander Vassilev, *Spies: The Rise and Fall of the KGB in America.* New Haven: Yale University Press, 2010.

Haynes, John Earl and Harvey Klehr, *The Venona Project: Decoding Soviet Espionage in America.* New Haven: Yale University Press, 2011.

"Hear Willmoore Kendall." *Tulsa Tribune*, April 26, 1924, 2.

Heer, Jeet. "Racism and the Paradox of Anti-Democratic Populism," May 26, 2021, https://jeetheer.substack.com/p/racism-and-the-paradox-of-anti-democratic.

Heilman, Robert B. "The State of Letters: Baton Rouge and LSU Forty Years Later," *Sewanee Review* 88, no. 1 (1980): 126–43.

Heise, Kenan. "Irving P. Pflaum," *Chicago Tribune*, April 25, 1985, chicagotribune.com.

Herndon, Jeffrey C. "Voegelin's History of Political Ideas and the Problem of Christian Order." PhD diss., Louisiana State University, 2003.

"Highest U.S. Court." *Spokane Chronicle*, April 11, 1959, 59.

"Hobart Aide Hits Program." *Democrat and Chronicle*, October 25, 1940, 45.
"Hobart Faculty." *Star-Gazette*, February 26, 1941, 7.
"Honorary Degree." *Miami Daily News-Record*, June 16, 1941, 3.
House Vote #49 in 1947 (80th Congress), https://www.govtrack.us/congress.
House Vote #74 in 1947 (80th Congress), https://www.govtrack.us/congress.
House Vote #42 in 1957 (85th Congress), https://www.govtrack.us/congress.
Hsia, Chih-tsing, et al. *China: An Area Manual*. Volume I: *Geographical, Historical, and Military Background*, edited by Dave Nelson Rowe and WK. Chevy Chase, MD: Operations Research Office, 1953.
Hyneman, Charles S. "Charles S. Hyneman Papers," Indiana University Archives, Archives Online at Indiana University.
———. "In Memoriam: Willmoore Kendall," *P.S.* (Winter 1968): 55–56.
"It's Not Easy." *Tablet*, April 20, 1957, 4.
"Informal Tea." *Miami Daily News-Record*, November 16, 1931, 6.
"Jack Fischer, Amarillo." *Amarillo Daily News*, September 4, 1934, 5.
Jaffa, Harry. "Inventing the Past," *St. John's Review* XXXIII, no. 1 (Autumn 1981): 3–19.
———. Review of *The Basic Symbols of the American Political Tradition*, by WK and GWC. *Loyola of Los Angeles Law Review* 8, no. 2 (June1975): 471–505.
"Jaffa v. Bork: An Exchange." *National Review*, March 21, 1994, 56–59.
Jones, Stephen. *Oklahoma Politics in State and Nation, Volume I: 1907–1962* (Enid: Haymaker Press, 1974).
"J.R.R. Tolkien." *Pembroke College Record: 1973*.
"Judge Williams." *Miami Daily News-Record*, November 12, 1933, 6.
Judis, John B. *William F. Buckley, Jr.: Patron Saint of Conservatives*. New York: Simon and\ Schuster, 1988.
"Just Married." *Minneapolis Star-Tribune*, June 10, 1953, 9.
Kane, Harnett T. *Huey Long's Louisiana Hayride: The American Rehearsal for Dictatorship, 1928–1940*. New Orleans: Pelican, 1971.
"Katanga." *The Bee*, December 19, 1961, 8.
Kelly, Daniel. *Living on Fire: The Life of L. Brent Bozell, Jr.* Wilmington, DE: ISI Books, 2014.
"Kendall Goes." *Luther Register*, November 12, 1915, 1.
Kendall, Katherine A. "Katherine A. Kendall Papers," Social Welfare Archive, University of Minnesota Archives and Special Collections.
"Kendall Lauds." November 16, 1933, *Kiowa County Review*, 8.
"Kendall-Miller." *Stanford Daily*, April 16, 1959, 1.
Kendall, Nellie, ed., *Willmoore Kendall Contra Mundum*. New Rochelle, NY: Arlington ———House 1972.
"Kendall Reads." *Kiowa County Record*, May 4, 1933, 1.
"Kendall Rally." *Hartshorne Sun*, May 14, 1914, 1.
"Kendall Review." *YDN*, March 13, 1958, 4.
"Kendall-Sibley Debate." *Stanford Daily*, March 1, 1959, 1.
Kendall Student. Name Withheld. Interview with Author. November 17, 2016.

Kendall Student. Name Withheld. Interviews with Author. August 28, 2018 and September 28–29, 2018.
Kendall Student. Name Withheld. Interview with Author. September 28, 2018.
"Kendall to Challenge," *YDN*, February 17, 1958, 1.
"Kendall to Speak." *Okemah Semi-Weekly Herald*, July 3, 1936, 5.
"Kendall Transferred." *Miami Daily News-Record*, November 7, 1932, 1.
"Kendall Urged." *Lawton News*, July 28, 1920, 1.
"Kendall Will Take." *Daily Oklahoman*, October 27, 1940, 18.
Kendall, Willmoore. "American Conservatism and the 'Prayer' Decisions." *Modern Age* 8, no. 3 (Summer 1964): 245–59.
———. [Alan Monk]. *Baseball: How to Play it and How to Watch It*. Girard, KS: Little Blue Books, 1929.
———. "The Bill of Rights and American Freedom." In *What is Conservatism?*, edited by Frank S. Meyer, 41–64. New York: Holt, Rinehart, and Winston, 1964.
———. "Bipartisanship and Majority-Rule Democracy." Reprint. *World Affairs* 147 (Winter 1984–85): 201–10.
———. "Bolivian Follies," *NR*, October 6, 1956, 11–13.
———. "e The Civil Rights Movement and the Coming Constitutional Crisis." In Willmoore Kendall *Contra Mundum*, edited by Nellie Kendall, 362-85. New Rochelle, NY: Arlington House, 1972.
———. "Comment on McClosky's *Conservatism and Personality*," *American Political Science Review* 52, no. 2 (June 1958): 506–10.
———. *The Conservative Affirmation*. Chicago: Regnery, 1963.
———. "Do We Want an Open Society?" *NR*, January 31, 1959, 491–93.
———. "The Function of Intelligence," *World Politics* 1, no. 4 (July 1949): 542–52.
———. "How to Read Milton's Areopagitica." *Journal of Politics* 22, no. 3 (August 1960): 439–73.
———. "How to Read Richard Weaver: Philosopher of 'We the (Virtuous) People.'" *Intercollegiate Review* 2, no. 1 (September 1965): 77–86.
———. "Intolerable?" *NR*, October 25, 1958, 279–80.
———. Introduction to *A Communist Party in Action: An Account of the Organization and Operations in France*, by A. Rossi (Angelo Tasca), v–xxiv. Translated and Edited by WK. New Haven: Yale University Press, 1949.
———. "Introduction: How to Read Rousseau's *Government of Poland*." In *The Government of Poland*, by Jean-Jacques Rousseau, ix–xxix. Translated by WK. Indianapolis: Bobbs-Merrill, 1972.
———. "Introduction: How to Read Rousseau's *The Social Contract*." In *The Social Contract*, by Jean-Jacques Rousseau, vii–xiii. Translated by Willmoore Kendall. Chicago: Henry Regnery Gateway Edition, 1954.
———. *John Locke and the Doctrine of Majority Rule*. Urbana: University of Illinois Press, 1941.
———. "John Locke Revisited." *Intercollegiate Review* 2, no. 4 (January–February 1966): 217–234.
———. Letter. *YDN*, October 24, 1957, 2.

———. "The Majority Principle and the Scientific Elite," *Southern Review* (Winter 1939): 463–73.

———. "Men on the Job." *New Republic*, August 18, 1941, pp. 226–27.

———. "Moon-Struck Madness." *NR*, June 13, 1956, 20–21.

———. "On the Preservation of Democracy for America," *Southern Review* (Summer 1939): 53–68.

———. "The Open Society and Its Fallacies," *American Political Science Review* 54, no. 4 (December 1960): 972–79.

———. "The People Versus Socrates Revisited: The Perplexities of the Athenian Jury System Are Our Own Problem," *Modern Age* 3, no. 1 (Winter 1958–59): 98–111.

———. "Pio Baroja: A Study." Master's Thesis. Northwestern University, 1928.

———. "Prolegomena to Any Future Work on Majority Rule." *The Journal of Politics* 12, no. 4 (November 1950): 694–713.

———. "Review of *Parliamentary Government in England*, by Harold Laski." *Journal of Politics* 1, no. 2 (May 1939): 220–22.

———. "Review of *Prophets and Peoples*, by Hans Kohn." *Journal of Politics* 8, no. 3 (August 1946): 425–27.

———. "Spain Talks Back to the '*Times*.'" *NR*, July 20, 1957, 87–88.

———. Statement. *YDN*, May 14, 1948, 4.

———. "Summons to Revolution." *New Republic*, June 30, 1941, 895–96.

———. "The Two Majorities," *Midwest Journal of Politics* 4, no. 4 (November 1960): 317–45.

———. "Viela Has a Plan." *Tulsa Tribune*, March 28, 1923, 4.

———. "What is Conservatism." *Modern Age* 6, no. 4 (Fall 1962): 53–66.

———. "*Whose* American Conscience?" *NR*, April 20, 1957, 383–84.

———. "Wife of a Confessed Whipper." *Tulsa Tribune*, August 25, 1923, 1.

———. "Willmoore Kendall Collection." Archives and Special Collections. University of Dallas.

———. "Willmoore Kendall Papers." Hoover Institution. Library and Archives.

Kendall, Willmoore, Sr. "Average Child." *Tulsa Tribune*, November 16, 1923, 13.

———. "Church's Share." *Hartshorne Sun*, October 31, 1912, 9.

———. "Let Me Live," *Weatherford Democrat*, August 24, 1916, 5.

———. "Man Who Brought Light," *Miami Daily News-Record*, August 22, 1930, 3.

Kendall, Willmoore and FW. "Cicero and the Politics of Public Orthodoxy." *Intercollegiate Review* 5, no. 2 (Winter 1968–69): 84–100.

Kendall, Willmoore and George W. Carey. *The Basic Symbols of the American Political Tradition*. Baton Rouge: Louisiana State University Press, 1970.

———. "How to Read *The Federalist*." Introduction to *The Federalist Papers*. New Rochelle, NY: Arlington House, 1966.

———. "The 'Intensity Problem' and Democratic Theory." *American Political Science Review* 62, no. 1 (March 1968): 5–24.

———. "The 'Roster Device': J.S. Mill and Contemporary Elitism." *Western Political Quarterly* 21, no. 1 (March 1968): 20–39.

———. "Towards a Definition of 'Conservatism.'" *Journal of Politics* 26, no. 2 (May 1964): 406–22.
Kendall, Willmoore and James MacGregor Burns, "James MacGregor Burns *vs.* Willmoore Kendall." In *Dialogues in Americanism*, 101–141. Chicago: Regnery, 1964.
Kendall, Willmoore and Morris Q. Sibley. *War and the Use of Force—Moral or Immoral, Christian or Unchristian: A Debate at Stanford University*. Denver: Swallow Press, 1959.
Kendall, Willmoore, Lawrence F. O'Donnell, and John Ponturo. *Eighth Army Psychological Warfare in the Korean War*. Baltimore: Operations Research Office, 1951.
Kent, Edward A. "Required Readings," *YDN*, December 14, 1955, 2.
Kerbel, Josh and Anthony Olcott, "Synthesizing with Clients, Not Analyzing for Customers," *Studies in Intelligence* 54, no. 4 (Extracts, December 2010): 11–27.
Kim, Sora and Eric Haley. "Propaganda Strategies of Korean War-Era Leaflets," *International Journal of Advertising* 36 (May 2017): 1–21.
Kirschner, Don S. *Cold War Exile: The Unclosed Case of Maurice Halperin*. Columbia: University of Missouri Press, 1995.
"Klansmen Visit Church." *Mangum Star*, August 17, 1922, 1.
Klehr, Harvey and John Earl Haynes. *The Early Cold War Spies: The Espionage Trials That Shaped American Politics*. Cambridge, UK: Cambridge University Press, 2006.
Koch, John. "Faculty Clash," *YDN*, April 18, 1950, 1, 3.
Kotlowski, Dean J. "Limited Vision: Carl Albert, The Choctaws, and Native Self-Determination," *American Indian Culture and Research Journal* 26, no. 2 (Spring 2002): 17–43.
"Ku Klux Klan Commends." *Mangum Star*, August 24, 1922, 1.
"KVOO To Broadcast." *Miami Daily News-Record*, June 5, 1930, 6.
La Forge, Toby. "Boy Scout Tribune," *Tulsa Tribune*, July 29, 1923, 51.
"Latin Airmen." *The Evening Courier*, May 21, 1945, 3.
"Leader Backs." *Democrat and Chronicle*, February 26, 1941, 30.
Lemisko, Lynn Speer. "The Historical Imagination: Collingwood in the Classroom." *Canadian Journal of Social Studies* 38, no. 2 (Winter 2004), https://files.eric.ed.gov/fulltext/EJ1073911.pdf.
"Lions Prepare." *Miami Daily News-Record*, March 14, 1930, 6.
Lind, Michael. "Selling Out Strauss." A Review of *Leo Strauss and the American Right*, by Shadia B. Drury. *Washington Monthly*, November 1997, 52–54.
Litke, Justin Blake. "American Exceptionalism: From Exemplar to Empire." PhD diss., Georgetown University, 2010.
"Little Daily." *Stillwater Gazette*, November 16, 1937, 1.
"Little Giant Dies at Age 91." *Daily Oklahoman*, February 6, 2000, 13A.
Lloyd, Kent M. Lloyd, Introduction to *War & the Use of Force—Moral or Immoral, Christian or Unchristian—A Debate at Stanford University* by Willmoore Kendall and Mulford Q. Sibley (Denver: Swallow Press, 1959.
"Local Items." *Hartshorne Sun*, November 8, 1917, 5.

"Local Mention." *Advance Democrat*, July 11, 1918, 5.
"Locals." *Miami Daily News- Record*, June 19, 1931, 6.
Macdonald, Dwight. "On the Horizon: Scrambled Eggheads on the Right." *Commentary*, April 1956, https://www.commentarymagazine.com/articles/on-the-horizon-scrambled-eggheads-on-the-right/.
"Mangum Boy." *Mangum Star*, May 25, 1922, 1.
"Mangum Prodigy." *Daily Ardmoreite*, August 9, 1922, 3.
March, Luke. "Left and Right Populism Compared: The British Case." *British Journal of Politics and International Relations* 19, no. 2 (May 2017): 282–303.
"Marriage Announcement." *Sooner State Press*, July 20, 1935, 3.
Mason, Yvona Kendall, ed. *The Oxford Years: The Letters of Willmoore Kendall to His Father*. Bryn Mawr, PA: Intercollegiate Studies Institute, 1993.
McCallum, R.B. "Willmoore Kendall, 1932–35." *Pembroke College Record*, 1966–67.
McCarthy, Daniel. "The Constitution Versus Calhoun: Why Harry Jaffa is Still Wrong About Willmoore Kendall," *American Conservative*, September 23, 2013, https://www.theamericanconservative.com.
"McCarthy Censure." *YDN*, November 19, 1954, 3.
"McCarthy and His Enemies," *YDN*, April 22, 1954, 2.
"McCarthy Debate," *YDN*, April 12, 1954, 1.
McCarthy, Shaun P. *The Function of Intelligence in Crisis Management: Towards an Understanding of the Intelligence Producer-Consumer Dichotomy*. Aldershot, UK: Ashgate, 1998.
"McCarthy Succumbs." *YDN*, May 3, 1957, 1.
"McCord-Kendall," *Stanford Daily*, April 9, 1959, 1.
McGirr, Lisa. "Now That Historians Know So Much About the Right, How Should We Best Approach the Study of Conservatism." *Journal of American History* 98, no. 3 (December 2011): 765–70.
McKenna, George, ed., *American Populism*. New York: G.P. Putnam's Sons, 1974.
McManus, John F. *William F. Buckley: Pied Piper for the Establishment*. Appleton, WI: John Birch Society, 2002.
McMinn, Betty. "Vice President of Scarabia," *Campus*, January 31, 1940, 2.
"Memorandum for the Central Director of Collection and Dissemination," November 19, 1946, Central Intelligence Group, cia.gov.
"M.E. Revival." *Foss Enterprise*, July 14, 1916, 1.
"Methodist Church Notes." *Mangum Star*, July 13, 1922, 6–7.
"Methodist Church Notes." *Mangum Star*, September 28, 1922, 5.
"Methodist Pastor." *Mangum Star*, October 12, 1922, 4.
"Methodists Agree." *Miami Daily News-Record*, April 19, 1939, 2.
"Miami Minister." *Daily Oklahoman*, March 4, 1932, 14.
Michie, Allan C. and Frank Ryhlick. *Dixie Demagogues*. New York: Vanguard, 1939.
Miller, John Perry. "The Economist Speaks." *YDN*, October 15, 1951, 5.
Milburn, George. "The Apostate," in *Short Stories from the New Yorker*. New York: Simon and Schuster, 1940.
———. *No More Trumpets and Other Stories*. New York: Harcourt, Brace, 1933.

———. "Oklahoma," *Yale Review* XXXIV (March 1946): 515–26.
———. *Oklahoma Town* (Freeport, NY: Books for Libraries, 1931.
"Money Spent On Wars," *Tulsa Tribune*, July 23, 1923, 11.
Morgan, Chris. "Willmoore Kendall Catches Fire," *Jacobite*, August 22, 2019, jacobitemag.com.
Mudde, Cas and Cristóbal Rovira Kaltwasser. *Populism: A Very Short Introduction*. Oxford: Oxford University Press, 2017.
Mueller, Jan Werner. *What is Populism?* Philadelphia: University of Pennsylvania Press, 2016.
Mulloy, D.J. *Enemies of the State: The Radical Right in America from FDR to Trump*. Lanham, MD: Rowman & Littlefield, 2018.
———. *The World of the John Birch Society: Conspiracy, Conservatism, and the Cold War*. Nashville: Vanderbilt University Press, 2014.
———. "On the 'Calhounism' of Willmoore Kendall," in *WKM*, 99–139.
Murley, John A. and John E. Alvis, eds., *Willmoore Kendall: Maverick of Conservatives*. Lanham, MD: Lexington Books, 2002.
Nash, George H. *The Conservative Intellectual Movement in America Since 1945*. New York: Basic Books, 1976.
———. "The Place of Willmoore Kendall in American Conservatism," in *WKM*, 3–15.
———. "Willmoore Kendall: Conservative Iconoclast (I)," *Modern Age* 19, no. 2 (Spring 1975): 127–35.
———. "Willmoore Kendall: Conservative Iconoclast (II)," *Modern Age* 19, no. 3 (Summer 1975): 236–48.
"National Prohibition." *Advance Democrat*, July 4, 1918, 1.
"New Methodist." *Mangum Star*, November 9, 1922, 1.
"New Warden." *McCurtain Gazette*, January 31, 1923, 2.
"Notices." *Mangum Star*, November 17, 1921, 4.
"Not Guilty." *Hartshorne Sun*, June 18, 1914, 1.
"Nov. 11 Speaker." *Waxahachie Daily Light*, October 30, 1941. 1.
Nugent, Mark. "Willmoore Kendall and the Deliberate Sense of the Community," *Political Science Reviewer* 36 (2007): 228–65.
"Obituary of Louise Cowan." *New York Times*, November 19, 2015, B14.
Oklahoma United Methodist Archives, Archives and Special Collections, Dulaney-Browne Library, Oklahoma City University.
"Oklahoma Child Prodigy." *Ardmore Daily Press*, September 15, 1922, 1.
"Oklahoman Coming." *Waxahachie Daily Light*, October 23, 1941, 1.
Olcott, Anthony. "Revisiting the Legacy: Sherman Kent, Willmoore Kendall, and George Pettee-Strategic Intelligence in the Digital Age." *Studies in Intelligence* 53, no. 2 (June 2009): 21–32.
Oliver, Revilo P. "Revilo P. Oliver Online Papers." http://www.revilo-oliver.com/papers/.
———. *The Jewish Strategy*. Earlysville, VA: Strom, 2005.
"On the Verdict." *YDN*, October 17, 1949, 4.
O'Sullivan, John. "When Liberalisms Collide: What the Hungarian prime minister meant by 'Liberal Democracy.'" *National Review*, October 20, 2014. NewsBank.

Owen, Christopher H. "The Man From Bug Tussle," *Chronicles*, February 2021, pp. 40–43.

———. "Pondering the People: Willmoore Kendall's Path from Progressive to Conservative Populism." In *Walk Away: When the Political Left Turns Right*, edited by Lee Trepanier and Grant Havers. Lanham, MD: Lexington Books, 2019).

———. "Sooner State 'Boy Wonder:' The Oklahoma Roots of Willmoore Kendall's Thought." *Chronicles of Oklahoma* 97, no. 1 (Spring 2019): 72–91.

Park, Richard, Jr., "Memorandum for the President," March 12, 1945, https://www.futile.work/uploads.

Payne, Stanley G. *Spain's First Democracy: The Second Republic, 1931–1936*. Madison: University of Wisconsin Press.

Pemantle, Oscar H. *Contrasting Arguments: The Culture War and the Clash in Education*. New York: Peter Lang, 2019.

———. Interview with the Author. Email, June 29, 2019.

———. "Trial by Drury." Unpublished Manuscript in Possession of the Author, 2019.

Phillips-Fein, Kim. "'As Great an Issue as Slavery or Abolition': Economic Populism, the Conservative Movement, and the Right-to-Work Campaigns of 1958." *Journal of Policy History* 23, no. 4 (2011): 491–512.

———. "Conservatism: A State of the Field." *Journal of American History* 98, no. 3 (December 2011): 723–43.

Pierson College, Yale University. Fellows Records. Manuscripts and Archives, Yale University Library.

"Plan for Peace." *Hammond Times*, May 15, 1944, 6.

Portillo, Sulma M. "Unequal Benefactors and Beneficiaries: The Utilitarian Inadequacy of Mill's Arguments for Freedom." PhD., diss., University of Windsor, 2007.

Postell, Joseph. "Philosopher Kings or the Sense of the Community? Jaffa, Kendall, and the Problem of Majority Rule." *Anamnesis* 7 (2018): 50–69.

"Political Union Award." *YDN*, January 12, 1950, 1, 6.

Power, M. Susan. "Willmoore Kendall: The Early Years: A Review of *The Oxford Years*, edited by Yvona K. Mason." *Modern Age* 38 (Fall 1995): 82–87.

"Prodigy Here!" *Tulsa Tribune*, November 26, 1922, 3.

"Professors Will Debate." *San Mateo Times*, May 2, 1959, 15.

"PU Holds Meeting." *YDN*, February 11, 1949, 1.

"PU to Broadcast Discussion Series." *YDN*, October 16, 1948, 1.

Ranney, Austin and Willmoore Kendall. "Democracy: Confusion and Agreement." *Western Political Quarterly* 4, no. 3 (September 1951): 430–39.

———. *Democracy and the American Party System*. New York: Harcourt, Brace, 1956.

"Rather Be Right?" *YDN*, January 25, 1949, 12.

"R.B. McCallum." *Pembroke College Record: 1973*.

"Recovery Road," *Miami Daily News-Record*, January 4, 1934, 6.

"Regents Name Six." *Minneapolis Star*, July 12, 1946, 9.

Regnery, Henry. "Henry Regnery Papers." Hoover Institution. Library and Archives.

———. *Memoirs of a Dissident Publisher*. Chicago: Regnery, 1985.
———. "The Stormy Sage of Northford." *National Review*, September 1, 1978, 1084–86.
Reinsch, Richard M., II. "A Question of Patriotism." *Law and Liberty*, 2018. www.lawliberty.org.
———. "A Tale of Two Majorities." *Law and Liberty*, August 31, 2016, www.lawliberty.org.
Report on the Possible Uses of the Polygraph and Supplemental Report of the Examination of Korean Nationals and Communist Chinese, ORO-S-85. Chevy Chase, MD: Operations Research Office, 1951.
Resnick, Paul. "Kendall Cites." *YDN*, April 24, 1957, 1.
"Rev. Kendall Speaks." *Miami Daily News-Record*, March 1, 1931, 3.
"Rev. W. Kendall's July 4th Address." *Hartshorne Sun*, July 17, 1913, 1.
"Rev. Willmoore Kendall." *Daily Oklahoman*, June 7, 1942, 25.
Revised Summary of ORO Projects, Special Studies and Field Operations, Volume I, DTIC AD0007783. Chevy Chase, MD: Operations Research Office, 1952.
"Rhodes Scholar." *Sooner State Press*, April 6, 1935, 2.
Richards, Jack S. and Theodore S. Rogers. *Approaches and Methods in Language Teaching*, 3rd ed. Cambridge, UK: Cambridge University Press, 2014.
"Right Think." *YDN*, February 9, 1959, 2.
"Robert S. Cohen (1923–2107)," http://www.bu.edu/cphs/about/robert-cohen/.
Roosevelt, Kermit. Introduction to *War Report of the O.S.S.* New York: Walker, 1976.
Rousseau, Jean Jacques. *The Government of Poland*. Translated and with an Introduction by Willmoore Kendall. Indianapolis: Bobbs-Merrill, 1972.
———. *The Social Contract*. Translated and with an Introduction by Willmoore Kendall. Chicago: Henry Regnery Company, 1954.
Rothbard, Murray N. *Strictly Confidential: The Private Volker Fund Memos of Murray N. Rothbard*, ed. David Gordon. Auburn, AL: Ludwig von Mises Institute, 2010.
Rowland, Donald. *History of the Office of the Coordinator of Inter-American Affairs: Historical Reports on War Administration*. Washington, DC: GPO, 1947.
Schramm, Wilbur. *The Nature of Psychological Warfare*. Chevy Chase, MD: Operations Research Office, 1954.
Schrock, Thomas. Interview with Author. Email, October 31, 2017.
———. Interview with Gayle McKean, February 3 and February 4, 2016, https://wslamp70.s3.amazonaws.com/leostrauss/s3fs-public/interviews/pdf/Schrock%20Interview.pdf.
"Scholar and Athlete." *New York Times*, October 8, 1922, x9.
Sehlinger, Peter J. and Hamilton Holman. *Claude G. Bowers: Spokesman for Democracy*. Indianapolis: Indiana Historical Society, 2000.
Sellars, Nigel. "Wobblies in the Oil Fields: The Suppression of the Industrial Workers of the World in Oklahoma." In *An Oklahoma I Had Never Seen Before: Alternative Views of Oklahoma History*, edited by Davis D. Joyce. Norman: University of Oklahoma Press, 1994.

Semple, Robert B. "Kendall, Weiss." *YDN*, October 22, 1957, 1, 3.
Serum, Kristin. "Freedom of Speech." *Minneapolis Star*, April 7, 1967, 6.
"Shakespearian Studies." *Miami Daily News-Record*, September 11, 1931, 6.
Shauer, Frederick. "The First Amendment as Ideology." *William and Mary Law Review* 33, no. 3 (1992): 853–69.
"Similarity of Political Parties." *Arizona Daily Star*, April 14, 1958, 12.
Sivek, Susan Currie. "Editing Conservatism: How *National Review* Magazine Framed and Mobilized a Political Movement." (2007). Linfield University. http://digitalcommons.linfield.edu/mscmfac_pubs/4.
Smith, Connie. Interview with Author, Dallas, Texas, September 28, 2018.
Smith, Diana. "Kendall, Ogg Opposed," *Stanford Daily*, January 14, 1959, 1.
Smith, J. Allen., *Growth and Decadence of Constitutional Government*. New York: Holt, 1930.
Smith, Pat. Interview with Author. Dallas, Texas, September 28, 2018.
Smith, R. Harris. *OSS: The Secret History of America's First Central Intelligence Agency*. New York: Lyons Press, 2005.
Smith, Russell Jack. *The Unknown CIA: My Three Decades With the Agency*. Washington, DC: Pergamon Brassey's International Defense Publishers, 1989.
"Society Mask." *Daily Oklahoman*, November 28, 1925, 1.
"Some Generalities," *YDN*, June 10, 1957, 2.
"Sooner Named," *Daily Oklahoman*, April 15, 1946, 21.
Souza, Carlos Roberto de. "Para la defensa de las Americas: The Pictorial Magazine *En Guardia* in Nelson A. Rockefeller's Propaganda Campaign for Latin America during World War II," 2011. https://core.ac.uk/reader/86445257.
Spracher, William C. "National Security Intelligence Professional Education: A Map of U.S. Civilian University Programs and Competencies." PhD diss., George Washington University, 2009.
Stone, Robert L. "Professor Harry V. Jaffa Divides the House: A Respectful Protest and A Defense Brief." *University of Puget Sound Law Review* 10 (1987): 471–505.
"Students at Hobart." *Democrat and Chronicle*, March 1, 1941, 21.
"Students for Wallace." *YDN*, April 17, 1948, 1, 3.
Tait, Joshua A. "The Right, With Lincoln: Conservative Intellectuals Interpret Lincoln, c. 1945–1989." Master's Thesis. University of Canterbury, 2013.
Tanenhaus, Sam. "Choosing Sides: The Writers and Politicians Who Sculpted Today's Extreme Divisions," *New Republic*, November 2018.
Teachout, Terry. "Such, Such Were the Joys." *National Review*, August 28, 1995, 44–45.
Teter, Michael. "Gridlock, Legislative Supremacy, and the Problem of Arbitrary Inaction," *Notre Dame Law Review* 88, no. 5 (June 2013): 2217–32.
Thomas, Mike. "Looking Down," *YDN*, October 24, 1957, 2.
Thomas, Hugh. *The Spanish Civil War*. New York: Harper, 1961.
"Through the Spiritual Vision." *Lawton News*, May 18, 1919, 1.
"Tribune Cub Reporters." *Sooner State Press*, September 26, 1936, 2.
Troy, Thomas F. *Donovan and the CIA: A History of the Establishment of the Central Intelligence Agency*. Frederick, MD: University Publications of America, 1981.

"Tulsa." *Tulsa Tribune*, July 26, 1923, 16.
"Tulsa's Blind Prophet." *Tulsa Tribune*, April 26, 1924, 2.
Turner, Steven. *George Milburn, Southwest Writers Series*. Austin: Steck-Vaughn, 1970.
"Two Letters," *YDN*, October 17, 1957, 2.
"Two to Watch." *YDN*, January 7, 1958, 2.
"Typewriter Makes." *New York Herald*, August 6, 1922, 18.
United States. Office of the Coordinator of Inter-American Affairs. Coordination Committee for Columbia Records. 1943.
"U. of R. Faculty Members." *Richmond Times-Dispatch*, September 17, 1941, 7.
"U.S. Communists." *YDN*, March 24, 1950, 1.
U.S. Government Manual, Summer 1944. Washington, DC: Office of War Information, 1944.
U.S. Government Manual, 1945, 2d ed. Washington, DC: Government Information Service, 1945.
U.S. State Department Register, December 1, 1946. Washington, DC: Government Printing Office, 1947.
"UWF, PCA Heads." *YDN*, January 16, 1948, 1, 5.
"Varsity Debaters." *YDN*, May 14, 1949, 1.
"Victory Dinner." *Miami Daily News-Record*, February 28, 1937.
"View With Alarm," *YDN*, October 12, 1957, 2.
Voegelin, Eric. "Eric Voegelin Papers." Hoover Institution. Library and Archives.
"Walton Addresses." *Mangum Star*, October 5, 1922, 1.
"Walton Advised." *Tulsa Tribune*, May 1, 1923, 5.
"Warning." *Miami Daily News Record*, February 24, 1930, 1.
Weaver, H.S. "Bozell, Vecchione." *YDN*, January 22, 1948, 1–2.
"Weiss-Bozell." *YDN*, March 4, 1953, 1.
"Wet, Dry Chiefs." *Kiowa County Review*, November 2, 1933, 1.
"Wets Invited." *Kiowa County Record*, July 6, 1933, 1.
Weyl, Nathaniel. "Nathaniel Weyl Papers." Hoover Institution. Library and Archives.
White, William S. "Apostles of the Right." A Review of *The Conservative Affirmation*, by Willmoore Kendall. *New York Times*, October 20, 1963, 12–13.
Wilhelmsen, Alexandra. Interview with Author. Irving, Texas, September 28, 2018.
"Will Discuss Freedom," *The Times Record*, May 2, 1958, 54.
Williams, Stephen. Letter. *YDN*, October 17, 1957, 2.
Williams, Meredith. "Miami Minister," *Daily Oklahoman*, March 4, 1932, 14.
Wills, Garry. *Confessions of a Conservative*. Garden City, NY: Doubleday, 1979.
———. "Domini Canis." Review of *The Conservative Affirmation*, by WK. *Modern Age* 7, no. 4 (Fall 1963): 438–42.
Wilson, Francis Graham. "Francis Graham Wilson Papers." University of Illinois Archives.
———. "The Political Science of Willmoore Kendall." *Modern Age* 16, no. 1 (Winter 1972): 38–47.
Wimsatt, William K., Jr., "A Conservative View," *Yale Daily* News, October 16, 1951, 5.

Winchell, Mark Royden. *Cleanth Brooks and the Rise of Modern Criticism.* Charlottesville: University Press of Virginia, 1996.

———. "An Extended Family." *Southern Review* 31, no. 2 (Spring 1995): 197–218.

Winks, Robin W., *Cloak and Gown: Scholars in the Secret War, 1939–1961.* New York: Collins-Harvill, 1987.

Wise, David and Thomas P. Ross. *The Espionage Establishment.* New York: Random House, 1967.

"WITV Facts." *Fort Lauderdale News*, February 23, 1956, 54.

Woods, Kevin M. "Creating the Capacity for Innovation: U.S. Army 1945–1960." PhD diss., University of Leeds, 2011.

"Youngest H.S. Graduate." *Mangum Star*, May 25, 1922, 1.

"Yvona Kendall." *Daily Oklahoman*, November 26, 1939, 57.

Index

Page references for figures are italicized

abolitionism, 22, 180
Albert, Carl B., 44, 48, 161, 184, 201–8
alcohol and alcoholism, 8, 14, 44, 85, 87, 140, 142, 152–53, 156–59, 161–62, 171, 185, 188; Antabuse (disulfiram), 85, 152, 156, 158, 161; treatment for, 152–53, 156, 161–62
Alsop, Joseph and Stewart, 125, 127
Andrade, Juan, 8, 57–59, 86
Andrade, Maria Teresa, 57–59, 86
anti-communism, xvi, 1, 6, 92, 100, 112, 131, 143, 151, 171, 177, 184
anti-Semitism, 45, 160
Aquinas, Thomas, St., xii–xiii
Ardmore, Oklahoma, 15–16, 195
Aristotle, 2–3, 7, 164–65, 179, 193, 203–4, 207
Athanasius, St., xv, 2
Augustine of Hippo, St., xii, xv
Axis Powers, 80, 82–84

Barnes, Harry Elmer, 79–80
Barnett, Victor, 21, 50
Baroja, Pio, 26
Beard, Charles A., 64, 79–80, 102
Bellow, Saul, 66, 194
Berdahl, Clarence, 62, 93

Berns, Walter, 136
Bible, xv, 16–17, 81, 183
Bill of Rights, 6, 63, 105, 142, 158, 181–82
Bogotá, Colombia, 82–85
Boorstin, Daniel, 45–46
Boudin, Louis B., 64
Bowers, Claude G., 46–49
Bozell, L. Brent, Jr., 7, 105–6, 116, 137, 152–54, 156–57, 161, 177–78, 181, 194
Bozell, Patricia Buckley, 152–53, 161–62, 177
Braden, Carl, 158
Brooks, Cleanth, 5, 62–64, 67, 71, 86, 104, 109, 111, 116, 156
Brooks, Edith "Tinkum," 71, 86, 156
Brunsdale, Anne (Kendall), 112, 116–17, 128–30, 140, 162, 186
Buchan, John, 43
Buckley, F. Reid, 105, 153
Buckley, William F., Jr., xvii, 3, 7, 99–100, 102–6, 112, 114–17, 124, 127–29, 131, 137, 142–43, 152–62, 165, 176–78, 181, 185–86, 191, 194–95
Bugtussle, Oklahoma, 44, 201–8

bureaucracy and bureaucrats, 7, 47, 80, 84, 87, 89–91, 107, 112–13, 127, 135, 138
Burke, Edmund and Burkeanism, 2–3, 42, 173, 193
Burnham, James, 123, 127, 158, 160, 191
Burns, James MacGregor, 157, 178, 184

Calhoun, John C., 102, 191
capitalism and business, 4, 6, 26, 47–48, 57–58, 83, 101, 149, 158, 205
Carey, George W., 117, 158, 161, 188–91
Carlism and Carlists, 150–51
Cartagena, Colombia, 83–84
Catholics and Catholicism, xi, 2, 20, 48, 57–58, 83, 129, 140, 150, 165, 171, 177–78, 182, 186–87, 194, 206
Central Intelligence Agency (CIA), xi, 7, 89, 107–10, 112, 156
Central Intelligence Group (CIG), 89–90, 92
Cerny, Karl, 158
Chiang Kai-shek, 113, 125, 157
Chicago, 14, 16, 19, 28, 35–38, 58, 62, 65–66, 71, 86, 136
Childers, Charles C., 23
China and the Chinese, xiii, 110–12, 125
Christianity and Christians, xii–xv, 20, 43, 114, 124, 139, 157, 164, 172, 188–89
Cicero, 150, 180
Civil Rights Act of 1957, 205
Civil Rights Act of 1964, 180, 205, 207
Claremore, Oklahoma, 14, 26, 28
Clay, Henry, 191
clear and present danger doctrine, 104–6, 130, 133, 161
Cold War, xi–xvi, 1, 9, 89, 100, 108, 111, 116, 194
Cole, G.D.H, 45, 48
Colley, Nathaniel S., 103–4, 106

Collingwood, R.G., 8, 41–42, 67, 102, 128
communism and communists, xiii, xv, 2, 42, 48–49, 57–58, 60, 62, 70–72, 89–92, 99, 103–6, 108, 112, 116, 125–26, 130, 132–33, 138–39, 157, 159–61, 177, 181. *See also* anti-communism; Stalinism; Trotskyism
Congress, 7, 63, 104, 148–49, 177–80, 182, 184, 189, 191, 203–8; plenary power of, 178, 191, 204–6
Corbett, P.E., 92, 101, 103
Cowan, Donald A., 171–73, 175, 184
Cowan, Louise, 171–72, 175, 194
Crutcher, Anne, 87, 92
Crutcher, Leon, 87, 92

Dahl, Robert, 101, 103, 149, 151, 155, 161, 188
Daily Oklahoman, 40, 45, 51
de Alvarez, Leo Paul, 173, 191, 193–94
Declaration of Independence, 137, 142, 190
democracy, xv, 1–2, 4, 6, 23, 48, 58, 63–65, 68–70, 100, 107, 115, 125, 132–37, 148–49, 151, 178–79, 182–84, 188, 193, 203–4, 208; importance of deliberation in, 6, 135, 179, 189–91, 204, 206–8; representative, 6, 132, 135, 148–49, 189–90, 203–4
Democratic Party and Democrats, 18, 21–24, 46–49, 58, 70, 92, 127, 139, 183, 202–7
Dennis, Lawrence, 70, 80, 107
dictatorship, 7, 107, 116, 151, 156–57
domestic tranquility, 6, 180, 193
Dominican Republic, 156–57, 184
Donovan, William J., 80, 90–91
Driver, Cecil, 93, 101, 103, 106

Eddy, William A., 69–70, 80
Eisenhower, Dwight D., 127, 138, 143, 159, 207
elites and elitism, 4–6, 42, 47, 62–64, 99, 108, 132, 179, 189

equality, xiv, 48, 62, 127, 134–35, 164, 178–79, 190–93, 205
Erler, Don, 184–85
Eufaula, Oklahoma, 16, 51
Evans, Medford, 138, 159
Evanston, Illinois, 15–16, 26, 38, 117; Orrington Hotel, 26, 38, 117

Fairlie, John, 62, 66
Fandal, Damian, 172, 186–87, 193–94
fascism, xi, 64–65, 70, 106–7
Federal Bureau of Investigation (FBI), 71, 91, 104
The Federalist, 8, 189, 193
Fesler, James W., 111, 113–14, 137
Finer, Herman, 101, 103
Fischer, John, 5, 45, 123–25, 161
Fort Sill, Oklahoma, 23, 25
freedom, xiv–xv, 4, 6, 68, 105, 115, 190; academic, 70, 103, 114, 138, 157; limits on, 105, 115, 133, 136, 138, 147–48, 157; of speech, 104, 113, 133, 136, 147–48, 157. *See also* liberty and rights
free enterprise and free markets. *See* capitalism
Furniss, Edgar S., 111, 130

Galbraith, Evan, 154
Galbraith, Nancy, 154
Garner, James Wilford, 59–60, 62, 66
Garrett Theological Seminary, 15–16, 27
general welfare, 6, 193
Georgetown University, 158, 161–62
God and Man at Yale, 100, 114–15, 117, 162
Goldwater, Barry M., 1, 157, 177, 183–84
Graham, Billy, 1, 139
Grant, Edward, 44–45
Great Depression, 4, 39–40, 59, 87
Griswold, A. Whitney, 131, 155

Halperin, Maurice, 91

Hamilton, Alexander, 48, 151, 178
Harper, Fowler, 104–5
Hart, Jeffrey, 2, 137, 185
Hobart College, 66, 69–70, 111
Hobbes, Thomas, 67, 156, 164
House Un-American Activities Committee (HUAC), 158, 160
Humphrey, Hubert H., 61, 92, 194
Hyneman, Charles S., 60–64, 66, 71, 79–80, 82, 92–93, 100, 103, 109, 111, 113, 117, 124, 141, 143, 150, 152, 156, 158, 175, 187, 194

Idabel, Oklahoma, 17, 25
Inter-American Defense Board (IADB), 85–88, 91
Irish, Marian, 181

Jaffa, Harry V., 172, 183, 191
Jews and Judaism, xv, 20, 45–46, 73. *See also* anti-Semitism
John Birch Society, 159–60
judges and judicial supremacy, 7, 61, 63, 136, 138, 179–80, 182–83, 208
justice, xiii, 6, 178, 180, 182–83, 190, 193
just war theory, xiii, xv, 22

Kendall, Gennessee Adams, 23, 27, 51
Kendall, Katherine Tuach, 8, 37, 41, 44–45, 57–58, 60–62, 65–66, 71, 73, 81–82, 86–87, 112, 186
Kendall, Nellie Cooper, xvi–xvii, 8, 140, *141*, 150, 154, 161–62, 185–86, 194–95
Kendall, Pearl Garlick, 15–16, 24–26, 35, 72–74, 82, 112, 156, 176, 194
Kendall, Walter Chiles (grandfather), 15, 23, 27
Kendall, Walter Earl (brother), 25, 50, 82, 176
Kendall, Willmoore, Jr.: absolute majoritarianism, 2–3, 64, 100, 105, 107, 131, 134, 137; battle-line metaphor, 7, 164; behaviorism,

opposition to in political science, 130, 136, 139, 165, 172; cigarette smoker, 9, 44, 157–58, 173, 184; close reading/textual analysis, 8, 67–68, 79, 107, 109, 116, 128, 139, 147, 151, 190–91; "congressional majority," 148–49, 204; consensus, need for political, 4, 116, 135, 149, 180, 182, 189, 192, 206–7; conservative populist theorist, 2–7; debater and speaker, xi–xvii, 7, 70, 103–4, 117, 130–33, 138–39, 141, 157–59, 161, 178–80, 186; deliberation and the deliberate sense of the community, 5, 148–49, 178, 180, 184, 186, 189–91, 204, 206–8; "Great Bureaucracy," 132–33; intelligence officer, xi, 1, 7–9, 74, 79–93, 106–13, 191; isolationist, 49, 64–65, 70–72, 79–80, 82; journalist, 8, 21, 25–27, 36, 43–44, 46–47, 49–51, 57–58, 124–28, 161–62, 176–77; local government and localism, 6, 63–64, 83–84, 101, 117, 136, 148–49, 179–80, 183, 203–6; marriage annulments, 129, 154, 162, 186; notoriety in academia, 60, 106, 115, 139, 142–43, 147, 149, 180; orthodoxy, need for political, social, and academic, 102, 106, 115, 130–31, 138, 148, 150, 163, 177, 179, 190; prodigy, 9, 15, 18–19, 25, 40; southerner, 24, 165, 181; teacher, xvi, 7, 9, 14, 37, 39–40, 44, 59–61, 66, 70–72, 91, 99–102, 106–7, 114–15, 117, 130–31, 137, 141–42, 162, 172–76, 179, 182–88, 193–95; tribune, 2, 4–5, 9, 194; writing style, 2, 26, 36, 39, 41, 64, 115, 127–28, 151, 162, 164, 188, 190

Kendall, Willmoore, Sr., xii, xvii, 14–29, 35–36, 40–47, 50–51, 59–60, 64–65, 70–74, 91, 154; advice giving, 25, 36, 43–44, 46, 50–51, 64, 70, 91, 128; blindness, 15–18, 23, 73; as orator, 16–18, 22–24, 41, 73; politics and political views, 17–18, 20–24, 47, 65, 71–72; religious views, 16–17, 20, 46

Kennedy, John F., 127, 159, 175–76, 181, 183, 206

Kent, Sherman, 107–8, 111

Key, V.O., 103, 106, 113

Keynes, John Maynard and Keynesianism, 2, 47–48, 114, 157–58

King and Country Debate, 42–43

Kirk, Russell, 3, 132, 185, 191–92

Kirkpatrick, Evron, 90, 92–93

Korean War and Korea, xi, 7, 109–10, 112, 150

Ku Klux Klan, 14, 20–22

Langer, William, 90, 108

Latin America, 7, 45, 50, 80–85, 88, 90–91, 126

Lawton, Oklahoma, 16, 18–19, 21, 23

liberals and liberalism, 3, 5–7, 62, 85, 92, 104–5, 114, 116, 139, 142, 155, 157–60, 163, 205–6; cultural and political dominance of, 1, 3, 99–100, 102, 106, 123, 125, 131–33, 178; distinct from communism, 125, 159–60; Kendall as critic of, 1, 6–7, 58, 85, 92, 99, 104, 107, 123–27, 132–33, 139, 149, 158, 163–65, 171, 177–79, 182, 184, 186–87, 191

libertarians and libertarianism, 2, 6, 115, 132, 143, 203

liberty, xiii, 1–2, 4, 6, 68–69, 116, 132, 138, 147, 178, 183, 190, 193. *See also* rights and freedom

Lincoln, Abraham, xiii, 1, 22, 48, 190–91

Lippmann, Walter, 43, 46, 49, 108, 125

Locke, John and Lockeanism, 1, 6, 42, 66–69, 79, 88, 100, 128, 151, 163–65, 185, 188, 190

Los Angeles State College, 162, 171

Louisiana State University, 8, 60–67, 70–71, 101, 172, 189
loyalty program and loyalty oaths, 92, 99–100, 104, 107–8, 116
Luther, Martin, xv, 22, 70

Macdonald, Dwight, 5, 123
Madison, James and Madisonianism, 3, 7, 142, 149, 151, 178–79
Madrid, xvi, 45–46, 49–51, 57–58, 126, 142, 150, 153, 188
Mangum, Oklahoma, 15, 18–21, 181
Mansfield, Harvey, Sr., 147
Marxism. *See* communism
Mason, Yvona Kendall, 15, 20–21, 24–25, 27, 51, 82, 85, 88, 92, 112, 115–16, 129, 154, 156–57, 159, 162, 176, 185–86
McAlester, Oklahoma, 23, 28, 205
McCallum, R.B., 41–42, 48, 124, 186
McCarthy, Joseph and McCarthyism, 1, 3, 99, 106, 113, 116, 124, 130–31, 143, 158, 160–61; *McCarthy and His Enemies*, 116–17
McClellan, James B., 172, 180
McClosky, Herbert, 107, 139
McCormack, John, 206–7
Mencken, H.L., 26–27
Methodism and Methodists, xii, 13–18, 21–23, 27, 46, 72–73, 80, 86, 206
Meyer, Frank, 149, 177
Miami, Oklahoma, xii, 36
Milburn, George, 21–22, 26–28, 45, 60
Mill, John Stuart, 1, 6, 70–71, 116, 132–33, 147–48, 151, 189
Milton, John, 100, 150
more perfect union, 178, 180, 193
Mumford, Lewis, 102, 125
Murley, John, 194
Murray, John Courtney, 192
Murray, William H. "Alfalfa Bill," 23, 47

Nash, George H., 3, 7

National Review, xi, 5, 7, 100, 123–31, 137, 140, 149–50, 152–54, 156, 158–62, 176–77, 188; "The Liberal Line," 7, 125, 140
Nazis and Nazism, xiii–xv, 83, 87, 109
New Critics, 8, 67
New Deal, 7, 40, 47, 59, 70, 80, 102, 114, 203, 205
Niemeyer, Gerhart, 129, 177, 188
Nixon, Richard, 181, 207
Northford, Connecticut, 117, 129–30, 137, 140, 155–56, 162
Northwestern University, 15–16, 20–21, 24–26, 35, 39, 73, 117

Office of Strategic Services (OSS), 80, 88–91
Office of the Coordinator of Inter-American Affairs (CIAA), 72, 74, 80–84, 88–91
Oklahoma A&M University, 25–26
Oklahoma City, 21, 28, 35–36, 73
Oklahoma City University, 72–73
Oklahoma Military Academy, 14, 26
Oliver, Revilo P., 40, 66, 80, 112, 124, 127, 159–60, 176, 194
Operations Research Office (ORO), 109–13, 115, 137, 155, 162
Ortega y Gasset, José, 61, 102, 163
Oxford University, 8, 40–52, 57, 59–60, 72, 80, 101, 165, 186; Pembroke College, 41–42, 44, 49, 186

pacifism and pacifists, xi–xvii, 23, 27, 43, 49, 65, 71, 126, 140, 157, 164
Palo Alto, California, xi, xv–xvi, 140, 142
Park, Richard, Jr., 88
Park, Willard Z., 91
Parry, Stanley, 129, 157
Pemantle, Oscar, 131
Penniman, Howard, 92, 103
the people, xiii–xiv, 1–7, 62–63, 65, 69, 100–101, 117, 132–33, 135, 179, 190, 192–93, 203; American,

2, 62–63, 102, 130, 132, 180; versus experts, 63–65, 102, 108, 115, 117, 132, 179–80; sovereignty and will of, 1, 3–6, 63–65, 100, 106, 132–35, 149, 179–80, 182, 191, 204; wisdom and virtue of, xiii–xiv, 65, 69, 117, 193–94
Pettee, George, 109, 111, 113
Phillips, Leon C., 70, 91
Plato, 67, 136, 164
political parties and partisanship, 108, 134–35, 138–39, 178, 204–6, 208
populism, 2–7, 88
private property, 48, 70, 135, 179, 188, 192
prohibitionism, 17–18, 39, 48, 180
propaganda, 7, 47, 65, 80–84, 109–11, 115, 123, 125, 128, 163
psychological warfare (psywar), xi, 1, 7, 109–12

race and racism, 6–7, 20–21, 28, 47, 127, 181
Ranney, Austin, 115, 134–35, 137, 181
Rayburn, Sam, 206–7
Regnery, Henry, 163, 185, 187, 191
Relm Foundation, 140, 151, 155, 185
Republican Party and Republicans, 2, 18, 22, 46–48, 58, 70, 86, 105, 108, 112, 125, 127, 139, 177, 183, 194, 207
Rhodes Scholarship and Rhodes Scholars, 35–36, 40–41, 43–46, 49–50, 60, 62
rights, xii, 3, 5, 20, 100, 107, 182, 190; civil, 7, 22, 104, 106, 127, 177, 180–84, 186, 205, 207; and duties, 68–69, 147–48, 164–65, 188, 192; individual, 6, 68–69, 79, 107, 133, 188–90, 193; natural, 63, 67–68, 137, 172, 182, 188, 190–92; state's, 2, 180, 182
Rockefeller, Nelson A., 72, 74, 80, 84, 90

Roosevelt, Franklin D., 1, 43, 46–48, 65, 72, 79–80, 83, 86, 88, 102, 124
Röpke, Wilhelm, 185
Rossiter, Clinton, 132, 134, 163, 192
Rothbard, Murray, 2, 132, 143, 145n22
Rousseau, Jean-Jacques and Rousseauianism, 1–4, 7, 63–64, 88, 100, 105, 115–16, 131–32, 142, 149, 151, 164, 185, 193
Rubìn, Daniel, 38
Rusher, William, 162, 176

Schlesinger, Arthur M., Jr., 102, 116, 125
Schweitzer, Albert, 1, 139
segregation, 21, 61, 177, 181, 203
Sibley, Mulford Q., xi–xvii, 80, 140, 142, 157, 179, 194
Smith, J. Allen, 64, 135, 149
Smith Act, 104–5, 107
Smultea, Ilie, 131
socialism and socialists, xi, xii, 22, 47–49, 51, 57–58, 60, 70–71, 85, 140, 157
Socrates, xiv, 1, 132–34, 147, 151, 164
Southern Agrarians, 62, 171
Soviet Union, xiii, xv–xvi, 87–88, 91, 103–4, 109–11, 127, 138, 157, 159, 171, 175–76
Stalinism and Stalinists, 2, 48, 57, 59, 62, 72, 90, 105
Stanford University, xi, xv–xvii, 124, 140–42, 149–50, 155, 173
Stillwater, Oklahoma, 16, 25, 72, 84
Strauss, Leo and the Straussians, 2–3, 7, 136–37, 139, 141, 150–51, 162–63, 172, 184, 186, 188, 190, 193
Supreme Court, 133, 138, 178–79, 182–83

Terman, F.E., 140, 142
Trotskyism and Trotskyists, 2–3, 8, 57, 59, 62, 71–72, 91, 123
Trujillo, Flor de Oro, 156

Index

Trujillo, Rafael, 156, 175
Truman, Harry S, 88–90, 99, 106, 108, 112, 183, 205
Tulsa, Oklahoma, 13–14, 17, 21–23, 25, 27–28, 36, 45, 50–51, 58, 181
Tulsa Race Massacre, 13, 21, 27, 181
Tulsa Tribune, 13–14, 21–22, 25–27, 50, 128
tyranny, xiv–xv, 134, 142, 193

United Press International, 50–51, 57–58, 72, 83
United States Constitution, 6, 47, 63, 67, 137–38, 149, 191–93, 207; preamble and purposes of government, 6, 193
United States State Department, 47, 88–91, 99, 109, 113
University of Dallas, 4, 6, *68*, 165, 171–76, 180, 182–87
University of Illinois, xii, 35–41, 59–60, 62, 67, 124
University of Minnesota, xi, 88–91
University of Oklahoma, xii, 22, 25–27, 45, 91
University of Richmond, 71

Vandenberg, Hoyt, 90
Van Horne, John, 36, 40
Vecchione, Pasquale J., 105
Voegelin, Eric, 2–3, 79, 103, 106, 124, 136–37, 141, 151, 182, 186–90, 193

Walker, Edwin A., 159
Wallace, George C., 3, 179, 182

Wallace, Henry A., 103–5
Walsh, J. Raymond, 69–70, 80
Walton, John C., 21–23
war, xi–xvi, 110–11, 116, 127, 139, 180–81; civil, 180–81, 191; nuclear, xiii–xv, 127, 139
Ware, Richard, 151
Warren, Robert Penn, 62–64, 67, 111
Weatherford, Oklahoma, 16, 22
Weaver, Richard, 128, 133, 163, 187, 193–94
Weiss, Paul, 63, 138, 157
Wells, Henry, 103
Wells, H.G., 42
Western Civilization, xii–xiii, xv, 152, 164, 189
Weyl, Nathaniel, 91, 181
Wilhelmsen, Frederick D., 150–51, 172, 188, 194
Wills, Garry, 181
Wilson, Charles Banks, 201, *202*, 208
Wilson, Francis Graham, 66, 81, 92–93, 152, 159–62, 165, 171, 180
World War I, 17, 20, 22–23, 27, 70, 79, 87
World War II, xi, 1–2, 59, 71–72, 74, 79–88, 110, 150

Yale Daily News, 99, 104–5, 114, 130–31, 138
Yale University, xi, xvii, 7, 89, 92–93, 99–109, 111–17, 123, 129–31, 136–40, 142, 150, 154–55, 158, 162–63, 172, 184

About the Author

Christopher H. Owen is a professor of history at Northeastern State University in Tahlequah, Oklahoma. His previous work includes *The Sacred Flame of Love: Methodism and Society in Nineteenth-Century Georgia*. In spring 2015, he met Willmoore Kendall in the pages of an anniversary edition of *God and Man at Yale*.

www.ingramcontent.com/pod-product-compliance
Lightning Source LLC
Chambersburg PA
CBHW061710300426
44115CB00014B/2634